DIRECTORIES
FOR THE CITY OF
CHARLESTON,
SOUTH CAROLINA

FOR THE YEARS
1830–31, 1835–36, 1836, 1837–38, AND 1840–41

James W. Hagy

CLEARFIELD

Printed for
Clearfield Company, Inc. by
Genealogical Publishing Co., Inc.
Baltimore, Maryland
1997

Reprinted for
Clearfield Company, Inc. by
Genealogical Publishing Co., Inc.
Baltimore, Maryland
2002

International Standard Book Number: 0-8063-4678-7

Made in the United States of America

CONTENTS

INTRODUCTION

This is the fourth volume of city directories for Charleston, South Carolina. It represents a continuing effort to republish the directories of the city prior to the Civil War. The first volume contained the city directories for the years 1782, 1785, 1790, 1801, and 1802 as well as the census reports for 1790 and 1800. This appeared under the title of *People and Professions of Charleston, South Carolina, 1782-1802* (Baltimore: Clearfield, 1992). The second volume was *City Directories for Charleston, South Carolina for the Years 1803, 1806, 1809 and 1813* (Baltimore: Clearfield, 1995). The third volume was *Charleston, South Carolina City Directories for the Years 1816, 1819, 1822, 1825, and 1829* (Baltimore: Clearfield, 1996).

These city directories, except for one, have separate sections for those people living in the Charleston Neck. At the time the city limit ended at the southern side of Boundary St. (now Calhoun). The area above that was the Neck which continued up the peninsula to The Lines (now Line St.). The Neck was governed by commissioners who were elected by people who lived there and who were qualified to vote for state legislators. The area was more thinly settled than the city and most houses did not have numbers. For protection, the citizens of the Neck carried out patrol duty under the leadership of the commandant of the Charleston Neck Rangers.

Both the city and the Neck had a considerable number of Free People of Color and slaves. Slaves were never listed in the city directories and the Free People of Color appeared in all of the directories included here, although some lists are very short..

Some of the city directories contain valuable information in addition to the usual listings such as (1) streets, lanes, alleys and courts; (2) teachers at Charleston College; (3) public buildings; (4) churches, chapels, and meeting houses; (5) commercial establishments; (6) insurance offices; (7) banks; (8) benevolent and charitable institutions and societies; (9) public amusements; (10) literary institutions; (11) public offices; (12) newspapers; (13) police of the city of Charleston; (14) officers of fire companies; (15) officers of Charleston Neck; (16) officers of the Customs House; (17) the harbor pilots; (18) the commissioners of public schools in Charleston; (19) commissioners of the Cross Roads and Poor of Charleston Neck; (20) justices and notaries; (21) officers of military units; (22) officers of lodges; and (23) consuls.

The entries were sorted by WordPerfect, a computer software program, which does not always sort listings as is traditionally done. For example, "M" followed by an apostrophe appears at the end of the entries for the letter "M" and "St." is treated as "St." rather than "Saint."

Street numbers in these directories create a problem as many houses were not numbered and the people compiling the volumes arbitrarily assigned numbers to them. At least one publisher gave houses different numbers from those displayed on the place. Therefore different numbers may appear for the same building.

Justices of Quorum Unis held magistrates' court in the city for the trial of criminal cases relating to free persons of color and for small claims, domestic attachments, and distress warrants for rent.

Some abbreviations found herein are: Al. = Alley; btw. = between; Cont'd. = Continued; cr. = corner; e. = east when not part of a name such as the east side of King St.; E. = east when part of a name such as East Bay St.; FPC = Free Person of Color; Ln. = Lane. = north; off. = Office; op. = opposite; res. = residence; s.= when not part of a name such as s. Meeting St.; S.= south when part of a name such as South Bay St.; S.C. = South Carolina; Sq. = Square; St. = Street or Saint; w. = west; Whf. = Wharf.

Copies of this book and those listed above may be ordered from: Clearfield Company, 220 East Eager St., Baltimore, Maryland 21202, Tel. 410-625-9004.

This book is dedicated to Johnnie Belcourt and the memory of Mary Garnier Ward.

The 1830–31 Directory

Morris Goldsmith, a Jewish resident of the city who was a deputy United States marshal at the time took the census of 1830 in Charleston and then compiled this directory entitled *Directory and Strangers' Guide, for the City of Charleston and Its Vicinity, From the Fifth Census of the United States* (Charleston: Printed at the Office of the Irishman, 1831). It contains 3,102 entries. As well as the names of people, their professions, and addresses, Goldsmith included information such as the names of the justices of the peace, the commissioners of various organizations such as the Orphan House, the Marine Hospital, the Market, the Work House and Streets and Lamps. He also lists historical events of the city and gives information on the free schools and such. He listed first the whites within the city limits, then the free persons of color within the city, next the whites in the Neck area, and finally the free persons of color in the Neck. All four groups have been combined here in one alphabetical listing. He explained that the Neck contained 10,054 persons and that the people living there were not subject to any of the ordinances of the city, it being governed by a board of commissioners. The Neck began on the north side of Boundary (now Calhoun) St. He noted that the suburbs there were quite picturesque and healthy. Three churches were to be found in the Neck as the area was "too distant from the city" for the people "to devote regular attendance to religious service" south of Boundary Street.

Aarons, Moses, 29 Boundary St.
Abbott, Simon B., n. side Mary St., Neck
Aberdell, John, Carpenter, 39 Wall St.
Abrahams, Elias, Dry Goods Store, 300 King St.
Abrahams, Moses, Clothing Store, 95 E. Bay St.
Adams, David, Mrs., Widow, 122 Queen St.
Adams, Jasper, Rev., Professor, 54 St. Philip St.
Addison, Edward, Cabinet Maker, 48 State St.
Addison, Francis, Mrs., 36 Wall St.
Addison, Henry, Blacksmith, 12 Wall St.
Addison, Joseph, Shipwright, Wentworth St.
Addison, Thomas, Planter, Hudson St., Neck
Adger, James, Merchant, 78 E. Bay St.
Adger, James, Merchant, King St. s. side, btw. Wolf & Spring Sts., Neck
Adrian, William, State Constable, Battery, E. Bay St.
Affanasseife, Daniel, Clerk, 269 King St.
Aiken, Ann, Widow, 11 Cumberland St.
Aiken, James, Meeting St., cr. Line St., Neck
Aiken, Thomas, M. D., 5 Cumberland St.
Aiken, William, Jr., Planter, cr. King & Ann Sts., Neck
Aiken, William, Planter, cr. King & Ann Sts., Neck
Aimar, Sebastian, Dry Goods & Grocery Store, 199 E. Bay St.
Ainger, Joseph M., Cooper, 12 Amen St.
Aires, Anthony, Fruit Store, 2 Market St.
Airs, Mary, Mrs., 27 Archdale St.
Alberts, Henry, Clerk, cr. St. Philip & George Sts.
Aldert, Henry, Pilot, 48 State St.
Aldert, Sikee, Pilot, 7 Stoll's Al.

Aldrich, Robert, Wharfinger, 15 Tradd St.
Alexander, Abraham, Dry Goods Store, w. side King St., 2 doors n. of Mary St., Neck
Alexander, David, President, Union Insurance Co., 3 Logan St.
Alexander, John J., Accountant, 19 Horlbeck's Al.
Alexander, Samuel, Harbor Master, res. 63 Queen St., off. 10 Gillon St.
Allan & Johnson, Factors, 10 Crafts' S. Whf.
Allan, Robert M., Factor, res. 46 Tradd St.
Allen, Ellen, 13 Wentworth St., F.P.C.
Allen, James, Grocery, e. side King St., near Ann St., Neck
Allen, S. & M. & Co., Exchange Brokers, 6 Broad St.
Allen, William, Commission Merchant, 52 E. Bay St.
Allerdick, Henry, Grocery, 83 Tradd St.
Allrenne, Ann, 33 Anson St., F.P.C.
Alston, Charles, Planter, 2 Ladson's Court
Alston, T. W., George St.
Alston, Thomas, Jr., Planter, 223 E. Bay St.
Alston, William, Planter, 25 King St.
Ancrum & Oliver, Tutors, 211 E. Bay St., F.P.C.
Ancrum, William Washington, n.w. cr. Church & S. Bay Sts.
Anderson, Henry, Capt., 13 Anson St.
Anderson, James, Cooper, 95 Wentworth St., F.P.C.
Anderson, Robert, Dry Goods Store, 147 King St.
Andrews, Louisa, Widow, 35 Hasell St.
Andrews, Warren, Factor, Kunhardt's Whf.
Angel, Justus, Planter, 124 Tradd St.
Angus, John, Blacksmith, Amherst St., Neck
Annelly, Thomas, Cooperage, Vanderhorst's Whf., res. 50 E. Bay St.
Anthony, J. C., Tallow Chandlery, Mary St., near King St., Neck
Anthony, Mary, Widow, Cannonborough, near Boundary St., Neck
Arms, Elizabeth, Mrs., 1 George St.
Armstrong, Archibald, Ship Carpenter, 15 Middle St.
Armstrong, William, Clerk, 19 Wentworth St.
Arnold, J. W. B., Tailor, 137 King St.
Arnold, L., Merchant, 128 E. Bay St.
Arnold, Louisa, cr. State St. & Unity Al.
Artman, Peter, Coach Maker, 5 Archdale St.
Artope, George, Engineer, w. side Nassau St., Neck
Ashby, John, Boarding House, 23 Elliott St.
Ashby, Thomas, Planter, 6 Liberty St.
Ashe, John, Boarding House, 17 Elliott St.
Ashe, John S., Hon., 5 Friend St.
Ashly, Matilda, 11 West St.
Assalit, Joseph, Professor of Languages, 23 Tradd St.
Atchison, John, Livery Stables, Church St., op. Cumberland St
Atwell, George E., Jeweller, 250 King St.
Aubin, Joseph, Wine & Liquor Store, 174 E. Bay St.
Aufterheide, C. F., Grocery, 60 Market St.
Auld, Donald, Medical Student, 31 Society St.
Auld, Emeline, Miss, 31 Society St.
Aveilhe, S. E., Miss, 173 Meeting St.
Axson, Jacob, City Attorney, off. 104 Church St., res. 19

Meeting St.
Axson, John, Planter, s. side Charlotte St., Mazyckborough, Neck
Axson, -----, Mrs., Boarding House, 85 Church St.
Axson, Sarah, Mrs., Boarding House, n.w. cr. Church & Cumberland Sts.
Babcock, S. & Co., Booksellers, 290 King St.
Babson, Ann R., Widow, 1 Berresford St.
Bachman, J., Rev., Pastor, German Lutheran Church, w. side Pinckney St., Cannonborough, Neck
Bacot, Daniel D., 10 Orange St.
Bacot, Peter, Cashier, Bank of U. S., 11 Archdale St.
Bacot, Thomas W., Sr., Post Master, n.e. cr. King & Tradd Sts.
Badger, James, Clerk, Planters & Mechanics Bank, 47 Beaufain St.
Bailey, Amity, Watch Maker, cr. King & Beaufain Sts.
Bailey, Henry, Attorney, 12 St. Michael's Al.
Bailey, William, Teacher, 8 Guignard St.
Baird, E., Mrs., Wolf St., Hampstead, Neck
Baker, Barnard E., 16 Legare St.
Baker, Calvin, Commission Merchant, 18 Vendue Range
Baker, Edward B., 87 Boundary St.
Baker, Gregory & Co., Hat Warehouse, 286 King St.
Baker, Martha, Dyer & Scourer, 167 Meeting St.
Baker, Mary, Widow, 87 Boundary St.
Baker, N., 96 Tradd St.
Baker, R. S., Rev., n.e. cr. Broad & Friend Sts.
Ball, Ann, Mrs., 89 Church St.
Ball, E., M. D., 222 Meeting St.
Ball, Eliza, Widow, 292 E. Bay St.
Ball, John, Planter, 27 Hasell St.
Ball, Nathaniel, Tailor, Charlotte St., Mazyckborough, Neck, F.P.C.
Ball, Timothy, Mariner, 48 State St.
Ballard, Joseph, Fancy Chair Store, 157 King St.
Ballintine, Alexander, Harness Maker, 119 Meeting St.
Ballund, Alexander, Grocer, 111 Church St.
Bamfield, James, 17 George St.
Bamfield, Thomas, 16 George St.
Bampfield, George, Alexander St., Wraggborough, Neck
Bancroft, James, Merchant, 167 E. Bay St.
Banks, Charles, Accountant, 2 George St.
Barbot, A., Merchant, 85 Church St.
Barelli, John, Turner, 17 Berresford St., F.P.C.
Barguet, Barbara, 113 Meeting St., F.P.C.
Barker, J. Sanford, Merchant, 20 Society St.
Barker, James, Truss Maker, 28 Pinckney St.
Barksdale, R. B., Mrs., 10 Meeting St.
Barksdale, Thomas, Planter, 71 Wentworth St.
Barns, Henry, Cannon St., Cannonborough, Neck
Barns, W. B., Inspector of Customs, 118 Meeting St.
Baron, Elizabeth, Widow, 123 Tradd St.
Baron, John, 26 Society St.
Barrelli, J. A., Merchant, 13 Champney St., res. 127 King St.
Barrelli, John, Fruit Store, 65 Broad St
Barrett, Isaac, Factor, Kunhardt's Whf., res. n.e. cr. King & Boundary Sts.
Bartless, Mary, Widow, 2 Washington St.

Bartlett, Hiram, Boot & Shoe Store, 209 King St.
Bartlett, William, Iron Monger, 44 King St.
Barton, Aaron, Carpenter, 10 St. Philip St.
Barton, Mary, Miss, 52 Wentworth St.
Battersby, Joseph, Merchant, Chisolm's N. Whf.
Battimand, Edward, Barber, 221 E. Bay St., F.P.C.
Bauch, Peter, Confectioner, 237 Meeting St.
Bauxbaum, Elizabeth, Widow, 126 Queen St.
Bay, Andrew, State Assessor, 7 Logan St.
Bay, Elihu H., Hon., 7 Logan St.
Bazil, John, Fruit Store, 27 Tradd St., F.P.C.
Beach & Cook, Dry Goods Store, 341 King St.
Bearman, Frederick, 228 Meeting St.
Beaufort, Frederick, Butcher, Cannon St., Cannonborough, Neck
Beaupe, J. H., Grocer, 227 E. Bay St.
Becais, Benjamin, Gunsmith, 83 Market St.
Becais, Mary, 83 Market St.
Becau, Entunne, Tailor, 19 Guignard St.
Beck, R. M., 106 Market St.
Becker, Daniel, Grocer, cr. George & Coming Sts.
Becker, Hans, Grocer, s.e. cr. Wentworth & St. Philip's Sts.
Beckley, John, Planter, Radcliffborough, Neck
Beckman, A., Paper Hanger, s.e. cr. Meeting & Pinckney Sts.
Beckman, C. J., Corn Grist Mill, n. side Boundary St., Neck
Beckman, F. A., Accountant, 21 St. Philip St.
Bee & Carter, Brokers & Commission Merchants, 15 Broad St.
Bee, Barnard E., 114 Tradd St.
Bee, F. C., Widow, 121 Broad St.
Bee, J. Simons, Broker, 9 State St., res. 4 Friend St.
Bee, James M., Accountant, 10 Water St.
Bee, Price, Cooper, 72 Tradd St.
Bee, Robert, Cooper, cr. E. Bay St. & Kiddell's Whf., res. 70 Tradd St.
Bee, W. R., 121 Broad St.
Bee, William, Clerk, S. C. Society, 72 Tradd St.
Beers, Booth & St. John, Exchange Brokers, 104 E. Bay St.
Behrman, Charles, Grocery, s.w. cr. Church & Market Sts.
Bell, David, 23 Society St.
Bell, James, Carpenter, Henrietta St., Neck, F.P.C.
Bell, William, Bricklayer, 46 Society St.
Bellingall, Margaret, 19 Archdale St., F.P.C.
Bellinger, John, M. D., St. Philip St., op. Liberty St.
Bellinger, Joseph, M. D., 37 Society St.
Bellmore, Ann, Judith St., Neck, F.P.C.
Belson, Mary, Widow, e. side King St., btw. Wolf & Spring Sts., Neck
Bement & Milliken, Wholesale Grocers, 130 E. Bay St.
Bement, Edward, Merchant, 212 Meeting St.
Benjamin, Philip, 15 St. Philip St.
Bennett, E. S, M. D., w. end Beaufain St.
Bennett, Henry, Mrs., Widow, n.e. end Smith St.
Bennett, Joseph, City Treasurer, 3 New St.
Bennett, Joseph, Steam Sawmills, E. Bay St., op.

Wentworth St.
Bennett, Swinton, Mrs., Widow, 134 King St.
Bennett, Thomas, Lumbermills, Cannonborough, Neck
Benoist, A., Baker, King St., near Line St., Neck
Benoist, Daniel, Merchant, 251 E. Bay St.
Benoist, Petit & Co., Fancy Store, 188 Meeting St.
Bensadon, Jacob, Teacher, 36 Hasell St.
Benson, Laurence, 171 Meeting St.
Benson, William G., Grocer, 27 King St.
Bentham & Dunkin, Attorneys, 65 Meeting St.
Bentham, Robert, Attorney, Radcliffborough, Neck
Berbant, Samuel, Tailor, 353 King St.
Bermingham, J., Rev., n.e. cr. Broad & Friend Sts.
Bermingham, T., Rev., n.e. cr. Broad & Friend Sts.
Bernard, Horace, Merchant, 7 Society St.
Berney, Rebecca, Widow, Radcliffborough, near St. Paul's
    Church, Neck
Berney, Robert, Broker, 1 State St.
Berney, William, cr. Anson & Guignard Sts.
Berrett, William H., Bookseller, n.w. cr. Broad & State
    Sts.
Berry, John, Millinery, 329 King St.
Berry, Peter, Confectioner, 251 King St.
Berry, Robert H., Dry Goods Store, 221 King St.
Bertrand, E., Mrs., Radcliff St., Neck
Bessart, P. G., Clerk, 20 Mazyck St.
Betner, Peter C., Boarding House, 36 Elliott St.
Bianchi, G., Carver & Gilder, 138 King St.
Birch, Weller & Co., Dry Goods Merchants, 270 King St.
Bird, J. S., Fancy Store, 22 Broad St., res. King St.
Bird, William, Ship Carpenter, 17 Pinckney St.
Birnie, William & George, Hardware Merchants, 21 Broad
    St.
Bishop, S. N., Merchant, 6 Magwood's Whf.
Black, Alexander, Superintendent of the Rail Road, 103
    Wentworth St.
Black, Alexander W., Merchant, 105 E. Bay St.
Black, Elizabeth, Mrs., Widow, 13 Bull St.
Black, James, Merchant, Spring St., Neck
Black, John, Merchant, 21 Broad St.
Black, William P., Baker, 195 King St.
Blackwood, John, Accountant, 86 Tradd St.
Blackwood, John, Merchant, Chisholm's N. Whf., res.
    Montague St., near Coming St.
Blackwood, Thomas, President, Planters & Mechanics
    Bank, 14 Pitt St.
Bladgeworth, Charlotte, 28 Wentworth St., F.P.C.
Blaimyer, Caroline, Radcliffborough, near St. Paul's
    Church, Neck
Blain, E., Mrs., Cannonborough, Neck
Blain, William S., Editor, "Irishman" & Teacher, 26 State
    St.
Blair, Andrew, Wheelwright, Meeting St., near Henrietta
    St., Neck
Blake, Charles, Commission Merchant, 141 E. Bay St.
Blake, Edward, 8 King St.
Blake, John H., Broker, 20 Broad St., res. 301 E. Bay St.
Blake, John, Tanner, n. side John St., Neck
Blamyer, William, w. end Cannon St., Neck
Blanchard, John, Shoe Maker, 135 E. Bay St.

Blaney, Joseph, State Constable, 24 Market St.
Blondeau, E., Hatter, 6 Queen St.
Bloomfield, John, 8 Friend St.
Blum, John A., Grocery, 117 Broad St.
Blum, Mary, Widow, King St., w. side, btw. Mary &
    Cannon St., Neck
Blumeau, Jean, Carpenter, 109 Church St.
Boag, William S. & Co., Druggists, 285 King St.
Boatwright, Hilleary, & Co., Commission Merchants, 149
    E. Bay St.
Bohlen, Johan, Grocery, cr. Archdale St. & Swinton's Ln.
Bond, Henry, Wheelwright, 57 State St.
Bondo, Heloise, Jewellery & Fancy Goods, 156 King St.
Bonneau, E., Miss, w. side Charlotte St., Neck
Bonneau, John, Factor, 12 Church St.
Bonneau, Symmes, 7 Church St.
Bonner, E. M., Milliner, 118 King St.
Bonner, John, Cabinet Maker, 118 Church St.
Bonnetheau, E., n. side Boundary St., Neck
Bonnetheau, Elizabeth, Mrs., Widow , 5 State St.
Bonnetheau, Henry B., Accountant, 5 State St.
Bonnetheau, James N., Printer, 5 State St.
Borch, Fanny, Hampstead, Neck, F.P.C.
Bordenave, John, Hair Dresser, 142 Meeting St.
Borno, Adele, 36 Anson St., F.P.C.
Bosse, Vincent, Billiard Room, w. side King St., above
    John St., Neck
Bostan, Peter B., Baker, w. side King St., btw.
    Vanderhorst & Warren Sts.
Boucheneau, Charles, w. end Magazine St.
Bourne, N. G., Baker, 40 Elliott St.
Bours, Luke, Accountant, 76 Church St.
Bousquet, Peter, Dry Goods Store, 183 King St.
Bowen, Ann, Grocery, e. end Laurens St.
Bowen, Nathaniel, Right Rev., D. D., Elliott St., w. side
    Cannonborough, Neck
Bowles, Abiel, Teacher, College St.
Bowman, Lynch, Miss, 22 Beaufain St.
Bowman, Mary Ann, 176 Church St.
Boyce & Henry, Factors, Fitzsimons' Whf.
Boyce, Ker, Factor, 20 Hasell St.
Boyd, J., Judith St., Radcliffborough, Neck
Boyden, Andrew, 230 Meeting St.
Boylston, Henry, M. D., cr. King & Hudson Sts., Neck
Brady, Edward, Grocery, 247 E. Bay St.
Brady, Edward, Grocery, s.e. cr. Boundary & Wall Sts.
Brady, John, Bricklayer, 16 Anson St.
Brailsford, Edward, M. D., 39 Tradd St.
Brailsford, Elizabeth, 12 Hasell St.
Brailsford, Elizabeth, Widow, 2 S. Bay St.
Brailsford, William, Factor, 80 King St.
Brainerd, Henry, 103 Meeting St.
Brainerd, Lavinia, 103 Meeting St.
Brandon, David P., Upholsterer, 77 Meeting St.
Branen & M'Intyre, Grocers, 266 King St.
Brase, Peter, Grocery, Stores, 97 & 108 Tradd St.
Braserman, Isabella, 27 Wall St.
Breffeahl, J. M., Gunsmith, 148 Meeting St.
Breman, C., Factor, 195 Meeting St.
Bremar, Henry, Dentist, 23 Pinckney St.

Bremer, Otto P. D., Grocery, s.w. cr. Queen & Mazyck Sts.

Brenan, C. & D., Factors, Fitzsimons' Whf.

Brewster, C. Starr, Dentist, 156 King St.

Brier, B. B., College St., F.P.C.

Bringloe, Richard, Shopkeeper, 65 Church St.

Brisbane, Mary, Widow, 29 Meeting St.

Brisbane, William, Planter, w. end Beaufain St.

Britton, Elizabeth, School Mistress, 49 Pinckney St.

Britton, T., Shoemaker, King St., near Vanderhorst St., Neck

Broadfoot, Frances, Widow, 296 E. Bay St.

Brocklebank, William, Plasterer, s.e. cr. Meeting & Henrietta Sts., Neck

Brodie, Robert H., Founder, 133 Coming St.

Brodie, Robert, Measurer of Lumber, 39 Meeting St.

Broughton, Ann, Miss, 49 Anson St.

Broughton, George J., Planter, n. side Boundary St., Neck

Brow, Harriett, Widow, 13 St. Michael's Al.

Brown & Weissinger, Dry Goods Etc., w. King St., btw. Cannon & Mary Sts., Neck

Brown, A. II., 56 E. Bay St.

Brown, Adam J., Pyrotechnist, 106 Wentworth St.

Brown, Alexander, Merchant, e. side St. Philip St., btw. Cannon & Mazyck Sts., Neck

Brown, Anna, Widow, 27 Society St.

Brown, Archibald, Widow, 13 Archdale St.

Brown, Chancy, 5 Clifford's Al., F.P.C.

Brown, Charles T., s.w. cr. Anson & George Sts.

Brown, Charlotte, 125 Wentworth St., F.P.C.

Brown, E., Boarding House, 10 Beason's Al.

Brown, Edward, 19 St. Michael's Al.

Brown, Eliza, Mantuamaker, 92 Market St.

Brown, Elizabeth, 35 St. Philip St.

Brown, George, Ship Carpenter, 35 St. Philip St.

Brown, Horatio, Bricklayer, 35 St. Philip St.

Brown, J., Barber, 225 King St., F.P.C.

Brown, James, 79 Church St.

Brown, James, Mrs., Washington St., Mazyckborough, Neck

Brown, Jane, Mrs., e. end Laurens St.

Brown, John B., Hat Store, 17 Broad St.

Brown, John, Cabinet Maker, 88 King St., F.P.C.

Brown, Joshua, Mrs., Boarding House, 56 E. Bay St.

Brown, June, 264 E. Bay St., F.P.C.

Brown, M., Rev., Pastor, St. Mary's Catholic Church, res. n.e. cr. Wentworth & St. Philip Sts.

Brown, M., Shoe Maker, 48 Anson St., F.P.C.

Brown, Moses, Barber, 57 Elliott St., F.P.C.

Brown, Peter, Barber, 10 Elliott St., F.P.C.

Brown, Polly, Charlotte St., Mazyckborough, Neck, F.P.C.

Brown, Richard, 16 Society St.

Brown, Robert C., Notary Public, 95 E. Bay St., res. 47 Tradd St.

Brown, Robert E., Factor, 79 Church St.

Brown, Robert, Factor, 79 Church St.

Brown, Sidney, Printer, 35 St. Philip St.

Brown, Tunis & Co., Factors, Roper's Whf.

Brown, William, 14 Burns Ln.

Brown, William, Boarding House, 11 Beason's Al.

Brown, William, Planter, 79 Church St.

Bryan, John, Planter, n.w. cr. Hasell & Anson Sts.

Bryan, Jonathon, Dry Goods Store, 335 King St.

Buckhester, J. A., 73 Boundary St.

Buckle, Mary Ann, Widow, 261 King St.

Buckmyer, Cornelius, Merchant, 28 Holbrick's Al.

Buckmyer, John C., Merchant, res. 24 Society St.

Buckner, Eliza, Mrs., 15 Bull St.

Buckner, J. H., Accountant, 28 Horlbeck's Al.

Budd, Sarah, Widow, 80 Church St.

Budd, Thomas, Capt., 52 Tradd St.

Buerhaus, H. D., Tailor, 21 Queen St.

Buist, Arthur, Rev., Teacher, 6 St. Michael's Al.

Buist, George, Attorney, 11 Hasell St.

Buist, Mary, Widow, 5 Church St.

Buliock, Eliza, Mrs., School Mistress, 105 Church St.

Bull, John, Grocery, n. side Boundary St., Neck

Bull, -----, Mrs., Widow, 10 Lamboll St.

Bull, Rose, Charlotte St., Mazyckborough, Neck, F.P.C.

Bull, Samuel, Boot & Shoe Store, 271 King St.

Bullwinkle, George, Grocery, cr. Wentworth & St. Philip Sts.

Bulow, John J., Planter, n. cr. King & Cannon St., Neck

Bunch, D., Millinery, 263 King St.

Bunch, Dennis, Butcher, Hampstead, Neck

Bundrock, Charles, Grocery, cr. King & Lamboll Sts.

Burch, Sarah, Widow, 42 Wentworth St.

Burckmyer, J. C. & Co., Merchants, 140 E. Bay St.

Burdell, R. F., Grocer, cr. E. Bay & Tradd Sts., res. Beaufain St.

Burden & Joor, Factors, Chisholm's N. Whf.

Burden, Kinsey, Jr., Factor, 15 Meeting St.

Burden, Kinsey, Sr., Planter, 15 Meeting St.

Burdges, S. B., Tavern, 18 Queen St., cr. State St.

Burger, Samuel, Tax Collector, 70 Queen St.

Burges, James S., Printer, 44 Queen St.

Burgoyne, William, Druggist, 2 Broad St., res. 2 Water St.

Burie, Daniel, Blacksmith, 127 Meeting St.

Burk, John, Carpenter, 9 Middle St., F.P.C.

Burke, J. H., Pilot, 3 Stoll's Al.

Burke, Richard, Pilot, Church St., op. Stoll's Al.

Burke, Rosalie, Hampstead, Neck

Burnham, Thomas, n. side Boundary St., Neck

Burnham, William, Locksmith, 59 Pinckney St.

Burns, J. M., Bootmaker, 108 Church St.

Burns, Mary, Mrs., 15 Minority St.

Burrell, William, Bootmaker, 52 Broad St.

Burrows, Ellen, 102 Wentworth St., F.P.C.

Burrows, Frederick, Pilot, 36 Meeting St.

Busing, J. D., Grocery, Montague St.

Bussacker, Charles, Dry Goods Store, 307 King St.

Bussey & Hawley, Grocers, 2 Vendue Range

Busson, P. F., Spring St., Neck

Buswell, M., Grocer, Gadsden's Whf.

Butler, Charles P., Goldsmith, 135 King St.

Butler, Eliza, Mrs., 32 Laurens St.

Butler, Nelly, Judith St., Neck, F.P.C.

Butler, Robert, Capt., 59 Boundary St.

Byrne, A., Rev., n.e. cr. Broad & Friend Sts.

Cabeuil, Louis, Tailor, 95 Church St.

Cabeuil, Louisa E., Shopkeeper, 91 Church St.
Cain, William D., Shoemaker, 181 Church St.
Calder, James, Merchant, Chisolm's N. Whf., res. 23 Meeting St.
Caldwell, William A., Vendue Master, 25 Vendue Range
Callender, H., Widow, 7 Water St.
Calton, James, Dr., 17 St. Michael's Al.
Calvert, Eliza, Mrs., 16 Guignard St.
Calvo, Rachael, 114 Queen St.
Cambridge, St. John, Printer, 14 Wall St.
Cameron, Ann, Boarding House, 100 Queen St.
Campbell, A.W., Factor, 2 New St.
Campbell, Isaac M., M. D., 93 Broad St.
Campbell, James, Grocer, cr. State & Chalmers Sts.
Campbell, John, s.e. cr. Meeting & Ann Sts., Neck
Campbell, Peter, Tavern, 202 King St.
Campbell, Rose, 33 St. Philip St., F.P.C.
Campbell, Samuel, Barber, 209 E. Bay St., F.P.C.
Cannon, George, Dry Goods Store, 320 King St.
Cannon, Jane, King St., near Line St., Neck
Canter, Emanuel, Clerk, 79 King St.
Canter, Rebecca, Widow, 2 Savage St.
Cantwell, P., Factor, Gadsden's Whf.
Capers, L. G., Dry Goods Store, 338 King St.
Capers, Thomas F., Planter, 45 Meeting St.
Capers, William, Rev., 232 Meeting St.
Capers, William, Rev., n.e. cr. Coming & Boundary Sts., Neck
Cardoza, David, 99 E. Bay St.
Cardozo, Isaac, 99 E. Bay St.
Cardozo, J. N., 99 E. Bay St.
Carew, Edward, n.e. cr. Wall & Laurens Sts.
Carivenc, -----, Madame, 224 Meeting St.
Carlisle, Margaret, Widow, 6 Anson St.
Carman, M., Milliner, 301 King St.
Carmand, Francis, Woolen Draper & Men's Mercer, 86 Queen St.
Carmil, John, Butcher, w. side Meeting St., btw. Columbus & Wolf Sts., Neck
Carnochan, Richard, Merchant, 1 Crafts' S. Whf.
Carpenter, C., Butcher, s. side Cannon St., Neck
Carpenter, James, Butcher, s. side Cannon St., Neck
Carr & Riley, Tailors, 146 King St.
Carr, G. D., Boarding House, 34 Queen St.
Carrere, C. J., Accountant, 107 Broad St.
Carrere, Eliza, Widow, 107 Broad St.
Carrol, C. R., Attorney, 74 Broad St.
Carroll, B., Jr., Radcliffborough, n.w. end, Neck
Carroll, Bartholomew, Planter, Radcliffborough, n.w. End, Neck
Carroll, Charles R., Attorney, Radcliffborough, n.w. end, Neck
Carroll, R. W., Hair Dresser, 4 Queen St.
Carson, Elisha, Merchant, e. side King St., btw. Wolf & Spring Sts., Neck
Carson, William, Grocer, 144 King St.
Carson, William, Planter, 90 Tradd St.
Carston, John, Scavenger, 30 Society St.
Cart, John, Bookkeeper, Planters & Mechanics Bank, res. 53 Meeting St.

Cart, John, Measurer of Lumber, 38 Bull St.
Casey, T. E., Coachmaker, 5 Chalmers St.
Caskin, John, Carpenter, Charlotte St., Neck
Cason, James, Grain Store, 58 Market St.
Cassady, Patrick, Livery Stables, 142 Church St.
Cassin, Conly, Notary Public, Gadsden's Whf.
Cassin, Mary, Mrs., e. end Laurens St.
Catherwood, J., Watchmaker, 63 Broad St.
Cauley, William, Tailor, 55 State St.
Causse, Elizabeth, Mrs., 7 Price's Al.
Caw, Peter, Watchmaker, 78 Meeting St., res. 18 Friend St.
Cay, John E., 183 E. Bay St.
Chamberlin, J. & Co., Importers of China, Glass & Crockery, 277 King St.
Chandler, Muldrowe, Widow, 46 St. Philip St.
Chapeau, J. B., Confectioner, 128 Church St.
Chapman, James, Merchant, 76 King St.
Chapman, Thomas, Merchant, 51 E. Bay St.
Chartrand, Philip, Tivoli Garden, Meeting St., near Line St., Neck
Chase, P. S., Shoe Store, 80 Meeting St.
Chasteau, D. C., Druggist, 176 Meeting St.
Chate, Catharine, Widow, 5 Pinckney St.
Chazel, Eliza R., Widow, 6 Anson St.
Cheeseborough & Campbell, Factors, 54 E. Bay St.
Cheeseborough, J. W., Factor, 2 New St.
Cheves, Eliza, 39 Hasell St., F.P.C.
Cheves, Langdon, Planter, Pinckney St., Cannonborough, Neck
Chew, T. R., Blacksmith, Lucas St., Cannonborough, Neck
Chiffelle, Thomas P., Export & Coastwise Inspector, 181 Queen St.
Childs, Robert, 143 Meeting St.
Chisolm, George, Jr., 22 Legare St.
Chisolm, George, Sr., Factor, 25 E. Bay St.
Chisolm, Robert T., Sawmills, w. end Tradd St., res. 2 Meeting St.
Chisolm, S., Tavern, s.w. cr. King & George Sts.
Chisolm, William, Tailor, 7 Smith's Ln., F.P.C.
Chitty, Richard, Butcher, cr. Nassau & Wolf Sts., Neck
Chrietzberg, Clara, Shopkeeper, 72 Market St.
Chrietzberg, Conrad, Grocer, 12 King St.
Chrietzberg, George, Baker, 42 King St.
Christopherson, C., Grocer, 12 King St.
Chupein, L. Y., Millinery, 158 King St.
Chupein, Lewis, Mineral Water Establishment, 13 Broad St.
Chur, George, Grocer, 26 Market St.
Clancy, John, Grocery, w. side King St., near Warren St., Neck
Clark & Thompson, Attorneys, 116 Church St.
Clark, B., Dry Goods Store, 163 King St.
Clark, Charles, Engineer, 8 Maiden Ln.
Clark, Charles, Grocer, cr. E. Bay & Tradd Sts.
Clark, J. R., Boundary St., n.e. end, Neck, F.P.C.
Clark, Mary, Mrs., 31 Guignard St.
Clark, Richard, Pilot, 6 Stoll's Al.
Clarke, E., n. side Boundary St., near Meeting St., Neck
Clarkson, Elizabeth, Widow, Bull St., near Coming St.

5

Clarkson, Emanuel, Student at Law, Bull St., near Coming St.

Clawson, John, Clerk, 2 Archdale St.

Clayton, David, Wagon Yard, King St., near Radcliff St., Neck

Cleapor & Fields, Sail Makers, Price's Whf.

Cleapor, Agnes, Mrs., 27 Laurens St.

Cleary, Catherine, Widow, Vernon St.

Cleary, N. G., Planter, 85 Wentworth St.

Clement, Sarah, Widow, 97 Queen St.

Clements, S., Mrs., St. Philip St., near Cannon St., Neck

Clifford, Henry, Factor, Middle St.

Clissey, A., Dry Goods Store, 182 King St.

Clissey, Raymond, Store Keeper, 98 King St.

Clough, James B., Merchant, 188 E. Bay St.

Clouson, John, Patroon, 26 Beaufain St.

Clyde, Thomas M., Tanner, Amherst St., n. side Hampstead, Neck

Cobia, F. I., Butcher, Reid St., s. side, btw. King & Meeting Sts., Neck

Cobia, Henry, Merchant, 132 E. Bay St., res. 82 Wentworth St.

Coburn, Anna, Mrs., 12 Middle St.

Cochran, Alexander, Accountant, e. end Society St.

Cochran, C., Planter, w. end Cannon St., Cannonborough, Neck

Cochran, Margaret, Dry Goods Store, 120 King St.

Cochran, Samuel, Tailor, Elizabeth St., Neck, F.P.C.

Cochran, T., Mrs., Widow, w. end Cannon St., Cannonborough, Neck

Cochran, T., Mrs., Widow, w. end Cannon St., Cannonborough, Neck

Coffey, B. J., Grocer, s.e. cr. Market & State Sts.

Cogdell, J. S., Naval Officer, 46 Meeting St.

Cogdell, R., Mrs., cr. Pitt & Rutledge Sts.

Cogdell, R. W., Teller, Bank of the State, cr. Broad St. & Gadsden Al.

Cogswell, H. & Co., Dry Goods Store, 324 King St.

Cohen, David D., Planter, Montague St.

Cohen, Hartwig, King St., op. Tobacco St.

Cohen, Hyam, Sutler, 12 Orange St.

Cohen, Mordecai, Planter, 103 Broad St.

Cohen, Moses, Widow, 74 King St.

Cohen, Myer M., Attorney, 70 Broad St., res. 57 E. Bay St.

Cohen, Nathan A., Clothing Store, 169 E. Bay St.

Cohen, Philip, Broker & Commission Merchant, 57 E. Bay St.

Cohen, Solomon J., Dry Goods Store, 356 King St.

Cohler, Archibald, Stevedore, 24 Mazyck St., F.P.C.

Cohrs, H. A., Dry Goods Store, 322 King St.

Colburn, F. A. & Co., Dry Goods Store, 86 Broad St.

Colburn, James S., Dry Goods Store, 86 Broad St.

Cole, Eliza, St. Philip St., btw. Vanderhorst & Warren Sts., Neck

Cole, John, Butcher, Nassau St., Neck

Cole, John, Clerk, 8 St. Philip St.

Cole, Joseph, Planter, 8 St. Philip St.

Cole, Sarah, 19 St. Philip St.

Coleman, Richard, Shop Keeper, 63 Tradd St.

Coleman, Wright & Co., Wholesale Saddlery, 292 King St.

Collier, William, Inspector of Customs, 14 Wentworth St.

Collins, John, Dryer & Courier, 169 Meeting St.

Colson, Owen, Planter, 168 King St.

Colton, Thomas, Tailor, 94 Market St.

Colzy, Angelique, Widow, 111 Church St.

Condy, Jeremiah, Merchant, 122 E. Bay St., res. 100 Meeting St.

Condy, Thomas D., Attorney, 98 Meeting St., res. 9 Church St.

Conner, Daffy, Henrietta St., Neck, F.P.C.

Conner, John, Saddler, 271 King St.

Conner, Samuel, Gristmill, 64 Market St., res. 33 Hasell St.

Connolly, Elizabeth, Widow, 35 Pinckney St.

Connolly, J., Grocer, 14 S. Bay St.

Cook, D., Wagon Yard, e. side King St., btw. Mary & Reid Sts., Neck

Cook, J. A., Grocery, Radcliffborough, near St. Paul's Church, Neck

Cook, Otto, Grocer, n.e. cr. Anson & Laurens Sts.

Cooper, Mary, Mrs., 23 St. Philip St.

Cooper, N., Shoe Store, 143 King St., res. 63 Anson St.

Cooper, T. J., 125 Queen St., F.P.C.

Cooper, William, Shoe Maker, 64 Church St., F.P.C.

Copes, T., Pilot, 5 Stoll's Al.

Coram, Charlotte, Mrs., 43 George St.

Corbett, Elizabeth, Miss, 4 Logan St.

Corbett, James, Dry Goods Store, 330 King St.

Corbett, John, Planter, cr. Lynch & Bull Sts.

Corbett, Thomas, Jr., Planter, cr. Lynch & Bull Sts.

Corbett, Thomas, Planter, cr. Lynch & Bull Sts.

Corby, John, Blacksmith, O'Neale & Bird's Whf.

Corcoran, Jane, Grocer, 62 King St.

Cordes, R. N., Mrs., n. side Charlotte St., Neck

Cords, Richard, Carpenter, Henrietta St., Neck, F.P.C.

Corlies, Peter, Grocer, 16 Wall St.

Cormick, Thomas, Factor, 21 Vanderhorst's Whf., res. 64 Church St.

Corrie, Sam, Wheelwright, e. side King St., btw. John & Ann Sts., Neck

Cot, Julia, 75 Boundary St., F.P.C.

Cotchett, George, Factor, Edmondston's Whf., res. Fort St., near S. Bay St.

Cotes, Christopher, Factor, 19 Wentworth St.

Courtenay, Edward S., Magistrate & School, St. Philip St., btw. Warren & Radcliff Sts., Neck

Courtney, H., Mrs., Boarding House, 56 Broad St.

Courtney, Lydia, Widow, cr. Church & Elliott Sts.

Cowan, John, Cabinet Maker, 157 Meeting St.

Cowan, Maria, 34 Beaufain St.

Cox, George, Seed Store, 212 King St.

Cox, Thomas, Shoemaker, Chapel St., Neck, F.P.C.

Crafts, H. B., Mrs., e. side Coming St., btw. Vanderhorst & Boundary Sts., Neck

Cramer, George, Tavern, 55 Queen St.

Crane, Henry, Grocer, 248 E. Bay St.

Crawford, John, Planter, 1 Rutledge St.

Crawford, Lewis, Meeting St., near Municipal Guard House, Neck

Crawley, Hannah, Widow, 78 Broad St.

Cripps, C. A. & C., Misses, 45 Meeting St.
Cripps, Hester, Widow, 27 E. Bay St.
Crocker, D. & Co., Merchants, Magwood's Whf., res. 23 Tradd St.
Crocker, Hester, cr. Archdale St. & Swinton's Ln.
Croft, George, Capt., 9 Cumberland St.
Crofts, Arnoldus, 13 Liberty St.
Cromwell, Samuel, Bricklayer, 19 Back St.
Cross, Charles K., Clerk, 145 E. Bay St.
Cross, George W., Attorney, 2 Waring's Row, res. 44 Meeting St.
Cross, William, Bricklayer, 64 Beaufain St.
Crovat, L. J., 281 King St.
Crovat, Peter, Paint Store, 269 King St.
Crowley, Ann, Mrs., 102 St. Philip St..
Crozier, Alexander, 48 King St.
Crozier, William, Grocer, 48 King St.
Cruger, Henry N., Attorney, 4 Short St.
Cruger, Lewis, Attorney, 4 Short St.
Cruger, Nicholas, Merchant, 4 Short St.
Cruickshanks, D., Tanner, 22 Queen St.
Cruickshanks, Robert, Tailor, 24 Berresford St.
Cruickshanks, William, King St., e. side, btw. John & Hudson Sts., Neck
Cullum, Sarah, Widow, 45 Beaufain St.
Cummings, R. G., w. side St. Philip St., near Line St., Neck
Cunningham, A. F., Printer, 36 Queen St.
Cunningham, A. J., Watchmaker & Jeweller, 278 King St.
Cunningham, Andrew, Carpenter, 45 Beaufain St.
Cunningham, Richard., Hon., State Senator, n. side Charlotte St., Neck
Curtis, Ann, Widow, 39 Coming St.
Curtis, E. M., Carpenter, Queen St., near Medical College
Curtis, Thomas, M. D., 11 Liberty St.
Cushan, Eliza, 17 Anson St.
Cuthbert, James, Planter, 6 Smith St.
Deming & Bulkley, Furniture Ware Store, 218 King St.
Dalcho, Frederick, D. D., 19 New St.
Daley, William, Grocery, 156 Meeting St.
Damascin, Martin, Grocery, 45 King St.
Darby, Harriett, Mrs., Washington St., Neck
Darby, John, Silversmith, 27 Archdale St.
Dard, Peter, Coachmaker, 18 Laurens St.
Darrell, E. B., Mrs., Widow, Pitt St.
Darrill, Ann H., Miss, 5 Society St.
Dart, Bella, Mantuamaker, 18 Pitt St., F.P.C.
Dart, Benjamin, 55 Tradd St.
Dasher, Claus, Grocery, 139 E. Bay St.
Dasoux, Harriet, 32 St. Philip St., F.P.C.
Datty, Julia, Miss, Female Academy, 21 Legare St.
Dauesne, P., Teacher of French, Charleston College
Davega, Isaac, Dry Goods Store, 215 King St., res. 29 George St.
Davega, Moses, 169 Meeting St.
Davenport & Rice, Wholesale Boot & Shoe Store, 105 King St.
Davenport, C. A., Boot & Shoe Store, cr. of King & Clifford Sts.
Davenport, S. & Co., Merchants, 6 Crafts' Whf.

Davidson & M'Nicoll, Merchants, cr. of Crafts' N. Whf. & E. Bay St.
Davidson, M. E., Mrs., Boarding House, Ellery St., op. Church St.
Davidson, William, Merchant, 296 E. Bay St.
Davis, Eliza, 50 Anson St., F.P.C.
Davis, George Y., Merchant, 52 E. Bay St.
Davis, Henry, Vendue Master, 331 King St.
Davis, Jacob, Painter, 34 Tradd St.
Davis, Jane, Mrs., Boarding House, 45 E. Bay St.
Davis, John, Capt., 37 E. Bay St.
Davis, M. E., Mrs., n.w. end Cannonborough, Neck
Davis, Margaret, Boarding House, 102 Queen St.
Davis, Martha, Widow, 7 Clifford St.
Davis, Martha, Widow, cr. John & Meeting Sts., Neck
Davis, Rene P., Sausage Maker, 5 Maiden Ln.
Davis, Thomas, Capt., 75 Church St.
Davis, W. T., n.w. end Cannonborough, Neck
Daws, Elsy, 32 Anson St., F.P.C.
Dawse, H. P., Factor, Roper's Whf., res. 69 Church St.
Dawson, C. W., Mrs., s. side Ann St., Neck
Dawson, Charles, Planter, 120 Broad St.
Dawson, J. C., Accountant, 11 New St.
Dawson, J. Drayton, Attorney, 5 Waring's Range, res. 34 Bull St.
Dawson, John, Jr., Inspector of Customs, Ann St., Neck
Dawson, Octavius, Outdoor Clerk, State Bank, 13 Bull St.
Dawson, S. P., Accountant, 11 New St.
Dawson, Samuel, Carpenter, Henrietta St., Neck
Dawson, W. A., Accountant, 11 New St.
Dawson, William, Planter, 7 Rutledge St.
Day & Edgerton, Drapers & Tailors, 262 King St.
Day & Hubbell, Coachmakers, 68 Wentworth St.
Day, F., Millinery, 284 King St.
Deas & Brown, Factors, 6 Kiddell's Whf.
Deas, E. H., M. D., 119 Church St.
Deas, Henry, Hon., State Senator, 7 Friend St.
Deas, John M., cr. E. Bay & Minority Sts.
Deas, Maria Mary, Ann St., Neck, F.P.C.
Deas, Seaman, Planter, King St., btw. Hudson & John Sts., Neck
Deas, Thomas H., Planter, s. side John St., Neck
Dease, John, Watchmaker, 18 State St.
DeBow, John, Coachmaker, 202 Meeting St.
DeBow, Mary, Widow, 12 Amen St.
DeCamps, James, Broker, 102 King St.
DeCosta, Jane, e. side King St., near Ann St., Neck
Deery, J., Shoe Store, 174 E. Bay St.
DeGafferally, A., Wood & Lumber Measurer, 6 Middle St.
Dehon, Sarah, Widow, 43 Meeting St.
Deignan, Mary, Lucas St., Cannonborough, Neck
Dekrief, Richard, Barber, Nassau St., Hampstead, F.P.C., Neck
DeLaMotta, Jacob, M. D., 88 Broad St., cr. King St.
Delaney, Michael, Pilot, 62 Church St.
DeLang, Martha, Widow, 218 E. Bay St.
DeLarge, Mary, 25 Pinckney St., F.P.C.
DeLelisseline, F. A., Attorney, 116 Wentworth St.
DellaTorre, A., Looking Glass Store, 65 Broad St.
DeLorme, A., Grocery, 8 Champney St.

7

DeLorme, J. F. & Son, Upholsterers, 24 State St.
Dempsey, Massy, 1 Cumberland St., F.P.C.
Dempsey, Miles, Bank Coffee House, 129 E. Bay St.
Dempsey, Thomas, Grocery, 12 Champney St.
Dener, Christianna, Widow, 31 Mazyck St.
Dennehy, Jeremiah, Printer, 97 Market St.
Dennis, Thomas S., M. D., 3 George St.
Dennisson, H. C., Mrs., n.e. cr. Pitt & Wentworth Sts.
Denoon & Highet, Bakers, 85 Queen St.
Dent, Ann, Widow, cr. Pitt & Montague Sts.
Deromas, Eugene, Store Keeper, w. side King St., op. Ann St., Neck
DeSaussure, Charles, Factor, 35 Meeting St.
DeSaussure, H. A., Attorney, 35 Meeting St.
DeSaussure, H. W., Hon., 35 Meeting St.
Descoudres & Co., Grocery, Wine & Liquor Store, 281 King St.
Desel, C. M., Radcliffborough, Neck
Deveaux, Jane, Widow, w. side Meeting St., btw. Wolf & Reid Sts., Neck
Deveaux, Portias, Accountant, w. side Meeting St., btw. Wolf & Reid Sts., Neck
Deveaux, T. E., Attorney, Spring St., Neck
DeVillers & Poirter, Grocery, n.e. cr. Queen St.
DeVillers, Louis, Music Store, 91 Broad St.
Dewees, John, Factor, Mary St., Wraggborough, Neck
Dewees, John, Wine Store, 70 E. Bay St.
Dewees, Joseph, s.e. cr. Charlotte & Alexander Sts., Neck
Dewees, William, Factor, 4 Wall St.
Dewitt, William, Carpenter, w. end Magazine St.
Deye, Benjamin, 16 Church St.
Dibble, A. C., Hat Store, 37 Broad St.
Dick, James, Autioneer & Commission Merchant, 23 Vendue Range
Dickinson, Francis, Planter, Alexander St., Wraggborough, Neck
Dickson, J. R., Grocery, 207 E. Bay St.
Dickson, John, M. D., 31 Coming St.
Dickson, S. D., Grocery, 201 E. Bay St.
Dickson, S. Henry, M. D., cr. Hudson & Meeting Sts., Neck
Dickson, Thomas, King St., near Columbus St., Neck
Dieckman, J. H., Grocery, Hampstead, Neck
Dile, Jane, Dry Goods Store, 158 King St.
Dill, Anthony, John St., Neck, F.P.C.
Dixon, John, Merchant, w. side King St., near Ann St., Neck
Dixon, Robert, Bricklayer, 31 Pinckney St.
Dodd & Barnard, Merchants, 183 E. Bay St.
Dogget, S. W., Teacher, 236 Meeting St.
Don, Alexander, Printer, 52 Society St.
Donegan, J., Boot & Shoemaker, 237 King St.
Doret, A. M., Goldsmith, 115 King St.
Dorrill, Robert, Factor, 25 State St.
Dotterer, Thomas, Engineer, cr. Motte & Anson Sts.
Doucin, M., Boot & Shoe Store, cr. Meeting & Market Sts.
Dougherty, J., Plasterer, 16 Bull St.
Dougherty, Joseph, Grocery, 27 S. Bay St.
Doughton, Francis, Fruit Store, 312 King St.

Doughty, James M. E., w. cr. Elliott & Bridge Sts., Neck
Doughty, William, cr. George & St. Philip Sts.
Douglas, Margaret, 75 Meeting St., F.P.C.
Douglass, Benjamin, M. D., Pritchard's Whf.
Douglass, Campbell, Grocery, 141 Meeting St.
Douglass, John, Wolf St., Neck
Dowling, Archibald, Grocery, 3 King St.
Dowling, Elizabeth A., Widow, 17 Society St.
Downie, Robert, Tin Plate Worker, 59 Broad St.
Drayton, Alfred, 3 Rutledge St.
Drayton, Charles, M. D., w. end Montague St.
Drayton, John, Mrs., Widow, w. end Bull St.
Drayton, Mary, 9 West St., F.P.C.
Drayton, Susan, 22 Berresford St., F.P.C.
Drayton, William, Hon., Member of Congress., res. 4 Gibbes St.
Drege, Peter, Clothing Store, n.e. cr. Queen & E. Bay Sts.
Drewes, Wilson, Mrs., Widow, 55 Coming St.
Duboc, Francis, Dry Goods Store, 187 King St.
Dubois, E., Mrs., Upholsterer, 90 Queen St.
Duffield, John, Merchant, Chisolm's N. Whf.
Duffus, John, Broker & Notary Public, 87 E. Bay St., cr. Church & Water Sts.
Duffy, James, Grocery, 10 S. Bay St.
Duffy, Neil, Tavern, 46 Queen St.
Duggan, Thomas, Bricklayer, St. Philip St., near Lines, Neck
Duhadway, -----, Mrs., Millinery, 106 King St.
Duhn, Henry, Grocery, 15 Back St.
Dukes, Francis, Grocery, s. cr. King & Columbus Sts., Neck
Dukes, W. C., Factor, Edmondston's Whf., res. cr. Anson & Society Sts.
Dumont, Maria Adelaide Rosignol, 128 Meeting St.
Dunkin, Benjamin F., Attorney, Radcliffborough, Neck
Dunlap, William, Clerk, 22 Broad St.
Dunn, J. E., Storekeeper, 68 Market St.
Dupont, Francis, Paper Hanger, 162 King St.
Dupont, Joseph, Shopkeeper, 90 Meeting St.
DuPrat, Sarah, 129 King St., F.P.C.
Dupree, A., Widow, 88 Tradd St.
Dupree, Julianna, 12 Society St.
DuPree, James, e. side Meeting St., btw. Mary & Ann Sts., Neck
Duprey, Antionette, Widow, 30 Hasell St.
Duquereron, F., Merchant, 3 Fraser's Whf. res. 19 Tradd St.
Durand, Victor, Clothing Store, 155 E. Bay, res. 38 Queen St.
Durban, A., Hatter, 67 Queen St.
Duryea, Jacob, Boarding House, 9 Queen St.
Duryen, E. S., Printer, 9 Queen St.
Duval, Peter, Grocery, Cannon St., Neck
Dwight, Eliza, Pastry Cook, 85 Broad St., F.P.C.
Dwyer, Patrick, Grocery, 74 Tradd St.
Eager, Robert, Clerk, cr. Wentworth & Coming Sts.
Eager, Sarah, Mrs., 115 Wentworth St.
Eason, Christiana, 37 Hasell St.
Eason, Robert, Ship Carpenter, 35 Anson St.

Easterby, George, Capt., 87 E. Bay St.
Eaton, Amaziah, Boarding House, cr. State & Amen Sts.
Eaton, R., s.w. cr. Maiden Ln. & Guignard St.
Eaton's, -----, Miss, Seminary, 19 George St.
Eckhard, George B., Attorney, 31 George St.
Eckhard, Jacob, Jr., 37 Society St.
Eckhard, Jacob, Sr., Musician, 31 George St.
Eckhoff, George H., n. side Boundary St., Neck
Eddings, William, Carpenter, 12 Smith St., F.P.C.
Eden, William, 51 Beaufain St.
Edgerton & Allen, Academy, 127 Wentworth St.
Edmondston, Charles & Co., Merchants, Edmonston's Whf.
Ednard, Jane, 27 St. Philip St., F.P.C.
Edwards, Charles E., M. D., 123 Wentworth St.
Edwards, Edward H., Planter, 11 Meeting St.
Edwards, G. B., 14 Legare St.
Edwards, George, Planter, 14 Legare St.
Edwards, Henry, n.e. end Boundary St., Neck
Edwards, James, 22 Wall St.
Efler, John, Butcher, Cannon St., Neck
Eggart, Julia, 34 St. Philip St., F.P.C.
Egleston, George W., Attorney, w. end Radcliffborough, Neck
Ehney, Mary, Miss, 28 Magazine St.
Ehney, P. M. C., Inspector of Customs, 9 Pinckney St.
Ehney, William, Tailor, Charlotte St., Mazyckborough, Neck
Elder, James, Tanner, John St., Neck
Elfe, Albert, Carpenter, 42 George St.
Elfe, B., Miss, e. end Chapel St., Neck
Elfe, Edward, M. D., 175 Meeting St.
Elfe, George, Printer, 61 Church St.
Elfe, Isaac, Accountant, 175 Meeting St.
Elfe, Robert, Attorney, off. 5 Fireproof Building, res. 175 Meeting St.
Elfe, William, Accountant, 175 Meeting St.
Elford, A. L., Mrs., Widow, cr. Meeting St. & Lines, Neck
Elford, James, Mathematic Instrument Maker, 119 E. Bay St.
Elliott, Alexander, 5 Coming St., F.P.C.
Elliott, Barnard, Mrs., 10 George St.
Elliott, Benjamin, Attorney, 20 Legare St.
Elliott, Daphne, 2 Smith's Ln., F.P.C.
Elliott, Stephen, Jr., Attorney, 22 St. Michael's Al., res. 2 Short St.
Elliott, Thomas O., Attorney, 194 Church St., res. 90 Church St.
Elliott, William, Accountant, 20 Legare St.
Ellis, Mary, Seamstress, cr. Maiden Ln. & Guignard Sts.
Ellis, Moses J., Accountant, 25 St. Philip St.
Ellis, Noah J., Printer, 25 St. Philip St
Elmore, Stent, Painter, Vernon St.
Elsworth, J. T., Gauger, 3 Boundary St.
Elwig, Peter, Carpenter, w. end Beaufain St., F.P.C.
Emanuel, Isaac, Auctioneer, 302 King St., res. 7 Meeting St.
Emery, Elizabeth, Widow, 2 Unity Al.
Emmett, Sarah, Seamstress, 7 Middle St., F.P.C.
England, Alexander, Planter, 54 Tradd St.

England, John, Right Rev., Bishop of Charleston, cr. Wentworth & St. Philip Sts.
English, James, Carpenter, S. Bay St.
Esdra, Adelph, Watchmaker, 115 E. Bay St.
Esnard, Peter, Grocery, 85 Church St.
Eude, Louis, Coffee House, 141 E. Bay St.
Evan, James, Stone Cutter, 40 Coming St.
Evan, John, Gold & Silversmith, 214 King St.
Evans, Charles, Turner, 118 Meeting St.
Evans, J. H., Millwright, Gadsden's Whf.
Evans, Laycraft, Carpenter, 81 Queen St.
Evans, Sarah, e. end Hampstead, Neck
Everingham, John, Mrs., Widow, 244 E. Bay St.
Evern, Fayette, 3 Maiden Ln., F.P.C.
Eyland, James, Jewellery & Fancy Goods, 172 King St.
Faber, H. F., Planter, Charlotte St., Neck
Faber, Joseph W., Attorney, Charlotte St., Neck
Fable, John, Grocery, s.w. cr. St. Philip & Cannon Sts., Neck
Fair, Pleasant, Cannon St., Cannonborough, Neck
Fair, William, 20 Mazyck St.
Fairchild, R., Tavern, 274 King St.
Farley, John, Teacher, 1 Bull St.
Fasbender, John, Watchmaker, 112 Meeting St.
Fash, Leonard, Grocery, 158 Meeting St. & 5 Vendue Range
Fayolle, Peter, Dancing Master, 82 King St.
Fayolle, Theodore B., Musician, 80 King St.
Fechtman, John, Grocery, 10 Smith's Ln.
Feeny, Luke, Store Keeper, 17 Archdale St.
Fell, Thomas D., Tinner, 100 Market St.
Fell, W., Mrs., Boarding House, 48 Broad St.
Fenn, Townsend & Hull, Dry Goods Store, 242 King St.
Ferguson, Ann, Widow, n. cr. King & John Sts., Neck
Ferguson, E. M., Widow, 10 Orange St.
Ferguson, James, Planter, n. cr. King & John Sts., Neck
Ferguson, John, Tailor, 23 Broad St.
Ferguson, Maria, Seamstress, 22 Boundary St., F.P.C.
Ferrett, J. T., Fruit Store, 42 Market St.
Ferrit, Charles, Tailor, 44 Coming St.
Fillette, F., Dry Goods Store, 159 King St.
Fink, Jane, Seamstress, 42 St. Philip St., F.P.C.
Finley, Rush, M. D., 69 Broad St.
Finley, William P., Attorney, 69 Broad St.
Fits, John, Butcher, Hampstead, Neck
Fitzsimons, Charles, State Constable, 58 Elliott St.
Fitzsimons, Christopher, Merchant, 22 Hasell St.
Fitzsimons, Thomas, Carpenter, Henrietta St., Neck
Flagg, H. C., Attorney, 64 Wentworth St., off. State House Sq.
Flanagan, Emma, Boarding House, Philadelphia St.
Fleig, Francis, Musician, 26 Hasell St.
Fleming, J. H., Ship Joiner, O'Neale & Bird's Whf.
Fleming, Joseph H., 15 Hasell St.
Fleming, Patrick, Storekeeper, 228 E. Bay St.
Flemming, James, Grocery, 18 Tradd St.
Flemming, Robert, Grocery, e. side King St., btw. Wolf & Spring Sts., Neck
Flemming, Ross & Co., Wholesale Grocery, cr. E. Bay St. & Vendue Range

Flemming, Thomas, Merchant, 18 George St.
Flemming, Thomas, Wholesale Dry Goods Store, 317 King St.
Floderer, John, Grocery, 66 Church St.
Fludd, John, Planter, 11 Church St.
Fogartie, Ann, Miss, School Mistress, 25 Wall St.
Fogartie, George, Planter, 16 Middle St.
Fogartie, Henry, w. end Boundary St., Neck, F.P.C.
Fogartie, J., 25 Wall St.
Folker, Rebecca, Mrs., 6 St. Philip St.
Follin, A., Storekeeper, cr. Meeting & Columbus Sts., Neck
Follin, A., Tobacconist, 152 Meeting St.
Follin, Joseph, Tobacconist, 234 E. Bay St.
Forbes, John, Tinner, 11 Tradd St.
Ford & Desaussure, Attorneys, 41 Broad St.
Ford & Huger, Attorneys, 8 Waring's Range
Ford, B., Chapel St., Neck
Ford, Jacob, Attorney, 201 Meeting St.
Ford, Peggy, Washington St., Neck, F.P.C.
Ford, Timothy, Mrs., Widow, 42 Meeting St.
Fordham, Richard, Blacksmith, back of Exchange, E. Bay St.
Forrest, Charity, Widow, 5 Hasell St.
Foster, W. B., D. & C. Clerk, Bank of the State of S. C., res. 5 Clifford St.
Fougeres, -----, Marquis, French Consulate, 141 Church St.
Fourgeaud, Arnold, Baker, 18 Guignard St.
Francis, Edward, Livery Stables, 122 Church St.
Francis, George M., Pilot, 18 Church St.
Francis, John, Barber, 10 Smith's Ln., F.P.C.
Francis, John, Barber, 312 King St., F.P.C.
Franklin, Eliza, Henrietta St., Neck, F.P.C.
Fraser, Charles, Attorney, 53 King St.
Fraser, F., Mrs., Widow, 99 Tradd St.
Fraser, J. & Co., Factors, Fraser's Whf.
Fraser, John, Factor, 41 E. Bay St.
Frazer, Charles P., Factor, cr. Wharf & Vernon Sts., res. 10 Laurens St.
Frazer, J. J., Bathing House & Factor, e. end Laurens St.
Frazer, James, Farmer, w. side King St., op. Ann St., Neck
Frazer, John J., Factor, John St., btw. Meeting & King Sts., Neck
Frazer, -----, Widow, Mrs., Boarding House, 10 Laurens St.
Frazer, William, Accountant, 53 Wentworth St.
Frederick, Adolph, Mariner, 72 Church St.
Freeman, Peter, Planter, 5 Legare St.
Freeman, William, Grocery, 3 Tradd St.
Friel, Ellen, Mrs., Boarding House, 133 Church St.
Friend, James, Carpenter, 23 Boundary St.
Frier, Charles, Planter, 94 Wentworth St.
Frost, Edward, Attorney, n.w. cr. Meeting & Tradd Sts.
Frost, H. R., M. D., 23 Archdale St.
Fulda, F. L. W., Grocery, s.w. cr. George & St. Philip's Sts.
Fuller, Benjamin, Planter, King St., btw. John & Ann Sts., Neck

Fuller, Oliver, Capt., Insurance Inspector, 105 Meeting St.
Furman, C. M., Master in Equity, 1 Waring's Range, res. 5 King St.
Furman, Josiah, Factor, 52 King St.
Furman, Marvin & Co., Factors & Commission Merchants, 68 E. Bay St.
Furr, Catherine, Widow, 17 Coming St.
Furr, John P., Turner, 15 Burns Ln.
Fursman, H., Boarding House, 13 Beadon's Al.
Furth, Joseph, Dealer in Clothing, 5 Archdale St.
Gabeau, Eliza, Widow, 36 St. Philip St.
Gadsden, C., Rev., Mazyckborough, Neck
Gadsden, Christopher, Mrs., Widow, 16 S. Bay St.
Gadsden, Fisher, Factor, Gadsden's Whf.
Gadsden, John, Mrs., Widow, 11 Meeting St.
Gadsden, Rebecca, Widow, 124 Meeting St.
Gadsden, T. N., Broker, 134 King St.
Gadsden, Thomas, Attorney, off. 104, res. 28 Church St.
Gaillard, A. T., Factor, 6 New St.
Gaillard, D. S., U. S. Military Store Keeper, 2 Court House Sq.
Gaillard, Eleanor, 5 Price's Al.
Gaillard, Mazyck & Sons, Factors, Chisolm's N. Whf.
Gaillard, Peter, Sr., Planter, 310 E. Bay St.
Gaillard, S. T. & Co., Grocery, 73 E. Bay St.
Gaillard, Theodore, City Marshal, 52 King St.
Gallagher & M'Intyre, U. S. Garden, 129 Meeting St.
Galliot, A., Tobacconist, 13 Elliott St.
Gandouin, Izadore, Hat Store, 111 E. Bay St.
Ganini, Jacob, Fruit Store, 37 Market St.
Gannt, Thomas John, Register in Equity, 54 King St.
Garden, Adam, 9 Clifford St., F.P.C.
Garden, Jack, Livery Stables, 7 Chalmers St., F.P.C.
Garden, John, Pinckney St., near Cannon St., Neck, F.P.C.
Garden, Margaret, 56 King St., F.P.C.
Garden, Martha, 28 Mazyck St., F.P.C.
Gardner, Margaret, 2 Anson St.
Gardner, Margaret, Seamstress, 49 Meeting St., F.P.C.
Gardner, Mary, 3 Cumberland St., F.P.C.
Garrett, Ann, Widow, 115 Meeting St.
Gates, John, Butcher, s. side Cannon St., Neck
Gates, Thomas, Butcher, s. side Cannon St., Neck
Gates, Thomas S., Rev., Charlotte St., Mazyckborough, Neck
Gatewood, W. C., Clerk, 25 Broad St.
Gauth, Peter, Radcliffborough, near St. Paul's Church, Neck
Gauthier, F., Teacher of French, 10 Coming St.
Gaylord, Norman, Tavern, 85 Queen St.
Gear, John, St. Philip St., above Boundary St., Neck
Geddes, Gilbert C., Planter, 19 Society St.
Geddes, James, Attorney, n.w. cr. King & Mary Sts., Neck
Gelzer, Sarah, Widow, w. side King St., op. Columbus St., Neck
George, Elizabeth, 12 Guignard St.
George, John, Cryer of the Court, 177 E. Bay St.
George, Rachael, Mrs., Tavern, 177 E. Bay St.
Gerard, Peter, Clothing Store, 179 E. Bay St.
Gerard, Peter G., Tailor, 222 King St.

Gerkins, Christopher, Grocery, n.e. cr. Meeting & Wentworth Sts.
Gerry, Grandison, 25 Society St.
Gervais, Paul T., Rev., Planter, 7 Lamboll St.
Gibbes & Waring, Factors, 3 Roper's Whf.
Gibbes, Arthur S., s. side Meeting & Ann Sts., Neck
Gibbes, Benjamin S., Factor, n.w. cr. Elizabeth & John Sts., Neck
Gibbes, Edward, Factor, 7 Savage St.
Gibbes, Edwin, Notary Public, 87 Tradd St.
Gibbes, Elizabeth, Widow, 67 Church St.
Gibbes, Joseph S., Factor, S. Bay St., res. 6 Gibbes St.
Gibbes, M. G., Attorney, 47 Meeting St.
Gibbes, R. R., Planter, s. side Meeting & Ann Sts., Neck
Gibbes, Robert, Jr., Planter, w. side Meeting St., 2 Doors below Ann St., Neck
Gibbes, William H., 81 Broad St.
Gibbon, George & Co., Merchants, 8 Gillon St.
Gibbon, George, Merchant, 78 Queen St.
Gibbs, C. & J., Merchants, 15 Vendue Range
Gibbs, Paul C., Merchant, Gibbes Whf., res. 17 Meeting St.
Gibson, Alexander, Merchant, 3 Crafts' Whf., res. 69 Meeting St.
Gibson, J. G., Salesman, 80 Anson St.
Gibson, James, Coachmaker, 226 Meeting St.
Gibson, William, Accountant, 12 Broad St.
Gibson, William H., Grocery, 164 King St. & 105 E. Bay St.
Gidiere, J. J., Dry Goods Store, 358 King St.
Gidiere, John M., Music Store, 340 King St.
Gidiere, Margaret, Dry Goods Store, 358 King St.
Giese, Charles, Grocery, 88 Meeting St.
Gilbert, Catherine, 9 Water St.
Gilchrist, Margaret, Alexandria St., Neck, F.P.C.
Gilchrist, R. B., Attorney, 3 Washington St., res. 3 Society St.
Gildersleeve, Benjamin, D. D., 40 St. Philip St.
Giles, Mary, Boarding House, 11 Broad St.
Giles, O. J., Clerk, Commission of Streets & Lamps, e. side King St., btw. Ann & Mary Sts., Neck
Giles, Robert, 8 Gibbes St.
Gilliland, Margaret, Widow, 351 King St.
Gilliland, W. H., Auctioneer, 320 King St.
Gilman, Samuel, D. D., 7 Archdale St.
Gist, Sarah, Widow, 38 Meeting St.
Gitsinger, Benjamin R., Printer, 6 State St.
Gitsinger, William S., Carver & Gilder, 6 State St.
Gladding, George, Butcher, n. side Cannon St., Neck
Gleason, H. G. & Co., China & Crockery Store, 264 King St.
Glen, John, Teller, Planters & Mechanics Bank, n.w. cr. Reid & Meeting Sts., Neck
Glenn, Rachel, Alexandria St., Neck, F.P.C.
Glieze, Henry, M. D., 120 Meeting St.
Glover, Henry C., M. D., 52 Society St.
Glover, Joseph, M. D., 5 Rutledge St.
Gnech, -----, Mrs., Dry Goods Store, 192 King St.
Godard, Rene, Merchant, 53 E. Bay St., res. 125 King St.
Goddard, George, Merchant, 18 Vanderhorst's Whf.

Godet, Ann, Seamstress, 4 Liberty St.
Godfrey, Catharine, Mrs., Gadsden's Whf.
Godfrey, Eleanor, 20 Anson St.
Godfrey, W. W., Bookkeeper, 11 Anson St.
Godfry, Richard, Radcliffborough, Neck
Goldsmith, Abraham, Synagogue Yard, Hasell St.
Goldsmith, Frances, Widow, 38 Hasell St.
Goldsmith, Henry, 129 Wentworth St.
Goldsmith, Joseph H., 129 Wentworth St.
Goldsmith, Morris, Deputy U. S. Marshal, 129 Wentworth St.
Gonzalez, B., Merchant, 15 Champney St.
Good, Francis, Grocery, s. cr. Meeting & Wolf Sts., Neck
Goodman & Miller, Factors, Edmonston's Whf.
Gordon & Reid, Bakers, 53 Tradd St.
Gordon, Charles, w. end Cannonborough, Neck
Gordon, John, Planter, 218 Meeting St.
Gordon, William E., Master of Workhouse, Meeting St., near Reid St., Neck
Gospry, F. S., Radcliffborough, Neck
Gough, Caroline, 15 St. Philip St.
Gough, Edward, 4 New St.
Gough, John, Medical Student, 4 New St.
Gough, Margaret, 3 Clifford St., F.P.C.
Gough, Thomas, Student at Law, 4 New St.
Goulding, C., Widow, w. side King St., near Cannon St., Neck
Gouldsmith, Richard, Cabinet Maker, 203 King St.
Gourdin, Henry, Merchant, 44 E. Bay St.
Gourjan, Thomas, Meeting St., near Municipal Guard House, Neck
Gourman, Samuel, Grocery, cr. Rutledge & Wentworth Sts.
Gowan, Peter, 19 Friend St.
Gowan, Peter, Watch Maker, 78 Meeting St.
Gowan, Sarah, 61 Wentworth St., F.P.C.
Gradick, C. C., Grocery, w. cr. Elizabeth & John Sts., Neck
Graham, J. C., Market St.
Graham, Michel, cr. Meeting & Boundary Sts.
Graham, Sarah, 11 Coming St., F.P.C.
Granby, George, Dry Goods Store, 252 King St.
Granniss, G. B. & Co., Shoe Store, 240 King St.
Grant, Ann, Mrs., 9 Wall St.
Grant, Elizabeth, Mrs., 33 Horlbeck's Al.
Grapon, Mary, 33 Friend St., F.P.C.
Graves & Horlbeck, Druggists, 118 Church St.
Graves, Charles, Planter, 9 Archdale St.
Graves, Massy, Widow, Smith's Ln.
Gray, A. H., Painter, 42, res. 5 Broad St.
Gray, J. W., Commissioner in Equity, 5 Waring's Row, res. 220 E. Bay St.
Gray, J., Widow, 80 Market St.
Gray, John B., Teacher, 32 Wentworth St.
Gray, R., Mrs., w. side King St., op. Wolf & John Sts., Neck
Gray, Sylvanus, Merchant, Magwood's Whf.
Gray, William, Printer, 5 Queen St.
Greely, Catharine, 12 Berresford St.
Green, C. F., Grocery, cr. Meeting St. & Horlbeck's Al.

11

Green, Catharine, Boarding House, 68 State St.
Green, E., Mrs., Widow, Washington St., Neck
Green, T. P., Druggist, 187 E. Bay St.
Greenhill, Jane, Miss, Green St.
Greenland, Benjamin, M. D., 6 Back St.
Greenland, Eliza, Widow, 74 Tradd St.
Greenland, William, 21 Meeting St.
Gregory, J. Ladson, Attorney, off. Court House, res. 9 Friend St.
Gregson, William, Coach Maker, Green St.
Grieg, Alexander, Boarding House, 11 Market St.
Grimball, Paul C., Planter, w. side Cannonborough, near Bennett's Mills, Neck
Grimke, John, M. D., 50 St. Philip St.
Grimke, Mary, Widow, 297 E. Bay St.
Grimke, T. S. & Henry, Attorneys, 72 Broad St.
Grimke, Thomas S., Attorney. 38 S. Bay St.
Groning, Lewis, Mrs., Widow, 125 Tradd St.
Gros, John, Cabinet Maker, 191 Meeting St.
Groves, Elizabeth, Dry Goods Store, 191 King St.
Gruber, Margaret B., Widow, e. side Meeting St., btw. Wolf & Columbus Sts., Neck
Guierra, Ufemme, Meeting St., near Hudson St., Neck
Guilbert, E., Professor of Music, 1 Wall St.
Guillet, Ellen, 3 Archdale St.
Guillett, James, Butcher, n. side Cannon St., Neck
Gunther, Philip, 6 Pitt St., F.P.C.
Guy, Mary, 4 Minority St.
Guy, William, Saddler, Meeting St., btw. Boundary & Henrietta Sts., Neck
Guy, William, Tailor, Boundary St.
Hagan, Rosanna, 28 Hasell St.
Hager, Johnson, Henrietta St., Neck, F.P.C.
Haig, David, Cooper, 204 Meeting St. & Crafts' Whf.
Haig, James, Attorney, 204 Meeting St.
Hall, Ann, Seamstress, 20 St. Philip St.
Hall, Charlotte, 24 Hasell St., F.P.C.
Hall, James, Boarding House, 11 Elliott St.
Hall, -----, Mrs., Dry Goods Store, 131 King St.
Hall, Susannah, Widow, 5 Court House Sq.
Hall, William, M. D., e. side Hampstead, Neck
Halliday, Eleanor, Widow, 42 Church St.
Hallsell, John, Butcher, Hampstead, Neck
Hamilton, A., Mrs., Female Academy, 78 Meeting St.
Hamilton, Alexander, Coach Trimmer, 39 Beaufain St.
Hamilton, Clarinda, 46 Pinckney St.
Hamilton, James, Grocery, 14 Tradd St.
Hamilton, James, Jr., Governor & Commander in Chief, 18 S. Bay St.
Hamilton, James, Sr., 2 Church St.
Hamilton, John, Clerk, 65 Market St.
Hamilton, John, Ship Carpenter, Guignard St.
Hamilton, S. H., Planter, Radcliffborough, Neck
Hammett, Caroline, 7 Wentworth St.
Hammett, Thomas, Wolf St., Neck
Hammill, Thomas, Wheelwright, 148 Church St.
Hammond, Ogden, Factor, Chisolm's S. Whf.
Hampton, D., Tailor, 198 King St., F.P.C.
Hampton, Daphne, 18 Anson St., F.P.C.
Hamye, C. H., Grocery, 17 Market St.

Hanckle, Christopher, Rev., Rector of St. Paul's, 115 Boundary St.
Handsberry, F., Painter, 65 Queen St.
Hannahan, John C., Cooper, 28 New St
Hannahan, R. S. H., Planter, 10 Bull St.
Hanscome, Thomas, Planter, 119 Tradd St.
Happoldt, Albert, Butcher, s. side Cannon St., Neck
Happoldt, C. D., Butcher, s. side, Cannon St., Neck
Happoldt, Charles M., 81 Market St.
Happoldt, Elizabeth, Widow, s. side Cannon St., Neck
Happoldt, John M., 17 Amen St.
Harby, Henry J., Blacksmith, 253 E. Bay St.
Harby, Rebecca, Widow, 253 E. Bay St.
Harkley, F., 115 Church St.
Harkley, Henrietta, 21 Wentworth St.
Harleston, E., Miss, 4 Logan St.
Harleston, Nicholas, Planter, Radcliffborough, Neck
Harmon, Louisa, 33 Wall St., F.P.C.
Harper, W. W., Baker, cr. King & Tradd Sts.
Harris, Isaac, Fruit Store, 41 Market St.
Harris, Jacob, Clothing Store, 205 E. Bay St.
Harris, R., Fruit Store, 130 King St.
Harrison, J., Boot Maker, 2 West St., F.P.C.
Harrison, J., Boot Maker, 35 Beaufain St., F.P.C.
Harrisson, Ann, Mrs., 91 Market St.
Harrisson, D. W., Bookstore, Chalmers St.
Harrisson, J., Paint & Oil Store, 170 E. Bay
Hart, Bella, Widow, 122 Meeting St.
Hart, N. H., Clerk, 206 King St.
Hart, Nathan, Hardware Store, 206 King St.
Hart, Samuel, Sr., Merchant, Cordes Whf.
Harth, William, Lumber Yard, 1 Gibbes Whf.
Hartshorne, Maria, 16 Magazine St.
Harvey, Ann, Widow, 252 E. Bay St.
Harvey, E. T., Wharfinger, 272 Church St.
Harvey, Edward, Dyer & Scourer, 82 Queen St.
Harvey, Josiah R., Planter, 9 Lynchs Ln.
Harvey, Samuel, Boarding House, 38 Elliott St.
Harvey, Susannah H., 9 Lynchs Ln.
Harvey, Thomas M., Boarding House, 53 Elliott St.
Harwood, R. & W. B., Fancy Dry Goods Store, 261 King St.
Hasell, C. B., Spring St., Neck
Hashagan, Henry, Grocer, Laurens St.
Haskell, C., Mrs., Pinckney St., Cannonborough, Neck
Haskell, William, Factor, Vanderhorst's Whf., res. 117 Boundary St.
Haslett, John, President, Fire & Marine Insurance Co., 68 Broad St.
Hatch, A. M. & Co., Wholesale Boot & Shoe Store, cr. King & George Sts.
Hatch, Eveline, Millinery, 33 King St.
Hatch, Mary W., 27 Pinckney St.
Hatch, Prince, Boat Builder, 36 Anson St.
Hatfield, Ann, Widow, n.w. cr. Beaufain & Coming Sts.
Hattier, William H., Fruit Store, Market St., op. Anson St.
Hauck, Henry, 58 Anson St.
Hauschildt, Peter, Grocery, 141 King St.
Hauschildt, Peter, Grocery, n.e. cr. St. Philip & Warren Sts., Neck

12

Haviland & Ashfield, Druggist, 304 King St.
Hayden, Jane, Mrs., America St., Hampstead, Neck
Hayne, Elizabeth, Widow, 21 Water St.
Hayne, P. H., Lt., U. S. Navy, n. end Lynch St.
Hayne, R. Y., Hon. U. S. Senator, 36 King St.
Hayne, W. A., Bank of State of S. C., res. cr. St. Philip &
    Vanderhorst Sts., Neck
Hayne, William E., U. S. Appraiser, 8 S. Bay St.
Headden, Joseph, Hair Dresser, 5 Tradd St.
Headwright, Henry, Burns Ln.
Hedderly, John, 29 King St.
Hedly, John, Accountant, n. side Boundary St., Neck
Heilbron, James & Co., Druggists, cr. Church & Elliott
    Sts.
Heilbron, James, 64 Church St.
Heimburger, J. G., 92 Wentworth St.
Helfrid, Diana, Grocery, 16 Tradd St.
Helfrid, John, Sr., State Constable, 74 State St.
Hemerly, John, Grocery, 14 Wall St.
Hendricks, F., Grocer, n. cr. King & Warren Sts., Neck
Henry, Alexander, Cashier, Bank of S. C., 136 Wentworth
    St.
Henry, Charles, Mary St., near King St., Neck, F.P.C.
Henry, Edward, Grocery, 7 Guignard St.
Henry, George, Factor, 1 Liberty St.
Henry, Jacob, Cabinet Maker, Charlotte St., Neck
Hephburn, Harriett, cr. Coming & Montague Sts.
Herckenrath & Lowndes, Merchants, Crafts' S. Whf.
Heriot & Simons, Factors, Kunhardt's Whf.
Heriot, B. D., Factor, w. end of Beaufain St.
Heriot, C., Mrs., Radcliff St., Neck
Heriot, G. W., Planter, Radcliffborough, Neck
Heriot, Roger, Notary Public, 87 E. Bay St., res. 32 Church
    St.
Hertz, Jacob, Dry Goods Store, 97 King St.
Hertz, H. M., Lumber Merchant, w. end of Beaufain St.
Hertz, H. M., Factor, King St., near John St., Neck
Hervey, George, Merchant, 48 E. Bay St.
Heulan, J. J., Professor of Music, 74 Church St.
Heyward, Arthur, Planter, 277 E. Bay St.
Heyward, Charles, Planter, 277 E. Bay St.
Heyward, Joseph, Mrs., Widow, 5 Logan St.
Heyward, Nathaniel, Planter, 277 E. Bay St.
Hichborn, W. H., 42 Tradd St.
Higham & Fife, Merchants, 75 E. Bay St.
Hill, C. G., Coach Maker, e. side Coming St., near St.
    Paul's Church, Neck
Hill, F. C., Painter, 9 Clifford St.
Hill, John, Clerk, 7 Queen St.
Hillard, Ann E., Widow, Boarding House, 62 Wentworth
    St.
Hillard, Oliver B., Grocery, 7 Vendue Range
Hilleary, William, Factor, Kunhardt's Whf.
Hillman, Ann, Boarding House, 69 E. Bay St.
Hilson, John, Grocery, Meeting St., near Reid St., Neck
Hinds, James, 11 Price's Al.
Hines, John H., Grocery, Lucas St., Cannonborough, Neck
Hinson, Elizabeth, 13 Guignard St.
Hinson, Thomas, Carpenter, 9 Berresford St.
Hislop, Hannah, 26 Laurens St.

Hitchingham, Elizabeth, 13 Guignard St.
Hobson, Abraham, Shoe Maker, 83 Broad St.
Hodgson, H., Grocery, 2 Anson St.
Hoff, J. C., Bookseller & Stationer, 84 Queen St.
Hoff, J. M., Clerk, Market, 15 George St.
Hoff, Philip, Bookseller, 10 Broad St.
Hogarth, Mary, 16 Wall St.
Hohn, C. F., Grocery, Gadsden's Whf.
Holbrook, J. Edwards, M. D., 61 Meeting St.
Holbrook, Moses, M. D., 64 Queen St.
Holland, John, Boarding House, 29 Tradd St.
Holloway, Richard, Carpenter, 36 Mazyck St., F.P.C.
Holloway, Richard, Jr., Carpenter, 35 Beaufain St., F.P.C.
Holmes & Waring, Attorneys, 2 St. Michael's Al.
Holmes, C. R., U. S. Appraiser, Champney St.
Holmes, Cato, Henrietta St., Neck, F.P.C.
Holmes, Charles R., Hudson St., Neck
Holmes, I. E., Attorney, Battery, E. Bay St.
Holmes, J. B., Factor, w. end Beaufain St.
Holmes, J. B., Mrs., Widow, Battery, E. Bay St.
Holmes, J. G., Attorney, Battery, E. Bay St.
Holmes, J. T. W. & Co., Dry Goods Store, cr. King &
    Queen Sts.
Holmes, J. T. W., 107 Queen St.
Holmes, John L., Merchant, 7 Mey's Whf.
Holmes, John, Mrs., Widow, 126 Tradd St.
Holmes, William, Factor, Cordes Whf., res. 113 Boundary
    St.
Holmes, William, M. D., Battery, E. Bay St.
Holowell, Lynde, Clerk, 336 King St.
Holton, Elizabeth, Pastry Cook, 15 Cumberland St., F.P.C.
Holton, Mary, Seamstress, 82 Wentworth St., F.P.C.
Holwell, T. W., Grocery, 65 Market St.
Honor, J. H., Accountant 29 Mazyck St.
Honor, Thomas, Bookbinder, 17 Beaufain St.
Hood, Caroline, n. side Boundary St., Neck
Hopkins, John, Merchant, 15 Wall St.
Horlbeck, D., Attorney, off. 49 Broad St.
Horlbeck, Elias, M. D., 184 King St.
Horlbeck, Henry, Bricklayer
Horlbeck, Henry, Jr., Bricklayer
Horlbeck, John, Bricklayer, 241 Meeting St.
Horry, Elias Lynch, Planter, w. end Broad St.
Horry, Elias, Planter, cr. Meeting & Tradd Sts.
Horry, Lucretia, Widow, cr. Pitt & Montague Sts.
Horsey, Thomas, Clerk, 231 King St.
Houston, William, Carpenter, 19 Middle St.
Howard, A. G., M. D., cr. Broad & State Sts.
Howard, Alexander, Barber, 32 Chalmers St., F.P.C.
Howard, Anna, 43 Tradd St.
Howard, James, Boarding House, 51 State St.
Howard, John, Bricklayer, Henrietta St., Neck
Howard, Ora, Shoe Store, n.e. cr. Meeting & Market Sts.
Howard, Richard, Cooper, Cordes Whf.
Howard, Richard, Cooper, Washington St., Neck
Howard, Robert, Broker & Commission Merchant,
    Kunhardt's Whf.
Howe, James, 5 King St.
Howe, John, Shoe Store, 115 Church St.
Howe, Mary, Grocery, 5 King St.

13

Howe, Philip, 5 King St.
Howell, James, Shoemaker, 64 George St.
Howland, Ward & Spring, Wholesale Dry Goods Store, 146 E. Bay St.
Howland, William, Dry Goods Store, 208 King St.
Huard, Stanislaus, Druggist, 34 Broad St.
Hubbell, S., Grocery, e. end Boundary St., Neck
Hubert, John, Carpenter, 7 Queen St.
Huger, Ann, Widow, cr. Broad & Mazyck Sts.
Huger, Benjamin J., Tailor, 42 Coming St., F.P.C.
Huger, Charlotte, 25 St. Philip St.
Huger, D. E., Jr., Attorney, 28 Meeting St.
Huger, D. E., Planter, 28 Meeting St.
Huger, Daniel, Broker, 4 State St.
Huger, John, Planter, 3 Meeting St.
Huger, Mary, Mantuamaker, 42 Coming St., F.P.C.
Huger, William, M. D., 28 Meeting St.
Hughes, J. D., Boarding House, 12 Bedon's Al.
Hughes, William, Accountant, 83 King St.
Hume, A., Dr., Planter, n.w. end Cannonborough, Neck
Hume, John, Planter, 136 Wentworth St.
Hume, Robert, Planter, 7 Lynch St.
Hume, William, Dr., Planter, King St., near John St., Neck
Humphreys, Ann, Mantuamaker, 110 Queen St., F.P.C.
Humphreys, John, Keeper, Poor House, Mazyck St.
Humphreys, Joseph, Tailor, 110 Queen St., F.P.C.
Hunt & Shand, Attorneys, 1 Court House Sq.
Hunt, Benjamin F., Attorney, Meeting St., op. Municipal Guard House, Neck
Hunt, Randall, Attorney, off. 4 Fireproof Building, res. 211 Meeting St.
Hunt, T. G., Attorney, 211 Meeting St.
Hunt, Thomas, M. D., 211 Meeting St.
Hunt, Thomas, Mrs., Widow, 211 Meeting St.
Hunter, John, Pinckney St., near Cannon St., Neck
Huntington, Robert, Planter, 36 Bull St.
Hurlbut, M. L., Teacher, S. C. School, res. 96 Church St.
Hurst, Charles, Inspector of Customs, 20 Middle St.
Hurst, Jefferson, Pump & Block Maker, 39 George St., Shop Gillon St.
Husser, William, cr. Pinckney & Cannon Sts., Neck
Hussy, Bryan, Mrs., 12 Stoll's Al.
Hutcherson, R. W. & Co., Dry Goods Store, 261 King St.
Hutchins, Shubael, Merchant, 142 E. Bay St.
Hutchinson, Leget, Planter, 1 New St.
Hyams, Catharine, Widow, 4 Clifford St.
Hyams, D., Mrs., Mantuamaker, 18 S. Bay St.
Hyams, Daniel, Radcliff St., Neck
Hyams, E. L., Jail, Magazine St.
Hyams, Henry, Tailor, King St., near Ann St., Neck
Hyams, M. D., Grocery, 17 S. Bay St.
Hyams, Rebecca, Widow, 2 Clifford St.
Hyams, Samuel, Jailer, Charleston District Jail, Magazine St.
Hyams, Solomon, Dry Goods Store, 196 King St.
Hyde & Cleveland, Wholesale Hardware Store, 289 King St.
Hyer, J. H., Carpenter, s.w. cr. Radcliff & St. Philip Sts., Neck
Icard, L., Tallow Chandler, e. side Meeting St., n. of

Mary St., Neck
Ilsley, Francis, Superintendent, Lee's Mills, w. end Beaufain St.
Inglesby, Betsy, Ann St., Neck, F.P.C.
Inglesby, J. S., M. D., 45 Tradd St.
Inglesby, William H., Attorney, 41 Tradd St.
Inglis, Ellen, Seamstress, 4 Chalmers St.
Inglis, Mary, 65 Anson St.
Ingliss, Thomas, Hair Dresser, 83 Meeting St., F.P.C.
Ingraham, D. N., U.S. Navy, cr. Laurens & E. Bay Sts.
Ingraham, G. H., Factor, Fraser & Co. Whf.
Ingraham, George, Factor, 28 Laurens St.
Ingraham, W. P., Planter, 1 Smith St.
Innis, John, Coach Trimmer, 119 Meeting St.
Irving, John B., 4 Short St.
Irving, William, Barber, 108½ King St., F.P.C.
Isham, Henry, Clerk, 338 King St.
Izard, Henry, Mrs., Widow, 25 Legare St.
Izard, Ralph, Mrs., 223 E. Bay St.
Jacks, Ann, Mrs., n. side Chapel St., Mazyckborough, Neck
Jackson, J. A., Millinery & Fancy Store, 297 King St.
Jackson, M. A., Millinery, 348 King St.
Jackson, Martha, Henrietta St., Neck, F.P.C.
Jackson, Rachel, 7 Cumberland St., F.P.C.
Jacobs, Catherine, 41 Boundary St., F.P.C.
Jacobs, Cecelia, Mrs., Shopkeeper, 243 E. Bay St.
Jacobs, Hyam, Cannonborough, near Cannon St., Neck
Jacobs, Moses, Clothing Store, 254 King St.
Jacoby, George, Grocery, 83 Church St.
Jager, Hans, Grocery, 27 Elliott St.
James, A. C., Mrs., 237 E. Bay St.
James, Henry, Factor, 38 Church St.
James, M., Shopkeeper, 31 King St.
Jamison, Maloney, Grocery, s.e. cr. Boundary & Meeting Sts.
Jaques, Richard, Clerk, 20 Pitt St.
Jaques, Thomas, Clerk, 20 Pitt St.
Jarcke, Nicholas, Grocery, cr. Pitt & Beaufain Sts.
Jarmonet, P., King St., btw. Mary & Warren Sts., Neck
Javain, P., Farmer, w. cr. St. Philip St. & Lines, Neck
Jeanerett, Mary, Widow, 68 Church St.
Jeffords, J. H., Sailmaker, 9 Minority St.
Jeffords, John, Shopkeeper, 11 Middle St.
Jenkins, Elias, Bricklayer, 6 Liberty St.
Jenkins, James, Accountant, 6 Liberty St.
Jenkins, John, 34 Horlbeck's Al.
Jenkins, Joseph, Student of Law, 17 Rutledge St.
Jenkins, Phoebe, 17 Rutledge St.
Jenkins, T. J., Accountant, 6 Liberty St.
Jenkins, William, Student of Medicine, 17 Rutledge St.
Jervey, Blake & Waring, Auctioneers & Brokers, 20 Broad St.
Jervey, James, U. S. District Clerk., 37 Laurens St., op. Wall St.
Jervey, John, Ann St., Neck, F.P.C.
Jervey, Thomas H., Surveyor, Custom House, res. 53 Church St.
Johnson, A., Boot & Shoe Maker, 13 Tradd St.
Johnson, Ann, n. side Boundary St., btw. Meeting &

Elizabeth Sts., Neck
Johnson, Camilla, Pastry Cook, 84 Broad St., F.P.C.
Johnson, Edward, Wheelwright, 18 Beaufain St., F.P.C.
Johnson, Elizabeth, Dry Goods Store, 91 King St.
Johnson, Flora, 18 Pinckney St., F.P.C.
Johnson, H., Boot & Shoe Store, 230 King St.
Johnson, -----, Iron Foundary, Eason's Whf.
Johnson, J. A., M. D., s.e., cr. Warren & St. Philip Sts., Neck
Johnson, James, 32 Beaufain St., F.P.C.
Johnson, James S., Grain Merchant, Mey's Whf.
Johnson, James, Tallow Chandler, Chapel St., Neck
Johnson, John, Jr., Col., 22 Society St.
Johnson, Joseph, 114 Queen St.
Johnson, Joseph, Dr., President, U. S. Bank, res. 51 Church St.
Johnson, Louisa, Cannonborough, Neck, F.P.C.
Johnson, -----, Miss, Store, 348½ King St
Johnson, Nathaniel, Carpenter, 11 Minority St.
Johnson, Sarah, Mantuamaker, 95 Wentworth St., F.P.C.
Johnson, -----, Shoe Store, 117 E. Bay St.
Johnson, Sophia, Henrietta St., Neck, F.P.C.
Johnson, T., Painter, 6 Tradd St.
Johnson, Thomas, Farmers Hotel, 226 King St.
Johnson, Timothy, Tavern, w. side King St., btw. Ratcliff & Mary Sts., Neck
Johnson, William, Hon., Pinckney St., Cannonborough, Neck
Johnston, Ann, Mrs., Shopkeeper, 55 State St.
Johnston, E. A., Tailor, 328 King St., F.P.C.
Joiner, C., Mrs., Thomas St., Cannonborough, Neck
Joiner, Mary, Thomas St., Cannonborough, Neck
Jones, Abraham, Cabinet Maker, 13 Beaufain St.
Jones, Charlotte C., 95 Wentworth St., F.P.C.
Jones, E. S., Dr., St. Philip St., Radcliffborough, Neck
Jones, Elias, Rice Mills, Meeting St., near Ann St., Neck
Jones, Henry, 51 Tradd St.
Jones, Isaac, State Constable, Savage St.
Jones, Jehu, Boarding House, 67 Broad St., F.P.C.
Jones, Jehu, Jr., Tailor, 27 Beaufain St., F.P.C.
Jones, Jeremiah, Alexander St., Neck, F.P.C.
Jones, M., Mrs., Grocery, 107 King St.
Jones, M., Mrs., s.e. cr. Meeting & Reid Sts., Neck
Jones, R., Widow, 71 Broad St.
Jones, Samuel, Mrs., Widow, 1 Guignard St.
Jones, Thomas S., Warren St., Radcliffborough, Neck
Jones, William, Carpenter, 57 King St.
Jones, Wiswald, Commission Merchant, 18 Vendue Range, res. 82 Meeting St.
Jordon, Christopher, Coach Maker, 17 Anson St.
Joseph, Joseph J., Shopkeeper, w. side King St., btw. Radcliff & Mary Sts., Neck
Joshua, Peter, Grocery, 25 Market St.
Jouvele, Louis, Tinner, 94 Market St.
Joye, D. G., Grocery, 117 Church St.
Joye, Peter, John St., Neck
Joyner, Joshua, Shopkeeper, 151 Meeting St.
June, C., cr. State & Linguard Sts.
Just, George, Wharf Builder, 34 Hasell St.
Kanapau, C., Clerk, Lucas Mills, Neck

Kane, Christopher, Grocer, 39 Anson St.
Kane, Dennis & Co., Dry Goods Store, 332 King St.
Keckley, J., M. D., cr. Radcliff & King Sts., Neck
Keith, Charlotte, Miss, 2 Lamboll St.
Keith, Henry, Henrietta St., Neck, F.P.C.
Keith, Mathew I., 2 Lamboll St.
Keller, Jacob, 19 Market St.
Kelly, Eliza, Store Keeper, 92 Church St.
Kelly, Eliza, Widow, 10 Stoll's Al.
Kelly, M. A., Dry Goods Store, 4 Horlbeck's Al.
Kelly, Michael, Broker, 5 State St., res. 37 Tradd St.
Kelly, William, Fancy Chair Store, 169 King St.
Kelly, William, Plasterer, 11 College St.
Kennedy, Ann, Grocery, 74 Market St.
Kennedy, Edward, Deputy Collector of Customs, 18 Mazyck St.
Kennedy, James, Grocery, 117 Queen St.
Kennedy, James, Shipwright, 37 Wall St.
Kennedy, Lionel H., Attorney, Waring's Row, res. Tradd St.
Kennedy, William, Boarding House, 21 Elliott St.
Kennifec, Daniel C., Accountant, 175 E. Bay St.
Ker, John C., Merchant, 3 Chalmers St., res. 214 Meeting St.
Kerr, George, Hay Store, 12 Price's Whf., res. Laurens St.
Kerr, T. J., Wharfinger, Laurens St.
Kerrison, C. & E. L., Dry Goods Store, 211 King St.
Kershaw, Charles, Factor, res. 30 Meeting St.
Kershaw, Lewis & Co., Factors, 56 E. Bay St.
Kershaw, Newman, Wharfinger, 29 E. Bay St.
Kester, Mary, Seamstress, 46 King St., F.P.C.
Ketchum, Joel, Jr., Dry Goods Store, 231 King St.
Kick, William, Store Keeper, 242 E. Bay St.
Kiddell, Arthur, 35 Broad St.
Kiddell, Charles, Merchant, Kiddell's Whf., res. 35 Broad St.
Kiels, C., Coming St., near St. Paul's Church, Neck
King & M'Cready, Attorneys, St. Michael's Al.
King, Eliza, Confectionary, 11 St. Philip St., F.P.C.
King, John, 136 Church St.
King, John, Coach Maker, cr. State & Queen Sts.
King, John, Jr., 136 Church St.
King, Leonard, Carpenter & Umbrella Manufactory, 84 Meeting St.
King, Margaret, Mrs., 10 Clifford St.
King, Mitchell, Attorney, res. cr. Meeting & George Sts.
King, W. S., Printer, 63 Broad St.
Kingdom, Henry, Coming St., near St. Paul's Church, Neck
Kingman, Eliab, Jr., Clerk, 201 E. Bay St.
Kingman, Eliab, Steward, Orphan House
Kingman, Hannah, 16 Berresford St.
Kingman, John, Clerk, 100 Wentworth St.
Kingman, John, Teacher, Orphan House
Kinloch, Frederick, Teacher, cr. Montague & Pitt Sts.
Kinloch, George, Grocery, 20 Meeting St.
Kinloch, Richmond, Millwright, 15 Bull St.
Kinsey, F., Mrs., Dry Goods Store, 247 King St.
Kippenberg, Mary Ann, Mrs., 5 Anson St.
Kirk, C. W., Bricklayer, Minority St.

Kirk, John, 131 E. Bay St.
Kirkland, M., St. Phililp's St., near Cannon St., Neck
Kirkpatrick, E., 60 Church St.
Kirkpatrick, J. & Co., Factors, Edmonston's Whf.
Kirkpatrick, J., 4 Meeting St.
Kittleband, John, Carpenter, 2 Logan St.
Klinck, John, Grocery, Stores, 26 St. Philip St. & cr.
Boundary & Coming Sts.
Kneply, Solomon, Blacksmith, 15 Chalmers St.
Knox, John F., Ship Carpenter, 9 Anson St.
Knust, Sarah, Widow, 15 Coming St.
Knuth, John, Grocery, 18 State St.
Kohlman, J. H., Grocery, 73 Tradd St.
Kohnke, C. F., Grocery, cr. Anson & Society Sts.
Koster, Casper J., Grocery, 61 State St.
Kottmeyer, Henry, Grocery, n.e. cr. Wall & Minority Sts.
Kriete, Frederick, Grocery, 2 Archdale St.
Kugely, Martha, Widow, 34 Mazyck St.
Kugly, Jacob, Butcher, Amherst St., Hampstead, Neck
Kunhardt, William, Kunhardt's Whf., res. 22 George St.
Labasse, Mary, Meeting St., above Municipal Guard
House, Neck
Labat, Catherine, Widow, 29 George St.
Labat, Isaac C., Dry Goods Store, 352 King St.
Labatat, Isaac, Painter, King St. Road, Neck
Labatute, Z., s.w. cr. Meeting St. & Lines, Neck
Laborde, Francis, Livery Stables, 54 Society St.
Labruce, Catherine, Mrs., 13 Rutledge St.
Lacombe, Joseph, Cigar Maker, 211 E. Bay St.
LaCosta, A., King St., near Ann St., Neck
Lacoste, Adel, Milliner, 179 King St.
Lacoste, C. J. A., China Store, 160 King St., Dry Goods
Store, 149 & 158 King St.
Ladeveze, Victor, Dry Goods Store, 185 King St.
Ladson, J. H., Factor, S. C. Insurance Co. Whf., res. 8
Meeting St.
Ladson, Susan, Widow, 89 Tradd St.
Lafar, David B., Cooper, Magwood's Whf., res. 58 Queen
St.
Lafar, John J., 58 Queen St.
Laffan, Edmund, Factor, Fraser & Co. Whf.
Laffiteau, P. S., Accountant, 20 Pinckney St.
Lafon, John, Cooper, 198 E. Bay St.
Lamb, James, Merchant, 51 E. Bay St., res. 61 Tradd St.
Lambert, William C., Mattress Store, 59 Queen St.
Lamotte, J., Blacksmith, 75 Market St.
Lance, Francis, Broker & Vendue Master, 7 State St., res.
23 Friend St.
Lance, M. H., Rev., Judith St., Mazyckborough, Neck
Lance, William, Attorney, 26 St. Michael's Al., res. 108
Queen St.
Landreth, Robert, Seed Store, 241 King St.
Langlois, Maria, School Mistress, cr. Pitt & Montague Sts.
Lankanaw, J. H., Grocery, cr. Pinckney & Doughty Sts.,
Neck
Lanneau, Bazile, Jr., Merchant, 127 E. Bay St., res. 49
Tradd St.
Lanneau, Bazile, Sr., Pitt St.
Lanneau, C. H., Tannery, w. end Beaufain St., res. Pitt
St.

Lapene, John A., w. side King St., near Radcliff St., Neck
Lapont, Mary, 9 Maiden Ln., F.P.C.
Laporte, Rene, Farmer, Bee St., Cannonborough, Neck
LaRoche, Mary, Mrs., Planter, Lucas St., Cannonborough,
Neck
LaRousseliere, Louis, Druggist, 184 Meeting St.
Lason, Catharine Ann, Clifford's Al., F.P.C.
Latham, Daniel, Distiller, 3 Hasell St.
Laurens, Edward R., Planter, 290 E. Bay St., cr. Laurens
St.
Laurens, Eliza, Planter, 290 E. Bay St., cr. Laurens St.
Laval, Jacint, Factor, William's Whf., res. cr. Anson &
Pinckney Sts.
Laval, William, U. S. Measurer, 9 West St.
Lawton, J. & C., Dry Goods Merchants, 80 E. Bay St.
Lawton, R. B., Tavern, 25 Queen St.
Lawton, William M., Factor, Chisolm's S. Whf., res. S. Bay
St.
Lazarus, Benjamin D., Merchant, 9 Champney St., res. 93
Tradd St.
Lazarus, Catherine, Dry Goods Store, 268 King St.
Lazarus, Marks, 93 Tradd St.
Lazarus, Michael, Merchant, 93 Tradd St.
Lea, William, Pilot, 5 Smith Ln.
Leach, Jane, Grocery, 232 King St.
Leader, Mary, Widow, 3 Berresford St.
Leake, Joanna, Boarding House, 73 E. Bay St.
LeBatt, Mary, 200 Meeting St., F.P.C.
Lebby, Thomas, Printer, 21 Amen St.
Lebleux, F., Dyer & Scourer, 92 King St.
LeCaron, Charles, Merchant, Edmondson's Whf.
Lecat, Francis, Professor of Music, 79 Meeting St.
Lee, Benjamin, Accountant, 13 College St.
Lee, Edward, Barber, 61 Broad St., F.P.C.
Lee, Eliza, Pastry Cook, 76 Tradd St., F.P.C.
Lee, Elsey, Pastry Cook, 51 Wentworth St., F.P.C.
Lee, F. J., Custom House, 24 Hasell St.
Lee, Isaac M., off. 20 Broad St., res. cr. Pitt & Boundary
Sts.
Lee, J. W. & Co., Hat Stores, 160 & 287 King St.
Lee, Mary Ann, Clifford St.
Lee, Paul S. H., Pinckney St., w. side, Cannonborough,
Neck
Lee, Sarah, Accoucher, 44 Beaufain St.
Lee, -----, Sawmills, Harleston's Green, w. end Beaufain
St.
Lee, Stephen, Radcliff St., n.w. end Radcliffborough,
Neck
Lee, Stephen, Teacher, res. cr. Pitt & Boundary Sts.
Lee, Thomas, Hon., U. S. District Judge & President, State
Bank, res. cr. Pitt & Boundary Sts.
Lee, William, M. D., res. cr. Pitt & Boundary Sts.
Lee, William, M. D., 13 College St.
Leefe, Benjamin, Commission Merchant, off. 7 Broad St.,
res. 120 Queen St.
Leefe, Harriet, Widow, 120 Queen St.
Legare & Egleston, Attorneys, 45 Broad St.
Legare & Rice, Attorneys, 70 Broad St.
Legare, Charles, Henrietta St., Neck, F.P.C.
Legare, D., Planter, cr. Guignard & Anson Sts.

16

Legare, Hugh S., Attorney General, 30 Bull St., off. 45 Broad St.
Legare, J. B., Attorney, 15 Hasell St.
Legare, James, Mrs., Widow, 54 Coming St.
Legare, James, Planter, e. end Hampstead, Neck
Legare, Mary, Mrs., 93 Boundary St.
Legare, S. & J., Factors, Chisolm's S. Whf.
Legare, S. P., Mrs., cr. Pinckney & Bridge Sts., Neck
Legare, Solomon, Factor, 3 Gibbes St.
Legare, Thomas, M. D., cr. St. Philip & Vanderhorst Sts., Neck
Legare, Thomas, Planter, 40 S. Bay St.
Legare, William, Planter, Nassau St., Neck
Lege, J. M., Dancing Master, 62 Queen St.
Legg, Maria, Seamstress, 23 Wentworth St.
Lehre, Ann, Widow, 96 Tradd St.
Lehre, Thomas, Jr., State Treasurer, 5 Fireproof Building
Leland, Joseph & Brothers, Merchants, 159 E. Bay St.
Leman, James, Nassau St., Neck
Lemser, John L., Butcher, n. side Cannon St., Neck
LePrince, A., Dry Goods Store, 185 King St.
LeSeigneur, Vincent, M. D., 52 Church St.
Lesene, Charles R., Cannon St., s. side, Radcliffborough, Neck
Lessesne, Henry, Accountant, 18 Archdale St.
Lessesne, Thomas, Accountant, 18 Archdale St.
Lessesne, W. J., Teacher, 39 Society St.
Letchmere, Henry, 20 Church St.
Levy, Aaron, Dealer in Clothing, 75 State St.
Levy, Barnard, Printer, 97 King St.
Levy, Elias, Gauger, Queen St., near Medical College
Levy, Emanuel, Dry Goods Store, 245 King St.
Levy, George, Shopkeeper, 26 New St.
Levy, J. C., Merchant, Champney St., res. 279 E. Bay St.
Levy, Joseph, Printer, 55 State St.
Levy, Lyon, Accountant, 55 E. Bay St.
Levy, Lyon, Jr., Shoemaker, 36 Hasell St.
Levy, Moses C., 211 King St.
Levy, Reuben, 55 State St.
Lewis, Cecilia H., Grocery, 209 E. Bay St.
Lewis, Isaac, 36 Wentworth St.
Lewis, Jane, 5 Bull St., F.P.C.
Lewis, John, Boot & Shoe Maker, Liberty St., F.P.C.
Lewis, John, Factor, 12 Meeting St.
Lieure, Peter, Clothing Store, 103 E. Bay St.
Lightburn, E., Mrs., Elliott St., w. side, Cannonborough, Neck
Lindburg, Nicholas, Shopkeeper, 60 State St.
Lindsay, William, Merchant, 17 Wentworth St.
Lindsey, Samuel, Shoemaker, Philadelphia St.
Lindsy, James, Horse Dealer, 11 Amen St.
Ling, Philip, Coach Maker, 21 Guignard St.
Ling, Robert, Coach Maker, 84 Market St.
Lining, Charles, Planter, 17 Legare St.
Lining, E. B., Planter, St. Philip St., near Cannon St., Neck
Lining, Richard, Planter, 17 Legare St.
Liston, Henry, Cooper, Amen St., F.P.C.
Litle, James, Cotton Gin Manufacturer, 159 Meeting St., res. 30 Archdale St.

Little, Robert, Lumber Merchant, Fraser & Co. Whf.
Little, Robert, Lumber Merchant, Charlotte St., Neck
Livingston, Jane, 241 Meeting St.
Livingston, Philip, 17 Water St.
Livingston, R.Y., n. side Cannon St., Neck
Lloyd, Dianna, 104 King St., F.P.C.
Lloyd, John, Printer, 13 Amen St.
Lloyd, John, Store Keeper, 33 George St.
Lloyd, Joseph, Store Keeper, 33 George St.
Lloyd, Mary J., Widow, 36 Bull St.
Lloyd, William, Broker & Commission Merchant, 29 Broad St., res. 33
Lloyd, William, Venitian Blind Maker, 144 Meeting St.
Locke, G. B., Grocery, cr. Cordes St. & Prioleau's Whf.
Lockwood, Joshua, Jr., Teller, State Bank, 75 Broad St.
Lockwood, T. P., Young Ladies Seminary, 3 Washington St.
Logan, C. M., Broker, 97 Broad St.
Logan, Daniel, Accountant, 46 St. Philip St.
Logan, G. W., Attorney, 6 Waring's Range, res. 7 Lynch St.
Logan, George, M. D., 26 Archdale St.
Logan, Sarah, 22 Guignard St., F.P.C.
Logan, William, Librarian, Charleston Library Society, Pinckney St., Cannonborough, Neck
Lopez, Priscilla, Widow, 10 Stoll's Al.
Lopez, Samuel, Dry Goods Store, cr. King & Boundary Sts.
Lord, Archibald, Porter, U. S. Bank, 2 State St.
Lord, Maria, 13 West St.
Lord, Mary E., Widow, 17 Bull St.
Lord, Richard, Collector, 10 Berresford St.
Lord, Samuel, Accountant, 178 E. Bay St.
Lovegreen, Andrew A., Dry Goods Store, 326 King St.
Lovell, -----, Mrs., Widow, 241 E. Bay St.
Lovering, Ann, Grocery, 10 King St.
Lowden, J., Merchant, 13 Crafts' S. Whf., res. 56 Meeting St.
Lowe, R. C., Sail Maker, 245 E. Bay St., Loft, Fitzsimons' Whf.
Lowndes, James, Planter, 14 Meeting St.
Lowndes, Pinckney, Planter, 118 Tradd St.
Lowndes, Thomas, Planter, 112 Broad St.
Lowndes, William, Mrs., Widow, 118 Tradd St.
Lowrey, Charles F., Printer, 32 Horlbeck's Al.
Lowrey, Charles, Tailor, 32 Horlbeck's Al.
Lubeck, Caroline, 7 Maiden Ln., F.P.C.
Lubkin, Luder, Grocery, s.e. cr. Anson & Boundary Sts.
Lucas, Jonathan, Jr., Merchant, 65 E. Bay St.
Lucas, Jonathon, Jr., Merchant, w. end Cannonborough, Neck
Lucas, William, Planter, w. end Wentworth St.
Ludlow, John R., China & Crockery, 233 King St.
Lurdens, Ann, 94 King St., F.P.C.
Lynah, James, Planter, St. Philip St., near Cannon St., Neck
Lynch, Caroline, Millinery, 255 King St.
Lynch, Francis, Draper & Tailor, 242 King St.
Lyon, George, Watchmaker, 143 E. Bay St.
Lyons, Thomas, Gadsden's Whf.
Macaulay, George, 94 Church St.

Mackey, Eliza, 13 Coming St., F.P.C.
Mackey, John, Store Keeper, 29 Church St.
Mackie, Abel, Boat Builder, E. Bay St., near Market St.
Mackie, Hervey & Co., Merchants, 48 E. Bay St.
Mackie, James, Mazyck St., near Queen St.
Macnamara, John, Vendue Master, Vendue Range, res. 1 Anson St.
Magarth, John, Merchant, Fitzsimons' Whf., res. 197 Meeting St.
Magson, Sol I., St. Philip St., near Lines, Neck
Magwood, J. A., Merchant, 11 Smith St.
Magwood, Simon, cr. Smith & Bull Sts.
Maille, Peter, Goldsmith, 114 Meeting St.
Main, A. R., Dry Goods Store, 213 King St.
Main, E., Miss, Millinery, 259 King St.
Main, William B., Ship Carpenter, 17 Wall St.
Mair, Thomas, Merchant, 60 E. Bay St.
Mairs, Levy, 117 King St.
Mairs, Simon, Wine & Liquor Store, 117 King St.
Malcolm, Elizabeth, Widow, St. Andrew's Hall, Broad St.
Mallery, Lewis, Shoe Maker, 91 E. Bay St.
Manigault, Charles, Planter, S. Bay St.
Manigault, G. H., Planter, 16 Meeting St.
Manigault, Gabriel, Planter, s.e. cr. Meeting & John Sts., Neck
Manigault, Joseph, Planter, s.e. cr. Meeting & John Sts., Neck
Manigault, Peter, Attorney, 5 Waring's Row
Manigault, Peter, Attorney, s.e. cr. Meeting & John Sts., Neck
Manly, Basil, Rev., 38 King St.
Mann, John, 39 Boundary St.
Mann, Rebecca, 39 George St., F.P.C.
Manning, Joseph, M. D., cr. Society & E. Bay St.
Manson, George, Ship Carpenter, Marsh's Whf.
Manude, Amelia, 65 George St.
Marchant, P. S., Planter, e. end Hampstead, Neck
Marion, M., Mrs., Widow, Pinckney St., Cannonborough, Neck
Marion, S., Mrs., 13 Queen St.
Markey, John, Tavern, 3 Market St.
Markins, John, Columbus St., Neck
Markley, B., Planter, cr. Warren & St. Philip St., Neck
Markley, John, Coach Maker, 53 Broad St.
Marks, J. B., Notary Public, 6 Clifford St.
Marks, Joseph, Merchant, 10 Queen St.
Marks, Mark, Deputy Sheriff, 6 Clifford St.
Marley, Ellen, 29 Archdale St.
Marsh, Abraham, Drayman, 109 Boundary St., F.P.C.
Marsh, James, Ship Carpenter, 222 E. Bay St.
Marsh, -----, Ship Yard, Gadsden's Whf.
Marsh, William, Wharfinger, 11 Pinckney St.
Marshall, John, Factor, Gadsden's Whf., res. 13 Middle St.
Marshall, Mary, Widow, 97 Broad St.
Marshall, Thomas, 74 Tradd St.
Martigniat, Joseph, Grocery, 178 Meeting St.
Martin, C. W., Blacksmith, America St., Hampstead, Neck
Martin, Jacob, Blacksmith, Burns Ln.
Martin, John N., Blacksmith, e. side of King St., btw. Reid & Wolf Sts., Neck

Martin, Joseph, Henrietta St., Neck, F.P.C.
Martin, L. V., Bricklayer, e. Coming St., btw. Boundary & Vanderhorst Sts., Neck
Martin, Robert & Co., Factors, 7 Kiddell's Whf.
Martin, Thomas, Attorney, 74 Broad St.
Marvin, Aaron, Factor, 74 King St.
Massias, A. A., District Paymaster, U. S. Army, 387 E. Bay St., off. 106 Broad St.
Massot, H., Watchmaker, 11 Queen St.
Masterson, Michael, Grocery, 5 Market St.
Mathews, H. B., Shoe Maker, 22 St. Philip St., F.P.C.
Mathews, Isaac, Livery Stables, Broad St., res. 103 Queen St., F.P.C.
Mathews, Jane, Charlotte St., Neck, F.P.C.
Mathews, John, Carpenter, 3 Friend St., F.P.C.
Mathews, Peter, 43 Boundary St., F.P.C.
Mathews, Sarah, 43 Boundary St., F.P.C.
Mathey, C., Watchmaker, 173 King St.
Mathiessen, C. F., Dry Goods Store, 175 King St.
Mathiessen, John, Accountant, 232 E. Bay St.
Matiria, Francis, cr. Meeting & Mary Sts., Neck
Matthews & Bonneau, Factors, Kiddell's Whf.
Matthews, David, Shoemaker, n. cr. Nassau & South Sts., Hampstead, Neck
Matthews, James, Factor, 51 Anson St.
Matthews, Maria, Widow, 26 Meeting St.
Matthews, William, Planter, s.e. cr. Elizabeth & Charlotte Sts., Neck
Maugin, F., Mariner, Lucas St., Cannonborough, Neck
Maul, Mary, Widow, 36 Beaufain St.
Maxton, John, Baker, 17 Tradd St.
Maxwell, D., 15 Amen St.
Maxwell, Harriet, 91 Meeting St.
Maxwell, R., Pastry Cook, w. end Beaufain St., F.P.C.
May, John, Cabinet Maker, 59 Queen St.
Maybank, M. S., Mrs., n. cr. Nassau & South Sts. Hampstead, Neck
Mayer, Samuel, Ship Carpenter, 237 E. Bay St.
Maynard, John, Baker & Grocery, 49 St. Philip St.
Mayrant, Diana, Mary St., Neck, F.P.C.
Mazyck, A. H., Attorney, 94 Wentworth St.
Mazyck, Edward, 94 Wentworth St.
Mazyck, Henry, Planter, Cannonborough
Mazyck, Mary, Widow, 61 Church St.
Mazyck, Philip, M. D., 94 Wentworth St.
Mazyck, Theodore, Accountant, 187 Meeting St.
Mazyck, William, Factor, 94 Wentworth St.
Mazyck, William, Factor, e. end Judith St., Neck
McAnally, J., Grocery, s.w. cr. Broad & King Sts.
McBarney, J. R., Storekeeper, s. cr. King & Bridge Sts., Neck
McBeth, John, Carpenter, 61 Meeting St., F.P.C.
McBride, Mary, Widow, 58 Church St.
McCall, Emeline, 62 State St., F.P.C.
McCall, Joseph P., Accountant, cr. Church & Water Sts.
McCally, Sarah, Widow, 88 Anson St.
McCants, Ann, 10 Savage St.
McCarter, J. J., Bookstore, 310 King St.
McCarter, John, Turner, Burns Ln.
McCartney & Gordon, Hardware, 18 Broad St.

McCay, Joseph, Mrs., Widow, 50 King St.
McCay, Thomas, Accountant, 50 King St.
McCloud, Cato, Charlotte St., Neck, F.P.C.
McCollum, John, 70 State St.
McCormick, John & Co., Dry Goods Store, 249 King St.
McCormick, Timothy, 24 New St.
McCready, Edward, Attorney, 97 Meeting St.
McCready, James, Accountant, 348 King St.
McCready, Jane, Mrs., 97 Meeting St.
McCready, William, Abstract Clerk, Custom House, 348 King St.
McCune, Mary, Radcliffborough, near St. Paul's Church, Neck, F.P.C.
McDermont, Edward, n. side Boundary St., e. end, Neck
McDonald, Alexander, Grocery, s.e. cr. King & George Sts.
McDonald, Hugh, Merchant, 191 E. Bay St.
McDonald, J. C. W., M. D., cr. Coming & Beaufain Sts.
McDonald, Sarah, Boarding House, 191 E. Bay St.
McDow, William, Teacher, Montague St.
McDowall, Andrew, Dry Goods Store, 145 King St.
McDowall, Mary, Widow, 55 Wentworth St.
McElheny, Susannah, Widow, n. end Lynch St.
McElmoyle, William, Factor, S. Bay St., res. 82 King St.
McFeeters & Wanless, Saddlers, 224 King St.
McGann, P., Watchmaker, 24 Queen St.
McGillivray, A. H., Vendue Master & Broker, 9 Chalmers St.
McGinniss, Elijah, Clerk, 14 Mazyck St.
McGinniss, Joseph, s. side Charlotte St., Neck
McGrainigaw, Eliza, Henrietta St., Neck
McGregor, A., w. side King St., btw. Radcliff & Warren Sts., Neck
McHugh, Francis, Student at Law, 49 Beaufain St.
McIntosh, Betsy, Alexander St., Neck, F.P.C.
McIntosh, Daniel, Grocery, w. side King St., btw. Radcliff & Mary Sts., Neck
McIntosh, Rebecca, 2 Wentworth St.
McIntyre, Charles & Co., Wholesale Dry Goods Store, 275 King St.
McIntyre, Charles, Merchant, 74 Wentworth St.
McKee, Abel, Ship Joiner, 150 Church St.
McKee, John, Bricklayer, 3 Bedon's Al.
McKee, Mary, 99 King St., F.P.C.
McKegan, John, Blacksmith, 235 Meeting St.
McKegan, John, Blacksmith, Burns Ln.
McKegan, Neil, Grocery, 61 Market St.
McKenrue, A., Mrs., s. cr. Reid & Amherst Sts., Hampstead, Neck
McKensie, Richard, Saddlery, 135 Church St.
McKenzie, A., Shoe Maker, 7 Queen St.
McKenzie, J., Carolina Coffee House, 91 E. Bay St.
McKinley, Peter, Carpenter, 25 Water St.
McKinney, Christopher, 8 West St.
McKinney, Laurence, Wheelwright, 121 Queen St.
McLean, George, Butcher, Cannon St., Neck
McLean, Samuel, Butcher, Spring St., Neck
McLean, Susan, Widow, w. end Bull St.
McLean, Thomas, Blockmaker, w. end Bull St.
McMillan, John, 12 Vendue Range, res. Ellery St., op.

Church St.
McMillan, Sarah Ann, Widow, 30 Bull St.
McMillan, Thomas, Carpenter, Gadsdens Whf.
McNamee, James, Boot & Shoe Maker, 112 Church St.
McNeil, Daniel, Capt., Doughty St., Neck
McNeil, John, King St., cr. Wolf St., Neck
McNeill & Blair, Grocers, 44 Broad St.
McNeill, Henrietta, Widow, 41 King St.
McNellage, John, Sail Maker, Loft, Kunhardt's Whf., res. Reapers Al.
McNicol, Daniel, Merchant, 60 E. Bay St.
McOwen, Patrick, Accountant, 39 St. Philip St.
McPherson, J. E., Planter, 289 E. Bay St.
McPherson, O. L., Planter, 289 E. Bay St.
McPherson, Susan, Widow, 94 Broad St.
Meacher & Halmes, Grain Merchants, cr. Market & E. Bay Sts. & 8 Tradd St.
Meacher, Thomas, Grain Merchant, res. Mey's Whf.
Mead, A., Grocer, Kiddell's Whf.
Mealy, John, 17 St. Philip St.
Mease, J. B., Dry Goods Store, 151 King St.
Meeker, William, Coach Maker, 57 Wentworth St.
Memminger, C. G., Attorney, 61 Meeting St.
Menlove, Edward, Merchant, 7 Fitzsimons' Whf.
Merritt, J. H., Merchant, 112 E. Bay St.
Merritt, James, Factor, 7 Bull St.
Mey, Ann, 66 King St., F.P.C.
Mey, J. H., Merchant, 3 Mey's Whf.
Meyer, John, 40 Broad St.
Michel, Francis, cr. Laurens & Wall Sts.
Michel, J., Magistrate's Office, 90 E. Bay St.
Michel, John, Magistrate, St. Philip St., near Vanderhorst St., Neck
Michel, William, M. D., 183 Meeting St.
Middleton, Arthur, Planter, 249 E. Bay St.
Middleton, F., Boarding House, 6 Tradd St.
Middleton, Henry, Planter, E. Bay St., s. cr. Vernon St.
Middleton, J. J., Planter, E. Bay St., s. cr. Vernon St.
Middleton, O. H., Planter, Montague St.
Middleton, Thomas, Factor, 10 Meeting St.
Mieslane, Hans, Grocery, s. side Cannon St., Neck
Mignot, R., Confectioner, 170 King St.
Miles, Edward, Doughty St., Neck
Miller, A. E., Printer, 4 Broad St.
Miller, Abraham, Out Door Clerk, Bank of State of S. C.
Miller, Catharine, Mrs., e. side Mary St., Neck
Miller, Charles E., Merchant, Chisolm's Whf., res. 52 Anson St.
Miller, George A., Teacher, 22 Mazyck St.
Miller, J. B., n. cr. Reid & Amherst Sts., Neck
Miller, J. C., Factor, Willams Whf
Miller, J. P., Bricklayer, 6 Orange St.
Miller, James A., Assistant Marshal, res. Theatre
Miller, James A., Factor, Vanderhorst St., Neck
Miller, John C., Merchant, e. end Mary St., Neck
Miller, John, Grocer, 4 Tradd St.
Miller, M., Goldsmith, 150 King St.
Miller, Ripley & Co., Wholesale Dry Goods Store, 310 King St.
Miller, Robert S., Baker, 143 Meeting St.

19

Miller, Stent, Printer, 96 Market St.
Miller, William H., Tailor, 58 Queen St.
Miller, William, Hampstead, Neck
Miller, William, Merchant, 50 Anson St.
Milliken & Gilliland, Auction Stores, 17 & 19 Vendue
Range
Milliken, Thomas, Auctioneer & Commission Merchant,
Charlotte St., near Elizabeth St., Neck
Mills, E. S., Mrs., Pinckney St., Cannonborough, Neck
Mills, O. & S., Commission Merchants, 26 Vendue Range
& Napier's Row
Mills, Otis, Merchant, cr. Meeting & Queen Sts.
Mills, P. V., Mrs., Widow, 39 Market St.
Mills, T., Mrs., Boarding House, cr. Church & Tradd Sts.
Mills, Thomas, Mrs., Widow, 40 Tradd St.
Milne, Andrew, Planter, 14 Rutledge St.
Mintzing, J. F., 26 Friend St.
Miott, C., Hotel, cr. King & Society Sts.
Miott, Edward, Boat Builder, 15 College St.
Mishaw, F., Coming St., above Boundary St., w. side,
Neck, F.P.C.
Mishaw, John, 120 Meeting St.
Mishaw, John, Shoemaker, Coming St., above Boundary
St., w. side, Neck, F.P.C.
Missroon & Utley, Mathematical Store, 89 E. Bay St.
Missroon, James, Capt., E. Bay St., near Battery
Mitchell, Ann, 2 George St., F.P.C.
Mitchell, Ann, 29 Beaufain St., F.P.C.
Mitchell, Ann, Widow, 81 Market St.
Mitchell, Charlotte, 222 Meeting St.
Mitchell, J. D., Ordinary, Charleston District, 5 Fireproof
Building, res. 134 Wentworth St.
Mitchell, J. H., Quorum Unis, 27 Guignard St.
Mitchell, J. W., Attorney, 27 Guignard St., off. 84 E. Bay
St.
Mitchell, James & Son, Coopers, 76 E. Bay St.
Mitchell, James, 50 Meeting St.
Mitchell, James S., 50 Meeting St.
Mitchell, Rebecca, Widow, Washington St., Gadsden's
Whf.
Mitchell, Sarah, 18 Swinton's Ln, F.P.C.
Mitchell, T., Fruit Store, 182 E. Bay St.
Mithchell, Jane, 14 Pinckney St., F.P.C.
Moderen, J., Boat Builder, 218 E. Bay St.
Moffett & Caulder, Dry Goods Store, cr. King St. &
Horlbeck's Al.
Moffett, A., 6 Beaufain St.
Moise, Aaron, Accountant, 256 E. Bay St.
Moise, Abraham, Attorney, 72 Broad St., Res, 84 Tradd
St.
Moise, Abraham, Clerk, 256 E. Bay St.
Moise, Columbus, Clerk, 256 E. Bay St.
Moisson, L., Gunsmith, 16 State St.
Molant, Sarah, 45 Boundary St., F.P.C.
Moles, Margaret, Store, n. cr. King & Radcliff Sts., Neck
Monar, Louis, Hair Dresser, 12 Queen St.
Monefeldt, -----, Mrs. & Miss, Young Ladies Academy,
Beaufain St., near Coming St.
Monies, Jane, Mantuamaker, 84 Meeting St., F.P.C.
Monk, S. P., Teacher, S. C. Society School, 52 Meeting St.

Monquey, Honore, Factor, 40 Bull St.
Montague, Catharine, 90 Wentworth St.
Montesque, R., Tin Plate Worker, 189 E. Bay St.
Montgomery & Platt, Merchants, cr. Edmonston's &
Kiddell's Whf.
Mood, Christian, Silversmith, 8 Smith St.
Mood, Edmund M., Mast Block & Pump Maker, 270 E.
Bay St.
Mood, John, Storekeeper, 11 Liberty St.
Mood, P. & Co., Gold & Silver Smiths, 191 King St.
Moody, Eleanor, Seamstress, 47 Anson St., F.P.C.
Moody, James G., Cannon St., Cannonborough, Neck
Mooney, Ann, Store Keeper, 14 King St.
Mooney, Mary, Widow, 21 Horlbeck's Al.
Moore, Catherine, Widow, cr. Smith & Bull Sts.
Moore, Eleanor S., s. side Vanderhorst St., Neck
Moore, I. C., Carpenter, e. side Meeting St., btw. Reid &
Mary Sts., Neck
Moore, J. D., Hair Dresser, 27 Broad St.
Moore, Philip, Factor, w. end Montague St.
Moore, R., St Philip St., btw. Boundary & Vanderhorst
Sts., Neck
Moore, T. B., St. Philip St., above Boundary St., F.P.C.,
Neck
Moorhead, James, Grocery, 284 King St., cr. Society St.
Mordecai, Isaac, Dry Goods Store, 234 King St., res. w.
end Beaufain St.
Mordecai, J. D., Grocer, 89 Market St.
Mordecai, M. C., Vendue Master, 21 Vendue Range, res.
89 Market St.
Mordecai, R., Widow, 16 Guignard St.
Mordecai, Thomas W., Accountant, w. end Beaufain St.
Morecock, E., Mrs., Boarding House, 24 Broad St.
Moreland, Andrew, Factor, S. Bay St.
Morgan, Benjamin, 14 Middle St.
Morgan, Isaac, Printer, 1 Bull St.
Moriarty, M., Dry Goods Store, 283 King St.
Morison, Simon, Cabinet Maker, 174 Meeting St.
Morris, C. G., Merchant, 82 E. Bay St., res. n.w. cr. of E.
Bay & Wentworth Sts.
Morris, Edward, Rice Store, 20 Vendue Range
Morris, T., Jr., Porter, Bank of S. C., 123 Church St.
Morris, William, Watchmaker, 206 King St.
Morrison, J., Mrs., 85 Market St.
Morrison, John, Mrs., Widow, 70 Tradd St.
Morrison, Joseph, Planter, Lucas St., Cannonborough,
Neck
Morrison, Richard T., Mary St., Neck
Morrison, Sarah, Widow, 60 Wentworth St.
Morry, William, Planter, Lucas St., Cannonborough, Neck
Mortimer, Edward C., M. D., 56 Anson St.
Moser, Philip, M. D., New St.
Moses, Isaiah, Planter, e. side King St., btw. John &
Hudson Sts., Neck
Moses, Israel, Vendue Master, 28 Vendue Range, res.
Beaufain St.
Moses, Jacob, Storekeeper, 64 State St.
Moses, Levy, Coming St., near St. Paul's Church, Neck
Moses, Reuben, Clothing Store, 276 King St.
Moses, Simon, Dry Goods Store, e. side King St., btw.

John & Ann Sts., Neck
Moses, Solomon, 79 Wentworth St.
Mosiman, J., Watchmaker, 13 Queen St.
Moss & Cassidy, Tailors, 311 King St.
Moss, J. D., Widow, 63 Wentworth St.
Motta, J. A., Confectioner, 121 King St.
Motte, Isaac, Mrs., Widow, 24 Meeting St.
Motte, Mary W., Widow, 34 Church St.
Moulen, Jane, Storekeeper, cr. King & Warren Sts., Neck
Moultrie, James, M. D., 12 Cumberland St.
Moultrie, Justina, 120 Wentworth St., F.P.C.
Moultrie, -----, Mrs., 125 Boundary St.
Moultrie, William M., M. D., 110 Broad St.
Mouzon, Charles, Planter, 8 St. Philip St.
Mowry, H., Boot & Shoe Store, 142 King St.
Mowry, S. & Co., Merchants, 134 E. Bay St., res. 10 State St.
Muckenfuss, Henry, Bricklayer, 120 Wentworth St.
Muckenfuss, Henry W., Accountant, 120 Wentworth St.
Muckenfuss, S. T., Mechanic, 120 Wentworth St.
Muggridge, M., Globe Tavern, 216 King St.
Muir, Jane, Boarding House, 24 Broad St.
Muir, William, Shoemaker, 14 Bull St., F.P.C.
Mullens, John, Pilot, 1 Stoll's Al.
Munds, Israel, Rev., 43 State St.
Munds, Robert, Teacher, 43 State St.
Munroe, M. E., Grain Merchant, 14 Vendue Range, res. cr. Boundary & St. Philip Sts.
Munroe, Margaret, Widow, 81 Church St.
Murden, Jeremiah, Merchant, Kunhardt's Whf.
Murden, -----, Mrs. & Daughters, Seminary, n.w. cr. Meeting & Hasell Sts.
Murphy, L. C., Mrs., Boarding House, 359 King St.
Murray, Ann E., Dry Goods Store, 81 King St.
Murray, C. B., Clerk, 81 King St.
Murray, James L., Grocery, S. Bay St.
Murray, Robert, Tailor, 46 Broad St.
Murrell, J. J., Planter, 23 Middle St.
Mushington, William, 140 King St., F.P.C.
Myers, D., Capt., s. side Charlotte St., Neck
Myers, John, Capt., Grocery, Gadsden's Whf.
Myles, Ann, 112 Tradd St.
Myles, Jane, Accoucher, 11 Queen St.
Naser, Frederick, City Scavenger, 29 Mazyck St.
Nathans, Henry, State Constable, 6 Hasell St.
Nathans, Nathan, Dry Goods, Etc., King St., btw. John & Hudson Sts., Neck
Nauman, William, Hardware, 232 King St.
Nedderman, F. S., Sail Store, 90 Market St.
Neil, Henry, Planter, 7 St. Philip St.
Nell, M., Mrs., Hampstead, Neck
Nell, Stephen, Accountant, Hampstead, Neck
Nell, William S., Baker, 186 Meeting St.
Nelme, J. W., 19 Pinckney St.
Nelson, John, Blacksmith, 4 Middle St.
Nelson, Mary, Widow, 65 King St.
Neufville, Benjamin, Printer, 86 Anson St.
Neufville, John, Attorney, 86 Anson St.
Neufville, William, Accountant, 86 Anson St.
Neve, W., Grocery, n.w. cr. Alexander & Charlotte Sts., Neck

Neve, William, Grocery, 1 Elliott St.
Neville, H. W., Cabinet Maker, 65 Wentworth St.
Neville, J., Grocery, 11 King St.
Neville, Joshua, Cabinet Maker, 7 Wentworth St.
Newbold, Samuel, Pilot, 12 Water St.
Newbury, Mary, 40 George St.
Newhall, Edward, 152 King St.
Newton, Cordelia, 129 Queen St., F.P.C.
Newton, Elizabeth, 47 Pinckney St., F.P.C.
Newton, Mary, Widow, Cannon St., Neck
Newton, P., Cannon St., Neck
Newton, William, Merchant, Fraser & Co. Whf.
Newton, William, Merchant, w. end Cannon St., Neck
Neye, Harmon, Grocery, n.e. cr. Boundary & Meeting Sts., Neck
Nicholson, Alexander, Wheelwright, cr. Meeting & Coming Sts.
Nicholson, James, e. side Pinckney St., Cannonborough, Neck
Nooney, Francis, Rigger, 5 Wentworth St.
Norman, E., Shopkeeper, 25 Tradd St.
Norris, Agnes, Widow
Norris, J. C., Accountant, Mercury Office, 10 Magazine St.
North, E. W., M. D., off. 91 Meeting St., res. 44 Montague St.
North, John, Attorney, 111 Broad St.
North, Pricilla, 16 Mazyck St., F.P.C.
North, Richard, M. D., 44 Montague St.
North, Webb & Co., Factors, Chisolm's Whf.
Norton, -----, Mills, Gadsden's Whf.
Nowell, A., Mrs., Widow, e. side Alexander St., Neck
Nowell, John L., e. side Alexander St., Neck
Nowell, Lionel C., Planter, e. side Alexander St., Neck
O'Conner, Patrick, Factor, Gadsden's Whf.
O'Driscol, -----, Miss, School, 98 Tradd St.
O'Gorman, Mary, Teacher, 11 Friend St.
O'Hanlon, Charles, Eagle Tavern, 133 E. Bay St.
O'Hara, Henry, Broker, 24 New St.
O'Hear, James, Factor, 4 Cumberland St.
O'Hear, Joseph, Planter, 4 Cumberland St.
O'Neale & Bird, Ship Builders, O'Neale & Bird's Whf.
O'Neale, Charles, Merchant, w. side King St., op. Wolf St., Neck
O'Neale, James, Shop Keeper, 67 State St.
O'Neale, John, Boat Builder, 4 Wentworth St.
O'Neil, Edmund, Grocery, 63 Market St.
O'Neill, John, Butcher, s. side Cannon St., Neck
O'Neill, Patrick, Butcher, s. side Cannon St., Neck
O'Wen, J. L., Dentist & Dry Goods Store, 148 King St.
Oakes, S. & Son, Sugar Store, 53 Queen St.
Oakley, R. S., Druggist, 152 King St.
Oakley, William, Millinery, 301 King St.
Ogden, G. W., Capt., Pritchard's Whf.
Ogden, W. S., Shoe Store, e. side King St., near Spring St., Neck
Ogier, Ann, Widow, John St., Neck
Ogier, Thomas, 53 Beaufain St.
Ogilby, William, British Consul, 39 E. Bay St.
Ogleby, William, Barber, 343 King St., F.P.C.

Ohlson, Christopher, Tavern, 171 E. Bay St.
Olds, Welcome, 85 Coming St.
Oliphant, David, Painter, n.e. cr. Meeting & Society Sts.
Oliver, John, 95 Wentworth St., F.P.C.
Olney, G. W., Merchant, 13 Vendue Range
Oppenheim, H. W., Grocery, s.e. cr. Market & Church Sts.
Osburn, Margaret, Widow, 32 S. Bay St.
Ottolengui, A., Merchant, 91 Market St.
O'Hear & Desaussure, Factors, 6 Roper's Whf.
O'Neale, James, House Carpenter, 13 Back St.
Palmer, B. M., Rev., 82 Broad St.
Parish, Corning & Co., Wholesale Dry Goods Store, 265 King St.
Parker, Charles, Surveyor, 6 St. Michael's Al., res. Anson St., op. Laurens St.
Parker, Eliza, Miss, 19 Legare St.
Parker, Henry, Pilot, 44 Church St.
Parker, John, Jr., Planter, s. side Ann St., Neck
Parker, John M., Factor, 35 E. Bay St.
Parker, John, Sr., Planter, e. side St. Philip St., btw. Cannon & Mary Sts., Neck
Parker, Peter G., 6 George St.
Parker, Peter G., Planter, Chapel St., Neck
Parrara, Domingo, Grocery, Market St., near E. Bay St.
Parrara, Emanuel, Grocery, Market St., near E. Bay St.
Parsons, Hannah, Alexander St., Neck, F.P.C.
Parsons, J. D., School, 7 Tradd St.
Parsons, William, Painter, 266 E. Bay St.
Passaligne, Louis, s.w. cr. Boundary & Wall Sts.
Patrick, Casimer, Merchant, Kunhardt's Whf., res. e. end Society St.
Patrick, Philip, Notary Public, 234 E. Bay St.
Patterson & Magwood, Merchants, Magwood's Whf.
Patterson, George H., 42 Church St.
Patterson, Hugh, 31 Laurens St.
Patterson, James, Grocery, 71 E. Bay St.
Patterson, James, Merchant, 14 Queen St.
Patterson, John, Accountant, 231 E. Bay St.
Patterson, Samuel, Merchant, 25 Rutledge St.
Patton, William, Wharfinger, 26 Laurens St.
Paul & Brown, Grocery, 47 Broad St.
Payne, Harriett, Mrs., 3 Hasell St.
Payne, John W., w. side King St., btw. Bridge St. & Lines, Neck
Payne, M., Washington St., Wraggborough, Neck, F.P.C.
Payne, Robert K., Surveyor, Court House Sq.
Payne, Robert K., Surveyor, Hampstead, Neck
Payne, William & Son, Brokers & Auctioneers, 28 Broad St.
Pearce, Eugenius, 103 Queen St.
Pearce, Harriett, Widow, 41 Society St.
Pearson, Margaret, Miss, 13 Bull St.
Peigne, James L., Clerk, 196 E. Bay St.
Peixotto, Solomon C., King St., op. Municipal Guard House
Pelmoine, F. S., St. Michael's Al.
Pelot, Mary C., Meeting St., near Wolf St., Neck, F.P.C.
Pelser, Hannah, 17 College St.
Pemble, David, Store Keeper, 161 E. Bay St.

Pennal, Robert, Grocery, 358 King St.
Pennington, Ann Eliza, Widow, Burns Ln.
Penot, R., Ladies Shoe Store, 63 Broad St.
Pepoon & Eckhard, Attorneys, Chalmers St.
Perkins, Daniel, Merchant, 17 New St.
Perkins, E. G., Shoemaker, 270 E. Bay St.
Perman & Bacon, Grocery Store, 63 E. Bay St.
Perman, Isabella, Widow, 63 E. Bay St.
Peronneau & Finley, Attorneys, 69 Broad St.
Peronneau, W. H., 109 Tradd St.
Peronneau, William, 36 S. Bay St.
Perrinchief, F., s. side Radcliff St., Neck
Perry, E. D., Planter, 44 Broad St.
Perry, Edward, Mrs., Widow, 44 Broad St.
Perry, J., w. side Cannon St. & Lines, Neck
Perry, Stevens, Attorney, 14 Water St.
Perry, William, Baker, 20 Queen St.
Perry, William, Boarding House, 29 Elliott St.
Peters, George, 47 Society St.
Peters, James, Teacher, 8 Price's Al.
Peters, Jane, w. side Cannonborough, Neck
Peters, Sarah H., Teacher, 47 Society St.
Petigru & Cruger, Attorneys, 16 St. Michael's Al.
Petigru, James L., Attorney, 111 Broad St.
Petit, E., Confectioner, 118 Meeting St.
Petit, F., Dry Goods Store, 227 King St.
Petivall, J. B., Engineer, 14 Hasell St.
Petsch, Jane, School, 14 Liberty St.
Pezant, John L., Merchant, 183 E. Bay St.
Pezant, Louis, Grocery, 79 Boundary St.
Pezant, Peter, Capt., 7 Wall St.
Philips, Aaron, 55 Church St.
Philips, Benjamin, 18 Beaufain St.
Philips, Dorothy, Widow, 132 Queen St.
Philips, Edward, Rev., 52 Beaufain St.
Philips, John, Attorney, 52 Beaufain St.
Philips, Martha, 10 Guignard St.
Philips, Otis, 52 Beaufain St.
Philips, St. John, M. D., 52 Beaufain St.
Phillippe, Hannah P., 113 Queen St.
Phillips, Ann, 84 Coming St., F.P.C.
Phinney, -----, Boarding House, 8 Queen St.
Picault, F. D., Clerk, 42 State St.
Picault, V., Mrs., Boarding House, cr. E. Bay St. & Vendue Range
Pillans, J. C., Carpenter, 43 Hasell St.
Pilsbury, H., Widow, 19 Hasell St.
Pinckney, C. C., Planter, cr. Elizabeth & Chapel Sts., Neck
Pinckney, Diana, cr. Berresford St., F.P.C.
Pinckney, Edward, Planter, 25 King St.
Pinckney, Eliza, 26 Berresford St., F.P.C.
Pinckney, H. L., Hon., 98 Church St.
Pinckney, Harriett, 223 E. Bay St.
Pinckney, Maria H., Miss, 223 E. Bay St.
Pinckney, Miles, Mrs., Widow, 44 Coming St.
Pinckney, Robert Quash, Surveyor, Cannonborough, near Bennett's Mills, Neck
Pinckney, Roger, Planter, 54 Meeting St.
Pitray & Viel, Merchants, 182 E. Bay St.
Pitray, L. A., Merchant, 12 George St.

Place, H., Boarding House, 34 Elliott St.
Plane, William A., Charleston District Sheriff & Boarding House, 18 Elliott St.
Plumeau, J. F., Teller, Bank of S. C., 94 King St.
Pogson, Milward, Rev., cr. Pitt & Wentworth Sts.
Pohl, Joseph, Ann St., Neck, F.P.C.
Pohl, Joseph, w. side King St., btw. Bridge & Lines, Neck
Poincignon, E., Tinner, 19 Queen St.
Poincy, V., Brass Founder, 2 Amen St.
Poinsett, Henry, Henrietta St., Neck, F.P.C.
Poinsett, Joel R., Planter, Pinckney St., Cannonborough, Neck
Poirier, P., Grocery, 42 Queen St.
Poland, Oliver, Boarding House, 23 Elliott St.
Pope, Mary Ann, Elizabeth St., Neck, F.P.C.
Porcher, F. Y., M. D., 45 Queen St.
Porcher, G., Mrs., Judith St., Neck
Porcher, Mary, Mrs., Widow, n. side Boundary St., Neck
Porcher, Philip, Planter, 111 Broad St.
Portee, William L., Grocery, 47 E. Bay St.
Porter, John, Grocery, 115 Broad St.
Porter, L., Capt., Pritchard's Whf.
Potter, Jane, Mrs., Widow, 13 Bull St.
Poujet, C., M. D., 19 Wall St.
Poultom, Rachel, Widow, 54 Church St.
Powell, Martha, Widow, 11 Legare St.
Poyas, Catherine, Widow, 47 Meeting St.
Poyas, E. A., Mrs., Widow, 67 Tradd St.
Poyas, F. D., Gunsmith, 63 Queen St.
Poyas, James, Ship Carpenter, 30 S. Bay St.
Pratt, George, Merchant, 14 Broad St.
Pratt, John, Capt., 14 Church St.
Prele, John F., Confectioner, 309 King St.
Prendergast, M., 88 Queen St.
Preston, J., Merchant, 175 E. Bay St.
Preston, John, Grocery, 130 Church St.
Price, A. D., Widow, 71 Church St.
Price, Betsey, Mantuamaker, 38 Coming St., F.P.C.
Price, Thomas, Officer, Union Bank, res. e. end Society St.
Price, William, 51 Beaufain St.
Price, William, Wharf Owner, Price's Whf. res. 307 E. Bay St.
Prince, Charles, Jr., 325 King St.
Prince, Charles, Tinner, 114 King St.
Prince, John, Porter, Planters & Mechanics Bank, Bank Yard, E. Bay St.
Pringle, Ann, Miss, Cannonborough, Neck
Pringle, E. J., Planter, 25 King St.
Pringle, George, Dry Goods etc., w. side King St., btw. Bridge St. & Lines, Neck
Pringle, J. J., Planter, 25 King St.
Pringle, James R., Hon., Intendent of Charleston & Collector of Customs, 2 Orange St.
Pringle, R. R., Planter, 25 King St.
Pringle, Robert A., Mrs., 91 Meeting St.
Pringle, William B., Planter, 25 King St.
Prioleau, Philip, M. D., 220 Meeting St.
Prioleau, Samuel, Mrs., Widow, Court House Sq.
Prioleau, T. G., M. D., 135 Meeting St.

Prithchard, Paul, Jr., Shipwright, 6 Hasell St.
Proctor, William, Merchant, 13 St. Michael's Al.
Proileau, Samuel, Hon., Recorder, 2 Church St.
Pundt, John, Grocery, cr. Smith & Bull Sts.
Purcell, Ann, Mrs., Green St.
Purse, Robert, Cabinet Maker, 3 Coming St.
Purse, William, Cabinet Maker, 10 Liberty St.
Purse, William, Sr., Jeweller, 58 Broad St.
Purvis, J. R. & Co., Factors, 5 Kiddell's Whf.
Quash, Albert, Barber, 195½ Wentworth St., F.P.C.
Quash, Francis D., Planter, 19 Rutledge St.
Quash, Robert H., Factor, 4 Kiddell's Whf., res. 91 Boundary St.
Query, H., Mrs., Boarding House, 279 King St.
Quin, John, n. side Boundary St., Neck
Quinan, B., Northern Warehouse, 257½ King St.
Quinby, Elizabeth, 44 George St.
Quinby, Joseph, Shipwright, 29 Wall St.
Quinlan, Mary, Widow, 49 Beaufain St.
Quinlon, John, 41 King St.
Radcliff, Maria, 49 Wentworth St.
Rain, Thomas, n.w. cr. Meeting & Reid Sts., Neck
Rame, C., Confectioner, 165 Meeting St.
Ramsay, David, Mrs., Widow, 32 Meeting St.
Ramsay, H. L., Miss, Seminary, 74 Broad St.
Ramsay, James, M. D., 181 Meeting St.
Ramsay, John, M. D., 101 Broad St.
Randall, Ann, 6 Greenhill St.
Raoul, William, Planter, 5 Greenhill St.
Rast, John, Dry Goods & Grocery, 339 King St.
Ravenel, Catharine, Widow, 64 Broad St.
Ravenel, Daniel, Cashier, Planters & Mechanics Bank, 56 Tradd St.
Ravenel, E., M. D., 131 Meeting St.
Ravenel, Henry, Surveyor, 1 Short St.
Ravenel, William, Factor, 64 Broad St.
Ravenel, William, Factor, Chisolm's N. Whf.
Ravina, J. D., Teacher, 18 Queen St.
Raynal, W. T., Dry Goods Store, 143 King St.
Read, John Harleston, Planter, 135 Wentworth St.
Recli, Carlo, Grocery, 3 Vendue Range
Redding, William F., Lottery & Exchange Office, 109 E. Bay St.
Redfern, John, Boot & Shoe Maker, 9 Tradd St.
Redheimmer, Peter, Farmer, n. side Spring St., Neck
Redman, James, Blacksmith, 26 Bull St.
Redmond, M., Tavern, 147 E. Bay St.
Redmond, William, Merchant, Fraser's Whf., Res 18 Legare St.
Reedy, James, Carpenter, 26 Chalmers St.
Reeves, A. P., Architect, 96 Tradd St.
Reeves, Eliza, Mrs., Teacher of Music, 11 Back St.
Reeves, Solomon, Carpenter, 17 Coming St.
Reicks, Claus, Grocery, cr. Meeting & Pinckney Sts.
Reicks, Gerd, Grocery, cr. King St. & Burns Ln.
Reid, Andrew, Grocery, n.e. cr. Meeting & Wentworth Sts.
Reid, Eliza, Widow, 104 Meeting St.
Reid, George, 23 Legare St.
Reid, George, cr. Clifford & Archdale Sts.

Reid, Mary, Widow, 49 E. Bay St.
Reid, William, M. D., 31 Meeting St.
Reighton, Mary, e. end Boundary St., Neck, F.P.C.
Reigne, John, Baker, 195 E. Bay St.
Remley, Paul, Bricklayer, 1 Society St.
Remmington, Sarah, Cannon St., Neck
Renald, John, Alexander St., Neck
Renney, B., Radcliffborough, near St. Paul's Church, Neck
Requier, Augustus, Confectioner, 112 Meeting St.
Reynolds, Ann, Widow, Cannonborough, Neck
Rice, William, 78 Broad St.
Rich, John, Grocery, 75 Market St.
Richards, Charles, Bricklayer, 265 E. Bay St.
Richardson, Robert, Bell Hanger, 92 Meeting St.
Richers, Henry, Grocery, 288 E. Bay St.
Ridgeway, Benjamin T., Millwright, e. end Chapel St.,
   Neck
Righton, I., M. D., n. side Charlotte St., Neck
Righton, Joseph, Cooper, cr. Roper's Whf. & E. Bay St.,
   res. 5 Water St.
Riley, C. H., Grocery, 13 Magazine St.
Riley, William, Printer & Bookseller, 110 Church St.
Ring, D. A., Oil Store, 114 E. Bay St.
Ripley, B. & Co., Paint & Oils Store, 88 E. Bay St. & 17
   Champney St.
Ripley, H., Judith St., Neck
Ripley, Samuel P., Shopkeeper, 13 George St.
Ritchie, Euphane, Nurse, 53 Tradd St.
Rivers, John, Carpenter, 55 St. Philip St.
Rivers, John, Ship Carpenter, 23 Water St.
Rivers, Mary G., Maiden Ln.
Rivers, Prioleau, Clerk, 32 Coming St.
Rivers, William H., Printer, 135 Wentworth St.
Rivers, William, Planter, 9 Orange St.
Riviere, J. P., Dry Goods Store, 175 King St.
Roach, Edward, Deputy City Treasurer, 38 Pinckney St.
Roach, Henry, Grocery, cr. King & John Sts., Neck
Roach, William, Clerk, Council, 13 Society St., off. City
   Hall
Robb, James, Grocery, 190 & 192 King St.
Robbins, E. & C., Wholesale Hardware, 305 King St.
Robens, Anthony, Fruit Store, 35 Market St.
Roberds, S. G., Painter, 119 King St.
Robert, Alexander, Teacher, 9 Friend St.
Roberts, Stephen, Capt., 33 Pinckney St.
Roberts, William, Inspector of Customs, 25 Middle St.
Robertson, J. T., 105 Broad St.
Robertson, J. W. R., Accountant, 23 Rutledge St.
Robertson, James, Clerk, 8 Clifford St.
Robertson, James, Merchant, 64 E. Bay St.
Robertson, James, Merchant, 7 Meeting St.
Robinson, Alexander, Secretary Fire & Marine Insurance
   Co., 23 E. Bay St.
Robinson, Betsey, Chapel St., Neck., F.P.C.
Robinson, John F. & Co., Merchants, Edmondston's Whf.
Robinson, John, Merchant, Judith St., Neck
Robinson, Randall, Teller, U. S. Bank, Pinckney St.,
   Cannonborough, Neck
Robinson, T. H., Vendue Master, 29 Pinckney St. & 160
   E. Bay St.

Robinson, William & S. T., Attorneys, 8 Waring's Row
Robinson, William, 86 Tradd St.
Robinson, William, Grocery, 132 Church St.
Robinson, William, Grocery, 93 E. Bay St.
Roche, E. L., Tailor, 30 Broad St.
Roddy, Martin, Grocery, 15 & 17 Queen St.
Rodgers, Charles, 9 Coming St., F.P.C.
Rodgers, John B., 122 Wentworth St.
Rodgers, John, Carpenter, 38 State St., F.P.C.
Rodgers, John R., 31 King St.
Rodgers, Louis, Wheelwright, Savage St.
Rodgers, Thomas, Carpenter, 122 Wentworth St.
Roger, Thomas, Merchant, 95 Meeting St.
Rogge, Conrad, Grocery, cr. Church & Cumberland Sts.
Rolando, F. G., Cooperage, 6 Champney St., res. 71 Tradd
   St.
Rolang, Catharine, 95 King St.
Rooney, Paul, Grocery, 14 Elliott St.
Roorbach, O. A., Bookstore, 296 King St.
Roper, B. D., Planter, 30 Church St.
Roper, Benjamin, Carpenter, 18 Wall St., F.P.C.
Roper, Elias, Tailor, F.P.C.
Roper, Thomas, 163 E. Bay St.
Rose, A. M., Miss, 21 George St.
Rose, Arthur, Planter, Charlotte St., Neck
Rose, F., Fruit Store, 13 Anson St.
Rose, Henry, Merchant, Kunhardt's Whf.
Rose, Hugh, Planter, 298 E. Bay St.
Rose, James, Planter, n.e. cr. E. Bay & Laurens Sts.
Rose, John, w. end Beaufain St.
Rose, William, w. end Beaufain St.
Ross, James, Merchant, State St., near Queen St.
Ross, Samuel, Store Keeper, 27 Market St.
Rote, Polly, Mrs., 41 Pinckney St.
Roumillat, E., Saddler, s. cr. Meeting & Wolf Sts., Neck
Roumillat, G. W., Confectioner, 71 Meeting St.
Roumillat, U., Confectioner, 48 Broad St.
Roupell, Mary, Miss, 102 Tradd St.
Roupell, Sarah, Widow, 43 Meeting St.
Rouse, Christopher, Tanner, e. side Ann St., Neck
Rouse, James W., 72 Market St.
Rout, G. W., Accountant, 14 Friend St.
Roux, Henry, Collector, 162 Meeting St.
Roux, Lewis, Notary Public & Quorum Unis, off. 101 E.
   Bay St., 162 Meeting St.
Rowarth, George F., Supintendent, City Burial Ground, cr.
   Doughty & Thomas Sts., Cannonborough, Neck
Ruddock, Susannah, Widow, 39 King St.
Ruff, William, Surgical Instrument Maker, 179 King St.
Rumph, G. H., s. cr. Meeting & Wolf Sts., Neck
Russell, James, n. side Boundary St., Neck
Rutledge, E., Mrs., Lucas St., Cannonborough, Neck
Rutledge, Edward, Mrs., Widow, cr. Lamboll & Legare
   Sts.
Rutledge, Frederick, Mrs., Widow, 117 Tradd St.
Rutledge, H. A., Attorney, 119 Church St.
Rutledge, John, Planter, n. cr. E. Bay & Laurens Sts.
Ryan, J., Boarding House, Elliott St.
Ryan, Laurence, Attorney, 72 Church St.
Salomon, Sarah, Clothing, 193 & 191 E. Bay St.

Saltar, T. R., Ship Carpenter, 59 State St.
Saltus, F. W., 3 Back St.
Salvo, Corado, Fruit Store, 98 King St.
Sampson, Abigail, Clothing Store, 205 E. Bay St.
Sampson, Jane, Clothing Store, 186 E. Bay St.
Sampson, Sarah, Dry Goods Store, 217 King St.
Sanders, John, Wolf St., Neck
Sanders, Swinder, Planter, 25 Coming St.
Sanders, William, Farmer, Nassau St., Neck
Santure, Philip, Confectioner, 269 King St.
Sasportes, Catherine, Alexandria St., Neck, F.P.C.
Sass, E. G., Clerk of Weights & Measures, 79 Queen St.
Sass, Jacob, 79 Queen St.
Sass, Ludwig W. & Co., Grocers, cr. King & Queen Sts.
Savage, Ann, Dry Goods Store, 180 King St.
Savage, Henrietta, 31 Beaufain St., F.P.C.
Savage, Sarah, Widow, 14 Orange St.
Sawyer, William, Dry Goods Store, 362 King St., cr. Boundary St.
Saxton, D. P., 30 George St.
Saylor, Samuel S., Factor, Kunhardt's Whf., res. 37 Meeting St.
Schaffer, C. G., cr. Ellery St. & Maiden Ln.
Schaffer, Frederick, Carpenter, w. end Pitt St.
Schaffner, Frederick, Grocery, cr. Montague & Pitt Sts.
Scharenberg, Christian, Grocery, cr. Montague & Pitt Sts.
Schirer, John, Carpenter, 12 Archdale St.
Schirer, Mary C., Widow, 1 State House Sq.
Schirmer, Jacob F., Cooperage, Kiddell's Whf.
Schmidt, John W., M. D., 53 Church St.
Schnider, C., Clerk, e. end Boundary St.
Schnierle, John, Carpenter, 11 Friend St.
Schnierle, John M., Carpenter, 11 Friend St.
Schram, Eliza, Boarding House, 18 Elliott St.
Schrier, John, Accountant, s. cr. King & Cannon Sts., Neck
Schriner, John H., Merchant, Kunhardt's Whf., res. 43 Society St.
Schriven, Thomas, Planter, e. end Hampstead, Neck
Schroder, M., Millinery, 257 King St.
Schroder, William, Grocery, cr. Queen & Friend Sts.
Schulte, Henry, Grocery, cr. Mazyck & Magazine Sts.
Schulte, J. H., Grocery, 64 Market St.
Schulte, John, Clerk, 16 Archdale St.
Schulz, John, Capt., 20 Laurens St.
Schwartz, Mary, Widow, e. side Coming St., near Boundary St., Neck
Scott, Margaret, Widow, 7 Mey's Whf.
Scott, Morgan, Grocery, 26 Church St.
Scott, Rebecca, w. side Meeting St., near Municipal Guard House, Neck
Scott, Thomas, Gauger, 21 Magazine St.
Seabrook, Thomas B., Planter, 18 Rutledge St.
Sebeck, Conrad D., Grocery, 16 Archdale St.
Sebring, Edward, Draper & Tailor, 32 Broad St.
Seilaff, Charles W., Grocer, 36 Archdale St.
Seixas, Abraham, Accountant, 99 E. Bay St.
Selin, Peter, Fruit Store, 33 Market St.
Selin, Peter, Grocery, n. cr. Meeting & Reid Sts., Neck
Senet, Joseph, Blacksmith, 11 Market St.

Seyle, Samuel, 220 King St.
Seymour, R. W., Attorney, 57 Meeting St.
Seymour, William W., 135 Queen St., F.P.C.
Shackleford, Eliza, 48 Society St.
Shacte, John, Clerk, 350 King St.
Shaffer, F., Carpenter, n. end Coming St., Neck
Shand, Peter J., Attorney, res. 38 Bull St.
Shanks, Charles, Boot Maker, 43 Broad St.
Shanly, Daniel, Grocery, 70 King St.
Shannon, John, Dry Goods Store, 102 Church St.
Shaw, Margaret, 111 Boundary St., F.P.C.
Shaw, Sarah, Seamstress, 29 Beaufain St., F.P.C.
Shea, Brown, Shoe Maker, 38 State St.
Shea, Richard, Henrietta St., Neck
Shecut, J. L. E. W., M. D., 110 Wentworth St.
Shecut, W. H., Fancy Store, 173 King St.
Shegog, William, Grocery, 62 Market St.
Sheively, Charles, Painter, 230 Meeting St.
Shelton, L. N., Wholesale Grocery, 120 E. Bay St.
Shephard, James, Harness Maker, 246 King St., res. 21 Coming St.
Shephard, John, Harness Maker, 246 King St., res. 21 Coming St.
Sheppard & Johnston, Grocers, n.w. cr. King & Tradd Sts.
Sheridan, J. J., Upholsterer & Cabinet Maker, 155 Meeting St.
Shime, Alexander, Millwright, Gadsden's Whf.
Shoolbred, James, Planter, 46 Coming St.
Shoolbred, John, Planter, Radcliffborough, near St. Paul's Church, Neck
Shrewsbery, Edward, Shipwright, Charlotte St., Mazyckborough, Neck
Sibley, George B. R., Ironmonger, cr. Pinckney St. & Maiden Ln.
Siddons, Joseph, Store Keeper, 139 King St.
Siegling, John, Music Warehouse, 109 Meeting St.
Signess, John, 16 Washington St.
Sigwald, John, Carpenter, 100 Boundary St.
Sigwald, Mary, Widow, Burns Ln.
Sillman, John H., Capt., 29 Laurens St.
Simmons, Joseph, Grocery, 1 Broad St.
Simmons, Stephen, Capt., 1 Anson St.
Simms & Duryea, Editors, City Gazette, off. 8 Broad St.
Simms, W. G., Magistrate & Editor, City Gazette, e. side King St. btw. Ann & Mary Sts., Neck
Simonds, J. W., Druggist, 357 King St.
Simons, Amelia, Alexandria St., Neck, F.P.C.
Simons, Anthony, Farmer, Hampstead, Neck
Simons, Benjamin B., M. D., 303 E. Bay St.
Simons, Benjamin P., Painter, 83 Broad St., res. 14 Smith St.
Simons, Charles, Engraver, Columbus St., Neck
Simons, Edward, Planter, 5 Orange St.
Simons, G., 18 Magazine St., F.P.C.
Simons, G., Factor, w. end Bull St.
Simons, K. L., Mrs., Widow, 7 Orange St.
Simons, Keating & Sons, Factors, 4 Roper's Whf.
Simons, Maurice, Jr., Register of Mesne Conveyance, 5 Fireproof Building, res. 1 Middle St.

Simons, Maurice, Planter, cr. Anson & Society Sts.
Simons, S. L., 40 Bull St.
Simons, Thomas Y., M. D., 48 Meeting St.
Simson, Lydia M., Ellery St., F.P.C.
Sineath, W. J., Hampstead, Neck
Sinkler, William, Planter, Pinckney St., Cannonborough, Neck
Sires & Nelme, Grocers, 9 Vendue Range
Sitern, John, Engineer, 11 Boundary St.
Sitly & Muntzing, Sawmills, w. end Queen St.
Sitly, Henry, 21 Friend St.
Sitly, John, Bricklayer, 88 Market St.
Skirving, B., Mrs., cr. Bull & Coming Sts.
Slawson, Dorothia, Widow, 135 King St.
Slowson, Eliza, 32 Coming St.
Sluter, Jacob, Dry Goods Store, 238 King St.
Small, Robert, Clerk, 3 Beaufain St.
Smallwood, Martha, Widow, 22 Market St.
Smerdon, Pricilla, Mrs., 19 Society St.
Smiley, Andrew, 257 E. Bay St.
Smith, A. C. & W. H., Factors, 12 E. Bay St.
Smith, A. C., Factor, 26 Horlbeck's Al.
Smith, Benjamin, Mrs., Widow, 9 Legare St.
Smith, Benjamin, Paint Store, back of Exchange, res. Battery, E. Bay St.
Smith, Benjamin R., Merchant, Vanderhorst's Whf., res. 6 Hasell St.
Smith, Charles B., Boundary St.
Smith, Charles, Planter, 104 Queen St.
Smith, Daniel, Grocery, cr. Rutledge & Bull Sts.
Smith, Elizabeth, Miss, Amherst St., Hampstead, Neck
Smith, Grace, 119 Wentworth St., F.P.C.
Smith, Harris & Co., Wholesale Hardware, 313 King St.
Smith, J. A., Mrs., Widow, 15 Broad St.
Smith, J. M., Tavern, 43 E. Bay St.
Smith, J., Teller, State Bank, 118 Wentworth St.
Smith, James, Accountant, 16 Beaufain St.
Smith, Jane, 11 Cliffford's Al., F.P.C.
Smith, John, Clerk, St. Philip's Church, 12 Magazine St.
Smith, John R., Attorney, 16 St. Michael's Al.
Smith, Joseph H., Attorney, e. end Mary St., Neck
Smith, Ladson, Planter, 104 Queen St.
Smith, Loughton, Mrs., Widow, 185 E. Bay St.
Smith, Mary Ann, 7 West St.
Smith, Mary Ann F., 14 Berresford St.
Smith, Oliver, 155 Church St., F.P.C.
Smith, Q. H., w. side Washington St., Neck
Smith, Richard, Cabinet Maker, 55 Broad St.
Smith, Robert, Planter, 209 Meeting St.
Smith, Roger, Mrs., 14 Coming St.
Smith, Samuel, Mrs., Widow, 73 Broad St.
Smith, Samuel, Shoe Maker, 104 Market St.
Smith, Simon, Ann St., Neck, F.P.C.
Smith, T. L., Collector of Fines, 90 E. Bay St., res. 105 King St.
Smith, Thomas, Factor, Chisolm's N. Whf.
Smith, Thomas, Jr., Planter, Green St.
Smith, Thomas R., Planter, 15 New St.
Smith, Thomas, Tailor, 93 Wentworth St., F.P.C.
Smith, W. J., 12 Magazine St.

Smith, W. L., Planter, 185 E. Bay St.
Smith, Whiteford, cr. Archdale & Beaufain Sts.
Smith, William, 43 Beaufain St.
Smith, William, Factor, res. 90 Broad St.
Smith, William, Jr., Shipwright, cr. Smith's Whf. & Washington St., Neck
Smith, William Mason, Planter, 22 Meeting St.
Smith, William S., Clerk, Court of Common Pleas, res. 35 Laurens St.
Snitter, Charles, Barber, 91 Market St., F.P.C.
Snow, Richard, Henrietta St., Neck, F.P.C.
Snowden, Joshua L., Ship Chandler, 186 E. Bay St., res. 28 Society St.
Snowden, William E., Merchant, 184 E. Bay St., res. 291 E. Bay St.
Sollee, F. W., Teller, Union Bank, res. 97 Church St.
Sollee, Harriett, Widow, 97 Church St.
Solomon, Alexander, Store Keeper, 280 King St.
Solomon, Solomon, Dry Goods Store, 73 Market St.
Southworth, Edward, Academy, 61 Queen St.
Sparks, Rachel, Widow, 87 Queen St.
Sparnock, Henry, Inspector of Customs, 21 Wall St.
Spears, Archibald, 4 Orange St.
Speisseger, John, Repairer of Musical Instruments, 11 Hasell St.
Spencer, Maria, Widow, 116 Meeting St.
Spidle, John G., Carpenter, 14 Archdale St.
Sprecks, C., Grocery, 10 Market St.
Springer, S. C., Moss Dealer, S. Bay St.
Squires, Lanson, Blacksmith, Vernon St.
St. Amand, J. A., Coachmaker, 205 Meeting St., res. Society St.
Starr, E. P., Accountant, 203 Meeting St.
Stars, Charles, Grocery, e. end Laurens St.
Steedman, Charles J., Sheriff, Charleston District, Washington St., Neck
Steedman, Thomas, Alexander St., Wraggborough, Neck
Steel, William G., Lumber Yard, w. end Beaufain St.
Steele, William, Dry Goods Store, 354 King St.
Steike, John, Shoemaker, 89 Wentworth St.
Stent, John, Carpenter, 37 King St.
Stephens, Thomas, Printer, 131 E. Bay St.
Stephens, Thomas, Sr., Teller, Union Bank, 131 E. Bay St.
Stevens, D., Planter, 28 George St.
Stevens, Joel, Hardware, cr. E. Bay & Gillon Sts.
Stevens, Joseph M., Maj., 53 Church St.
Stewart, Angus, Carolina Coffee House, 20 Tradd St.
Stewart, James, Boot Maker, 48 Anson St.
Stewart, Jane, 1 Greenhill St.
Stewart, Robert, Bookkeeper, U. S. Bank, res. 13 Friend St.
Stewart, Robert, Carpenter, 14 Burns Ln.
Stiles, Copeland, Thomas St., Neck
Stillman, J., Grocery, 67 Market St.
Stock, John Y., Elliott St., w. side, Cannonborough, Neck
Stocker, James M., Merchant, 130 E. Bay St.
Stocker, Rebecca, Widow, 14 Laurens St.
Stocker, W. I., Boat Builder, 216 E. Bay St., res. 50 Anson St.
Stockfleet, John, Grocery, cr. Elizabeth & Henrietta Sts.,

Neck
Stoddard & Davis, Wholesale Shoe Store, 272 King St.
Stoll, Frederick, Grocery, Thomas St., Cannonborough, Neck
Stoll, J., Society St.
Stoll, Martha, 93 Wentworth St.
Stoll, Smart, Tailor, 30 Tradd St., F.P.C.
Stoll, William, Clerk, 29 Society St.
Stone, J., Confectioner, 228 King St.
Stone, Robert, Cannon St., Neck
Street, H. E., Planters Hotel, 141 Church St.
Street, Joseph, State Constable, 81 Wentworth St.
Street, T. & T., Merchants, 126 E. Bay St.
Strobel, Jacob, Keeper, Marine Hospital, 5 Back St.
Strobel, John, 17 Mazyck St.
Strobel, Martin, Attorney, 162 Meeting St.
Strobel, Thomas, Mary St., Neck, F.P.C.
Strohecker, C. C., Attorney, res. 22 Horlbeck's Al., off. 55 Meeting St.
Strohecker, George, Carpenter, res. 22 Horlbeck's Al.
Strohecker, Henry, Accountant, res. 22 Horlbeck's Al.
Strohecker, John, Hardware, 163 Meeting St., 22 Horlbeck's Al.
Strohmer, John, Inspector of Customs, 1 Berresford St.
Stroub, Henry, Carpenter, Burns Ln.
Stuat, Jane, Mantuamaker, 9 Wentworth St.
Sturgis, Josiah, 6 S. Bay St.
Sturken, Henry, Grocery, s.e. cr. Pinckney & Cannon Sts., Neck
Suares, A., Clerk, Henrietta St., Neck
Suares, David, Capt., Henrietta St., Neck
Suares, Judith, Widow, Henrietta St., Neck
Suau, Peter, Rice Store, 172 E. Bay St.
Sullivan, Daniel, 17 Chalmers St.
Sullivan, Mary, Widow, 72 Anson St.
Summerman, H., Store Keeper, s.w. cr. Elizabeth & Chapel Sts., Neck
Summers, Penelope, Boarding House, 9 Elliott St.
Summers, Rosa, Nurse, Smith's Ln., F.P.C.
Suraw, Joseph, Shoemaker, e. side King St., near Ann St., Neck
Surtis, Thomas, Pilot, 15 Water St.
Sutton, Mary, Widow, n. end Smith St.
Sweegan, Matthew, Grocery, 13 Market St.
Sweeny, Diana Pastry Cook, 4 Queen St., F.P.C.
Swift, William, Dry Goods Store, 336 King St.
Swinton, A. J., Mrs., Alexander St., Wraggborough, Neck
Swinton, Eliza, Miss, 17 Archdale St.
Swinton, Jane, Mrs., 5 Wall St.
Symmes, Charlotte, Mrs., Boarding House, 123 Church St.
Symmes, Thomas, Dry Goods Store, 253 King St.
Syphan, Sarah, Bridge St., Neck
Tally, Jane, Henrietta St., Neck, F.P.C.
Tally, Nicholas, Rev., cr. Pitt & Boundary St.
Talvande, A., Academy, 24 Legare St.
Tamplet, J. P., Mrs., 10 Back St.
Tanswell, W. N., Bell Hanger, 54 Queen St.
Taveau, Augustus, Planter, w. end Wentworth St.
Tavel, Julius, Accountant, 40 State St.
Taylor & Co., Tailors, 56 Broad St.

Taylor, F. H., Tailor, 51 Broad St.
Taylor, Josiah, Factor, 6 Lamboll St.
Taylor, M. S., Miss, Seamstress, 18 Middle St.
Taylor, Margaret, Seamstress, 16 Chalmers St., F.P.C.
Taylor, Martha, Seamstress, 3 West St., F.P.C.
Taylor, Mary, 20 Berresford St., F.P.C.
Taylor, Mary, Widow, 182 Meeting St.
Teasdale, Richard, Factor, Chisolm's N. Whf., res. Orange St.
Teel, Joseph, Book Store, 195 King St.
Telfer, Robert, Gauger, 123 King St.
Tennant, Charles, Planter, 62 Anson St.
Tennant, Thomas, Inspector of Customs, 29 Guignard St.
Tew, Eleanor, Widow, 80 Wentworth St.
Tew, Henry, Accountant, Radcliff St., Neck
Tew, William M., Carpenter, 80 Wentworth St.
Thacum, Thomas W., Carpenter, 3 Pitt St.
Thayer, E., Mrs., Widow, 91 Tradd St.
Thayer, Ebenezer, Theological Book Store & Circulating Library, 79 Broad St.
Thayer, S. B., St. Philip St., near Radcliff St., Neck
Thayer, Thomas W., Accountant, 27 Queen St.
Theus, Benjamin, Printer, 7 Broad St.
Theus, James, 7 Broad St.
Thomas, Emanuel, 98 Meeting St.
Thomas, Holwell, 77 Tradd St.
Thomas, John N., Cabinet Maker, 2 Minority St.
Thomas, Stephen, e. side Coming St. btw. Vanderhorst & Boundary Sts., Neck
Thomason, S. T., 12 West St.
Thompson, Ann, Seamstress, 42 Wentworth St.
Thompson, Anna, s. end Savage St., F.P.C.
Thompson, George, Blacksmith, cr. Meeting & Cumberland St.
Thompson, George, Bricklayer, 35 Hasell St.
Thompson, Hannah, Widow, 3 Court House Sq.
Thompson, John, Blacksmith, 52 Market St.
Thompson, John, Grocery, cr. Bull & Coming St.
Thompson, Joseph, Blacksmith & Grocery, 1 King St.
Thompson, Mary C., Widow, 25 Hasell St.
Thompson, -----, Mrs. Accoucher, 33 Meeting St.
Thompson, Robert C., Accountant, 3 Court House Sq.
Thompson, Sarah, 38 Coming St.
Thompson, William, Boarding House, 48 Queen St.
Thompson, William, Boarding House, 13 Elliott St.
Thomson & Co., Saddlers, 45 Broad St.
Thorne, W. T., 8 Beaufain St.
Thornehill, Catharine, Dry Goods Store, 225 King St.
Thurston, R., Factor, 1 Vanderhorst's Whf.
Thwing, Edward, Merchant, 19 State St.
Tidyman, Hester, Mrs., Widow, 3 Rutledge St.
Tidyman, Philip, Dr., 122 Broad St.
Tileston, William M. & Co., Wholesale Boot & Shoe Store, 306 King St.
Timmons & Graveley, Hardware, 165 E. Bay St.
Timmons, George, Porter, Ale & Beer Store, 74 E. Bay St., res. 3 Legare St.
Tinkham, S., Mrs., cr. King & Radcliff Sts., Neck
Tobias, Abraham, Vendue Master, Vendue Range, res. 101 Market St.

27

Tolck, J. D., Groceries, 3 Elliott St. & 59 Church St.
Toole, Patrick, Tailor, Chalmers St.
Toomer & Buist, Attorneys, 10 St. Michael's Al.
Toomer, A. V., M. D., Chapel St., Neck
Toomer, Henry B., Broker & City Assessor, off. 10 State St., res. Green St.
Toomer, Joshua W., Attorney, cr. Pitt & Bull Sts.
Toomer, M., Mrs., Mary St., Neck
Toppan, Edward, Dry Goods Store, 267 King St.
Torre, Ann, Widow, 21 New St.
Torrington, George, Grocery, E. Bay St. & Lynchs Ln.
Touchstone, F., Planter, St. Philip St., above Boundary St., Neck
Tovey, H. C., 285 E. Bay St.
Tovey, Henry & Son, Pump & Block Makers, 176 E. Bay St.
Tovey, Henry, 285 E. Bay St.
Trapier, Paul, 8 Short St.
Trapmann, Lewis, Merchant, res. 96 Wentworth St., Counting House, 79 E. Bay St.
Trescot, Caroline, Widow, 46 Beaufain St.
Trescot, Henry, Magistrate & Attorney, 97 Meeting St.
Trescot, William, Mrs., Widow, Coming St., above Boundary St., Neck
Trezevant, Diana, Nurse, 97 King St., F.P.C.
Trittau, G. H., Grocery, 175 Church St.
Trouche, Augustus P., Accountant, 186 King St.
Trout, Thomas, Accountant, 159 E. Bay St., res. 85 Tradd St.
Truchelut, F., Clerk, 86 Queen St.
Truesdel, David, Oyster House, 32 Queen St.
Tucker, John H., Planter, n.e. end Hampstead, Neck
Tucker, Joshua, Surgeon Dentist, 85 Meeting St.
Tunno, Adam, Merchant, 77 E. Bay St.
Tunno, Sarah, Widow, 5 Meeting St.
Tupper, T., Merchant, 183 E. Bay St., res. 50 Tradd St.
Turnbull, James, 20 Water St.
Turnbull, Joseph, Wentworth St., near Anson St.
Turnbull, Robert J., Planter, 1 Logan St.
Turner, Elizabeth, 26 Mazyck St., F.P.C.
Turner, George R., Sr., Doughty St., Cannonborough, Neck
Turner, Philada, 9 Coming St., F.P.C.
Turner, Sarah, 40 Pinckney St., F.P.C.
Turpin, Jane, n.e. end Boundary St., Neck, F.P.C.
Tyler, Joseph & Sons, Merchants, 138 E. Bay St., res. 76 Queen St.
Ulmo, A., M. D., Drug Store, 94 Meeting St.
Ulmo, E. E., Lt., Guard, n.e. cr. Hasell & Meeting Sts.
Ummensetter, John, Tanner, 55 Beaufain St.
Utley, Horace, Notary Public, 89 E. Bay St.
Uttermahl, L. W., 12 Burns Ln.
Valenet, S., Mantuamaker, 104 Market St.
Valentine, S., 117 King St.
Valk, Jacob R., Merchant, Kiddell's Whf.
Vanderhorst, Charlotte, 93 Market St., F.P.C.
Vanderhorst, R. W., Gen., Planter, Radcliffborough, Neck
Van Rhyn, John M., 22 Broad St.
Vanwelso, William, Wheelright, 4 St. Philip St.

Vardell, T. A., Widow, Vanderhorst St., near St. Paul's Church, Neck
Vardell, T. R., Bricklayer, Vanderhorst St., near St. Paul's Church, Neck
Vauce, Francis, Columbus St., Neck
Vauglin, Saffer, 15 Clifford's Al., F.P.C.
Vause, John T., Deputy Sheriff, 27 Mazyck St.
Veitch, William, Druggist, 223 King St.
Venning, J. M., Factor, Charlotte St., Mazyckborough, Neck
Venning, Robert, Factor, Williams' Whf., res. Society St., near Anson St.
Vernon, Nathaniel, Harleston's Green
Vesey, Susan, Alexandria St., Neck, F.P.C.
Vincent, Hugh E., Ship Chandler, 81 E. Bay St.
Vincent, W. J., Exchange Broker, 29 Broad St.
Vinro, J. W., Store Keeper, 44 Wentworth St.
Vinro, Sarah, Accoucher, 44 Wentworth St.
Vinyard, John, Planter, e. end Hampstead, Neck
Voglan, M., Cabinet Maker, 93 King St.
Vonghlan, Henry, Grocery, cr. E. Bay & Ellery Sts.
Vonholton, Tennis, Grocery, cr. Amen & Philadelphia Sts.
Wagner, Ann, Widow, 52 St. Philip St.
Wagner, Effingham, Accountant, 53 E. Bay St.
Wagner, J. J., Custom House Store Keeper, 118 Queen St.
Wagner, John, M. D., cr. Queen & Meeting Sts.
Wagner, Peter, Lafayette Coffee House, 153 E. Bay St.
Walker & M'Kenzie, Dry Goods Store, 290 King St.
Walker, C., Book Binder, 9 Broad St.
Walker, Elizabeth, Boarding House, 131 Church St.
Walker, Elizabeth, Pastry Cook, 239 King St., F.P.C.
Walker, Henry D., Carpenter, 24 Magazine St.
Walker, J. C., Reading Room, 7 State St.
Walker, John F., Factor, 7 Kiddell's Whf., res. 23 State St.
Walker, John, Planter, 14 George St.
Walker, Mary, e. side King St., 2 doors s. of Lines, Neck
Walker, Robert, Cabinet Maker, 125 Church St.
Walker, Thomas, Stone Cutter, 145 Meeting St.
Wall, Gilbert, Tailor, 89 Broad St., F.P.C.
Wallace, Agnes, Widow, 18 Friend St.
Wallace, Ann, 93 Church St.
Wallace, James, 15 St. Philip St.
Wallace, Thomas, Clerk, 18 Friend St.
Waller, William, Saddler, 89 Broad St.
Walpole, Horace, Planter, 82 Church St.
Walter, Jerry, Vendue Master, 15 Vendue Range
Walton, A. Y. & Co., Wholesale Hardware, 314 King St.
Ward, Francis, Clerk, City Court, 4 Middle St.
Ward, Harrit, 92 Tradd St.
Ward, John, Deputy Secretary of State, 4 Middle St.
Ward, Rose, Mrs., 69 Boundary St.
Ward, Sarah, Widow, 40 Meeting St.
Waring, D. J., Attorney, 2 George St.
Waring, Francis, Factor, 29 Hasell St.
Waring, Horatio S., M. D., 87 Wentworth St.
Waring, Jane, Widow, 101 Wentworth St.
Waring, Morton A., U. S. District Marshal, w. side St. Philip St., near Cannon St., Neck
Waring, Morton, Coastwise Inspector, Maiden Ln.
Waring, Thomas, Factor, 29 Hasell St.

Waring, Thomas, Mrs., 25 Friend St.
Waring, Thomas S., Accountant, w. side St. Philip St., near Cannon St., Neck
Warley, Charles, Factor, 12 Champney St., res. 60 Tradd St.
Warley, Charles, Wine Store, 35 Broad St.
Warley, Elizabeth, Miss, 30 Beaufain St.
Warner, Penelope, Widow, 44 Tradd St.
Warren, Elizabeth, Widow, 5 Lamboll St.
Washburn, A., Jr., Fancy Dry Goods Store, 299 King St.
Washington, William, Mrs., Widow, cr. Church & Fort Sts.
Waters, William, Clerk, 233 King St.
Watson, Ann, Seamstress, 14 Chalmers St., F.P.C.
Watson, Henry, Grocery, 186 Meeting St.
Watson, Stephen, Earthen & Chinaware, 66 E. Bay St.
Watton, Jane, Mary St., near King St., Neck
Waugh, Alexander B., Commission Merchant, 68 E. Bay St.
Webb, Daniel C., Factor, n. cr. Pinckney & Cannon St., Cannonborough, Neck
Webber, John W., 36 Coming St.
Webber, Samuel, 1 Pritchard's Whf.
Weed & Benedict, Hat Warehouse, 315 King St.
Weed, Joseph, Hatter, 29 Coming St.
Weinges, Rebecca, Store Keeper, cr. King & Cannon Sts., Neck
Weissinger, M., Mrs., w. side King St., near Cannon St., Neck
Welch, Isabella, Grocery, 32 Archdale St.
Welch, John, w. end Boundary St., Neck
Welch, Mary, 1 St. Philip St.
Well, Joseph T., Merchant, 162 E. Bay St., res. 180 E. Bay St.
Welling, William, Harness Maker, 119 Meeting St.
Wells, Hager, Mrs., Alexander St., Neck
Wells, Sarah, Seamstress, 45 State St.
Welsman, J., 88 Church St.
Wesner, Frederick., Capt., City Guard, cr. Queen & Mazyck Sts.
West, Charles H., Ship Chandlery, 79 E. Bay St.
West, Charles L., Oil & Tea Store, 124 E. Bay St.
West, Thomas, Planter, 121 Meeting St.
Westfeldt, C., Merchant, Chisolm's N. Whf.
Weston, E. R. & Co., Ironmongers, 22 Vendue Range
Weston, Francis, Planter, cr. Meeting & Wentworth Sts.
Weston, Paul, Dr., Planter, e. side Hampstead, Neck
Weston, Samuel, Tailor, 104 Queen St.
Wettegen, Conrad, Hampstead, Neck
Weyman, Edward, Mrs., Widow, 283 E. Bay St.
Weyman, Francis, Grocery, cr. Church St. & Lightwood Al.
Whales, E., w. end Cannon St., Cannonborough, Neck
Wheeler, Asa, Tavern, 272 King St.
Wheeler, Caroline, 19 Clifford St.
Wheeler, Stephen C., Merchant, 267 King St.
Whilden, Elias, Planter, Radcliffborough, Neck
Whilden, Joseph, 22 Magazine St.
White, Alston L., Teacher, S. C. School, Meeting St.
White, Charles L., 37 George St.
White, Eliza, Alexandria St., Neck, F.P.C.

White, George K., 21 Anson St.
White, George M., Clerk, 62 Anson St.
White, John, Alexander St., Neck
White, John, Factor, 216 Meeting St.
White, John, Stone Cutter, 42 Market St.
White, Mary, 26 Coming St., F.P.C.
White, W. H., Grocery, 44 Market St.
Whiteheart, Peggy, 2 Guignard St., F.P.C.
Whiting, D. H. W., Turner, 189 Meeting St.
Whiting, George J., Hat Warehouse, 229 King St.
Whitney, Archibald, Collector, 9 Society St.
Whitney, Mary, Store Keeper, 28 Queen St.
Whitridge, J. B., M. D., 2 Montague St.
Whitsel, F., Teacher, Lucas St., Cannonborough, Neck
Whittermore, C., Soap & Candle Manufacturer, w. side St. Philip St., btw. Warren & Radcliff Sts., Neck
Wienges, C., Grocery, cr. Pitt & Montague Sts.
Wienges, Jacob, Grocery, 31 Archdale St.
Wienges, John H., 88 King St.
Wigfall, Samuel, Washington St., e. end Boundary St., Neck
Wigfall, T., Sr., Planter, Washington St., e. end Boundary St., Neck
Wigfall, William M., Planter, Washington St., e. end Boundary St., Neck
Wightman, John, Jr., Painter, 199 Meeting St.
Wightman, Margaret, 85 Market St., F.P.C.
Wightman, William, 82 Meeting St.
Wilbur, William W., Comb Manufacturer, 166 King St.
Wilcox, Mary, n. side Boundary St., btw. King & Meeting Sts., Neck
Wilcox, Samuel, Boarding Officer, 19 Bull St.
Wilcox, William, Plasterer, 38 Coming St.
Wildman, N. H., Hat Warehouse, 279 King St.
Wiley, Samuel, Grocery, 15 Elliott St.
Wiley, Thomas, Grocery, 55 Elliott St.
Wiley, William, Grocery, Gadsden's Whf.
Wilkes, John, Merchant, 9 Crafts' S. Whf.
Wilkie, W. B. & G. W., Ship Chandlers, 61 E. Bay St.
Wilkie, William B., Cashier, Union Bank, 8 Liberty St.
Wilkins, M. L., Planter, Pinckney St., Cannonborough, Neck
Wilkinson, Willis, Dr., Planter, cr. Montague & Lynch Sts.
Williams, E., Chapel St., Mazyckborough, Neck
Williams, George P., Watch Maker, 169 Market St.
Williams, Isham, Planter, Williams' Whf.
Williams, John, Carpenter, Henrietta St., Neck, F.P.C.
Williams, Mary, 6 Clifford's Al., F.P.C.
Williams, S., Pilot, 113 Church St.
Williamson, E., Mrs., Millinery, 123 King St.
Williman, E., Mrs., w. end Boundary St., Neck
Willington, A. S., Editor, Courier, 281 E. Bay St.
Willis, Henry, Carpenter, Mary St., Neck
Willis, Mary, Boarding House, 227 King St.
Wilson & Ward, Cabinet Makers, 70 Wentworth St., F.P.C.
Wilson, A. J., cr. Pinckney & Bridge Sts., Neck
Wilson, Hugh, Sr., cr. Pinckney & Bridge Sts., Neck
Wilson, J., Mrs., Radcliffborough, Neck
Wilson, James, Seed Store, 236 King St.

Wilson, John L., Attorney, 12 State St.
Wilson, Robert, Capt., 5 Hasell St.
Wilson, Samuel, 67 Meeting St.
Wilson, Samuel, M. D., 19 New St.
Wilson, Susan, 21 Wentworth St.
Wilson, William H., City Sheriff, 100 Meeting St.
Wing, Sarah C., Widow, 87 Boundary St.
Winslow, Edward, Merchant, 12 Crafts' Whf.
Winthrop, Augustus, 115 Tradd St.
Winthrop, Charles, 115 Tradd St.
Winthrop, F. & C., Factors, 5 Champney St., 115 Tradd St.
Winthrop, F., 115 Tradd St.
Winthrop, Henry, M. D., 115 Tradd St.
Winthrop, J. A., Factor, 5 Fitzsimons' Whf., 115 Tradd St.
Winthrop, William, 115 Tradd St.
Wise, Edward, Boarding House, 6 Elliott St.
Wish, Ann, n. side Boundary St., Neck
Withers, Francis, Planter, s.w. cr. John & Meeting Sts., Neck
Witherton, Samuel, Accountant, 12 Middle St.
Witter, Eliza, Mantuamaker, 44 Anson St.
Wittker, William, Grocery, s. cr. Elizabeth & Henrietta Sts., Neck
Wolf, James, n.e. end Boundary St., Neck
Wolf, Rachel, Widow, 10 Stoll's Al.
Wonger, John, Paper Hanger, 8 Queen St.
Wood, A., Store Keeper, 40 King St.
Wood, Edward, State Constable, cr. Market St. & Reaper's Al.
Wood, Francis, Tavern, 10 Archdale St.
Wood, James, Engraver, Warren St., Neck
Wood, James P., Grocery, 210 King St.
Wood, Mary, Widow, Warren St., near St. Paul's Church, Neck
Woodrop, John, Merchant, 43 E. Bay St.
Woodruffe, -----, Mrs., Widow, 18 Pitt St.
Woodworth, George S., Assistant Keeper, Work House, Magazine St.
Woolet, Thomas, Boarding House, 15 Beadon's Al.

Woolf, Isaac, Dry Goods Store, 360 King St.
Woolf, R., Mrs., Clothing Store, 337 King St.
Woolf, Sarah, Dry Goods Store, 360 King St.
Wotherspoon, Robert, Merchant, 79 E Bay St.
Wotton, J. A., Teacher, 91 Anson St.
Wragg, E., Mrs., Widow, 185 E. Bay St.
Wragg, Middleton, & Co., Factors, Crafts' S. Whf.
Wragg, Samuel, Cashier, State Bank, Alexander St., Wraggborough, Neck
Wright & Brown, Merchants, 46 E. Bay St.
Wright, H., Mrs., Dry Goods Store, 174 King St.
Wright, J. J., Attorney, Bull St., near Pitt St.
Wright, R., Mrs., Bull St., near Pitt St.
Wright, Robert, Millwright, Bennett's Mills, Neck
Wurdeman, -----, Mrs., Dry Goods Store, 218 King St.
Wyatt, John, Ship Carpenter, 173 Church St.
Wyatt, Violetta, John St., Neck
Yates & McIntyre, Lottery Office, 25 Broad St.
Yates, Deborah, Widow, 3 Fort St.
Yates, E. A., Mrs., Widow, Washington St., Neck
Yates, Emma, Henrietta St., Neck, F.P.C.
Yates, J. D., Attorney, 104 Church St., res. 15 Church St.
Yates, Jeremiah A., 1 Ladson's Court
Yates, Thomas H., Carpenter, 47 Queen St.
Yeadon & McBeth, Attorneys, 18 St. Michael's Al.
Yeadon, Richard, 33 King St.
Yeadon, Richard, Jr., Notary Public & Attorney, 76 Wentworth St.
You, John C., Teacher, 4 Archdale St.
Young, Dinah, Widow, 77 Broad St.
Young, Edward, Tailor, Charlotte St., Mazyckborough, Neck, F.P.C.
Young, Joseph, Ship Chandlery, 194 E. Bay St., Res 263 E. Bay St.
Young, Mary, w. end Beaufain St., F.P.C.
Young, William, Grocery, 56 Church St.
Zealy, A. C., Mrs., Accoucher, 68 King St.
Zealy, William, Accountant, 68 King St.
Zylstra, John P., 149 E. Bay St.

The Directory for 1835-36

This is the next known directory after 1831. James Smith, a clerk, collected the information which was published and printed by Daniel J. Dowling as *The Charleston Directory; and Register, for 1835-6. Containing the Names, Occupations, and Residences of Persons in Business, &c. Collected by James Smith and The City Register; Consisting of A Variety of Useful Information, Connected with Our Trade and Commerce.* (Charleston: Daniel J. Dowling, 1835). The directory contains 3,597 records and the publisher promised to issue a directory and register annually. The directory listed first the white people in the city, next the white people in the Neck, then the free persons of color in business in the city, and lastly the free persons of color in business in the Neck. These four groups have been combined into one list here. Because many houses had no number, Dowling gave as exact a location as possible such as on King Street near Ann Street. This is especially true for the Neck as some areas there could be classified as rural.

Aarons, Moses, Grain Store, King St., btw. Warren & Morris Sts., Neck
Abbott, Samuel, Smith's Ln.
Abrahams, A. H., Merchant, 5 Pinckney St.
Abrahams, Elias, Salesman, King St., res. 45 Society St.
Abrahams, Hannah, Dry Goods Store, 217 King St.
Ackis, John, Bricklayer, 28 Pinckney St.
Adams, Ann, Widow, cr. E. Bay & Water Sts.
Adams, E., 124 Queen St.
Adams, George, Mrs., Widow, 37 Pinckney St.
Adams, Jasper, Rev., Prof., cr. Pinckney & Lucas Sts., Cannonborough, Neck
Adams, M. J., Mrs., Widow, 74 Anson St.
Addison, Francis, Mrs., Widow, 10 Pitt St.
Addison, George, Watchmaker, 235 King St.
Addison, Joseph, Ship Carpenter, 6 Wentworth St.
Addison, Thomas, w. end Montague St.
Adger, James, Merchant, cr. E. Bay St. & Boyce's Whf.
Adger, James, Merchant, King St., near Spring St., Neck
Adger, William, Merchant, King St., near Spring St., Neck
Aiken, William, Planter, Judith St., Neck
Aimar, S., Dry Goods Store, 199 E. Bay St.
Ainger, Joseph M., Cooper, cr. State St. & Lodge Al.
Akin, Thomas, M. D., 11 Cumberland St., res. 210 Meeting St.
Aldert, Sikee, Pilot, 7 Stoll's Al.
Aldrich, Robert, Wharfinger, 15 Tradd St.
Aldrich, Thomas R., M. D., 15 Tradd St.
Alexander, Abraham, Dry Goods Store, 340 King St.
Alexander, David, President, Union Insurance Co., res. 6 Logan St.
Alexander, Henry, M. D., 50 Meeting St., res. 6 Logan St.
Alexander, John J., Assistant Secretary, Union Insurance Co., res. 80 Queen St.
Alexander, Samuel, Harbor Master, res. 105 Queen St.
Allan & Johnston, Factors, Hamilton & Co. Whf.
Allan, Richard, M. D., 46 Tradd St.

Allan, Robert M., Factor, cr. Meeting St. & Price's Al.
Allan, William, Mrs., Widow, cr. Meeting St. & Price's Al.
Allen, J., Seamstress, Elizabeth St., Neck, F.P.C.
Allen, Mary, Widow, 13 Smith St.
Allen, -----, Mrs., Boarding House, 4 Champney St.
Allen, S. & M., Exchange Office, 6 Broad St.
Allen, William, Painter, 28 Smith's Lane
Allender, Willliam N., Book Binder, 7 Broad St.
Allerding, Henry, Grocer, 83 Tradd St.
Allison, James J., Rev., cr. Pitt & Boundary Sts.
Alston, Charles, Planter, 1 Water St.
Alston, W. A., Attorney, 2 Court House Sq.
Alston, William, Planter, King St.
Amelung, J. P. W., Academy, 73 Meeting St.
Ancrum, Jane, Widow, 15 Rutledge St.
Anderson, John, 3 Stoll's Al.
Anderson, Joseph, Engineer, Wolf St., Neck
Anderson, N. E., Millinery, 361 King St.
Anderson, Robert, Millinery, King St., near Ann St., Neck
Anderson, Thomas, Confectioner, Elliott St.
Andre, Rosalie, King St., near Columbus St., Neck
Andres, F., Grocer, Elizabeth St., Mazyckborough, Neck
Andrews, Louisa, Widow, 35 Hasell St.
Andrews, W., Factor, Magwood's S. Whf., res. 15 Society St.
Angel, Justus, Planter, 124 Tradd St.
Angus, John, cr. Meeting St. & Lines, Neck
Anthony, A., Tailoress, 272 E. Bay St.
Anthony, J. C., Tallow Chandler, cr. King & Reid Sts., Neck
Antonio, Aires, Tivoli Gardens, Neck
Appel, Conrad, Coffee House, op. Railroad, Neck
Arms, Elizabeth, Seminary, 16 George St.
Armstrong, Archibald, Mrs., 10 Minority St.
Armstrong, William G., Clerk, 19 Wentworth St.
Arnan, Michael, Blacksmith, 21 Middle St.
Arnold, J. W. B., Merchant Tailor, 137 King St.
Arnold, Louisa, cr. Archdale & Berresford Sts.
Artman, Peter, Coachmaker, 5 Archdale St.
Artope, George Engineer, Wolf St., Neck
Ashby, James A., Attorney, 72 Broad St.
Atwell, George E., Jeweller & Fancy Store, 250 King St.
Aubin, J. J., Porter & Liquor Store, 172 E. Bay St., res. 35 Montague St.
Aufterheide, C. F., Grocer, 60 Market St.
Augustin, Mary, Seamstress, 28 Mazyck St., F.P.C.
Auld, D. G., M. D., 23 Society St.
Aveilhe, Louisa, 160 King St.
Aveilhe, P. A., Capt., 183 E. Bay St.
Axson, Edward, Mrs., 43 King St.
Axson, Jacob, City Attorney, 104 Church St., res. 19 Meeting St.
Axson, John, Planter, Charlotte St., Mazyckborough, Neck
Axson, S., Mrs., Boarding House, 10 Cumberland St.
Babcock, S. & Co., Booksellers, 290 King St.
Babson, A. R., Widow, 2 Berresford St.
Bachman, John, Rev., w. side Pinckney St., Cannonborough, Neck
Bacon, Edward, 63 E. Bay St.

Bacot & Gibbes, Merchants, 13 Champney St.
Bacot, D. D., Factor, S. Bay St.
Bacot, P., Cashier, Branch U. S. Bank, 11 Archdale St.
Bacot, T. W., Assistant Postmaster, n.e. cr. King &
Tradd Sts.
Badger, J., Outdoor Clerk, Planters & Mechanics Bank,
res. Boundary & Washington Sts., Mazyckborough
Bagshaw, Elvira, Widow, 3 St. Philip St.
Bail, John, Boarding House, 13 Bedon's Al.
Bailey, Henry, Attorney, 83 Meeting St.
Bailey, J. S., Merchant, 45 E. Bay St.
Bailey, William, Teacher, 8 Guignard St.
Baily, Amity, Watchmaker, 243 King St.
Baily, Sarah, Widow, Philadelphia St.
Baker, Barnard E., 76 King St.
Baker, E., Brass Founder, res. 8 Wall St.
Baker, L., 201 Meeting St.
Baker, R. L., Druggist, cr. Broad & E. Bay Sts.
Baker, R. S., Rev., cr. Broad & Friend St.
Baker, Sproulls & Co., Hat Warehouse, 288 King St.
Ball, Alwyn, Mrs., Widow, Lucas St., Cannonborough,
Neck
Ball, Dyer, Teacher, 71 Queen St.
Ball, E. O., Planter, w. end Lynch St.
Ball, Eleanor, Miss, 67 Church St.
Ball, Isaac, Mrs., Widow, n.e. cr. E. Bay & Vernon Sts.
Ball, J., Mrs., Widow, 27 Hasell St.
Ballard, George, 87 Tradd St.
Ballund, Alexander, Distillery, 37 State St.
Bampfield, Joseph, Wheelwright, w. side King St., F.P.C.,
Neck
Bancroft, James & Co., Merchants, 164 E. Bay St., res.
Washington St., Mazyckborough
Banks, Harriet, Widow, res. 21 George St.
Banks, Hugh R., Merchant, 265 King St., res. 9 Hasell St.
Banks, William, Factor, res. 21 George St.
Baptiste & Jordan, Eating House, 21 Market St.
Barbot, A., Merchant, 53 E. Bay St.
Barguet, Barbara, Umbrella Maker, 113 Meeting St.,
F.P.C.
Barker, J. S., Merchant, 18 Society St.
Barker, S. G., Attorney, 98 Church St.
Barksdale, A., Widow, 11 Meeting St.
Barksdale, Thomas, Planter, 6 New St.
Barleet, William, Grocer, cr. Elizabeth & Boundary Sts.,
Neck
Barns, William B., Custom House, res. Charlotte St.,
Mazyckborough, Neck
Barnwell, W. H., Rev., 8 Logan St.
Baron, Alexander, M. D., 35 Meeting St.
Baron, Elizabeth, Miss, 101 Broad St.
Baron, Elizabeth, Widow, 26 Society St.
Barre, John, Wine Merchant, 45 Market St.
Barrelli, John, 63 Broad St.
Barrett, Jacob, 1 Pinckney St.
Barrett, Rachel, Widow, cr. King & Boundary Sts.
Bartless, Mary, Widow, 26 Middle St.
Bartlett, H. & F., Boot & Shoe Store, 209 King St.
Bartlett, William, 1 Longitude Ln.
Bartlett, William, Agent, Railroad, w. side Mary St., Neck

Barton, Jane, Widow, 8 Pitt St.
Bascome, Elizabeth, 6 Bull St.
Bass, Margaret, Seamstress, 49 Meeting St., F.P.C.
Baunay, Peter, French Goods Store, 177 King St.
Baxter, Amos, Millwright, n. side Boundary St., F.P.C.,
Neck
Bay, E. H., Hon., Judge, 1 Logan St.
Bay, John, Custom House, res. 84 Broad St.
Bazil, John, Fruit Store, 27 Tradd St., F.P.C.
Beaufort, Frederick, Butcher, Hampstead, Neck
Becaise, B. B., Gunsmith, 16 State St.
Becker, Daniel, Grocer, cr. of Wentworth & Coming St.
Becker, Hans, Grocer, s.e. cr. St. Philip & Wentworth
Sts.
Beckley, John, Planter, w. end Vanderhorst St., Neck
Beckman, F. A., Clerk, 21 St. Philip St.
Beckman, F., Grocer, cr. State St. & Unity Al.
Beckmann, A., Painter & Paper Hanger, 166 Meeting St.
Beckmann, C., 13 Smith St.
Bee, F. C., Widow, 11 Legare St.
Bee, J. M., Collector, 41 Tradd St.
Bee, J. S., Widow, 64 Wentworth St.
Bee, Joseph F., Planter, 85 Boundary St.
Bee, Robert R., Cooper, Hamilton & Co. Whf.
Bee, Thomas, 2 St. Michael's Al.
Bee, William C., Clerk, 64 Wentworth St.
Bee, William R., 11 Legare St.
Beers, J. D. & J. R. St. John, Exchange Office, 28 Broad
St.
Beers, James, Shoemaker, 245 E. Bay St.
Behrman, Charles, Grocer, cr. King & Broad Sts.
Beile, A. M., Widow, 83 Wentworth St.
Beile, J. P., Bookseller, 296 King St., res. 83 Wentworth
St.
Beile, Joseph, 32 King St.
Belcher, Elizabeth, Mrs., Boarding House, 6 State St.
Belin, A. H., Planter, 4 Short St.
Bell, David J., Clerk, 23 Society St.
Bell, David, Sr., Accountant, 23 Society St.
Bell, George, Merchant, 296 E. Bay St.
Bell, John L., Cooper, 23 Society St.
Bell, William, Bricklayer, 50 Society St.
Bellinger, J., M. D., 7 College St.
Belser, Mary, Widow, e. side King St., near Spring St.,
Neck
Bement & Milliken, Merchants, 136 E. Bay St.
Benjamin, Philip, 15 St. Philip St.
Benjamin, Solomon A., Clothing Store, 88 E. Bay St.
Bennett, Ann, Widow, 14 Smith's Ln.
Bennett, C. G., Printer, Radcliff St., near King St., Neck
Bennett, E. S., M. D., 145 Meeting St., res. w. end
Rutledge St.
Bennett, Margaret, Widow, Bedon's Al.
Bennett, Peter B., Grocer, Elliott St., near Church St.
Bennett, Peter, Radcliffborough, near Cannon St., F.P.C.,
Neck
Bennett, Richard, Carpenter, 56 King St.
Bennett, Thomas, Lumber Mills, w. end Cannonborough,
Neck
Bennett, W. J., res. w. end Cannonborough, Neck

Bennett, William J., Lumber Mills, E. Bay St., op. Wentworth St.

Benoist, A., Baker, cr. King & Reid Sts., Neck

Bensadon, Jacob, Fancy Store, 7 Tradd St.

Benson, Laurence, 171 Meeting St.

Benson, William, Clerk, 50 Anson St.

Benson, William G., Grist Mill, 27 King St.

Bentham & Holmes, Attorneys, 2 St. Michael's Al.

Bentham, Robert, Attorney, w. end Vanderhorst St., Neck

Bentley, R., Tailor, 6 Tradd St.

Berbant, Samuel, e. side King St., near Ann St., Neck

Berney, M., Mrs., Widow, 96 Church St.

Berney, William, 96 Church St.

Berrett, William H., Bookseller & Stationer, cr. Broad & State Sts.

Berry, H. A., Coachmaker, 19 Guignard St.

Berry, John, cr. State & Queen Sts.

Berry, Maria, Widow, 8 Friend St.

Bertrand, Peter, Carpenter, 98 Market St.

Bessent & Honor, Dry Goods Store, 244 King St.

Betts, James, Clerk, 7 Liberty St.

Beusse, J. H., Dry Goods Store, 227 E. Bay St.

Bianchi, G., Carver & Gilder, 138 King St.

Bigelow, Elizabeth, Widow, cr. St. Philip & Vanderhorst Sts., Neck

Bigelow, L., Tallow Chandler, cr. Radcliff & Warren Sts., Neck

Bingley, C. M., 15 Middle St.

Birch, P. N., Merchant, 272 King St., res. 79 Wentworth St.

Bird, J. S., Military & Fancy Store, 172 King St., res. 51 Wentworth St.

Bird, William, Ship Carpenter, 7 Lynch St.

Birnie, William & George, Merchants, 21 Broad St.

Bishop, S. N., Merchant, 2 Magwood's N. Whf.

Bizuel, J. P., Mariner, 26 State St.

Black, Alexander, 103 Wentworth St.

Black, Alexander W., Notary Public, 89, res. 55 E. Bay St.

Black, F. C., Merchant, Fitzsimons' Whf., res. 32 Society St.

Black, James, Carpenter, w. side Cannon St., Neck

Black, James, Merchant, 15 Magwood's S. Whf.

Black, William P., Bakery, 195 King St.

Blacklock, J. F., Merchant, Chisolm's N. Whf., res. 91 Tradd St.

Blackwood, -----, Seamstress, Henrietta St., Neck, F.P.C.

Blackwood, Caroline, Widow, 18 Montague St.

Blackwood, Thomas, President, Planters & Mechanics Bank, res. 18 Pitt St.

Blaimyer, Caroline, Miss, Elizabeth St., Mazyckborough, Neck

Blain, Andrew, Wheelwright, Meeting St., near Henrietta St., Neck

Blain, W. S., Teacher, 26 State St.

Blair, Hugh, & William, 44 Broad St.

Blake, Charles, Merchant, 4 Vendue Range

Blake, Edward, Teller, Bank of S. C., res. 5 Water St.

Blake, H. M. & E., Misses, 7 King St.

Blanchard, J. A., Mrs., Confectioner, 69 Church St.

Blaney, Josesph, 17 Berresford St.

Blum, A., Mrs., Widow, King St., op. Reid St., Neck

Blum, Frederick, Carpenter, w. side Wolf St., Neck

Blum, J. C., Commission Merchant, 30 Vendue Range

Blum, John A., Free School, Mary St., Hampstead, Neck

Blumeau, Jean, Carpenter, 101 Church St.

Boag, W. S. & Co., Apothecaries, 285 King St., res. 85 Wentworth St.

Bock, P., Grocer, cr. John & Elizabeth Sts., Neck

Bohles, L. E., Grocer, cr. Archdale St. & Swinton's Ln.

Boinest, Daniel, Merchant, 25 State St.

Bolchoz, Peter, Carpenter, 31 Beaufain St.

Bolchoz, Sophia, Mantuamaker, 31 Beaufain St.

Bolger, Ann, Dry Goods Store, 160 Meeting St.

Bolles, A., Teacher, 3 College St.

Bolles, Edwin A., Student of Divinity, 3 College St.

Bondeau, E., Baker, 46 Queen St.

Bonetheau, D., Watchmaker, w. side King St., near Amherst St., Neck

Bonetheau, E. W., Magistrate, res. Amherst St., Neck

Bonneau, A., Seamstress, 3 Anson St., F.P.C.

Bonneau, John, Factor, 13 Church St.

Bonnell, John, Capt., 14 Lynch St.

Bonner, E. M., Milliner, 116 King St.

Bonner, John, Cabinet Maker, 116 King St.

Boon, W. J, Bricklayer, 53 Meeting St.

Bordenave, John, Hair Dresser, 145 Meeting St.

Bosch, John H., cr. Wolf & Nassau Sts., Neck

Bosse, Vincent, Confectioner, w. side King St., near Radcliff St., Neck

Boucheir, John & Co., Grocers, 144 King St.

Boucheneau, Charles, Custom House, res. w. end Magazine St.

Boudo, H., Jewellery & Fancy Store, 156 King St.

Bourdon, Jane, 1 Mazyck St.

Bours, Luke, Accountant, 74 Church St.

Boutan, Peter B., Baker, King St., near John St., Neck

Bowen, Nathaniel, Right Rev., Elliott St., Cannonborough, Neck

Bowles, J. T., Printer, cr. Church & Lynch Sts.

Bowman, Ann, Widow, cr. E. Bay & Water Sts.

Bowman, Lynch, Miss, cr. Beaufain & St. Philip Sts

Bowman, Mary Ann, cr. State St. & Unity Al.

Bowman, Mary, Miss, cr. Beaufain & St. Philip Sts.

Boyce, Henry & Walter, Factors, 5 Boyce & Co. Whf.

Boyce, John, Jr., Grocer, 59 & 63 E. Bay St.

Boyce, Ker, Factor, res. 14 George St.

Boyce, Robert, cr. King & Society Sts.

Boyd, William, Merchant, res. 90 Society St.

Boylston, Henry, M. D., cr. King & Hudson Sts., Neck

Bradford, William, Ship Carpenter, Vernon St.

Bradley, J. C., e. side Radcliffborough, near Lines, Neck

Bradley, Margaret, Seamstress, 18 E. Bay St.

Brady, John, Bricklayer, extreme end Broad St.

Brady, John, Grocer, s.w. cr. King & Tradd Sts.

Brailsford, E., Miss, 12 Hasell St.

Brailsford, Elizabeth, 30 S. Bay St.

Brailsford, William, Factor, res. 48 King St.

Brandon, David P., Furniture Store, 77 Meeting St.

Branson, Ware, Sail Maker, 78 E. Bay St., res. 10 Lynch

St.
Brase, Peter, Grocer, 108 Tradd St.
Brauer, Peter, Grocer, 10 Smith's Ln.
Bremar, Henry, M. D., Alexander St., Wraggborough, Neck
Bremer, O. P. D., Clerk, res. 107 Church St.
Brenan, Charles, Factor, Fitzsimons' Whf., res. 3 Society St.
Breteau, P., Tailor, 147 Meeting St.
Brewer, A. G., Rev., 110 Wentworth St.
Brewster, C. R, Attorney, Radcliffborough, op. Duncan St., Neck
Bridges, John, Seaman's Boarding House, 23 Queen St.
Bringloe, R., Mrs., Milliner, 34 Tradd St.
Bringloe, Richard, Boat Builder, 34 Tradd St.
Brisbane, A. H., Col., 64 Tradd St.
Brisbane, Flora, Seamstress, 3 Cumberland St., F.P.C.
Brisbane, John, Planter, 64 Tradd St.
Brisbane, Mary, Widow, 29 Meeting St.
Brisbane, W. H., Rev., Editor, Southern Baptist, 26 Meeting St.
Brisbane, William, Planter, 14 Meeting St.
Brisson, P. F., Radcliffborough, Neck
Britton, -----, Mrs., Widow, 36 Pinckney St.
Broadfoot, Frances, Widow, 296 E. Bay St.
Broadfoot, William G., Merchant, 296 E. Bay St.
Brocklebank, William, Plasterer, Meeting St., near Ann St., Neck
Brodie, Robert H., 25 Coming St.
Brodie, Robert, Lumber Factor, Little's Whf., res. Charlotte St., Mazyckborough
Broughton, Alexander, 63 Wentworth St.
Broughton, Ann, Miss, 49 Anson St.
Broughton, George J., Meeting St. Road, Neck
Broughton, Sarah, Mrs., Widow, n. side Boundary St., Neck
Brow, Harriet, Widow, Seminary, 13 Cumberland St.
Brown, A. H., Attorney, 59 Meeting, res. 123 Tradd St.
Brown, Alexander, Merchant, w. side King St., btw. Cannon & Bridge Sts., Neck
Brown, Ann, Seamstress, Nassau St., Hampstead, F.P.C., Neck
Brown, Charles T., Planter, cr. Anson & George Sts.
Brown, E., Dressmaker, 92 Market St.
Brown, E., Mrs., Boarding House, 84 Broad St.
Brown, Eliza, cr. King St. & Smith's Ln.
Brown, F. T., Painter, 91 Church St.
Brown, George, 47 Broad St.
Brown, J. B. & L., Hat Warehouse, 17 Broad St.
Brown, James, Butcher, Amherst St., Hampstead, F.P.C., Neck
Brown, James, Clerk, 17 S. Bay St.
Brown, Jane, Pastry Cook, Elizabeth St., Neck, F.P.C.
Brown, John, Clerk, 118 King St.
Brown, Lavina, Mrs., Washington St., Mazyckborough, Neck
Brown, Louisa, 74 Wentworth St.
Brown, Magdalene, 96 Market St.
Brown, Malcolm, Boot & Shoe Maker, 45 Anson St., F.P.C.

Brown, Martha, Mrs., St. Philip St., near Orphan House, Neck
Brown, Mary, Widow, 13 Archdale St.
Brown, Moses, Hair Dresser, 44 King St., F.P.C.
Brown, Peter, Hair Dresser, 19 Elliot St., F.P.C.
Brown, R. E., 79 Church St.
Brown, Robert, Factor, 79 Church St.
Brown, Tunis & Co., Factors, Roper's Whf.
Brown, William, Grocer, n. cr. Meeting & Reid Sts., Neck
Brown, William W., Carpenter, Warren St., near King St., Neck
Browne, E. H., Pumpmaker, E. Bay St., near Hasell St., res. 44 Anson St.
Browne, Gabriel, Clerk, 35 St. Philip St.
Browne, Horatio, Bricklayer, 35 St. Philip St.
Browne, J. D., Superintendent, City Burial Ground, Thomas St., Cannonborough, Neck
Browne, R. C., Notary Public, 97 E. Bay St., res. 47 Tradd St.
Bruen, J. W., Teacher, 24 Pitt St.
Bruen, M. A. E., Milliner, 24 Pitt St.
Bruning, Henry, Grocer, cr. State St. & Unity Al.
Bryan, George S., Attorney, 9 Waring's Row
Bryan, John, Col., Planter, n.w. cr. Anson & Hasell Sts.
Bryan, Jonathan, Dry Goods Store, 335 King St.
Bryant, Charles S., N. side Boundary St.
Buckhester, J. A., State Constable, 73 Boundary St.
Buckner, Augustus, Fancy Dry Goods Store, 214 King St.
Buckner, Eliza, Widow, 29 Coming St.
Budd, Sarah, Widow, 78 Church St.
Budd, T. S., Capt., 53 E. Bay St.
Buist & Carroll, Attorneys, 73 Broad St.
Buist, Arthur, Free School, 30 Wentworth St.
Buist, George, Attorney, res. 116 Wentworth St.
Buist, George, Mrs., Widow, 5 Church St.
Bulet, Peter & Son, Confectioners, 354 King St.
Bull, William, 3 Logan St.
Bullen, Samuel, Clerk, 285 King St.
Bullwinkel, John, Grocer, cr. Elizabeth & Charlotte Sts., Neck
Bullwinkle, George, Grocer, cr. Wentworth & Pitt Sts.
Bulow, John J., Planter, N. cr. King & Cannon Sts., Neck
Bunch, Silas, Butcher, Meeting St., near Spring St., Neck
Bundrock, Charles, Grocer, cr. King & Lamboll Sts.
Burch, E. C., Factor, Roper's Whf., res. 74 King St.
Burch, -----, Mrs., Female Seminary, 120 Meeting St.
Burckmyer, C., Merchant, 124 E. Bay St., res. 5 New St.
Burckmyer, John C., Merchant, 140 E. Bay St., res. 24 Society St.
Burdell, Mary M., Widow, 33 Wall St.
Burdell, R. F., Merchant, 58 E. Bay St.
Burden, Kinsey, Jr., Planter, 114 Tradd St.
Burden, Kinsey, Planter, 114 Tradd St.
Burdges, Henry, Cabinet Maker, 10 Tradd St.
Burdges, S. B., New York & Baltimore House, cr. Queen & State Sts.
Burdges, William, Brass Founder, Market St., near Anson St.
Burford, Elizabeth, Widow, 10 Cumberland St.

Burger, Mary, Widow, 44 Beaufain St.
Burger, Nicholas, cr. Mazyck & Magazine Sts.
Burger, Samuel, Tax Collector, res. 73 Queen St.
Burges, J. S., Printer, 18 Broad St., res. 124 King St.
Burges, William, Blacksmith, Boundary St., near Anson St.
Burie, Daniel, Blacksmith, Elliott St., near Church St.
Burie, W. A., Blacksmith, Elliott St., near Church St.
Burke, A. M'Neill, 240 Meeting St.
Burke, J. H., Pilot, 4 Stoll's Al.
Burke, John, Custom House, res. 243 E. Bay St.
Burke, Martin, Dry Goods Store, 219 King St.
Burke, Samuel, Boat Builder, Williams' Whf., res. E. Bay St., op. Pritchard's Al.
Burnham, Thomas, Clerk, N. side Boundary St., Neck
Burnham, William, Locksmith, 34 St. Philip St.
Burns, Jacob, 23 Coming St..
Burns, James, Pilot, 48 E. Bay St.
Burrell, William, Bootmaker, 58 Broad St.
Burrell, William, Grocer, cr. Smith & Bull Sts.
Burrows, Frederick, Pilot, 12 Lynch St.
Burrows, Samuel, Pilot, 12 Lynch St.
Busing, J. D., Grocer, cr. Bull and Rutledge Sts.
Bussacker, Charles, 307 King St.
Butler, Charles, Goldsmith & Jeweller, 145 King St.
Butler, E., Widow, 15 Hasell St.
Butler, Robert, Capt., Mary St., Neck
Buxbaum, Eliza, Widow, 120 Queen St.
Byrne, A., cr. Wentworth & St. Philip St.
Bythewood, Matthew W., Sergeant, Guard, Wentworth St.
Cabeuil, L. R., Bathing Establishment, 99 Church St.
Caius, Susan, 25 St. Philip St.
Calcott, John, Factor, Chisholm's S. Whf.
Calder, Alexander, Planters Hotel, cr. Church & Queen Sts.
Calder, James & Co., Merchants, Chisholm's S. Whf.
Calder, James, 23 Meeting St.
Calder, James, Cabinet Maker, 104 Meeting St.
Calder, William, 19 George St.
Caldwell, J. M., Factor, Edmonston's Whf.
Caldwell, William A. & Son, Auctioneers, 25 Vendue Range, res. 103 Meeting St.
Calvert, T. H., Black & White Smith, Church St.
Cambridge, St. John, Printer, 10 Minority St.
Cameron, S. D., Sailmaker, cr. E. Bay St. & Fitzsimons' Whf., res. 50 Beaufain St.
Cammer, Peter, Farmer, 35 Wall St.
Campbell & M'Intire, Tavern, 202 King St.
Campbell, A. W., Factor, 56 E. Bay St., res. 2 New St.
Campbell, Ann, Widow, 72 State St.
Campbell, Caroline, Widow, 23 Laurens St.
Campbell, I. M., M. D., 97 Broad St.
Campbell, J. B., Attorney, 9 State St.
Campbell, James, 202 King St.
Campbell, James, Grocer, n.e. cr. State & Chalmers Sts.
Campbell, John, Mrs., Widow, e. side Meeting St., near John St., Neck
Campbell, Martha, 50 Beaufain St.
Campbell, Samuel, Hair Dresser, 83 King St., F.P.C.
Canaday, Henry, Planter, cr. Tradd & Legare Sts.

Cannon, George, Dry Goods Store, 332 King St.
Canter, Emanuel, Grocer, 89 Market St.
Canter, R., Widow, 144 King St.
Cantwell, Patrick, Inspector of Customs, res. Marsh St.
Capers, L. G., 22 Society St.
Capers, Thomas F., Planter, cr. E. Bay & Laurens Sts.
Carberry, John, Merchant, res. Charlotte St., Mazyckborough, Neck
Cardoza, Isaac, Weigher, Custom House, 50 Broad St.
Cardozo, J. N., Editor, Southern Patriot, 50 Broad St.
Carew & Childs, Steam Saw Mills, Washington St., Mazyckborough, Neck
Carew, Edward, Factor, 305 E. Bay St.
Carey, Eugene M., Apothecary, 106 Church St.
Carlisle, Margaret, 6 Anson St.
Carmand, Francis, Woollen Draper & Mercer, 86 Queen St.
Carnochan, Richard, Merchant, 1 Hamilton & Co. Whf, res. 52 Meeting St.
Carpenter, Ann, Mrs., s. side Bridge St., Neck
Carpenter, James, Butcher, n. side Cannon St., Neck
Carr, C. D., Tailor & Draper, 30 Broad St.
Carr, D. B., Boarding House, 30 Elliott St.
Carr, Robert, 6 Back St.
Carrere, Eliza, Widow, w. end Radcliffborough, Neck
Carrere, W. J., Accountant, w. end Radcliffborough, Neck
Carroll, B. R., w. end Bull St.
Carroll, Bartholomew, n.w. end Radcliffborough, Neck
Carroll, Edward, Attorney, n.w. end Radcliffborough, Neck
Carroll, R. W. & J. Hayden, Hairdressers, 4 Queen St.
Carroll, R. W., 4 Queen St.
Carson & Hamilton, Merchants, 118 E. Bay St.
Carson, Elisha, Factor, Edmonston's Whf., res. 35 Laurens St.
Carsten, John, City Scavenger, 30 Society St.
Carswell, J., Clerk, cr. Boundary & Wall Sts.
Cart, John, Jr., Planters & Mechanics Bank, n. side Boundary St., near Coming St., Neck
Cart, John, Sr., 28 Bull St.
Carter, Charles, Carter, Elizabeth St., Neck, F.P.C.
Carter, Jacob, Fancy Store, 245 King St.
Carter, Orlando, Factor, Gadsden's Whf.
Carter, Rebecca, Widow, 245 E. Bay St.
Carter, William, Broker & Auctioneer, 7 Broad St., res. 8 Beaufain St.
Casey, T. E., Coachmaker, 5 Chalmers St.
Caskin, John, Carpenter, Charlotte St., Neck
Cason, James, Manager of Omnibus, 92 Church St.
Cassady, P., Livery Stables, fronting Church & Queen Sts.
Cassin, J. D., Wood Factor, n. side Boundary St., Neck
Castion, Eugene, Cigar Maker, 139 King St., F.P.C.
Catherwood, J. J., Watchmaker, 63 Broad St.
Cattell, William, Planter, Cannons Road, Neck
Catto, William, 7 Wall St., F.P.C.
Caulier & Harper, Chemists & Apothecaries, 204 King St.
Cavidally, A., Professor of Languages, 33 King St.
Caw, Peter, Watchmaker, 78 Meeting St., res. 4 S. Bay St.
Cawse, A., 24 George St.

Cay, J. E., 183 E. Bay St.
Cay, Julia, Madam, 6 Wall St.
Chadwick, S., Merchant, 130 E. Bay, res. 13 Meeting St.
Chamberlin & Cobb, King St.
Champlin, Jackson, Bricklayer, w. end Magazine St.
Champlin, Oliver, w. end Magazine St.
Champlin, Samuel, Capt., Magazine Guard., w. end Magazine St.
Chandler, Catherine, Widow, 48 St. Philip St.
Chandler, John, 32 Archdale St.
Chandler, John, Rev., 99 Broad St.
Chandler, Marvin & Co., Fancy Store, 276 King St.
Chapeau, J. B., 128 Church St.
Chapman, Charles C. P., Writing Academy, 190 King St.
Chapman, James, Merchant, 85 Church St.
Chapman, Samuel, Pilot, 5 Stoll's Al.
Chapman, Thomas, Cashier, Bank of S. C., 51 E. Bay St.
Chapman, William, Merchant, 85 Church St.
Charier, F. N., Dry Goods Store, 338 King St.
Chase, P. S., Boot & Shoe Store, 142 King St.
Chasteau, C., M. D., 34 Queen St.
Chazal, E. C., Mrs., 46 Anson St.
Chew, Thomas R., Blacksmith, Lucas St., Cannonborough, Neck
Childs, Robert, Washington St., Mazyckborough, Neck
Chion, Mary, Dry Goods Store, 98 King St.
Chisholm & Taylor, Factors, Chisholm's S. Whf.
Chisholm, Alexander, Steam Saw Mills, w. end of Tradd St.
Chisholm, George, 22 Legare St.
Chisholm, George, Sr., Factor, 25 E. Bay St.
Chisholm, John N., Planter, 7 Meeting St.
Chisholm, Robert, Mrs., Widow, 9 Montague St.
Chisholm, Robert, Planter, 1 Meeting St.
Chison, Thomas, Tailor, e. side Cannon St., Neck, F.P.C.
Chitty, Charles C., 115 Queen St.
Chitty, J. W., Clerk, 138 Meeting St.
Chrietzberg, C., 19 Beaufain St.
Chrietzberg, George, Baker, 42 King St.
Christian, Elizabeth, 34 Wentworth St.
Christiansen, C., Grocer, cr. Meeting & Boundary Sts.
Christie, David L., 100 Church St.
Christie, Joanna, Widow, 100 Church St.
Christophersen, C., Grocer, 200 King St.
Chupein, J. M., Widow, 13 Broad St.
Chupein, L. Y., Millinery, 177 King St.
Chupein, L. Y., Mineral Water Establishment, 109 E. Bay St.
Chupein, T. L., Paper Hanger, 162 King St.
Church, Margaret, Umbrella Maker, 27 St. Philip St.
Church, S. H., Accountant, 306 King St.
Church, Susan, John St., near Mary St., Neck
Clancy, John, Grocer, King St., near Warren St., Neck
Clapp, J. B., Teacher, 17 Burns Lane
Clark, B. & Co., Dry Goods Store, 163 King St.
Clark, Charles, 12 Friend St.
Clark, Charles, Exchange Office, 13 Broad, res. 13 Society St.
Clark, Henry, Coachmaker, 87 Queen St.
Clark, John, Factor, w. end Tradd St.

Clark, John, Wagon Yard, s. cr. King & Cannon Sts., Neck
Clark, Joseph, Carpenter, 11 Minority St.
Clark, Mary, Widow, 87 Queen St.
Clark, Richard, Pilot, 45 Church St.
Clark, William, 125 Queen St.
Clark, William, Grocer, s.e. cr. Anson & Wentworth Sts.
Clarke, Charles, Grocer, 67 E. Bay St.
Clarke, William, Carpenter, 15 College St., F.P.C.
Clarken, John, w. side Spring St., Neck
Clarkson, Elizabeth, Widow, 4 Bull St.
Clarkson, Thomas B., Cannonborough, near Bennett's Mills, Neck
Clarkson, William, Planter, 4 Bull St.
Clasterier, S., Carpenter, Henrietta St., Neck
Clawson, Herman W., 23 Beaufain St.
Clayton, David, Dry Goods Store, King St., near Mary St., Neck
Cleapor & Fields, Sail Maker, Price's Whf.
Cleapor, John W., 8 Minority St.
Cleary, N. G., Planter, cr. Meeting & Ann Sts., Neck
Clement, Sarah, Mrs., Widow, St. Philip St., near Cannon St., Neck
Clement, W. & P., Factors, Gadsden & Co. Whf.
Clement, William P., Factor, St. Philip St., near Cannon St., Neck
Clemmons, N., Boarding House, 60 State St.
Clifford, Henry, Factor, Gadsden's Whf., res. 8 Middle St.
Clissey, Raymond, Bandbox Maker, 86 King St.
Clough, J. B. & Co., Merchants, 188 E. Bay St.
Clyde, Thomas M., Tanner, cr. Hanover & Amherst Sts., Neck
Coates, B. C., Academy, 90 Wentworth St.
Cobb, David W., Merchant, res. 195 Meeting St.
Cobia, Daniel, Rev., 8 George St.
Cobia, Elizabeth, Miss, 17 Montague St.
Cobia, F. J., Butcher, e. side Reid St., btw. King & Meeting Sts., Neck
Cobia, Henry, Clerk, 25 Society St.
Cobia, N., 122 Wentworth St.
Coburn, Peter, Ship Carpenter, e. side King St., near Ann St., Neck
Cochran, C. B., 118 Wentworth St.
Cochran, Eliza, Miss, Chalmers St., near Church St.
Cochran, Eliza, Mrs., Widow, w. end Cannon St., Cannonborough, Neck
Cochran, J. C., Planter, w. end Cannon St., Cannonborough, Neck
Cochran, M., Tailor, Charlotte St., Neck, F.P.C.
Cochran, Margaret, 120 King St.
Cochran, Samuel, Tailor, 351 King St., F.P.C.
Cochran, Thomas, Cabinet Maker, 95 Queen St., F.P.C.
Cochran, William, w. end Cannon St., Cannonborough, Neck
Cockfield, Benjamin, 13 Washington St.
Coffin, A. M., Mrs., cr. Broad & Savage Sts.
Coffin, George, Accountant, 84 Broad St.
Coffin, Thomas A., Planter, 289 E. Bay St.
Cogdell, John S., President, Bank of S. C., res. 46 Meeting St.

Cogdell, R. W., Teller, Bank of S. C., cr. Broad St. & Gadsden's Al.

Cohen & Springer, Merchants, 6 Gillon St.

Cohen, David D., Planter, 7 Rutledge St.

Cohen, E. A., 61 Meeting St.

Cohen, H., 19 Burns Ln.

Cohen, Henry S., Accountant, 160 E. Bay St.

Cohen, Hyam, Broker & Auctioneer, 77 Broad St., res. 78 E. Bay St.

Cohen, J., Jr., Merchant, Edmondston's Whf., res. 147 King St.

Cohen, Jacob, Charlotte St., Mazyckborough, Neck

Cohen, Laurence L., 61 Broad St.

Cohen, M. M., Attorney, 10 St. Michael's Al.

Cohen, Mordecai, 11 Champney St, res. 103 Broad St.

Cohen, Moses, Mrs., Widow, 147 King St.

Cohen, Myer, Corn Extractor, 77 Market St.

Cohen, Nathan A., Clothing Store, 169 E. Bay St.

Cohen, P. M. & Co., Druggists, 61 Broad St., Res 78 E. Bay St.

Cohen, P. S., 356 King St.

Cohen, S. I., Dry Goods Store, 356 King St.

Cohrs, H. A., Linen Store, 322 King St.

Colburn, B. P. & Co., Dry Goods Store, 234 King St.

Colburn, J. S., Dry Goods Store, n.e. cr. King & Broad Sts.

Colcock, C. J., Hon., cr. King & John Sts., Neck

Cold, D., Capt., 2 Hard Al.

Cole, John W., Butcher, Nassau St., Neck

Collier, W. R., Engineer, 15 Wentworth St.

Collins, J. B., Boarding House, 6 Elliott St.

Comings, Thomas, Engineer, Mary St., near King St., Neck

Condy, Thomas, U. S. Marshal, 3 Waring's Row

Conner, H. W., Merchant, res. 31 Society St.

Conner, Samuel, res. 33 Hasell St.

Connolly, Richard, 14 S. Bay St.

Cook, Daniel, Factor, Edmondston's Whf., res. King St., near Reid St.

Cook, Daniel, Factor, w. side King St., near Reid St., Neck

Cook, Daniel, Lumber Yard, w. end Montague St.

Cook, John A., Grocery, Mazyckborough, near Market St., Neck

Cook, Otto, Grocer, 69 E. Bay St. & cr. Anson & Laurens Sts.

Cook, Tobias, Wagon Yard, w. side King St., near Reid St., Neck

Cooper, G. W., Attorney, 57 Meeting St., res. cr. Washington & Inspection Sts.

Cooper, N., Boot & Shoe Store, n.w. cr. King & Queen Sts., res. 64 Anson St.

Copes, James, Pilot, 52 E. Bay St.

Copmann, P., Portrait Painter, 118 King St.

Coram, Charlotte, Widow, 55 George St.

Corbett, Elizabeth, Miss, 2 Rutledge St.

Corbett, James, Dry Goods Store, 330 King St.

Corbett, Mary, Widow, 24 S. Bay St.

Corbett, Thomas, Jr., 25 Lynch St.

Corbett, Thomas, Planter, 25 Lynch St.

Corby, John, Ship Blacksmith, Marsh's Whf., res. cr. Vernon & Washington Sts.

Cordes, Jacob, Grocer, n.w. end Boundary St., Neck

Cordes, Rebecca, Mrs., Widow, Charlotte St., Mazyckborough, Neck

Cordes, Richard, Butcher, Henrietta St., Neck, F.P.C.

Cories, Andrew, Baker, cr. St. Philip & Green Sts.

Cormier, Francis, Carpenter, Alexander St., Mazyckborough, Neck

Corrie, Samuel, Wheelwright, King St., btw. John & Ann Sts., Neck

Coster, George, Mariner, 43 Wentworth St.

Costillion, Michell, Fruit Store, 37 Market St.

Cotchett, George, Factor, Edmondston's Whf., res. 20 Church St.

Courtney, E. C., Mrs., Boarding House, 38 & 40 Broad St.

Courtney, E. S., Custom House, res. Battery, E. Bay St.

Cousins, Thomas, Accountant, 142 King St.

Cowan, J. B., Carpenter, 8 Whim Court

Cowan, John, Cabinet Maker, 157 Meeting St.

Cowan, Maria, Widow, 10 Clifford St.

Cowperthwaite, E. R., Chair Store, 179 King St., res. 3 Clifford St.

Cox, Daniel, Butcher, Henrietta St., Neck, F.P.C.

Crafts, G. I., Attorney, 72 Broad St.

Crafts, Harriet, Widow, 10 Logan St.

Cramer, George, Jr., n.e. cr. Church & Queen Sts., upstairs

Cramer, George, Tavern, n.e. cr. Church & Queen Sts.

Cramer, John, Capt., 143 Church St.

Crandell, Ann, Sausage Maker, 28 Beaufain St.

Crane, Henry, Grocer, 248 E. Bay St.

Cranston, Horatio, 33 Mazyck St.

Crask, William F., Printer, 114 King St.

Crawford, Grace, Widow, 4 Magazine St.

Crawford, J., Mrs., Widow, 6 Lynch St.

Crawford, John, Owner, Vanderhorst's Whf., res. 1 Rutledge St.

Crawford, Margaret, 4 Friend St.

Crawford, William, Cooper, 6 Lynch St.

Cregier, Ann, Widow, 31 Coming St.

Cripps, Ann, Widow, 50 Meeting St.

Crocker, D. & Co., Merchants, 128 E. Bay St.

Croft, George, Capt., 8 Pinckney St.

Cromwell, -----, Miss, Seminary, 125 King St.

Cromwell, Samuel, Bricklayer, 10 Back St.

Crone, E., Mrs., Widow, n. Boundary St., Neck

Cropp, A. B., Clerk, 9 Smith's Ln.

Cross, Charles K., 145 E. Bay St., res. 1 Society St.

Cross, George W., Attorney, 5 Waring's Row, res. 44 Meeting

Cross, William, Bricklayer, 6 Beaufain St.

Crouch, Charles, Attorney, St. Michael's Al., res. Queen St., near Medical College

Crovat, Gibbes, Ship Carpenter, 20 Laurens St.

Crovat, Lewis J., 281 King St.

Crovat, Peter, Paint Store, 269 King St.

Cruger, Lewis, Attorney, 8 Waring's Row

Cruickshank, Daniel, Tailor, 92 King St.

Cruickshank, Samuel, Hide & Leather Dealer, 22 Queen

St.
Cruikshank, M., Mrs., Widow, King St., near John St., Neck
Cruikshank, S., Tannery, Hanover St., Hampstead, Neck
Cubie, John, Grocer, 1 Back St.
Cudworth, John, Printer, 209 King St.
Cunningham, A. J., Jewellery & Fancy Store, 268 King St.
Cunningham, Richard, Col., 297 E. Bay St.
Curran, Daniel, Blacksmith, King St., near Mary St., Neck
Curry, James, Capt., Fort St.
Curry, Michael, 11 Anson St.
Curtis, Ann, 30 Coming St.
Curtis, Joseph, Carpenter, Inspection St.
Cuthbert, James, Planter, 5 Smith St.
Dacoster, William, Millwright, 10 West St., F.P.C.
Dalcho, F., Rev., 39 Meeting St.
Daley, William, Grocery, 156 Meeting St.
Dalgleish, Robert, Tin Plate Worker, 100 Market St.
Dalgleish, William, Bricklayer, cr. Queen & Mazyck Sts.
Dalton, F. C., Mrs., Boarding House, 75 Queen St.
Damascke, Martin, Grocer, 45 King St.
Daniels, J. R., 68 State St.
Daniels, William, Watchmaker, 268 King St.
Darby, Mary, Widow, 17 Horlbeck's Al.
Darley, George, 1 Gibbes St.
Darr, Susan, Mrs., Henrietta St., Neck
Darrell, Ann, Miss, 4 Hasell St.
Dart, Benjamin, 55 Tradd St.
Dascher, Claus, Grocer, 139 E. Bay St.
Davega, Isaac & Son, Dry Goods Store, 229 King St.
Davega, Moses, Merchant, 229 King St.
Davenport, William, Pilot, 12 Church St.
Davidson, James, Painter, 24 Tradd St.
Davidson, Thomas, Grocer, 21 S. Bay St.
Davidson, William, Merchant, res. 296 E. Bay St.
Davie, William J., Grocer, 49 King St.
Davis, Elvira, 5 Wentworth St.
Davis, Emery, Merchant, res. 84 Broad St.
Davis, G. Y., Merchant, 52 E. Bay St.
Davis, George, Capt., 6 Meeting St.
Davis, Henry, Auctioneer, 26 Queen St.
Davis, J. M., Mrs., Widow, cr. Pinckney & Cannon Sts., Cannonborough, Neck
Davis, J., Mrs., Boarding House, 95 Church St.
Davis, Jacob, Mrs., Widow, 38 Tradd St.
Davis, John, Boarding House, 279 & 281 King St.
Davis, John, Capt., 37 E. Bay St.
Davis, Moses, 213 Meeting St.
Davis, -----, Mrs., Dress Maker, Anson St., near Pinckney St.
Davis, Thomas, Capt., 75 Church St.
Dawes, H. P., Factor, Roper's Whf., res. 22 King St.
Dawson, Ann, Mrs., Widow, Ann St., Wraggborough, Neck
Dawson, Caroline, Widow, 5 Logan St.
Dawson, J. D., Magistrate, King St., near Warren St., Neck
Dawson, J. Drayton, Attorney, res. 9 Smith St.
Dawson, John, 32 Bull St.
Dawson, Octavius, State Bank, res. 7 Bull St.

Dawson, W. H., Broker, 38 Broad St., res. 7 Bull St.
Day, E. & Co., Merchant Tailors, 271 King St.
Day, Fisher, Millinery, 318 King St.
Day, Z., Carriage Warehouse, 68 Wentworth St.
Della Torre, A., Merchant, 181 E. Bay St., res. 65 Broad St.
Deas, C. D., Factor, Boyce & Co. Whf.
Deas, E. H., Dr., 119 Church St.
Deas, Henry, Hon., State Senator, 1 Friend St.
Deas, R. L., Butcher, Charlotte St., Mazyckborough, Neck, F.P.C.
Deas, Seaman, Planter, 60 Wentworth St.
Deas, Thomas H., Planter, n.e. cr. Society & Anson Sts.
Dease, John, Watchmaker, 88 E. Bay St.
Dease, S., Clerk, n.e. cr. Friend & Broad Sts.
Debogrin, John, Clerk, 6 West St.
Debow, John, Chair Maker, 202 Meeting St.
Debow, John, Jr., Blacksmith, n. side Boundary St., Neck
Debow, Mary, Mrs., Widow, cr. State St. & Lodge Al.
Debow, William G., Clerk, Rice Mill, George St.
DeCamps, James, Broker, 95 King St.
DeChoiseul, -----, Count, French Consul, 168 E. Bay St.
Deery, James, Boot & Shoe Maker, 103 Church St.
Dehon, Sarah, Mrs., Widow, 41 Meeting St.
Delacroix, G. W. & Co., Merchants, 71 E. Bay St.
Delamotta, Jacob, Dr., cr. King & Broad Sts.
Delaney, M. I., Pilot, 60 Church St.
Delang, Martha, Widow, 195 E. Bay St.
Delano, E. & J. B., Merchants, 159 E. Bay St.
Delarge, John, Tailor, Meeting St., Neck, F.P.C.
Delarge, Julia, Mantuamaker, Meeting St., Neck, F.P.C.
Delatorre, A., Merchant, 181 E. Bay St., res. 65 Broad St.
Deliessline, F. A., Attorney, res. 24 Mazyck St.
Dellinger & Losee, Crockery Merchants, 277 King St.
Deltmoldt, C. E., Surveyor & Engineer, 8 Waring's Row
Deming & Bulkley, Furniture Warehouse, 205 King St.
Dempsey, Miles, Clerk of Market, 129 Queen St.
Dener, Christiana, Widow, 33 Mazyck St.
Dener, George, Accountant, 139 Meeting St.
Dennehy, Jeremiah, Printer, 225 King St.
Dennis, Nathaniel, Tailor, 34 Beaufain St.
Denny, T. S., Dr., 213 King St.
Dent, Ann, Mrs., Widow, King St., near Hudson St., Neck
Depratt, Hannah, Fruit Store, 131 King St., F.P.C.
Dereef, Joseph, Wood Dealer, Mary St., Neck, F.P.C.
Dereef, Richard, Wood Dealer, Hanover St., Hampstead, Neck, F.P.C.
Descoudres, -----, & Co., Grocers, 281 King St.
Desel, Charles, M. D., Pitt St., above Boundary St., Neck
Desgraves, Peter, Farmer, Bee St., Neck
Dessaussure, Charles A., Factor, 6 Roper's Whf., res. 35 Meeting St.
Dessaussure, H. A., Attorney, 39 Broad St., res. 35 Meeting St.
Detolles & De Flanc, Mesdames, 18 Pinckney St.
Dettmers, H., Grocer, cr. Beaufain & Coming Sts.
Deveaux, J., Portrait Painter, 98 Meeting St.
Deveaux, M., Mrs., Widow, 31 Tradd St.
Deveaux, Porteous, 5 Minority St.
Deveaux, Thomas G., cr. Coming & Cannon Sts., Neck

Deveneau, E., Clerk, Railroad, res. 110 King St.
Devine, Joseph, Sausage Maker, e. side Market St., near King St.
Devion, C., Widow, 8 St. Philip St.
Dewar, W. S., Factor, 6 Fitzsimons' Whf.
Dewees, John, Mary St., Wraggborough, Neck
Dewees, John, Rice Stores, 78 & 178 E. Bay St.
Dewees, Joseph, Alexander St., Mazyckborough, Neck
Dexter, Edward, Ship Carpenter, 8 Bedon's Al.
Dexter, Mary, Mrs., Boarding House, 8 Bedon's Al.
Dibble, A. C., Hat Store, 37 Broad St.
Dick, James, Auctioneer, 23 Vendue Range, res. 39 Broad St.
Dick, William, State Constable, Charlotte St., Neck
Dickinson, E., E. Bay St., near Hasell St.
Dickinson, F., Planter, 12 Bull St.
Dickman, T. W., Dry Goods Store, 320 King St.
Dickson & Allen, Grocery, s.e. cr. Market St. & E. Bay St.
Dickson, Henry S., Dr., cr. Hudson & Meeting Sts., Neck
Dickson, Hillard & Co., Merchants, 201 E. Bay St.
Dickson, John, Dr., 50 St. Philip St.
Dickson, S. D., Merchant, res. 200 E. Bay St.
Dieckman, J. H., Grocer, Meeting St., near Wolf St., Neck
Dile, Jane, Dry Goods Store, 158 King St.
Dillingham, W. S., Dentist, 94 Meeting St.
Dinkins, L. J., Factor, 8 Fitzsimons' Whf.
Disher, Robert, e. side Pinckney St., Cannonborough, Neck
Disourney, Peter, 28 Wentworth St., F.P.C.
Divver, James, Academy, 124 Wentworth St.
Dixon & Wilkinson, Tallow Chandlers, King St., op. Ann St., Neck
Dobson, O. L., State Assessor, 4 Water St.
Dodd, E. K., John St., op. Mary St., Neck
Dodd, L. S., w. side Reid St., Neck
Dodd, William, Merchant, 136 E. Bay St.
Dodge, D. K., 55 Church St.
Doggett, S. W. & J. B. Clapp, Academy, 17 Burns Ln.
Doggett, S. W., Female Seminary, 236 Meeting St.
Don, Maria, Miss, 34 Society St.
Donegan, James, Grocer, cr. St. Philip & George Sts.
Donis, Emelie, Fruit Store, 164 King St., F.P.C.
Dorrill, E. R., Surveyor, res. cr. Lynch & Wentworth Sts.
Dorrill, John, Shoe Maker, 18 Washington St.
Dorrill, Robery, Factor, cr. Lynch & Wentworth Sts.
Dotterer, Thomas, 17 Wentworth St.
Doucin, M., Painter, 6 Clifford St.
Doucin, P. M., Clerk, 6 Clifford St.
Dougherty, J., Grocer, 27 S. Bay St., res. 95 Tradd St.
Dougherty, John, Jr., res. 95 Tradd St.
Dougherty, John, Planter, Washington St., Mazyckborough, Neck
Dougherty, Joseph, Plasterer, 14 Smith St.
Doughty, W. S., s. side Warren St., near Coming St., Neck
Doughty, William C., 21 Hasell St.
Douglas, Anthony, Accountant, 87 E. Bay St.
Douglas, Campbell, Grocer, 141 Meeting St.
Douglas, John, Mechanic, 84 Anson St.

Douglas, John, Tailor, 24 Berresford St., F.P.C.
Douglas, John, Wood Measurer, Washington St., Mazyckborough, Neck
Douglass, B., Dr., Surgeon Dentist, 227 King St.
Douglass, Joseph, Factor, 67 Queen St.
Dowling, Archibald, 7 Legare St.
Dowling, Daniel J., Printer & Stationer, n.w. cr. Church & Queen Sts.
Dowling, E. A., Mrs., Widow, 17 Society St.
Downie, Peter, Clerk, Planters Hotel, cr. Church & Queen Sts.
Downie, Robert, Tin Plate Worker, 59 Broad St.
Doyle, John, Ship Carpenter, 3 Liberty St.
Drayton, Alfred R., Rice Mills, King St. Road, Neck
Drayton, Charles, Dr., w. end Montague St.
Drayton, Emma, Miss, 87 King St.
Drayton, Hector, Drayman, Amherst St., Hampstead, Neck, F.P.C.
Drayton, John, Carpenter, 73 Anson St., F.P.C.
Drayton, Mary, Miss, 5 Smith's Ln.
Drege, Peter & Co., Clothing Store, 157 E. Bay St.
Drummond, J., Boot & Shoe Maker, Chalmers St., near Church St., F.P.C.
Drummond, James, Boot & Shoe Maker, King St., near Broad St.
Drummond, John, Boot & Shoe Maker, 51 Broad St.
Duboc, Francis, Store Keeper, 33 Queen St.
Dubois, Eleanor, Widow, 88 Queen St.
Due, Francis, Grocer, cr. King & Spring Sts., Neck
Due, Francis, Jr., Tin Plate Worker, cr. King & Spring Sts., Neck
Duff, John, Shoe Maker, cr. George & St. Philip Sts.
Duffus, J. A. & Co., Dry Goods Store, 222 King St., res. 129 King St.
Duffus, John, Notary Public, 87 E. Bay St., res. 129 King St.
Duffy, James, Ironmonger, 20 S. Bay St.
Dufour, J., Shop Keeper, cr. Meeting & Columbus Sts., Neck
Dufresne, P. F., Teacher of French, 122 Queen St.
Duggan, Thomas, Bricklayer, St. Philip St., near the Lines, Neck
Duke, Margaret, Widow, 6 Whim Court
Dukes, William C., Factor, Edmondston's Whf., res. King St., near Mary St., Neck
Dulen, Rene, 38 Maiden Ln.
Dunkin & Brewster, Attorneys, 65 Meeting St.
Dunkin, B. F., Attorney, w. end Radcliffborough, Neck
Dunlap, James, Tailor, 292 King St.
Dunlap, William, 132 Tradd St.
Dunlap, William, Clerk, 172 King St., res. 51 Maiden Ln.
Dunn, John E., Auctioneer, 27 Vendue Range, res. cr. Meeting & Market Sts.
Dunn, William, Dry Goods Store, cr. Meeting & Market Sts.
Dunstan, C., Pastry Cook, Nassau St., Hampstead, F.P.C., Neck
Dupont, Francis, Jr., Upholsterer & Paper Hanger, 147 King St.
Dupont, Francis, Sr., 74 Queen St.

Dupree, James, Carpenter, 25 Wall St.

Duquercron, F., Merchant, Fraser & Laffan's Whf., res. 19 Tradd St.

Durand, V. & Co., Charleston Clothing Store, 155 E. Bay St.

Durban, A., 29 Horlbeck's Al.

Durbec, E. & Co., Clothing Store, 228 King St.

Duryea, Jacob, Boarding House, 125 Church St.

Dutrieux, C., Baker, 85 E. Bay St.

Duval, John, Tin Plate Worker, cr. King & Warren Sts., Neck

Duval, Peter, Gardner, e. side Cannon St., Neck

Dwight, Caroline, Pastry Cook, 85 Broad St., F.P.C.

Eager, Robert, Merchant, 314 King St., res. 107 Wentworth St.

Eager, William, Clerk, 161 E. Bay St.

Eason & Dotterer, Foundry, Eason's Whf.

Eason, Dorothy, Mrs., 75 Wentworth St.

Eason, Robert, Wharf Owner, 35 Anson St.

Easterby, George, Capt., 87 E. Bay St.

Eckhard, G. B., Attorney, 2 Waring's Row, res. 31 George St.

Eckhard, Mary, Widow, 35 Society St.

Eckhard, Priscilla, Widow, 31 George St.

Edgerton, Edward, Tailor, res. 106 Church St.

Edmondston, C. & Co., Merchants, Edmondston's Whf.

Edmondston, Charles, res. Battery, E. Bay St.

Edwards, Daniel C., Planter, King St., near Spring St., Neck

Edwards, Edward H., Planter, 11 Meeting St.

Edwards, George, Planter, cr. King & Ann Sts., Neck

Edwards, Henry, Wood Dealer, Ann St., Neck, F.P.C.

Edwards, J. F., Planter, 34 Wall St.

Edwards, Jacob, Carpenter, Nassau St., Neck, F.P.C.

Egleston & Frost, Attorneys, 50 Broad St.

Egleston, George W., Attorney, Warren St., Radcliffborough, Neck

Ehlers, Carsten, Hampstead, Neck

Ehney, Elisha, Carpenter, 118 Meeting St.

Ehney, Francis, Mariner, n.e. cr. E. Bay & Hasell Sts.

Ehney, Mary, Widow, 28 Magazine St.

Ehney, William H., Dry Goods Store, 347 King St., res. 44 Montague St.

Elbridge, James, Butcher, cr. Hanover & Reid Sts., Neck

Elder, James, Tanner, John St., near Meeting St., Neck

Elfe, Albert, Carpenter, 53 George St.

Elfe, Edward, Dr., 108 Queen St.

Elfe, Eleanor, Miss, 104 Wentworth St.

Elfe, George, res. 108 Queen St.

Elfe, Isaac, 93 Boundary St.

Elfe, Robert, Attorney, 55 Meeting St., res. 93 Boundary St.

Elfe, William, 93 Boundary St.

Elford, James M., Telegraphic Office, 119 E. Bay St.

Elford, John., Wharfinger, res. 119 E. Bay St.

Elliot, B. S., Planter, 11 George St.

Elliot, Benjamin, Attorney, 20 Legare St.

Elliot, Thomas O., Master in Equity, 1 Waring's Row

Elliot, William S., Factor, 20 Legare St.

Elliott, William, Rev., Meeting St., near George St.

Ellis, J. G., Carpenter, 102 Market St.

Ellis, Mary, Widow, 102 Market St.

Elmore, Amelia, Mrs., Widow, Vernon St.

Elsworth, Foster, Blacksmith, 11 Boundary St.

Elsworth, Frederick, Blacksmith, 11 Boundary St.

Elsworth, John T., Gauger, Custom House, 11 Boundary St.

Elsworth, T., Mrs., Widow, cr. Boundary & Middle Sts.

Elwig, Peter, Carpenter, 64 Beaufain St., F.P.C.

Emery, Elizabeth, Mrs., Widow, 2 Unity Al.

England, Alexander, Jr., 12 Tradd St.

England, Alexander, Planter, 54 Tradd St.

England, John, Rt. Rev., Bishop of Charleston, n.e. cr. Broad & Friend Sts.

English, James, Ship Carpenter, 25 S. Bay St.

Enslow, J. L., Cooper, 94 E. Bay St., res. 119 S. Bay St.

Enston, William, Furniture Ware Room, 169 King St.

Esdra, Joseph, Mattress Store, 80 Market St.

Eude, Louis, French Coffee House, 141 E. Bay St.

Evans, Charles, Turner, 147 Meeting St.

Evans, James, 40 Coming St.

Evans, L., Cutler, 81 Queen St.

Evans, Susannah, Miss, 10 Pitt St.

Evans, William, Grocer, 210 King St.

Evans, William, Watchmaker, 267 King St.

Eveleigh, Thomas, Dr., cr. Smith & Montague Sts.

Everingham, Rebecca, Widow, 31 Mazyck St.

Everingham, -----, Widow, Queen St., near King St.

Ewan, John, Jewerly & Silversmith, 221 King St.

Eyland & Haydon, Jewerly & Military Goods, 267 King St.

Eyland, James, 78 Wentworth St.

Faber, H. F., Planter, Charlotte St., Neck

Faber, J. W., Attorney, Charlotte St., Neck

Faber, Mary, Widow, Charlotte St., Neck

Fabian, L., Mrs., Boarding House, s. cr. Church St. & St. Michael's Al.

Fair, Margaret, Widow, 20 Mazyck St.

Fairchild, R., Tavern, 274 King St.

Fanning, F. D., 313 King, res. 10 George St.

Farley, Elizabeth, 29 Archdale St.

Farley, J., Academy, 3 Bull St.

Farquharson, Elizabeth, Milliner, 115 King St.

Farr, Catherine, Widow, 16 Coming St.

Farrar, S. S., Wholesale Grocer, 168 E. Bay St.

Fasbender, J. H., Watchmaker, 112 Meeting St.

Fasbender, -----, Mrs., Grocery, 110 Meeting St.

Fash, Leonard, Grocery, cr. Meeting & Hasell Sts.

Fay, James, Washington Hotel, 147 E. Bay St.

Fay, Patrick, Grocer, 4 Champney St.

Fayolle, Peter, Dancing Master, 80 King St.

Fayolle, Theodore B., Music Master, 90 King St.

Fayssoux, Elizabeth, Widow, 66 Tradd St.

Feebrook, Christian, Grocer, 18 S. Bay St.

Feild, J., n.w. cr. Queen & State Sts.

Fell, Thomas D., Tin Plate Worker, 100 Market St.

Fell, William, Mrs., Boarding House, 86 Broad St.

Fenn, M. B., Dry Goods Store, 220 King St.

Ferguson, Eliza, Widow, 10 Orange St.

Ferguson, H. W., 23 Tradd St.

Ferguson, James, Planter, cr. King & John Sts., Neck

Ferrett, Charles, Tailor, 38 Coming St.
Ferrett, J. F., Fruit Store, 43 Market St.
Ferrett, Josephine, Miss, 192 Meeting St.
Ficken, Elias, Grocer, 125 Tradd St.
Fields, Nathaniel, Sail Maker, res. 29 Laurens St.
Fife, James, Merchant, 71 E. Bay St.
Fillette, Francis, Fancy Store, 159 King St.
Finagin & Lambert, Drapers & Tailors, 40 Broad St.
Findlay, Jemima, Seamstress, Henrietta St., Neck
Finely, W. P., Attorney, res. 17 Meeting St.
Fink, C. P., Grocer, 43 Beaufain St.
Finklay, James, Saddler, 16 Wentworth St.
Finley, J. E. B., Dr., 4 Church St.
Fishburne, Edward, Planter, cr. King & John Sts., Neck
Fishburne, M., Mrs., Widow, 136 Wentworth St.
Fisher, Jean M'J., Miss, 164 E. Bay St.
Fisher, Rebecca, 9 Coming St.
Fisher, S., Mrs., 164 E. Bay St.
Fisk, W., 299 King St.
Fitte, William, Blacksmith, Charlotte St., Neck
Fitzpatrick, Thomas, Clerk, 331 King St.
Fitzsimons, C., Mrs., Widow, Hasell St., op. Maiden Ln.
Fitzsimons, Charles, State Constable, 58 Elliott St.
Fleig, Francis, Professor of Music, 24 Beaufain St.
Flemming, Patrick, Grocer, 228 E. Bay St.
Flemming, Ross & Co., Wholesale Grocers, 167 E. Bay St.
Flemming, T., Merchant, 317 King St.
Flint, James, Commission Merchant, 9 Queen St.
Flynn, Edward P., Tailor, 12 Tradd St.
Flynn, William, res. 17 Mazyck St.
Fogartie, Ann, Miss, Free School, 23 Wall St.
Fogartie, Edward, Bricklayer, 23 Wall St.
Fogartie, Eliza, Seamstress, 41 Society St.
Fogartie, Samuel, Clerk, 23 Wall St.
Folger, Edward, 7 West St.
Folker, Thomas, John St., near King St., Neck
Follin, F., Clerk, 12 Boundary St.
Follin, Joseph, Cigar Maker, cr. Guignard St. & Maiden Ln.
Forbes, William P., Tin Plate Worker, 11 Tradd St.
Ford, Benjamin, Carpenter, 75 Boundary St.
Ford, E., Henrietta St., Neck
Ford, Elizabeth, Miss, Lucas St., Cannonborough, Neck
Fordham, Jane, Mrs., Widow, Vernon St.
Fordham, Richard, Blacksmith, cr. Exchange & E. Bay Sts., res. cr. Washington & Charlotte Sts., Mazyckborough
Forrest, John, Rev., 53 Beaufain St.
Fourgeaud, Arnold, Baker, 40 Elliot St.
Fox, Sarah, Widow, 41 George St.
Francis, David, Tailor, cr. Mary & Meeting Sts., F.P.C., Neck
Francis, Edward, Livery Stables, 127 Church St.
Francis, George, Pilot, 10 Stoll's Al.
Francis, James, Hair Dresser, King St., near Morris St., Neck, F.P.C.
Francis, John L., Hair Dresser, 312 King St., F.P.C.
Fraser, Ann, Widow, 13 Orange St.
Fraser, Charles, Attorney, 53 King St.
Fraser, Fredrick, Mrs., Widow, 99 Tradd St.

Fraser, J. & Co., Factors, Fraser & Laffan's Whf.
Fraser, James, Capt., w. side St. Philip St., Neck
Fraser, John, Merchant, res. 41 E. Bay St.
Frazer, Charles P., Wood Factor, e. end Laurens St.
Frazer, John J., Factor, John St., btw. King & Meeting Sts., Neck
Frazer, Lawerence, Bathing House, e. end Laurens St.
Freeman, William, Capt., 4 Longitude Ln.
Friday, William, Butcher, n. side Cannon St., F.P.C., Neck
Friend, John, Carpenter, Boundary St., op. Middle St.
Frierson, George, Dr., e. side Hampstead St., Neck
Fripp, A. P., Blacksmith, 15 King St., res. 9 Price's Al.
Frost, Edward, Attorney, res. 23 Archdale St.
Frost, Henry R., Dr., 63 Meeting St., res. 23 Archdale St.
Frost, N. M., Railroad Depot, Meeting St. Road, Neck
Fuller, Benjamin, Planter, St. Philip St., near Cannon St., Neck
Fuller, Oliver, Capt., Custom House, 107 Meeting St.
Fulmer, John, Amherst St., Hampstead, Neck
Furman, C. M., Cashier, Bank of State of S. C., res. 1 Ladson's Court
Furman, M., Seamstress, Henrietta St., Neck, F.P.C.
Fursman, James, Boarding House, 13 Bedon's Al.
Gabeau, Elizabeth, Widow, 36 St. Philip St.
Gadsden, Alexander E., Dr., 104 Church St.
Gadsden, Alston, 126 Queen St.
Gadsden, B. C., Planter, 126 Queen St.
Gadsden, C., Rev., cr. Alexander & Charlotte Sts., Neck
Gadsden, Christopher, Mrs., Widow, 12 S. Bay St.
Gadsden, George, n. side Boundary St., Neck
Gadsden, J. W., Widow, 126 Queen St.
Gadsden, James, Factor, 5 Meeting St.
Gadsden, T. N., Broker & Auctioneer, 12 State St., res. 24 Hasell St.
Gadsden, Thomas, Attorney, 104 Church St.
Gaillard, Augustus T., Factor, res. 9 Archdale St.
Gaillard, Cornelia, Widow, 66 Wentworth St.
Gaillard, Edwin, Mrs., Widow, w. side Cannonborough, Neck
Gaillard, James, Amherst St., Hampstead, Neck
Gaillard, Mary, 13 West St.
Gaillard, S. T., Planter, Elliott St., Cannonborough, Neck
Gaillard, Susan, Widow, Court House Sq.
Gaillard, Theodore, 66 Wentworth St.
Gaillard, W. S., 1st Lt., Citadel Guard, Neck
Gallagher, J. W., Factor, w. end Wentworth St.
Galliott, Alexis, Cigar Manufacturer, 95 E. Bay St.
Gamble, Margaret, Fruit Store, 110 King St.
Gamewell, William A., Rev., cr. Pitt & Boundary Sts., Neck
Gandouin, Izidore, Hat & Shoe Store, 111 E. Bay St.
Gantt & Gibbes, Broker & Auctioneers, 22 Broad St.
Gantt, T. J., Register in Equity, Court House, res. 54 King St.
Garcia, James R., Professor of Music, n. side Boundary St., Neck
Garden, A., 13 Clifford's Al.
Garden, Elias, Butcher, Ann St., near Meeting St., F.P.C., Neck

41

Garden, Jack, Livery Stables, Chalmers St., near State St., F.P.C.

Garden, John, Planter, e. side Pinckney St., Cannonborough, Neck

Garden, M. J., Seamstress, 23 Mazyck St., F.P.C.

Gardiner, J. H., Accountant, 161 E. Bay St., res. 286 King St

Gardiner, Margaret, Fruit Store, 110 King St.

Garrett, Ann, Widow, 115 Meeting St.

Gary, Jesse, Dry Goods Store, w. side King St., near Cannon St., Neck

Gates, George, Capt., w. end Beaufain St.

Gates, John, Butcher, s. side Cannon St., Neck

Gates, Thomas, Butcher, s. side Cannon St., Neck

Gatewood, William C., Agent of Lotteries, 26 Broad St.

Gauthier, F., Teacher of Spanish & French, 15 Coming St.

Geddes, Gilbert C., Planter, 24 Smith St.

Geddes, James, Attorney, n.w. cr. King & Morris Sts., Neck

Gefkin, E., Widow, 42 Anson St.

Gefkin, Henry C., 42 Anson St.

Geglar, Henry, 5 Lynch St.

George, John, Fruit Store, 39 Market St.

Gerard, Elizabeth, 17 West St.

Gerard, Peter G., Tailor & Draper, 29 Broad St.

Gerdts, Henry, Grocer, cr. Coming & Cannon Sts., Neck

Gerrits, H., cr. Boundary & Alexander Sts., Neck

Gervais, P. T., Rev., 8 Lamboll St.

Geyer, John S., Planter, Charlotte St., Neck

Geyer, Mary, Mrs., 17 Lynch St.

Geyer, R. C., Clerk, 17 Lynch St.

Geyer, W. J., Coach Maker, 58 Wentworth

Gianini, Jacob, Fruit Store, 63 Market St.

Gibbes & Waring, Factors, Hamilton & Co. Whf.

Gibbes, Benjamin S., Factor, cr. Elizabeth & John Sts., Neck

Gibbes, C. & J., Merchants, 10 Vendue Range

Gibbes, Charlotte, Widow, 4 State St.

Gibbes, Eliza, Widow, 67 Church St.

Gibbes, J. W., Merchant

Gibbes, John R., 23 Smith St.

Gibbes, Joseph S., Factor, 6 Gibbes St.

Gibbes, M. G., Broker, res. 51 Meeting St.

Gibbes, Mary P., Widow, res. 109 Broad St.

Gibbes, Paul, Mrs., Smith's Whf., Neck

Gibbes, Robert R., Planter, cr. Meeting & Ann Sts., Neck

Gibbes, S. W., Attorney, 24 St. Michael's Al., res. 109 Broad St.

Gibbes, Susannah, Widow, 51 Meeting St.

Gibbon, George & John, Merchants, 8 Gillon St., res. 12 New. St.

Gibson, Alexander & Co., Merchants, 60 E. Bay St.

Gibson, Alexander, 41 Coming St.

Gibson, D. C., Attorney, 12 St. Michael's Al.

Gibson, Elizabeth, Widow, 228 Meeting St.

Gibson, James G., Coach Maker, 228 Meeting St.

Gibson, William, Col., 4 Back St.

Gibson, William H., Clerk, 55 Wentworth St.

Gidiere J. M., Professor of Music, 338 King St.

Gidiere, Joseph J., Merchant, 336 King St.

Gidiere, Margaret, Dry Goods Store, 336 King St,

Giese, Charles, Grocer, 111 Meeting St.

Gilbert, Seth, Printer, s.w. cr. St. Michael's Al. & Church St.

Gilchrist, James, Clerk, Bank of S. C.

Gilchrist, M., Pastry Cook, Elizabeth St., Neck, F.P.C.

Gilchrist, R. B., Deputy Attorney, Waring's Row, res. cr. E. Bay & Society Sts.

Gildersleeve, B., Rev., Chalmers St., res. 40 St. Philip St.

Giles, Othniel J., Elizabeth St., Neck

Giles, Robert F., 2 Gibbes St.

Gilfillan, Alexander, Merchant, res. 9 Chalmers St.

Gillespie, Thomas, 30 Queen St.

Gilliand, W. D., Clerk, 310 King St.

Gilliand, W. H. & Co., Wholesale Dry Goods, 315 King St., res. 18 George St.

Gilman, Samuel, Rev., 60 Tradd St.

Gilmore, D. C., Shoe Store, cr. Church St. & St. Michael's Al.

Girardeau, Isaac, 6 Gibbes St.

Gist, Sarah B., Widow, 47 Beaufain St.

Gitsinger, Benjamin Russell, Printer, 4 Clifford St.

Gleason, H. B., Crockery Store, 264 King St., res. King St., near Hudson St.

Glen, John, Teller, Planters & Mechanics Bank, n.w. cr. Reid & Meeting Sts., Neck

Glenn, James, 97 Tradd St.

Glenn, Margaret, Widow, 97 Tradd St.

Glenn, Thomas, 97 Tradd St.

Glover, Joseph, Dr., 7 Rutledge St.

Glover, William, Boot & Shoe Maker, 200 Meeting St., F.P.C.

Gnech, M. E., Dry Goods Store, 188 King St.

Godard, Rene, President, Union Bank & Merchant, 53 E. Bay St., res. 127 King St.

Godet, Ann, 4 Liberty St.

Godfrey, E., Mrs., 20 Wentworth St.

Godfrey, William W., Accountant, 63 Beaufain St.

Goff, E., Mrs., Milliner, 168 King St., upstairs

Goldsmith, Abraham, 36 Hasell St.

Goldsmith, F., Widow, cr. Broad St. & Courthouse Sq.

Goldsmith, Henry, w. end Magazine St.

Goldsmith, Joseph H., 53 Church St.

Goldsmith, Morris, Deputy U. S. Marshal, w. end Magazine St.

Gonzalez, B., Merchant, 15 Champney St., res. 5 George St.

Gonzalez, John, 20 Market St.

Good, Francis, Grocer, s. cr. Meeting & Wolf Sts., Neck

Goodrich, Ann, Mrs., s. side Cannon Sts., Neck

Goodwin, E. M., 84 Wentworth St.

Gordon, C. P., U. S. Bank, res. w. end Cannonborough, Neck

Gordon, Catharine A., Mrs., Widow, Meeting St., near Reid St., Neck

Gordon, F., Mantuamaker, Warren St., near King St., Neck, F.P.C.

Gordon, John, Mrs., Wife of Col., Widow, 218 Meeting St.

Gorman, W. P., Boot & Shoemaker, 86 Broad St.

Gosprey, F., Carpenter, e. side Radcliffborough, Neck
Gough, Edward, 28 S. Bay St.
Gough, Emma, Widow, 28 S. Bay St.
Gough, Thomas, 28 S. Bay St.
Gouldsmith, Richard, Cabinet Maker, 293 King & 65 Wentworth Sts.
Gourdin & Smith, Merchants, Chisholm's S. Whf.
Gourdin, Henry, Merchant, res. cr. Meeting & S. Bay Sts.
Gourdin, R. N., Attorney, 22 St. Michael's Al.
Gourdin, Theodore, Dr., cr. Laurens & Wall Sts.
Gourgan, Theodore, Professor, Meeting St., near Henrietta St., Neck
Gowan, Peter, Watch Maker, 78 Meeting St., res. 4 S. Bay St.
Gradick, J. N., Carpenter, e. end Laurens St.
Graham, John L., Merchant, 298 King St.
Graham, Win C., Wentworth St., near Smith St.
Granby, George, Dry Goods Store, 252 King St.
Grand, Nicholas, Clerk, 31 Horlbeck's Al.
Granger, Mary, Mrs., Seamstress, n. side Boundary St., Neck
Granniss, George B., res. 240 King St.
Granniss, White & Co., Retail Shoe Store, 240 King St., Wholesale Store, 270 King St.
Grant, Eleanor, cr. Middle & Minority Sts.
Grant, Eleanor, Seamstress, cr. Middle & Minority Sts., F.P.C.
Grauman, Henrich, Tailor, King St., near Radcliff St., Neck
Graves & Finley, Druggists, 50 Broad St.
Graves, Charles, Planter, cr. Wentworth & Meeting Sts.
Graves, Daniel D., Dr., cr. Wentworth & Meeting Sts.
Gray, Albert H., Painter, Church St.
Gray, Francis, Carpenter, Henrietta St., Neck
Gray, J. W., Commissioner in Equity, 6 Waring's Row, res. 220 E. Bay St.
Gray, John B., Teacher, 220 E. Bay St.
Gray, R. A., Mrs., Henrietta St., Neck
Gray, Thomas, Painter, 28 Coming St.
Gray, William H., Printer, 4 Green St.
Gready, A. P., Fancy Wood Ware Store, 182 King St.
Green, J. F., Merchant, Chisholm's N. Whf.
Green, James F., Factor, res. Charlotte St., Mazyckborough, Neck
Green, T. P., Druggist, 187 E. Bay St., res. Alexander St, Mazyckborough
Greenhill, Elizabeth, Miss, 2 Greenhill St.
Greenland, Eliza, Widow, 64 Tradd St.
Greer, John M., Bookseller & Stationer, 161 King St.
Gregorie, J. Ladson, 2nd Lt., Guard at Citadel, Neck
Gregory, Aberdeen, Cooper, King St., near Warren St., Neck, F.P.C.
Gregory, O. H., cr. Meeting St. & Lightwood's Al.
Gregory, Richard, Carpenter, Meeting St., Neck, F.P.C.
Gregory, Titus, Cooper, Boundary St., near Meeting St., Neck, F.P.C.
Greig, Alexander, Grocer, 264 E. Bay St.
Greneker, Mary, Dry Goods Store, 225 King St.
Grierson, J. C., Custom House, res. Anson St., near Motte St.

Grierson, John, Custom House, cr. Anson & Motte Sts.
Grimball, J. R., Planter, 2 S. Bay St.
Grimball, P. C., Planter, 13 Rutledge St.
Grimke, Henry, Attorney, 72 Broad St., res. 297 E. Bay St.
Grimke, John, Dr., 54 St. Philip St.
Grimke, Mary, Widow, 297 E. Bay St.
Grimke, Thomas S., Mrs., Widow, 38 S. Bay St.
Groning, L., Mrs., Widow, e. side Coming St., near Warren St., Neck
Gros, J. F., Cabinet Maker, 191 Meeting St.
Gros, John, Clerk, Railroad, 191 Meeting St.
Groustine, J., Professor of Music, cr. Beaufain & St. Philip Sts.
Gruber, John, Bricklayer, Reid St., Hampstead, Neck
Gue, V. A., Jeweller, 80 Market St.
Guenveur, J. M., Teacher of French, 62 Broad St.
Guerard, Elizabeth, Mrs., Coming St., above Boundary St., Neck
Guerard, John, Planter, cr. Pitt & Bull Sts.
Guerin, John A., 155 E. Bay St.
Guerry, Grandison, Clerk, 18 Wentworth St.
Guerry, P. C., Clerk, 142 King St.
Guilbert, E., Professor of Music, 1 Wall St.
Guillaman, Peter, Farmer, King St., op. Columbus St., Neck
Guinness, Mary, w. end New St.
Guistetti, M., Military Ornament Maker, 234 King St.
Gullatt, E., 99 Market St.
Gullatt, Helen, 1 Archdale St.
Gurgerett, Marie, Widow, 5 Wentworth St.
Guy & Mathews, Commission Merchants, 184 E. Bay St.
Guy, Joseph, Carpenter, n. side Boundary St., Neck
Guy, Joseph, Saddler, w. side Meeting St., near Lines, Neck
Guynemer, Gustavus, King St., near Bridge St., Neck
Hacker, George, Carpenter, 3 Coming St.
Hagan, John, 191 E. Bay St.
Hagan, Rosanna, Widow, 8 Clifford St.
Hagood, J. W., Repairer of Musical Instruments, 205 King St.
Hague, Joseph C., Capt., 26 Smith St.
Hahnbaum, Elizabeth, Mrs., 226 Meeting St.
Haig, David, Cooper, 3 Bull St.
Haig, Mary, Widow, 204 Meeting St.
Hall, C., Mrs., Church St.
Hall, Daniel, Mrs., Widow, Court House Sq.
Hall, J., Fancy Dry Goods Store, 181 King St.
Hall, William, Dr., e. side Hampstead, Neck
Halliday, Eleanor, Widow, 42 Church St.
Halsey, E. L., Capt., Washington St., Mazyckborough, Neck
Halsted, J. S., Merchant, 275 King St.
Hamill, Thomas, Wheelwright, 146 Church St.
Hamilton, Alexander, Coach Trimmer, 103 Boundary St.
Hamilton, C. S., Merchant, 306 King St.
Hamilton, E., Young Ladies Seminary, 78 Meeting St.
Hamilton, James, Capt., Meeting St., near Tivoli Garden, Neck

Hamilton, James, Hon., State Senator, Church & Fort Sts.
Hamilton, John, Ship Carpenter, Hard Al.
Hammett, M. E., Mrs., w. side Columbus St., Neck
Hammett, Ripley, Wharfinger, 12 Pinckney St.
Hammond, Ogden, Planter, 12 S. Bay St.
Hamye, C. H., Marion Coffee House, 171 E. Bay St.
Hanahan, John C., w. end New St.
Hanahan, R. S. H., Planter, 19 Mazyck St.
Hanckel, C., Rev., 115 Boundary St.
Happoldt, Albert, Butcher, s. side Cannon St., Neck
Happoldt, C. D., Butcher, s. side Cannon St., Neck
Happoldt, C. L., Coach Trimmer, 21 Beaufain St.
Happoldt, J. M., Gunsmith, 117 Meeting St., 24
  Horlbeck's Al.
Happoldt, Paul, Bricklayer, e. side St. Philip St., near
  Lines, Neck
Harall Wright & Co., Saddlery Ware House, 295 King St.
Harbers, Claus, Grocer, cr. Pinckney St. & Maiden Ln.
Harby, H. J., Blacksmith, Church St., near St. Philip
  Church, res. 255 E. Bay St.
Harby, Rebecca, Widow, 255 E. Bay St.
Hard, B. F., 54 Society St.
Haris, John, Grocer, cr. King St. & Lines, Neck
Harleston, Sommers, Dr., e. end Radcliffborough, Neck
Harper, J. F., Wharfinger, 1 Vendue Range, res. 77 Tradd
  St.
Harper, James, Baker, s.e. cr. King & Tradd Sts.
Harper, W. W., 24 Horlbeck's Al.
Harrall, William, res. 7 Liberty St.
Harris, Abraham, 203 E. Bay St.
Harris, G. W., Dry Goods Store, 343 King St.
Harris, Isaac, Fruit Store, 41 Market St.
Harris, Jacob, Clothing store, 203 E. Bay St.
Harris, Rebecca, Fruit Store, 122 King St.
Harris, T. M., Boarding House, 8 Queen St.
Harris, Zachariah, Clerk, 203 E. Bay St.
Harrison, D. W., Book Depository, Chalmers St.
Harrison, J., Boot & Shoe Maker, 35 Beaufain St., F.P.C.
Harrison, John, 30 Queen St.
Hart, Daniel, Mrs., Widow, 213 Meeting St.
Hart, N. & Son, Hardware & Cutlery Store, 206 King St.
Hart, Richard, Wharfinger, w. side St. Philip St., near
  Boundary St., Neck
Hart S. N., 206 King St.
Hart, S., Sr., Auctioneers, n.w. cr. E. Bay St. & Vendue
  Range
Harth, David, 235 E. Bay St.
Hartman, Justus, Farmer, Meeting St. Road, Neck
Harvey, Edward, Dyer & Scourer, 82 Queen St.
Harvey, Edward T., E. Bay St., near Hasell St.
Harvey, M. A., 16 West St.
Harwood, E. & Co., Fancy Dry Goods Store, 261 King St.
Hasell, Andrew, Mrs., Widow, 48 Meeting St.
Haskett, Jane, 97 Queen St.
Haslett, J., Presidet, Fire & Marine Insurance Co., 59
  Church St.
Hasloop, Frederick, Grocer, 233 E. Bay St.
Hass, J., Boarding House, w. side King St., Neck
Hatch, Evelina, Milliner, 355 King St.
Hatch, Kimball & Co., Wholesale Shoe Store, 321 King St.

Hatch, Mary, Widow, 27 Pinckney St.
Hatcher, Thomas, 133 Church St.
Hattier, Achille, Confectioner, 89 Boundary St.
Hattier, W. H., Fruit Store, 73 Market St.
Hauk, J. H., Accountant, 59 Anson St.
Hauschildt, Peter, Tavern, n.e. cr. St. Philip & Warren
  Sts., Neck
Haviland, D. G. & Co., Druggists, 304 King St.
Hawie, Sarah, 43 State St.
Hayden, Jane, Mrs., Widow, America St., Hampstead,
  Neck
Hayden, Joseph, 67 King St.
Hayden, N., Merchant, res. 7 Liberty St.
Hayden, T. A., Printer, 44 Queen St.
Hayes, James, Rev., n.e. cr. Broad & Friend Sts.
Hayes, Richard H., Painter, 10 Tradd St.
Hayford, Ann, Dry Goods Store, 48 Anson St.
Hayne, Arthur P., Col., 14 Legare St.
Hayne, Elizabeth, Mrs., Widow, 27 Meeting St.
Hayne, Robert Y., Hon., 24 King St.
Hayne, William A., Bank of State of S. C., cr. St. Philip
  & Vanderhorst Sts., Neck
Hayne, William E., State Treasurer, 7 Church St.
Haynes, B., Tailor, n. Boundary St., Neck, F.P.C.
Hazelhurst, George A., Planter, 232 Meeting St.
Hearkley, William, Mariner, E. Bay St., next to cr. Hasell
  St.
Heath, Thomas H., 10 Boundary St.
Hedderly, James, Carpenter, 36 Montague St.
Hedderly, William, Grocer, 38 Montague St.
Hedley, John L., Wharfinger, n. side Boundary St., Neck
Heilbron, James, Broker & Auctioneer, 5 Broad St., res.
  76 Church St.
Heimsath, Frederick, Grocer, n. cr. Church & Water Sts.
Helfrid, John, State Constable, 74 State St.
Henahan, Betty, Pastry Cook, 16 Beaufain St., F.P.C.
Hencken, D., Grocer, cr. Wall & Minority Sts.
Hencken, Henry, Grocer, cr. Archdale & Beaufain Sts.
Henderson, Samuel, Merchant, King St., near Spring St.,
  Neck
Hendricks, Joseph, 135 E. Bay St.
Henry, Betsy, Shop Keeper, 40 Anson St., F.P.C.
Henry, George, Factor, res. Anson St., op. Laurens St.
Henry, Joel, Cabinet Maker, 28 Wentworth St.
Henry, S. W., Cabinet Maker, 105, res. 94 Meeting St.
Herbert, Michael, Boarding House, 51 State St.
Herckenrath & Lowndes, Merchants, 8 Hamilton & Co.
  Whf.
Heriot, Benjamin D., Factor, res. w. end Beaufain St.
Heriot, John R., Engineer, res. 21 Meeting St.
Heriot, R., Notary Public, 80 E. Bay St., res. cr. Anson &
  Guignard Sts.
Herron, John, Clerk, 99 St. Philip St.
Herron, Sarah, Widow, 83 Boundary St.
Hertz, H. M., Factor, w. end Beaufain St., res. King St.,
  near Hudson St.
Hertz, Isaac E., Accountant, 97 King St.
Hertz, Jacob, Dry Goods Store, 97 King St.
Hervey, George, Merchant, 48 E. Bay St., res. 81 Church
  St.

44

Hery, -----, Madame, Seminary, cr. Boundary &
Washington Sts.
Heyns, James, 11 Price's Al.
Heyward, Alice, Mrs., 117 Boundary St.
Heyward, Arthur, Planter, Charlotte St., Neck
Heyward, Charles, Planter, Chapel St., Wraggborough,
Neck
Heyward, Nathaniel, Planter, cr. E. Bay & Society Sts.
Hichborn, William C., Merchant, 128 E. Bay St., res. 40
Tradd St.
Higbam & Fife, Merchants, 75 E. Bay St.
Hilgen, Frederick, Grocer, 63 Anson St.
Hill, C. J., Rev., Henrietta St., Neck
Hill, F. C., Painter, 7 Clifford St.
Hill, John, Commission Merchants, 8 Tradd St.
Hill, Mary, Fancy Dry Goods Store, cr. King & Clifford
Sts.
Hillard & Thomas, Grocery Stores, 5 & 7 Vendue Range
Hillard, Oliver B., Grocer, res. 126 King St.
Hillard, William H., 23 Pinckney St.
Hillman, Ann, Boarding House, 69 E. Bay St.
Hilson, John, Grocer, e. side Meeting St., near Mary St.,
Neck
Hines, John H., Grocer, Lucas St., Cannonborough, Neck
Hines, Joseph A., Painter, n. side Boundary St., Neck
Hinson, Thomas, Carpenter, 10 Archdale St.
Hippias, P., Mrs., Smith's Whf., Neck
Hislop, Hannah, Mrs., Widow, 25 Laurens St.
Hobson, A., Boot & Shoe Maker, 7 Queen St.
Hodgson, H., Grocer, cr. Anson & Hasell Sts.
Hoefer, John G., Tailor, Elliot St., near Church St.
Hoff, Ann, Mrs., Widow, 15 George St.
Hoff, John C., 10 Back St.
Hoff, Philip, Bookseller & Stationer, 10 Broad St.
Hogarth, Henry, Cooper, Dewees' Whf., res. 24 Wall St.
Holbrook, J. E., M. D., 1 State St., res. 21 Legare St.
Holbrook, Moses, M. D., 64 Queen St.
Holcombe, John C., res. e. side Pinckney St.,
Cannonborough, Neck
Holcombe, Peck & Co., Merchants, Fraser & Laffan's Whf.
Holland, John, Dr., 11 Broad St.
Holmes & Rowland, Factors, Vanderhorst's Whf. & S. Bay
St.
Holmes, Ann, Mrs., Widow, 128 Tradd St.
Holmes, C. R., w. end Tradd St.
Holmes, Henry, 8 Mazyck St.
Holmes, I. E., Attorney, res. Battery, E. Bay St.
Holmes, J. G., Attorney, res. Battery, E. Bay St.
Holmes, J., Mrs., Widow, 104 Tradd St.
Holmes, John B., Mrs., Widow, Battery, E. Bay St.
Holmes, John L., Grain Merchant, 73 E. Bay St., res. 8 S.
Bay St.
Holmes, Sandiford, Church St., near the Battery
Holmes, W. A., M. D., res. Battery, E. Bay St.
Holmes, William, Butcher, w. side Radcliffborough, Neck
Holmes, William H., 113 Boundary St.
Holoway, Charles, Carpenter, Hanover St., Hampstead,
Neck, F.P.C.
Holoway, Richard, Carpenter, 33 Beaufain St., F.P.C.
Holt, Charles, Painter, 33 Wall St.

Holton, Margaret, Pastry Cook, res. 16 Cumberland St.,
F.P.C.
Holton, Thomas, Tailor, res. 16 Cumberland St., F.P.C.
Holwell, T. W., Accountant, 86 Church St.
Holwell, Thomas, Capt., Baptist Town
Honour, John H., 28 Archdale St.
Honour, Thomas, 17 Beaufain St.
Hopkins, C., John St., Neck
Hopkins, J. A., Cooper, 82 E. Bay St., res. 50 Meeting St.
Hopkins, J. M., 15 Wall St.
Hories, B., Grocer, cr. Anson & Ellery Sts.
Horlbeck, Daniel, Attorney, Hunt's Range, res. 54
Beaufain St.
Horlbeck, Edward, Bricklayer, 23 Horlbeck's Al.
Horlbeck, Elias, M. D., 184 King St.
Horlbeck, Henry, Bricklayer, 23 Horlbeck's Al.
Horlbeck, Henry, Jr., Bricklayer, 23 Horlbeck's Al.
Horlbeck, John, Bricklayer, cr. Meeting & Boundary Sts.
Horry, Mary S., Mrs., n.w. cr. Meeting & Tradd Sts.
Horry, Thomas, n.w. cr. Meeting & Tradd Sts.
Horsey, Samuel, Printer, res. cr. Anson & Society Sts.
Horsey, T. J., Teller, Planters & Mechanics Bank, res.
cr. Anson & Society Sts.
Hort, Elias B., Millwright, E. Bay St., near Hasell St.,
res. 1 Hasell St.
Horton, Eliza, Mrs., Widow, 14 Wall St.
Horton, James, Planter, n.e. side Hampstead, Neck
Horton, -----, Mrs., Widow, 14 Wall St.
Hoskin & Wood, Commission Merchants, 39 E. Bay St.
Houston, James, Tailor, 36 Coming St.
Houston, P., Surgeon Dentist, cr. King & Wentworth Sts.
Houston, William H., Carpenter, Charlotte St.,
Mazyckborough, Neck
Howard, A. G., M. D., n. cr. Church & Elliott Sts.
Howard, Alexander, Custom House, res. 109 E. Bay St.
Howard, -----, Mrs., 9 Tradd St., near Bedon's Al.
Howard, Richard, Cooper, Dewees' Whf.
Howard, Richard, Mrs., Widow, Washington St.,
Mazyckborough, Neck
Howard, Robert, 3 Pinckney St.
Howard, Robert, Lumber Dealer, Williams Whf., res. 80
Anson. St., F.P.C.
Howe, Philip, 5 King St.
Howe, Silas, Clerk, 209 King St., res. St Michael's Al.
Howell, Sidney, Merchant, res. 5 Liberty St.
Howland, B. J., Merchant, res. 27 Laurens St.
Howland, Ward & Taft, Merchants, 151 & 153 E. Bay St.
Howland, William, Dry Goods Store, 208 King St.
Howley, Charles, Clerk, s.w. cr. Queen & State Sts.
Huard, S., Druggist & Apothecary, 34 Broad St.
Hubert, C. N., Accountant, 75 E. Bay St.
Hubert, John, 16 State St.
Hubert, John, Carpenter, cr. E. Bay & Pinckney Sts.
Huchet, Charles, 38 Queen St.
Huchet, Theodore, Clerk, 38 Queen St.
Hudoff, Henry, Grocer, 141 King St.
Hudson, J. M., Dry Goods Store, 351 King St.
Huger, Alfred, Post Master, 114 Broad St.
Huger, Benjamin, Dr., 110 Broad St.
Huger, Benjamin T., Tailor, 103 King St., F.P.C.

45

Huger, Charlotte, Miss, 23 St. Philip St.
Huger, D. E., Hon., 28 Meeting St.
Huger, D. E., Jr., 28 Meeting St.
Huger, Daniel, 39 Coming St.
Huger, John, Planter, 3 Meeting St.
Huger, Mary, Mrs., Widow, 36 Bull St.
Hughes, Edward, 88 Tradd St.
Hughes, P. A., Carpenter, 60 George St.
Hughes, Thomas, Furniture Store, cr. Anson & Wentworth Sts.
Hughes, William L., Accountant, 88 Tradd St.
Hull, Townsend & Knevals, Clothing Store, 263 King St.
Hume, Alexander, Dr., King St., near Hudson St., Neck
Hume, John, Planter, 137 Wentworth St.
Hume, Robert, Planter, Lynch St., near Wentworth St.
Hume, William, Dr., w. side Pinckney St., Cannonborough, Neck
Humphreys, John, Master, Poor House, Mazyck St.
Humphries, Joseph, Tailor, 112 Queen St., F.P.C.
Hunt, B. F., Attorney, Hunt's Range
Hunter, John, cr. Pitt & Wentworth Sts.
Hunter, Margaret, 8 West St.
Hurkamp, John, Grocer, 95 Broad St.
Hurst, C. W., Blacksmith, e. end Hasell St.
Hurst, Charles, Inspector of Customs, 6 Stoll's Al.
Hurst, Jefferson, Carpenter, 39 George St.
Husman, H., Grocer, cr. Meeting & Water Sts.
Husser, Elizabeth, Widow, Boundary St., near Wall St.
Hussey, B. B., Bookseller & Stationer, 287 King St.
Hussey, B., Mrs., 9 Stoll's Al.
Hussey, Bryan, Engineer, 9 Stoll's Al.
Hutchinson, Anna, Mrs., 22 S. Bay St.
Hyam, Daniel, Store Keeper, 47 State St.
Hyams, Henry, Tailor, 10 Liberty St.
Hyams, Moses D., Grocer, 17 S. Bay St.
Hyams, Solomon, 194 King St.
Hyatt, Edmund & Co., Wholesale Dry Goods Store, 317 & 319 King St.
Hyatt, Edmund, res. 41 George St.
Hyatt, Nathaniel, res. 41 George St.
Hyde, Harris & Roosevelt, Wholesale Hardware Merchants, 289 King St.
Hyer, John H., Carpenter, Duncan St., Radcliffborough, Neck
Hyndman T. A., Wheelwright, Gadsden's Whf., res. Boundary St.
Inglesby, J. S., M. D., Church St., near Tradd St., Res, 45 Tradd St.
Inglesby, M. E., Mrs., Widow, 3 Orange St.
Inglesby, W. H., Attorney, 4 St. Michael's Al., res. 11 New St.
Inglesby, William, 45 Tradd St.
Inglis, Thomas, Hair Dresser, 81 Meeting St., F.P.C.
Ingraham, George H., Factor, Fraser & Laffan's Whf., res. 26 Laurens St.
Ingraham, Lousia, Mrs., Widow, 19 King St.
Ingraham, W. P., Planter, 1 Smith St.
Innis, John, Coach Trimmer, 119 Meeting St.
Irvine, Moses, Shoe Maker, 4 Logan St., F.P.C.
Irving, John B., Sheriff, Charleston District, res. w. end

Wentworth St.
Izard, Henry, Mrs., Widow, 25 Legare St.
Izard, Ralph, Mrs., Widow, 223 E. Bay St.
Jackson & Capers, Wholesale Dry Goods Store, 298 King St.
Jackson, Ann, Widow, 43 Coming St.
Jackson, George, 47 Society St.
Jackson, George, Tin Plate Worker, 283 King St.
Jackson, Henry, Bricklayer, Meeting St., near Mary St., Neck, F.P.C.
Jackson, Joel, Boundary St., near Anson St.
Jackson, John A., res. 298 King St.
Jackson, Joseph, Miniature Painter, 259 King St.
Jackson, M. A., Millinery, 187 King St.
Jacob, Matthew, Eating House, 13 Market St.
Jacobs, Cecelia, Dry Goods Store, 235 E. Bay St.
Jacobs, Hyam, Radcliffborough, near Cannon St., Neck
Jacobs, Moses, Clothing Store, 254 King St.
Jacobs, Myer, Col., 6 Society St.
Jacoby, George, Grocer, 83 Church St.
Jager, Hans, Grocer, cr. Elliott St. & Bedon's Al.
James, J. H., Pilot, 22 Tradd St.
James, John, Engineer, 274 E. Bay St.
James, Robert, Printer, King St., op. Price's Al.
James, William H., Ship Carpenter, King St., op. Price's Al.
Jamieson, J. W., Printer, 153 King St.
Jamieson, J. W., Tailor, 134 Queen St.
Jaques, George, Clerk, 5 St. Philip St.
Jaques, Thomas, Miller, Lucas St., Cannonborough, Neck
Jarcke, Nicholas, Grocer, cr. Beaufain & Pitt Sts.
Javain, Peter, Farmer, end St. Philip St., Neck
Jeannerett, C., Accountant, 164 E. Bay St.
Jeannerett, J. M., 164 E. Bay St.
Jeannerett, John C., Wharfinger, 70 Church St.
Jeffords, J. H., Sail Maker, 9 Minority St
Jeffords, John, 11 Middle St.
Jenkins, Christopher, Mrs., Widow, 15 Smith St.
Jenkins, Robert S., Planter, w. side Cannon St., Neck
Jenkins, T. C., w. end Montague St.
Jennings, John, Plasterer, 244 E. Bay St.
Jervey, J. P., M. D., res. 37 Laurens St.
Jervey, James, U. S. District Clerk, res. 37 Laurens St.
Jervey, T. H., Surveyor, Custom House, res. 53 Church St.
Jervey, Waring & White, Brokers, 20 Broad St.
Jervey, William, Attorney, Court House, res. 37 Laurens St.
Jervis, E., Painter, 22 Guignard St.
Jesup, Z. R., Boot & Store, 168 King St.
Jewell, Daniel., Cabinet Maker, n.e. cr. Meeting & Hasell Sts.
Jewett & Hamilton, Wholesale Dry Goods Store, 306 King St.
Johnson & Smith, Button Warehouse, 329 King St.
Johnson, A. & C., Misses, 24 S. Bay St.
Johnson, Alex, Boot & Shoe Maker, 23 Broad St.
Johnson, Ann, Mrs., Widow, 32 Coming St.
Johnson, B., Umbrella Maker, 248 King St.
Johnson, Elizabeth, Dry Goods Store, 91 King St.

46

Johnson, Flora, Seamstress, 72 Anson St., F.P.C.
Johnson, George, Carpenter, 91 King St.
Johnson, H. & L., Boot & Shoe Store, 139 Meeting St.
Johnson, H., Midwife, cr. Elizabeth & Boundary Sts., Neck, F.P.C.
Johnson, Hollis, Boot & Shoe Store, 230 King St.
Johnson, I. A., Mrs., Widow, e. cr. St. Philip & Warren Sts., Neck
Johnson, James S., Grist Mill, Market St., near Anson St., res. 99 Wentworth St.
Johnson, John, Mrs., Widow of Col., 56 Tradd St.
Johnson, Joseph, President, U. S. Bank, Apothecary Store, 11 Broad St., res. 51 Church St.
Johnson, L., Boot & Shoe Store, 117 E. Bay St.
Johnson, M., Seamstress, 7 Middle St., F.P.C.
Johnson, M'Kewn, w. side Pinckney St., Cannonborough, Neck
Johnson, Nathaniel, Carpenter, w. end New St.
Johnson, Peter, Painter, e. end Laurens St.
Johnson, Sarah, Seamstress, 72 Anson St., F.P.C.
Johnson, W., Boarding House, n. cr. State St. & Lodge Al.
Johnson, Walter, M. D., 81 Broad St.
Johnston, D. Pinckney, 9 Green St.
Johnston, David C., M. D., 99 Queen St.
Johnston, J. M. C., Clerk, 26 Broad St., res. 10 College St.
Johnston, James, Tallow Chandler, Chapel St., Neck
Johnston, P., Farmers Hotel, 226 King St.
Johnston, T. W., Tavern, King St., btw. Radcliff & Morris Sts., Neck
Jonas, William, Millwright, 63 Boundary St., F.P.C.
Jones, Abraham, Steward, Marine Hospital, Back St.
Jones, C., Dry Goods Store, 75 Market St.
Jones, Edward, Dr., w. side St. Philip St., near Warren St., Neck
Jones, H. J., Notary Public, 1 Gibbes St.
Jones, Harriet, Tailoress, Meeting St., near Reid St., Neck, F.P.C.
Jones, Isaac, State Constable, Pitt St., near Boundary St., Neck
Jones, John S., Hardware Store, 145 E. Bay St.
Jones, Kitty, Seamstress, N. Boundary St., Neck, F.P.C.
Jones, Lyndey, Pastry Cook, 77 Anson St., F.P.C.
Jones, Mary, Mrs., Widow, 1 Guignard St.
Jones, Mary, Widow, 31 Pinckney St.
Jones, Rachel, Mrs., Widow, 172 King St.
Jones, Richard, Collector, 19 Bull St.
Jones, Sarah, Mrs., Widow, 45 Market St.
Jones, Thomas S., e. side St. Philip St., near Warren St., Neck
Jones, W. H., Accountant, 1 Gibbes St.
Jones, W., Merchant, 142 E. Bay St., res. 80 Meeting St.
Jones, William, Carpenter, 8 Price's Al.
Jones, William H., Watch Maker, 297 King St.
Jones, William, Mrs., Widow, s. cr. Meeting & Reid Sts., Neck
Jones, William T., 60 King St.
Jordan, Christopher, Coach Trimmer, 53 Meeting St.
Jordan, Edward, Sail Maker, Dewees Whf., res. 13 St

Philip St.
Joseph, J., Butcher, s. side Cannon St., Neck
Joseph, J. J., Butcher, Meeting St., near Wolfe St., Neck
Joseph, Joseph, 121 King St.
Joshua, Peter, Grocer, 22 Market St.
Joye & Cheney, Grocers, 117 Church St.
Joye, Lydia, Mrs., Widow, 2 Wentworth St.
Joye, P. S., Capt., 31 Tradd St.
Judge, James, Dry Goods Store, 201 King St.
June, C., Boarding House, 10 Bedon's Al.
Just, George, Wharf Builder, 34 Hasell St.
Kalb, George, cr., Meeting & Spring Sts., Neck
Kalb, John, Meeting St., e. side, near Railroad, Neck
Kanapaux, J. D., Tinner, 19 Queen St.
Kanapaux, Joseph, Shoe Maker, 164 Meeting St.
Kanapaux, William, Jeweller, 99 Market St.
Kane, Christopher, Grocer, 250 E. Bay St.
Kane, J. F., 142 Church St.
Karck, Charles T., Grocer, 67 Market St.
Kean, William, Boarding House, Elliott St.
Keast, John, Boot & Shoe Maker, 108 King St.
Keckeley, E. O., Apothecary, cr. King & Morris Sts., Neck
Keckley, George, Iron Monger, 20 Beaufain St.
Keenan, Elizabeth, 105 King St.
Keenan, William, Engraver, 136 King St., res. 105 King St.
Keith, M. I., Register of Mesne Conveyance, 209 Meeting St.
Keith, S., Hay Store, Napier's Range
Kellers, C., Grocer, cr. Cumberland & Church Sts.
Kelley, Edward, Mariner, 9 Maiden Ln.
Kelly, M. A., Milliner, 22 Horlbeck's Al.
Kelly, Michael, Broker & Auctioneer, 13 State St.
Kelly, William H., Furniture Room, 165 King St.
Kelly, William, Plasterer, 8 College St.
Kelsey, C. & G. H. & Halsted, Wholesale Dry Goods Store, 275 King St.
Kennedy, A. J., Watch Maker, 49 Broad St.
Kennedy, Ann, Mrs., 71 Market St.
Kennedy, Edward, Measurer, Custom House, res. 18 Mazyck St.
Kennedy, James, Carpenter, 134 Queen St.
Kennedy, L. H., Attorney, cr. Tradd & Logan Sts.
Kent, E., n. side Boundary St., Neck
Keogh, Eliza, Mrs., Milliner, 25 State St.
Ker, J. C., Merchant, res. 15 Society St.
Ker, John, 38 St. Philip St.
Ker, Thomas J., Factor, Edmondston's Whf.
Kerrison, C. & E. L., Dry Goods Store, 211 King St.
Kerrison, Charles, 9 Smith's Ln.
Kerrison, Elizabeth, Mrs., Widow, 9 Smith's Ln.
Kerrison, William, Capt., 9 Smith's Ln.
Kershaw, Charles, 30 Meeting St.
Kershaw, Newman, Factor, Roper's Whf., res. 7 Lamboll St.
Ketchum, Joel & Co., Dry Goods Store, 241 King St.
Kiddell, Arthur, 2 Philadelphia St.
Kiddell, Charles, 36 Broad St.
Kimball, Moses, Merchant, 321 King St.
King, John, 136 Church St.

47

King, John, Clerk, Railroad, res. 22 Archdale St.
King, John, Wheelwright, 117 Meeting St.
King, Mitchell, Attorney, 25 St. Michael's Al., res. cr. George & Meeting Sts.
King, William A., Blacksmith, Chalmers St., near Church St.
King, William S., Assistant Editor, Courier, res. 18 Broad St.
Kingman, Eliab, Clerk, Railroad, 16 Mazyck St.
Kingman, James, 100 Wentworth St.
Kingston, Rebecca, Mrs., Widow, 31 Wall St.
Kinloch & Mordecai, Grain Merchants, 20 Vendue Range
Kinloch, Frederick, Teacher of Music, 13 Montague St.
Kinloch, George, res. 94 Tradd St.
Kinsey, Ann, Dry Goods Store, 247 King St.
Kirkland, Mary, Widow, e. side St. Philip St., Neck
Kirkpatrick, John & Co., Factors, Edmondston's Whf.
Kirkwood, William, Ship Carpenter, cr. Middle & Minority Sts.
Kirst & Co., Chemists & Apothecaries, 137 Meeting St.
Kittleband, George P., Clerk, 6 Lynch St.
Kittleband, Susan, Widow, 6 Lynch St.
Klinck, John & Co., Grocery Stores, 26 St. Philip St. & s.w. cr. Coming & Boundary Sts.
Knee, Harman, Grocer, s. cr. Meeting & Henrietta Sts., Neck
Knepley, E., Mrs., Boarding House, Chalmers St., near Church St.
Knepley, Solomon, Blacksmith, 106 Meeting St.
Knight, William K., Lt., City Guard, 51 Beaufain St.
Knox, Elizabeth S., Mrs., Widow, cr. E. Bay & Hasell Sts.
Knox, J. F. & Son, Shipwrights, Knox's Whf.
Knox, Walter, Carpenter, 1 Green St.
Knust, Sarah, Mrs., Widow, 17 Coming St.
Kohlman, J. H., Grocer, 73 Tradd St.
Kohne, Frederick, Mrs., Widow, extreme end Broad St.
Korniskey, J. S., Shop Keeper, 16 Tradd St.
Kotmeyer, E. H., Grocer, w. side King St., near Lines, Neck
Kramer, Frederick, Carpenter, s. side Radcliff St., Neck
Kugely, Martha, Widow, 34 Mazyck St.
Kunhardt, William, Factor, Edmondston's Whf., res. 54 George St.
Kyall, Peter, Mariner, 36 Wall St.
L'Engle, -----, Lt., U. S. A., cr. Anson & Guignard Sts.
Labat, Catherine, Widow, cr. Liberty & St. Philip Sts.
Labat, Isaac C., 22 Burns Ln.
Labatt, Mary, Seamstress, 56 Society St., F.P.C.
Labaussay, Mary, Widow, 95 Market St.
Laborde, Francis, E. Bay St., near Hasell St.
Labruce, Joseph, Mrs., Widow, e. side Hampstead, Neck
Lacassagne, Edouard, Hair Dresser, 154 King St.
Lachicotte, M., Widow, 17 Guignard St.
Lacoste, C. G. A., Fancy Store, 149 King St.
Lacoste, E., Radcliff St., near King St., Neck
Ladeveze, V., Mrs., Mantuamaker, 185 King St.
Ladeveze, Victor, 185 King St.
Ladson, J. H., Factor, Hamilton & Co. Whf., res. 8 Meeting St.
Lafar, Catharine, Widow, 2 Clifford St.

Lafar, David B., Cooper, 18 Vendue Range, res. 60 Queen St.
Lafar, John J., Assistant Steward, Orphan House, Neck
Laffan, Edmund, Factor, Fraser's Whf., res. 42 Bull St.
Laffiteau, S., Bookkeeper, cr. Church & Elliott Sts.
Lafon, John, 180 E. Bay St.
Lafourcade, J. B., 180 E. Bay St.
Lafrentz, Ernest, Grocer, cr. Coming & Bull Sts.
Lagley, William, 57 Queen St.
Laidler, William, Printer, res. 18 Broad St.
Lamb, James, Merchant, 51 E. Bay St., res. 61 Tradd St.
Lambers, Catharine, Widow, 97 Boundary St.
Lambert, William C., Mattress Store, 59 Queen St.
Lambkin, James, Stage Agent, Miott's Hotel, King St.
Lamotte, James, Blacksmith
Lance & Berney, Brokers & Auctioneers, 4 State St.
Lance, Francis, res. 13 Legare St.
Lance, M. H., Rev., Charlotte St., Mazyckborough, Neck
Lance, William, Attorney, 26 St. Michael's Al., res. 102 Broad St.
Landreth, Robert, Seed Store, 262 King St.
Lane, Samuel, Tailor, 48 Broad St.
Langlois, A., John St., Neck
Langlois, M. Z., Miss, Academy, Montague St., near Pitt St.
Langlois, Maria, Mrs., Academy, Montague St., near Pitt St.
Lankenau, J. H., Grocer, w. side Pinckney St., Cannonborough, Neck
Lanneau, Bazil, Merchant, 174 E. Bay St., res. 49 Tradd St.
Lanneau, C. H., Tanner, w. end Beaufain St., res. 1 Pitt St.
Lanneau, Fleetwood, Clerk, res. Planters & Mechanics Bank Yard
Lanneau, Peter, Accountant, 91 King St.
Lansdale, John S., 16 St. Philip St.
Lapenne, J. J., e. side King St., near Mary St., Neck
Laporte, Rene, Baker, 197 E. Bay St.
Laprince, A., Fancy Store, 207 King St.
Laroche, John G., 115 Queen St.
Laroche, Mary, Lucas St., Cannonborough, Neck
Larouselliere, Louis, 1 Beaufain St.
Lassen, Hans, Grocer, 19 Market St.
Latham, Daniel, Distillery, 2 Hasell St.
LaTourrette, James, Cap & Stock Manufacturery, 305 King St.
Latts, M., Mrs., Wife of Dr., Mary St., Neck
Laumonnier, Julia, Ladies' Seminary, 30 Horlbeck's Al.
Laurens, Edward R., Planter, e. side Pinckney St., Cannonborough, Neck
Laurens, Henry, Mrs., Widow, cr. E. Bay & Laurens Sts.
Laval, Jacint, 19 Pinckney St.
Laval, William, Comptroller General, res. 9 Beaufain St.
Lawton, J. & C., Merchants, 8 E. Bay St.
Lawton, R. B., Franklin Hotel, 25 Queen St.
Lawton, W. M., Factor, 3 Roper's Whf., res. 26 S. Bay St.
Lazarus, B. D., Merchant, 11 Champney St., res. 93 Tradd St.
Lazarus, Marks, res. 93 Tradd St.

Lazarus, Michael, Merchant, res. 103 Broad St.
Lea, John, Pilot, 6 Water St.
Lea, William P., Pilot, 6 Water St.
Leach, J., Grocery, 232 King St.
Leake, Joanna, Boarding House, 55 E. Bay St.
Leaumont, Margaret, Widow, 8 Minority St.
Leavitt, Horatio, 8 Church St.
Lebby, Thomas F., Printer, 26 Tradd St.
Lebby, -----, Widow, 26 Tradd St.
Lebleux, A., Dyer, 88 King St.
LeCaron, Charles, Merchant, Edmondston's Whf., res. 38 Meeting St.
Lecat, F., Professor of Music, 77 Meeting St.
Lee, Edward, Hair Dresser, 55 Broad St., F.P.C.
Lee, Elsy, Pastry Cook, w. side Hudson St., Neck, F.P.C.
Lee, Elvira, Pastry Cook, 72 Tradd St., F.P.C.
Lee, Francis J., Custom House, res. 20 Hasell St.
Lee, J. M'Pherson, Attorney, w. end Vanderhorst St., Neck
Lee, James, Mariner, 3 Stoll's Al.
Lee, James T., Teacher, res. Pitt St., near Boundary St.
Lee, John, Tailor, 72 Tradd St., F.P.C.
Lee, Lawrence, Dr., Pitt St., near Boundary St.
Lee, Stephen, 128 Wentworth St.
Lee, Thomas, Hon., U. S. District Judge, Pitt St., near Boundary St.
Lee, William, Alexander St., Mazyckborough, Neck
Leefe, Benjamin, Mrs., Widow, n. side Boundary St., Neck
Lefebre, Henry, Merchant, Edmondston's Whf.
Legare, Daniel, Dr., 3 Guignard St.
Legare, Hugh S., Mrs., 30 Bull St.
Legare, J. C. W., Planter, w. end Tradd St.
Legare, James, Factor, w. end Vanderhorst St., Neck
Legare, James, Mrs., Widow, 77 King St.
Legare, John B., Attorney, res. 17 Hasell St.
Legare, John D., 53 Anson St.
Legare, Mary, Mrs., Widow, 71 Boundary St.
Legare, O'Hear & Legare, Factors, Chisolm's N. Whf.
Legare, Thomas, Planter, 40 S. Bay St.
Legare, W. B., 4 Archdale St.
Lege, J. M., Dancing Master, 62 Queen St.
Legg, William, Tailor, 27 Coming St., F.P.C.
Legrix, J. P., Clerk, 157 E. Bay St.
Lehre, Thomas, Ordinary, res. 54 King St.
Leland, Dexter, Teacher, Philadelphia St., res. Court House Sq.
Leland, J. & Brothers, Merchants, Napier's Range, near Magwood's Whf.
Leman, James, Clerk, Nassau St., Neck
Lemassena, A., Sash & Blind Maker, 23 & 25 Tradd St.
LeMor, M., Boundary St.
Leparoux, F., Clerk, 157 E. Bay St.
Lequeux, Sims, Planter, Thomas St., Cannonborough, Neck
Lesene, Henry D., Attorney, 13 Archdale St.
Lesesne, Ann, Widow, 37 Society St.
Lesesne, Daniel, Clerk, 13 Archdale St.
Lesesne, William J., Teacher, 37 Society St.
Lesseigneur, V., Dr., 52 Church St.

Letchmere, Henry, 14 Church St.
Letiner, Edward F., Dr., 137 Meeting St.
Levan, Jacob, Carpenter, 147 Meeting St.
Levin, Emanuel, Clerk, 169 E. Bay St.
Levy, Aaron, Church St., near Market St.
Levy, Barnard, Printer, 97 King St.
Levy, David C., Merchant, cr. E. Bay St. & Williams Whf.
Levy, Elias, Gauger, 26 Vendue Range, res. 78 Broad St.
Levy, Elias, Jr., Accountant, King St., above Radcliffborough, Neck
Levy, Emanuel, Clerk, w. end Beaufain St.
Levy, J. A., Printer, cr. West & Mazyck St.
Levy, J. C., Merchant, 11 Champney St., res. 279 E. Bay St.
Levy, L., Clothing & Hat Stores, 205 E. Bay & 5 Market Sts.
Levy, Lyon, Mrs., Widow, 108 Broad St.
Levy, Lyon, Shoe Maker, 9 Pitt St.
Levy, Moses C., w. side Market St., near King St.
Levy, Moses, State Constable, Chalmers St., near Church St.
Levy, R., cr. West & Mazyck Sts.
Lewis & Robertson, Factors, 70 E. Bay St.
Lewis, Henry P., Tivoli Garden, Meeting St., Neck
Lewis, Isaac, 36 Wentworth St.
Lewis, John, 12 Meeting St.
Lewis, John, Boot & Shoe Maker, 11 Liberty St., F.P.C.
Lewis, John, Tailor, Ann St., Mazyckborough, Neck, F.P.C.
Lewis, Mary, Seamstress, Henrietta St., Neck, F.P.C.
Lieure, Peter, Clothing Store, 103 E. Bay St.
Limehouse, R. J., Attorney, 1 Court House Sq.
Limehouse, Robert, w. end Tradd St.
Lindergreen, Charles, Custom House
Lindershine, David, Ship Carpenter, n. side Boundary St., Neck
Lindsay & Haven, Merchants, 6 Hamilton & Co. Whf.
Lindsay, James, Livery Stables, Church St., op. Cumberland St.
Lindsay, William, Merchant, res. 173 E. Bay St.
Ling, Philip, Chair Maker, 82 Market St.
Ling, R., Mrs., Widow, 21 Bull St.
Lining, Charles, U. S. Bank, res. Friend St.
Lining, E. B., Planter, St. Philip St., near Vanderhorst St., Neck
Lining, Richard, 19 Legare St.
Lining, Thomas, Dr., Citadel, Neck
Linser, John L., Butcher, n. side Cannon St., Neck
Liston, Henry, Cooper, Amen St., near E. Bay St., F.P.C.
Litle, James, Saw Gin Man, 159 Meeting St., res. 30 Archdale St.
Livingston, Henry, Capt.,
Livingston, Philip, 3 Water St.
Livingston, R. Y., Accountant, 98 Anson St.
Lloyd, Joseph, Clerk, n. side Boundary St., Neck
Lloyd, Mary, Widow, 36 Bull St.
Lloyd, William, Broker & Auctioneer, 28 Broad St., res. 53 Tradd St.
Lloyd, William, Carpenter, 3 Magazine St.
Lloyd, William, Venetian Blind Maker, 84 Market St.

49

Locke, George B., Merchant, Dewees' Whf.
Lockwood, Joshua, Jr., Clerk, State Bank, 75 Broad St.
Lockwood, Joshua W., Engineer, 75 Broad St.
Lockwood, Stephen L., Accountant, 75 Broad St.
Lockwood, Thomas P., Seminary, s.w. cr. King & Boundary Sts.
Logan, C. M., 99 Broad St.
Logan, G. C., Millwright, e. end Hasell St.
Logan, George & T. M., Drs., Market St., near Archdale St.
Logan, George, America St., Mazyckborough, F.P.C., Neck
Logan, George C., Millwright, n.w. end Cannonborough, Neck
Logan, George, Dr., res. 21 Coming St.
Logan, George W., Attorney, 8 Waring's Row, res. 15 Lynch St.
Logan, N., Miss, cr. Archdale & Market Sts.
Logan, Thomas M., Dr., w. side Pinckney St., Cannonborough, Neck
Logan, William D., Ship Chandler, 198 E. Bay St., Res. cr. Minority & E. Bay Sts.
Logan, William, Librarian, Charleston Library Society, W. Side Pinckney St., Cannonborough, Neck
Lohman, D., Grocer, cr. St. Philip & Boundary Sts., Neck
Long, R., Mrs., Widow, 8 Wall St.
Lonsdale, Maria, 34 Coming St.
Lopez, David, Carpenter, Logan St., near Tradd St.
Lopez, John, Livery Stables, Chalmers St., near State St., F.P.C.
Lopez, P., Mrs., Widow, 1 Orange St.
Lord & Stocker, Merchants, 144 E. Bay St.
Lord, Archibald B., Porter, U. S. Bank, 2 State St.
Lord, Martha, Pastry Cook, Charlotte St., Neck, F.P.C.
Lord, Mary E., Widow, 69 Boundary St.
Lord, Richard, Teller, Bank of S. C., res. 10 Berresford St.
Lord, Samuel, Maiden Ln., near Hasell St.
Lovegreen, Andrew A., Dry Goods Store, 326 King St.
Lovell & Chapman, Grocers, s.w. cr. Church & Tradd Sts.
Lovell, Edward S., res. 5 Bull St.
Lovell, H. F., Mrs., Widow, 110 Tradd St.
Lovell, Lewis, 6 St. Philip St.
Lowden, John, Merchant, 70 E. Bay St., res. 54 Meeting St.
Lowe, R. C., Sail Maker, res. Gadsden's Whf.
Lowndes, Charles T., Merchant, 112 Broad St.
Lowndes, Edward T., Dr., 112 Broad St.
Lowndes, James, Sr., Planter, 14 Meeting St.
Lowndes, Rawlins, Planter, 112 Broad St.
Lowndes, Richard, U. S. A., 112 Broad St.
Lowndes, T. Pinckney, Planter, 116 Tradd St.
Lowndes, Thomas, Planter, 112 Broad St.
Lowndes, William, Mrs., Widow, 116 Tradd St.
Lowndes, William P., Planter, 112 Broad St.
Lowry, Catherine, Milliner, 113 Meeting St.
Lowther, Thomas, Dry Goods Store, 137 King St.
Lozier, John C., Grocer, 117 Queen St.

Lubkin, Luder, Grocer, cr. Anson & Boundary Sts.
Lucas, J., Jr., Merchant, Vanderhorst's Whf., res. w. end Cannonborough
Lucas, Jonathan, Jr., Lumber Mills, Lucas St., Cannonborough, Neck
Lucas, William, Planter, w. side Pinckney St., Cannonborough, Neck
Ludeke, Conrad, Butcher, e. Pinckney St., Cannonborough, Neck
Ludeke, Conrad, Grocer, cr. Market St. & Reaper's Al.
Lunquest, J. M., Goldsmith & Jeweller, 192 King St.
Lusher, J. O., Dr., n.e. cr. Church & Tradd Sts.
Lydakin, J., Widow, 5 Guignard St.
Lyles, William, Grocer, 78 Market St.
Lynah, James, Planter, 298 E. Bay St.
Lynch, Caroline, Milliner, 323 King St.
Lynch, F. C., Tailor, 323 King St.
Lynch, J. G., Printer, 26 Tradd St.
Lynch, Jane, Infant School, 106 Market St.
Lynch, Margaret, Mrs., Widow, Henrietta St., Neck
Lynes, J., Mrs., Warren St., near King St., Neck
Lyon, George, Jr., Watch Maker, 195 E. Bay St.
Lyon, George, Watch Maker, 143 E. Bay St.
Lyon, Oliver, Accountant, King St., near George St.
Lytle, John S., U. S. District Paymaster, 77 Broad St.
Macaulay, George, Planter, 94 Church St.
Macbeth, Catherine, Widow, res. 17 King St.
Macbeth, Charles, Attorney, res. 17 King St.
Macbeth, Hannah, Seamstress, 27 Meeting St., F.P.C.
Macbeth, James, Merchant, res. 44 Church St.
Macbeth, Robert, Clerk, 35 King St.
Mack, James, Clerk, Railroad, King St., near Mary St., Neck
Mackay, Alexander, Ship Joiner, King St., near Ann St., Neck
Mackey, John, Grocer, 33 S. Bay St.
Mackie, Mary, Mrs., Widow, cr. Church & Linguard Sts.
Madinger, Gottlieb, Clerk, 171 E. Bay St.
Maertons, F., Grocer, 206 Meeting St.
Magee, -----, Capt., 12 Church St.
Magness, E., Mrs., Widow, Church St., op. Amen St.
Magrath, A. G., Attorney, 45 Broad St., res. 197 Meeting St.
Magrath, J., Fraser & Co. Whf., res. 197 Meeting St.
Magwood, Charles A., Merchant, res. 13 Smith St.
Magwood, Simon, Col., cr. Smith & Bull Sts.
Main, A. R., Fancy Store, 243 King St.
Main, W. B., Ship Carpenter, 17 Wall St.
Mairs, Elizabeth, Mrs., Widow, 117 King St.
Mairs, Levy, 117 King St.
Makie, James, Seminary, 77 Broad St.
Malcolm, Elizabeth, Widow, St. Andrew's Hall., Broad St.
Mallery, Lewis, Boarding House, 36 Queen St.
Malone, T. W., Attorney, 72 Broad St., res. 226 King St.
Manigault, Ann H., Mrs., Widow, 16 Meeting St.
Manigault, C. D., Planter, w. side Pinckney St., Cannonborough, Neck
Manigault, Joseph, Planter, cr. Meeting & John Sts., Neck
Manigault, Peter, Attorney, cr. Meeting & John Sts., Neck
Manly, Basil, Rev., 26 King St.

Mann, John, Bricklayer, 39 Boundary St.
Mann, Rebecca, Mrs., 49 George St.
Manning, Joseph, Dr., cr. Society & E. Bay Sts.
Manson, George, Ship Carpenter, Gadsden's Whf.
Marchant, Sarah, Widow, w. end Cannonborough, Neck
Margart, J. H., King St. Road, Neck
Margrave, James, w. side Pinckney St., Cannonborough, Neck
Marienhoff, J. M., Grocer, 3 Elliott St.
Markey, John, Boarding House, 34 Tradd St.
Markley, B. A., Planter, w. end Radcliffborough, Neck
Markley, John, Coach Maker, 53 Broad St.
Markley, Thomas, s. side Cannon St., Neck
Marks, Joseph, Merchant, 10 Queen St.
Marley, Ellen, 33 Archdale St.
Marsh, James & Son, Shipwrights, Marsh's Whf., res. 222 E. Bay St.
Marsh, James, Ship Carpenter, Gadsden's Whf.
Marsh, William, Merchant, 1 Royce & Co. Whf., res. 116 Queen St.
Marshall, John, Factor, Gadsden's Whf., res. 13 Middle St.
Marshall, John T., Baker, 54 Tradd St.
Marshall, Mary, Widow, 99 Broad St.
Marshall, Thomas C., Wharfinger, 71 Tradd St.
Martignat, J., Cigar Store, 172 Meeting St.
Martin, C. W., Blacksmith, Meeting St., near Henrietta & America Sts., Neck
Martin, F., Boarding House, Elliot St.
Martin, J., Drayman, Henrietta St., Neck, F.P.C.
Martin, J. N., Bricklayer, 17 College St.
Martin, Jacob, Blacksmith, 50 Wentworth St., res. 13 Coming St.
Martin, Joe, Drayman, Zig Zag Al., F.P.C.
Martin, Joseph, 9 Market St.
Martin, L. V., Bricklayer, Coming St., Radcliffborough, Neck
Martin, Robert & Co., Factors, 3 Boyce & Co. Whf.
Martin, Robert, Factor, res. Charlotte St., Neck
Martin, Thomas, Attorney, 74 Broad St.
Martin, William, Rev., cr. Pitt & Boundary Sts., Neck
Mashburn, J. H., Custom House, 47 Anson St.
Mashburn, Nicholas, 47 Anson St.
Mason, George, 22 Lynch St.
Massot, H., Watchmaker, 11 Queen St.
Mathews, Bonneau & Co., Factors, Hamilton & Co. Whf.
Mathews, James, Factor, res. 52 Anson St.
Mathews, M. A., Mrs., Widow, 32 S. Bay St.
Mathews, Mary, Mrs., Widow, 52 Tradd St.
Mathews, P., Carpenter, 33 George St.
Mathews, Thomas, Mrs., Widow, 11 Church St.
Mathey, Charles, Watch Maker, 173 King St.
Mathiessen, C. F., Fancy Store, 175 King St.
Mathiessen, F. C., Accountant, 175 King St.
Mathiessen, William, 175 King St.
Matthews, David, Shoe Maker, Boundary St., near Meeting St., Neck
Matthews, H., Carter, Charlotte St., Neck, F.P.C.
Matthews, J. P., Merchant, res. cr. Clifford & Archdale Sts.
Matthews, John B., Tutor, 65 Boundary St., F.P.C.

Matthews, William, Planter, Charlotte St., Mazyckborough, Neck
Maxey, S. T., Bricklayer, cr. Washington & Boundary Sts., Neck
Maxey, Virgil, 5 Lynch St.
Maxton, John, Baker, 17 Tradd St.
Maxwell, Frances, Mrs., Widow, 18 Guignard St.
Maxwell, Harriet, Mrs., Widow, 89 Meeting St.
Maxwell, James, Carpenter, res. 119 King St., F.P.C.
May, John, Cabinet Maker, 68 Queen St.
May, Margaret, w. end Vanderhorst St., Neck
Maynard, Ann, Grocery, 194 Meeting St.
Mayrant, Charles, Radcliffborough, near Radcliff St., Neck
Mazyck, Alexander, 185 Meeting St.
Mazyck, Alexander, Attorney, res. 96 Wentworth St.
Mazyck, Catherine, 185 Meeting St.
Mazyck, Edward, res. 96 Wentworth St.
Mazyck, Gaillard & Mazyck, Factors, Chisolm's Whf.
Mazyck, Theodore, 185 Meeting St.
Mazyck, William, Factor, res. 96 Wentworth St.
Mazyck, William, Jr., Charlotte St., Mazyckborough, Neck
Meacher, Thomas, Grain Store, 202 E. Bay St., res. 40 Queen St.
Mead, Alfred, Grocer, Boyce & Co. Whf.
Meadows, Hanson, Pilot, 8 Stoll's Al.
Mealy, John, 17 St. Philip St.
Mechear, Francis, Carter, Wolf St., Hampstead, F.P.C., Neck
Mechie, Ellen, Pastry Cook, John St., Neck, F.P.C.
Medorne, George, 7 Wall St., F.P.C.
Meeker, Samuel, Carriage Repository, 190 Meeting St.
Meetze, Sarah, 123 Queen St.
Meislahn, Hans, Grocer, cr. Laurens & Middle Sts.
Melevear, Francis, Baker, Nassau St., Neck
Melton, W. A., Mariner, n. side Boundary St., Neck
Memminger, C. G., Attorney, 61 Meeting St., res. 138 Wentworth St.
Menard, P., Teacher, 21 Burns Ln.
Menlove, Edward, Merchant, 10 Fitzsimons' Whf., res. 16 Broad St.
Merritt, Jane, 11 Swinton's Ln.
Mey, J. H., Merchant, 2 Pinckney St.
Meyer, G., Butcher, e. side Radcliffborough, Neck
Meyer, J. H., Grocer, cr. Boundary & Coming Sts., & King St., near Reid St., Neck
Meyer, John, Back St.
Michel, Francis, Coroner, 90 E. Bay St., res. n.e. cr. Meeting & Hasell Sts.
Michel, John E., Goldsmith & Jeweller, 242 King St.
Michel, John, Quorum Unis, Broker & Auctioneer, 90 E. Bay St., res. St. Philip St., near Vanderhorst St.
Michel, Mary, Mrs., Widow, 4 Society St.
Michel, William, Dr., 184 King St.
Michell, F., Confectioner, 83 Market St.
Middleton, Arthur, Planter, 253 E. Bay St.
Middleton, Henry A., Planter, w. end Cannonborough, Neck
Middleton, Henry, Hon., Planter, extreme end Boundary St., Neck

Middleton, J. I., Planter, extreme end Boundary St.,Neck
Middleton, N. R., Planter, 117 Boundary St.
Middleton, Thomas, Planter, 9 Hamilton & Co. Whf., res. 10 Meeting St.
Mignot, R., Confectioner, 179 King St.
Miles, Edward, Capt., Lucas St., Cannonborough, Neck
Millar, A. E., Printer, 4 Broad St.
Millar, John C., Baker, 143 Meeting St.
Millar, R. S., Baker, 147 Church St.
Miller & Neyle, Merchants, Chisholm's Whf.
Miller & Spann, Factors, Edmonston's Whf.
Miller, Abraham, Porter, Bank of State of S. C., cr. Broad St. & Gadsden's Al.
Miller, C., Mrs., Widow, Mary St., Neck
Miller, Charles C., Clerk, Work House, Magazine St.
Miller, Charles E., Col., 52 Anson St.
Miller, Claudius, Clerk, 3 Beaufain St.
Miller, Jacob, Rope Maker, e. end Vanderhorst St., Neck
Miller, James A., City Marshal, 8 Short St.
Miller, John C., Factor, Mary St., Neck
Miller, John, Grocer, cr. E. Bay & Elliott Sts.
Miller, John M., Wharfinger, res. 56 Queen St.
Miller, John, Printer, 8 Short St.
Miller, Mathew, Jewelry & Fancy Store, 150 King St.
Miller, Ripley & Co., Wholesale Dry Goods, cr. King & Society Sts.
Miller, Robert, Merchant, res. 71 E. Bay St.
Miller, S. S., Printer, 5 Wall St.
Miller, William, Exchange Office, 28 Broad St., res. 11 College St.
Miller, William H., Clerk, 179 E. Bay St.
Miller, William H., Teacher, 15 Archdale St.
Milligan, William, Ironmonger, St. Philip St., near Cannon St., Neck
Milliken, Edward P., Clerk, 98 Church St.
Milliken, Thomas, Auctioneer, 17 Vendue Range, res. 98 Church St.
Milliken, William, Merchant, 136 E. Bay St.
Mills & Beach, Merchants, 26 Vendue Range
Mills, Gustavus, n.w. cr. Meeting & Queen Sts.
Mills, O. & S., Grain Merchants, Chisolm's Whf.
Mills, Otis, Merchant, n.w. cr. Meeting & Queen Sts.
Mills, Samuel S., 109 Meeting St.
Milne, Andrew, Planter, 14 Rutledge St.
Milnor, George H. & Co. Dry Goods Store, 324 King St.
Mintzing, Jacob F., 26 Friend St.
Miott, C. H., Merchant's Hotel, n.e. cr. King & Society Sts.
Miscally, D. W., Ord. Sergeant, City Guard, res. Marsh St.
Mishaw, John, Boot & Shoe Maker, 126 Meeting St., F.P.C.
Missroon, James, Navigation Store, 89 E. Bay St., res. 26 Marsh St.
Mitchell, Ann, Widow, 29 Beaufain St.
Mitchell, Betsy, Seamstress, Philadelphia St., F.P.C.
Mitchell, J. Y., 82 E. Bay St.
Mitchell, James D., 134 Wentworth St.
Mitchell, John A., Rev., 23 Queen St.
Mitchell, John W., Magistrate, 84 E. Bay St.

Mitchell, Margaret, Widow, 50 Meeting St.
Mitchell, Martha, Fancy Store, 183 King St.
Mitchell, Nelson, Attorney, 8 Waring's Row
Mitchell, Rebecca, Mrs., Widow, n.e. cr. Washington & Vernon Sts.
Mitchell, Sarah, Widow, 46 Coming St.
Mitchell, W. E., Pilot, 2 Lynch St.
Moderen, James, Boat Builder, 208 E. Bay St.
Moffett & Calder, Dry Goods Store, s. cr. King & Hasell Sts.
Moffett, Andrew, res. 24 Archdale St.
Moise, Aaron, Accountant, 10 Hasell St.
Moise, Abraham, Attorney, St. Michael's Al., res. 33 Laurens St.
Moise, Abraham, Jr., Clerk, 10 Hasell St.
Moise, C., Mrs., Widow, 8 Orange St.
Moise, Columbus, Clerk, 10 Hasell St.
Moise, Rebecca, Mrs., Widow, King St., above Radcliff St., Neck
Moise, Theodore S., Portrait Painter, 222 King St.
Moles, Margaret, Dry Goods Store, n. cr. King & Radcliff Sts., Neck
Monar, L., Widow, 12 Queen St.
Monefeldt, Maria H., Mrs., 150 King St.
Monefeldt, William S., Surgeon Dentist, 151 King St.
Monk, S. P., Teacher, S. C. Society School, res. 119 Broad St.
Monpoey, Honore, Factor, 40 Bull St.
Montague, Charles, 64 State St.
Montamat, L., Cigar Manufactory, 231 E. Bay St.
Montgomery, Andrew, Watch Maker, 193 King St
Montgomery, Cheeseborough & Co., Merchants, Hamilton's Whf.
Montisquieu, R., Tin Plate Worker, 189 E. Bay St.
Mood, E. M., Block & Pump Maker, 270 E. Bay St.
Mood, J. & P., Jewelers, 297 King St.
Mood, John, res. 37 George St.
Mood, William G., 145 King St.
Moodie, James G., St. Philip St., near Cannon St., Neck
Mooney, Ann, Dry Goods Store, King St., above Radcliff St., Neck
Moore, B. F., Millwright, Lynch St., near Water St.
Moore, Caroline, Mrs., Widow, 13 Wentworth St.
Moore, E. S., Mrs., Widow, Vanderhorst St., near Coming St., Neck
Moore, George A., Printer, res. Price's Al.
Moore, George H., Gunsmith, 65 Queen St.
Moore, J. L., Coach Maker, King St., op. Ann St., Neck
Moore, James, e. side Meeting St., Neck
Moore, Philip, w. end Montague St.
Moore, William B., Grain Store, King St., res. 4 Philadelphia St.
Moorhead, James, Grocer, 193 Meeting St.
Morand, John, Fisher, John St., Neck, F.P.C.
Morang, Mary, Widow, 52 King St.
Mordecai, Isaac, Dry Goods Store, 234 King St., res. 67 Beaufain St.
Mordecai, Joseph, res. 67 Beaufain St.
Mordecai, M. C., Auctioneer, 24 Vendue Range, res. 33 Meeting St.

Mordecai, Rhina, Mrs., Widow, 175 Church St.
Mordecai, Thomas W., Merchant, res. 23 S. Bay St.
Moreland, Andrew, Factor, 19 S. Bay St.
Morgan, Benjamin, Mariner, 14 Middle St.
Morgan, Eliza, 82 Wentworth St.
Morgan, J. B., Capt., Minority St., near E. Bay St.
Moriarty, Jane, Dry Goods Store, 213 King St.
Morison, Simon, Cabinet Maker, 87 Market St.
Morris, C. G., Merchant, 80 E. Bay St., res. cr. E. Bay &
  Wentworth Sts.
Morris, James, Merchant, 127 E. Bay St.
Morrison, J. D., Widow, 85 Market St.
Mortimer, S. H., Broker & Auctioneer, 6 State St.
Moses, Daniel, 24 Hasell St.
Moses, Isaiah, Planter, King St., btw. King & Hudson
  Sts., Neck
Moses, Israel, Dry Goods Store 194 King St., res. 22
  Beaufain St.
Moses, L. J., Auctioneer, res. n.w. cr. E. Bay St. &
  Vendue Range
Moses, M. L., 16 Swinton's Ln.
Moses, R. J., Dry Goods Store, 245 King St., res. 22
  Beaufain St.
Moses, Reuben, 278 King St.
Moses, Simon, Broker, 13 Magazine, res. 56 Beaufain St.
Moses, Solomon, City Marshal, 73 Wentworth St.
Mosimann, J., 21 Pinckney St.
Moss, Joseph & Co., Tailors & Drapers, 311 King St.
Motta, J. A., Confectioner, 121 King St.
Motte, D., Tinner, n. side Boundary St., Neck, F.P.C.
Motte, Frances, Widow, 40 Meeting St.
Motte, Francis T., 40 Meeting St.
Motte, J. Rhett, Dr., 9 State St.
Motte, Joseph, Shoe Maker, Charlotte St., Neck, F.P.C.
Moulan, Jane, Store Keeper, e. side King St., near Ann
  St., Neck
Moult, William, Jr., Merchant, 3 Magwood's N. Whf.
Moultrie, James, Dr., 12 Cumberland St., res. 15
  Montague St.
Moultrie, William, Dr., 8 Bull St.
Mousseau, Lucretia, Widow, 24 Society St.
Mousseau, P., Painter, 10 Wentworth St.
Mouzon, Charles, 4 St. Philip St.
Mouzon, Henry, Accountant, cr. Anson & Boundary Sts.
Mowry, S. & Co., Merchant, 130 E. Bay St.
Muckenfuss, Benjamin, Carpenter, w. end
  Cannonborough, Neck
Muckenfuss, Catherine, Mrs., 92 Wentworth St.
Muckenfuss, H. W., 113 Wentworth St.
Muckenfuss, Henry, Bricklayer, 120 Wentworth St.
Muggridge, Matthew, Globe Tavern, 216 King St.
Muggridge, W., Shoe Maker, 92 Church St.
Muir, Jane, Mrs., Boarding House, 24 Broad St.
Muir, Robert, Clerk, 49 Broad St.
Mulligan, Mary, Seminary, 11 Wentworth St.
Mullins, C. P., 18 Tradd St.
Mullins, John, Pilot, 1 Stoll's Al.
Munday, Mary, Dry Goods Store, 38 King St.
Munds, Israel, Rev., 41 State St.
Munro, M. E., Grain Merchant, 54 E. Bay St., res. 3

Bedon's Al.
Munro, M., Widow, 81 Church St.
Murden, Jeremiah, Merchant, 52 Society St.
Murden, John, 3 Stoll's Al.
Murden, -----, Mrs. & Misses, Seminary, 52 Society St.
Murdoch, James, Dry Goods Store, 237 King St.
Murphy, E., Mrs., Boarding House, 133 Meeting St.
Murphy, John, Poultry Vender, w. end Queen St.
Murphy, W. A., Dry Goods Store, 215 King St., res. 224
  Meeting St.
Murray, Ann E., Dry Goods Store, 81 King St.
Murray, Charles B., Accountant, 81 King St.
Murray, J. L., Clerk, Post Office, res. 14 S. Bay St.
Murray, James, Clerk, 37 Meeting St.
Murray, Robert, Tailor, 60 Broad St.
Murray, William C., Merchant, Chisolm's Whf., res. 13
  New St.
Murray, William, Capt., Planter, Lucas St.,
  Cannonborough, Neck
Murrell, Isaac S. K., Printer, 12 Middle St.
Murrell, Martha, 12 Middle St.
Mushington, Elizabeth, Pastry Cook, 140 King St., F.P.C.
Mushington, William, Hair Dresser, Chalmers St., near
  Church St., F.P.C.
Mushington, William, Tailor, 140 King St., F.P.C.
Myatt, Edward, 8 Swinton's Ln.
Myer, John, Warren St., near King St., Neck
Myers, David, Capt., 254 E. Bay St.
Myers, Eleazer, Cooper, 171 E. Bay St.
Myers, John, Capt., 249 E. Bay St.
Myles, Elizabeth, Mrs., St. Philip St., near Vanderhorst
  St., Neck
M'Alister, James, Carpenter, Chalmers St., near Church
  St.
M'Anally, Elizabeth, Widow, 125 Tradd St.
M'Berney, A. J., Dry Goods Store, 348 King St.
M'Bride, Eleanor, Widow, cr. E. Bay & Guignard Sts.
M'Bride, Mary, Widow, 58 Church St.
M'Bride, Patrick, Dry Goods Store, 348 King St.
M'Burney, Eliza, Widow, w. side Hudson St., Neck
M'Burney, J. R., Dry Goods Etc., cr. King & Bridge Sts.,
  Neck
M'Burney, William, Merchant, 317 King St.
M'Call, Joseph P., St. Philip St., near George St.
M'Call, Susanna, Widow, 18 Legare St.
M'Cants, Ann, Widow, s. end Savage St.
M'Carter, J., Bookseller, 308 King St.
M'Cartney & Gordon, Merchants, Broad St.
M'Cay, Frances, Widow, 10 Friend St.
M'Cay, Joseph, Clerk, 10 Friend St.
M'Clelland, Jackson, Dry Goods Store, 260 King St., res.
  28 Society St.
M'Clentic, R., Tin Plate Worker, 352 King St.
M'Collum, John, 70 State St.
M'Cormick, John, Clerk, 132 Queen St.
M'Cormick, T., Accountant, Magwood's N. Whf.
M'Crady, E., Attorney, 42 Broad St., res. 97 Meeting St.
M'Cready, William T., Custom House, res. 187 King St.
M'Culhum, Sarah, Widow, 88 Anson St.
M'Cully & Moore, Factors, Fraser & Co. Whf.

53

M'Donald, Alexander, Grocer, 316 King St.
M'Donald, Christopher, 62 King St.
M'Donald, Hugh, 191 E. Bay St.
M'Donald, Sarah, City Hotel, 191 E. Bay St.
M'Donnald, J. C. W., M. D., 65 Broad St.
M'Donnell, William, Dry Goods Store, 246 King St.
M'Dow, William, Teacher, Montague St.
M'Dowall, A. & Co., Dry Goods Store, 145 King St.
M'Dowall, Robert, Clerk, 29 Pitt St.
M'Ellienny, Susanna, Widow, 38 Bull St.
M'Elmoyle, William, Factor, Bailey's Whf, S. Bay St., res. s.w. cr. King & Tradd Sts.
M'Feeters, Andrew, Saddler, 224 King St., res. 2 Beaufain St.
M'Gillivray, E. B., Mrs., 17 Lynch St.
M'Ginley, Samuel, Carpenter, 17 Price's Al.
M'Ginnis, E., Clerk, 230 King St.
M'Guire, P. H., Merchant Tailor, 24 Queen St.
M'Hugh, Francis Q., Attorney, 87 Broad St., res. 49 Beaufain St.
M'Innes, Joseph, Millwright, Charlotte St., Mazyckborough, Neck
M'Intire, Elizabeth, Widow, 52 King St.
M'Intosh, D., Dry Goods Store, w. side King St., above Radcliff St., Neck
M'Intosh, William, Carpenter, cr. Pinckney & Doughty Sts., Cannonborough, Neck
M'Intyre, Anthony, Clerk, 3 Wentworth St.
M'Intyre, John, Dry Goods Store, 115 King St.
M'Intyre, Peter, 202 King St.
M'Kee, Abel, Ship Joiner, cr. E. Bay & Market Sts., res. 19 Pinckney St.
M'Kegan, John, Blacksmith, Burns Ln., res. 234 Meeting St.
M'Kensie, Andrew, Wheelwright, Boundary St., near Elizabeth St., F.P.C.
M'Kensie, Ann, Wagon Yard, cr. King & Bridge Sts., Neck
M'Kensie, Archibald, Saddler, cr. Chalmers & Church Sts.
M'Kensie, John, Butcher, e. side Columbus St., Neck
M'Kensie, Richard, Saddler, n.e. cr. King & Wentworth Sts.
M'Kensie, Thomas, Saddler, cr. Chalmers & Church Sts.
M'Kewn & Johnson, Wheelwrights, e. end Hasell St.
M'Kewn, William, Bricklayer, 57 George St.
M'Kewn, William T., Ship Carpenter, 57 George St.
M'Kinley, Peter, Carpenter, 7 Water St.
M'Kinney, B., Wheelwright, 121 Queen St.
M'Kinney, Bridget, Mrs., Widow, 121 Queen St.
M'Kinney, Christopher, Teller, U. S. Bank, res. 164 King St.
M'Lean, G. S., Butcher, s. side Cannon St., Neck
M'Lean, James, Tavern, 95 Church St.
M'Lean, William, Chalmers St., near Church St.
M'Leod, Cato, Carter, Charlotte St., Neck, F.P.C.
M'Master, J., Dry Goods Store, 353 King St.
M'Millan, John & Co., Factors, 5 Magwoods N. Whf.
M'Millan, John, Boarding House, 48 Queen St.
M'Millan, John, Commission Merchant, 10 Vendue Range

M'Millan, Thomas, Capt., 9 Bull St.
M'Namee, James, Boot & Shoe Maker, 112 Church St.
M'Neal, Henrietta, Widow, 41 King St.
M'Neill & Blair, Grocers, 77 E. Bay St.
M'Neill & Blair, Grocers & Importers of Wines, 44 Broad St.
M'Neill, Mary, 2 King St.
M'Nellage, John, Sail Maker, Gillon St., res. 1 Reaper's Al.
M'Nicol & Davidson, Merchants, cr. E. Bay St. & Hamilton & Co. Whf.
M'Owen, Patrick, Accountant, 41 St. Philip St.
M'Pherson, Elizabeth, Widow, 289 E. Bay St.
M'Pherson, James, Planter, 289 E. Bay St.
M'Pherson, -----, Misses, Milliners, 155 King St.
M'Whinnie, L. M., Mrs., Widow, 49 Broad St.
M'Whinnie, William, Clerk, 49 Broad St
Nabb, John, Capt., n.w. cr. Church & Broad Sts.
Napier, Thomas & Co., Rice Mills, Gadsden's Whf.
Nardin & Wood, King St., op. Guard House, Neck
Naser, Frederick, City Scavenger, 12 Coming St.
Nathans, Henry, State Constable, 36 Hasell St.
Nathans N., Dry Goods & Grocery, King St., btw. John & Hudson Sts., Neck
Naumann, William, Hardware Store, 294 King St.
Nayle, Philip A., Factor, res. 90 Tradd St.
Naylor, William, Accountant, 87 E. Bay St.
Nedderman, F. S., Oil Store, 90 Market St.
Neill, Andrew, Boot & Shoe Maker, 249 E. Bay St., F.P.C.
Nell, M. A. & U., Misses, Amherst St., Hampstead, Neck
Nelme, John W., 125 Wentworth St.
Nelson, John, Blacksmith, Middle St.
Neufville, Ann, Widow, 86 Anson St.
Neufville, B. S., Printer, 86 Anson St.
Neve, William, Duncan St., Radcliffborough, Neck
Neville, H. W., Cabinet Maker & Lumber Yard, 62 Wentworth St.
Neville, James, Tin Plate Worker, 92 Meeting St.
Neville, Joshua, Cabinet Maker, 69 Wentworth St.
Newbold, Samuel, Pilot, 12 Water St.
Newhall, Edward, Dry Goods Store, 140 King St., res. 76 Water St.
Newhall, Joseph, Shoe Store, 328 King St.
Newton, William, 74 Wentworth St.
Newton, William, Factor, Fraser & Co. Whf., res. w. end Cannon St., Cannonborough, Neck
Newton, William Merchant, w. end Cannon St., Neck
Nichols, J. H., Salesman, 321 King St.
Nicholson, James, e. side Pinckney St. Cannonborough, Neck
Nixon, John B., American Hotel, 99 E. Bay St.
Noel, A., Clerk, 157 E. Bay St.
Nooney, Francis, Rigger, E. Bay St., near Hasell St.
Nopie, William, Dyer & Scourer, 167 Meeting St.
Norman, G. A., Fancy Store, 25 Tradd St.
Norris, James C., America St., Hampstead, Neck
Norris, James, Hotel, cr. King & George Sts.
North, Edward, Dr., 101 Meeting St.
North, Edward W., Hon., M. D., Intendant of the City, Office 101 Meeting St., res. 44 Montague St.

North, R. B., Factor, res. 101 Meeting St.
North, Webb & Co., Factors, Chisolm's Whf.
Northrop, Claudian B., Attorney, 67 Meeting St.
Nowell, John L., e. side Alexander St., Neck
Nowell, Thomas S., Bookkeeper, Bank of S. C., res. 6 Mazyck St.
Nunan, Eliza, 16 George St.
O'Brien, Thomas, Boarding House, 131 Church St.
O'Connor, Elizabeth, Wentworth St., near Smith St.
O'Driscoll, Eleanor, Seminary, 96 Tradd St.
O'Hanlon, Charles, Eagle Tavern, 133 E. Bay St.
O'Hara, Charles, Physician, King St., near Columbus St., Neck
O'Hara, Martha, Widow, 10 Bull St.
O'Hear, James, Factor, cr. Pitt & Vanderhorst Sts., Neck
O'Hear, Joseph F., cr. Pitt & Vanderhorst Sts., Neck
O'Neal, James, Carpenter, 26 Magazine St.
O'Neall, James, Ship Carpenter, 6 Chalmers St.
O'Neill, Edmond, Grocer, Cannon St., Cannonborough, Neck
O'Neill, Francis, Merchant, 149 E. Bay St.
O'Neill, John, Butcher, s. side Cannon St., Neck
O'Neill, Patrick, Butcher, s. side Cannon St., Neck
O'Neill, Thomas, Boot & Shoe Maker, 13 Queen St.
O'Reilly, J. T., Accountant, cr. Clifford & Archdale Sts.
O'Wen, J. Leslie, Dry Goods, 148 King St.
Oakley, R. S., Druggist, 152 King St.
Oakley, William C., French Fancy Store, 301 King St.
Oberhausser, J., Druggist & Apothecary, 175 Church St.
Ogden, George W., Capt., 3 Hard Al.
Ogier, Sarah, Widow, 53 Beaufain St.
Ogier, T. L., Dr., cr. Broad & State Sts.
Ogier, Thomas, Mrs., Widow, cr. Broad & State Sts.
Ogier, W. H., Broker & Auctioneer, 7 Broad St., res. 53 Beaufain St.
Ogilby, William, British Consul, 168 E. Bay St., res. 42 Bull St.
Ogilvie, M., Clerk, 87 E. Bay St.
Ohlsen, Christian, Grocer, cr. Queen & Mazyck Sts.
Olandt, D., Grocer, cr. Queen & Friend Sts.
Oliphant, David, Painter, cr. Meeting & Society Sts.
Oliphant, E. L., Clerk, cr. Meeting & Society Sts.
Olive, P., Widow, 3 Wall St.
Oliver & Ancrum, Tailors, 241 E. Bay St., F.P.C.
Oliver, B. F., Shoe Maker, 4 Amen St.
Oliver, John, Carpenter, cr. Hanover & Amherst Sts., Neck, F.P.C.
Oliver, W. F., Shoe Store, 299 & 339 King St.
Olney, George W., Merchant, 9 & 11 Vendue Range, res. 18 E. Bay St.
Oppenheim, H. W., cr. King & Hudson Sts., Neck
Osborne, Catherine, Mrs., Widow, 32 S. Bay St.
Ostcliffe, John, Engineer, cr. Hanover & Reid Sts., Neck
Osterholtz, E. H., Grocer, n.e. cr. Meeting & Boundary Sts., Neck
Osterholtz, Frederick, Grocer, Lucas St., Cannonborough, Neck
Otis, J. A., Clerk, 81 Church St.
Otis, W. M., Clerk, 81 Church St.
Ottolengui, A., Auctioneer, 28 Vendue Range, res. 1 Pinckney St.

Owen, James, City Measurer, 9 Lynch St.
Owens, John, Gardener, Charlotte St., Neck
Oxlade, Thomas C., Jr., Watch Maker, 62 Broad St.
Oxlade, Thomas, Painter, 40 Queen St.
Page, G. W., Collector, 25 Queen St.
Page, John, Miller, 151 E. Bay St.
Palmer, Justus, Dry Goods Store, 19 E. Bay St.
Panknin, C. H., Apothecary & Chemist, n. cr. Church & Tradd Sts.
Pansin, C., Clerk, 157 E. Bay St., res. 110 Meeting St.
Parker & Brailsford, Factors, 13 Roper's Whf.
Parker, Charles, Capt., State Guard, Citadel, Neck
Parker, E. H., Mrs., Widow, 6 George St.
Parker, Elizabeth, Mrs., cr. Church & Water Sts.
Parker, F., Mrs., Widow, 16 Guignard St.
Parker, I. M., 48 King St.
Parker, John, Jr., Ann St., near Mary St., Neck
Parker, John M., Factor, res. 35 E. Bay St.
Parker, Orion, Capt., 7 Tradd St.
Parker, Rachel, Mrs., Chapel St., Wraggborough, Neck
Parker, Robert, Planter, Washington St., Mazyckborough, Neck
Parker, Sarah, Fruit Store, 118 Meeting St.
Parkerson, John, Bell Hanger, 11 Meeting St.
Parshall, Charles, Dry Goods Store, 255 King St.
Parsons, J. D., Teacher, Tradd St.
Parsons, W. S., Painter, Chalmers St., near Church St.
Passalaigue, Louis, Baker, cr. Boundary & Wall Sts.
Patinett, C., Miss, Mantuamaker, 167 King St.
Patrick, Casimir, Merchant, 116 E. Bay St., res. 3 Middle St.
Patrick, Philip, Clerk, Sheriff's Office, res. 30 Mazyck St.
Patten, George, Cabinet Maker, 90 Meeting St.
Patterson & Magwood, Merchants, Magwood's N. Whf.
Patterson, Hugh, Secretary, Union Insurance Co., 31 Laurens St.
Patterson, Samuel, end Rutledge St.
Patterson, William, Accountant, 248 E. Bay St.
Patton, William, Steam Packet Office, 6 Fitzsimons' Whf., res. cr. Laurens & Middle Sts.
Paul & Brown, Grocers & Importers Wines, 47 Broad St.
Paul, Elizabeth, Mrs., Warren, near King St., Neck
Payne, Henrietta, Widow, 30 S. Bay St.
Payne, J. S., Broker & Auctioneer, 1 State St., res. 19 Friend St.
Payne, Robert K., Surveyor, Hampstead, Neck
Payne, Sabina, Widow, 52 Wentworth St.
Peake, M., Mrs., 104 Market St.
Pearson, Benjamin E., Carpenter, 115 Broad St.
Pearson, Thomas, Watch Maker, 309 King St.
Peart, John S., 14 Liberty St.
Pecard, John, Mattress Maker, 8 Berresford St., F.P.C.
Pecare, Samuel, Clothing Store, 24 Market St.
Peigne, James L., Clerk
Pelmonie, F. L., Clerk, 42 St. Philip St.
Pelot, J. Alma, Classical & English Seminary, 234 King St.
Pemberton, G. O., Factor, 1 Tradd St.
Pemble, David, Fancy Store, 179 Church St.
Pennal, Robert, Grocer, cr. King & Boundary Sts.

Pepoon, B. F., U. S. Bank
Pepper, Daniel, Radcliffborough, near Boundary St., Neck
Pereira, Domingo, Grocer, 15 Market St.
Peronneau, Edward C., 1 Legare St.
Peronneau, H. W., Attorney, res. 101 Tradd St.
Peronneau, James, Dr., 36 S. Bay St.
Peronneau, Mazyck & Finley, Attorneys, Chalmers St., op. City Sq.
Peronneau, William, Custom House, 36 S. Bay St.
Perry, Joshua, Mrs., Widow, Washington St., Mazyckborough, Neck
Perry, Julia, 33 Horlbeck's Al.
Perry, Maria, e. end Vanderhorst St., Neck
Perry, Stephens, Attorney, 26 St. Michael's Al., res. 12 Water St.
Perry, William, Capt., 105 Church St.
Peters, C., Grocery, cr. Charlotte & Washington Sts., Neck
Peters, Jane, Miss, w. side Cannonborough, Neck
Peters, John H., Attorney, 1 Court House Sq., res. 27 Mazyck
Petigru & Lesesne, Attorneys, 8 St. Michael's Al.
Petigru, James L., 111 Broad St.
Petit, C. P., Saddler, King St., near Ann St., res. Radcliffborough, Neck
Petit, F., Confectioner, 188 Meeting St.
Petit, N. F., Tin Plate Worker, 88 Market St.
Petsch, Francis, Shoe Maker, 136 Queen St.
Petsch, J., Engineer, St. Philip St.
Petsch, J. H., School Mistress, 3 Liberty St.
Petsch, James, Millwright, 3 Liberty St.
Petsch, William, Blacksmith, 3 Liberty St.
Pettival, J. B., Surveyor
Peyssou, -----, Mrs., Hair Worker, 82 King St.
Pezant, John L., Merchant, 183 E. Bay St.
Pezant, Louis, Grocer, cr. Boundary & E. Bay Sts.
Pezant, Peter, Capt., 23 Wall St.
Phelon, E., Mrs., Widow, 88 Meeting St.
Philbrook, M. A., Boarding House, 85 Market St.
Philips, Aaron, Mrs., Widow, 93 Tradd St.
Philips, John, Attorney, 75 Broad St., res. 52 Beaufain St.
Philips, Margaret, Mrs., Widow, Philadelphia St.
Philips, Otis, Clerk, res. 52 Beaufain St.
Philips, St. John, Dr., res. 52 Beaufain St.
Phin, Alexander, Chemist, Chalmers St., op. the Depository
Picault, F. D., 155 E. Bay St., res. 34 Queen St.
Picault, V., Mrs., Boarding House, 14 Queen St.
Pickett, Carpenter & Co., Tin Ware Factory, 307 King St.
Pierce, Harriet, Mrs., Widow, John St., near St. Philip St., Neck
Pierce, J. S., Cabinet Maker, 42 Wentworth St.
Pierce, Phineas, Ice House, 132 Meeting St.
Piexotto, S. C., 36 Hasell St.
Pillans, J. C., Carpenter, 43 King St.
Pillans, R., Clerk, 43 King St.
Pinceel, Emanuel, Tinner, n. side Boundary St., F.P.C., Neck
Pincell, Charles, Shoemaker, 20 Archdale St., F.P.C.
Pinckney, Frances, Mrs., Widow, 23 King St.
Pinckney, H. L., Hon., Representative in Congress, 3 St.

Philip St.
Pinckney, Harriet, Miss, 223 E. Bay St.
Pinckney, Hopson, Dr., res. 84 Broad St., off. 63 Meeting St.
Pinckney, M. H., Miss, 223 E. Bay St.
Pinckney, Myles, Mrs., Widow, 40 Pitt St.
Pinckney, Robert Quash, Surveyor, 4 New St.
Pinckney, Thomas, Planter, 98 Broad St.
Pinckney, Thomas Shubrick, Bricklayer, 4 New St.
Pipard, P. F., Sexton, Catholic Church, res. 89 Wentworth St.
Pitary, Viel & Co., Merchants, 182 E. Bay St.
Pitray, Lewis A., 12 George St.
Place, Henry, Capt., 62 State St.
Plane, William A., Custom House, 12 State St.
Platt, Phillis, Seamstress, 24 Wentworth St., F.P.C.
Plumeau, J. F., 94 King St.
Plunkett, P. C., cr. Wentworth & Anson Sts.
Pogson, Milward, Rev., 132 Wentworth St.
Pohl, Joseph, cr. Cannon & Thomas Sts., Cannonborough, Neck
Poincignon, E., Tin Plate Worker, 19 Queen St.
Poincignon, John, Tin Plate Worker, 189 E. Bay St.
Poincy, Victor, Brass Founder, 2 Amen St.
Poinsett, Joel R., Hon., 96 Broad St.
Poirer, Peter, 155 E. Bay St., res. 9 Queen St.
Poland, Oliver, Boarding House, 23 Elliott St.
Police, Francis, Clothing Store, 179 E. Bay St.
Pollinot, Joseph, Tanner, 92 Meeting St.
Polock, Elias, 10 Beaufain St.
Poppenhein, John F., 6 Hasell St.
Porcher, Francis Y., Dr., cr. Church & Cumberland Sts.
Porcher, Harriet, 18 Friend St.
Porcher, Issac, Jr., Attorney, Court House Sq.
Porcher, P., Mrs., Widow, w. end Radcliffborough, Neck
Porcher, Thomas, Planter, 302 E. Bay St.
Porter, L. M., Capt., 91 Church St.
Porter, Sarah, Widow, 141 Church St.
Porter, William, Butcher, Nassau St., Hampstead, Neck
Porter, William D., Attorney, St. Michael's Al., res. 47 E. Bay St.
Porter, William L. & Son, Grocers, 53 Queen St., res. 47 E. Bay St.
Potter, Jane, Mrs., Coming St., near Boundary St., Neck
Pouget, C., Widow, 19 Wall St.
Poulnot, Joseph, Tanner, John St., Neck
Poyas, Catharine, Widow, 51 Meeting St.
Poyas, E. A., Widow, 67 Tradd St.
Poyas, Francis D., Gunsmith, 66 Queen St.
Poyas, James, Ship Carpenter, 37 S. Bay St.
Pregnet, Henry, Carpenter, 14 Tradd St.
Prendergast, Martin, Clerk, 167 E. Bay St.
Pressley, M. J., Miss, 45 George St.
Preston, James, Merchant, 175 E. Bay St.
Preston, John, Grocer, s.e. cr. Church & Chalmers Sts.
Prevost, Joseph, 30 Broad St.
Price, A., Miss, 2 West St.
Price, Eliza, Widow, 11 Green St.
Price, Thomas, Bookkeeper, Union Bank, res. 11 Society St.

Prince, A., Cooper, w. side Cannonborough, Neck
Prince, Charles, Sr., Tinner, 114 King St.
Prince, Edward, 2 Montague St.
Prince, Eliza, Mrs., John St., near Meeting St., Neck
Pringle, Edward. J., Planter, 62 Tradd St.
Pringle, Elizabeth, Mrs., Widow, 211 Meeting St.
Pringle, George, Merchant, e. side King St., Neck
Pringle, James R., Collector of Customs, 2 Orange St.
Pringle, John J., Planter, 62 Tradd St.
Pringle, Robert, Mrs., Widow, 19 Montague St.
Pringle, Robert R., Planter, 62 Tradd St.
Pringle, W. B., Planter, 25 King St.
Prioleau, Martha, Miss, 5 Logan St.
Prioleau, Philip G., Dr., 220 Meeting St.
Prioleau, Samuel, Hon., City Recorder, 2 Church St.
Prioleau, Thomas G., Dr., 135 Meeting St.
Prior, Seth T., cr. Meeting & Mary Sts., Neck
Pritchard, C. C., Dr., s.w. cr. E. Bay & Hasell Sts.
Pritchard, Paul, Jr. & Co., Shipwrights, Eason's Whf.
Pritchard, Paul, Jr., 17 Meeting St.
Pritchard, Paul, Sr., 6 Hasell St.
Pritchard, William, Ship Carpenter, Knox's Whf.
Pritchard, William, Sr., 30 Pinckney St.
Proctor, William, Merchant, res. 39 E. Bay St.
Prouting, Charles, Capt., 2 Longitude Ln.
Purcell, Ann, Widow, 5 Green St.
Purcell, J., Mrs., Widow. Pinckney St., Cannonborough, Neck
Purse, Henry W., Accountant, 168 E. Bay St.
Purse, Isaiah, Clerk, 7 Montague St.
Purse, Robert, Cabinet Maker, 32 Beaufain St.
Purse, T. F., Broker & Auctioneer, 7 Broad St., res. 15 Legare St.
Purse, William, 7 Montague St.
Purse, William, Mrs., Widow, St. Philip St., near Warren St., Neck
Purves, W. B., Cabinet Maker, 212 King St.
Putney, Reuben, Painter, 3 Wentworth St.
Pyatt, Mary, Mrs., Widow, cr. Charlotte & Meeting Sts., Neck
Quash, Albert, Hair Dresser, 193 E. Bay St., F.P.C.
Quash, Albert, Jr., cr. Queen & Church Sts., F.P.C.
Quash, Robert H., Factor, 18 Vanderhorst's Whf., res. 87 Boundary St.
Query, H., Mrs., Boarding House, 359 King St.
Quin, Mary, Widow, 8 Chalmers St.
Quinan, B., Mrs., Northern Ware House, 259 King St.
Quinby, Elizabeth, Widow, 59 George St.
Quinby, Joseph, Ship Carpenter, 29 Wall St.
Quinby, Lawrence, Carpenter, 59 George St.
Quinby, Thomas, Grocer, 11 Minority St.
Quinlan, Mary, Widow, 49 Beaufain St.
Rabb, Jacob, Pump Maker, Market St., near Fish Market
Radcliffe, John, Blacksmith, State St., near Market St.
Rain, Elizabeth, 34 Holbeck's Al.
Ralston, R., 60 Tradd St.
Rame, C., Confectioner, 155 Meeting St.
Ramsay, David, Mrs., Widow, 128 Queen St.
Ramsay, James, Mrs., Widow, 181 Meeting St.
Ramsay, John, Planter, 162 Broad St.

Ramsay, William G., Dr., E. Bay St., res. 7 New St.
Ramsay, William, Printer, 74 Broad St.
Ransone, T. S., Surgeon Dentist, 281 King St.
Rantin, C. A., Mrs., Widow, 26 Beaufain St.
Raoul, William, 7 Greenhill St.
Ravenel & Stevens, Factors, Chisholm's N. Whf.
Ravenel, C., Mrs., Widow, res. 64 Broad St.
Ravenel, Daniel, Cashier, Planters & Mechanics Bank, res. 17 George St.
Ravenel, Edmund, Dr., 42 Meeting St.
Ravenel, Henry, Auditor, Railroad Co., 1 Short St.
Ravenel, John, President, Railroad Co., res. 64 Broad St.
Ravenel, William, Merchant, 50 E. Bay St., res. 64 Broad St.
Ravina, J. D., Spanish Consul, Pro Tempore, 18 Queen St.
Raworth, M., Mrs., Widow, St. Philip St., near Vanderhorst St., Neck
Read, John H., Planter, cr. Wentworth & Rutledge Sts.
Read, William, Dr., 31 Meeting St.
Rechon, Lewis, Sail Maker, 1 Wentworth St.
Recli, Carlo, Medallion & Statue Maker, 45 Market St.
Redfern, John, Boot Maker, 9 Tradd St.
Redmond, Elizabeth, Shop Keeper, 26 Bull St.
Redmond, William & R., Merchants, Fraser & Laffan's Whf.
Reeder, Louisa, Mrs., King St., op. Columbus St., Neck
Reedy, James, Boarding House, 123 Church St.
Reeves, Matthew S., Professor of Music, Amherst St., Neck
Reeves, Solomon L., Carpenter, 18 Coming St.
Regnelia, John, 12 Clifford Al.
Reid & Belcher, Mesdames Female Seminary, 16 Cumberland St.
Reid, Benjamin, Wheelwright, Elizabeth St., Neck, F.P.C.
Reid, George B., Clerk, Bank of S. C., res. 2 Logan St.
Reid, George, Mrs., Widow, 49 E. Bay St.
Reid, James, City Marshal, 74 Church St.
Reid, S. E., Mrs., cr. Anson & Society Sts.
Reigne, John, 65 Church St.
Reigne, Peter, Baker, 46 Queen St.
Reilly, D., Tailor, 146 King St.
Reilly, Henry, Attorney, 95 Church St.
Reilly, Honoria, Mrs., Widow, 21 Society St.
Reilly, Thomas, Accountant, 95 Church St.
Remley, Catherine, Mantuamaker, 24 Hasell St., F.P.C.
Remley, P., Bricklayer, n. side Boundary St., Neck
Renay, B., Radcliffborough, near St. Paul's Church., Neck
Rennett, Joseph, Boarding House, 49 State St.
Requier, A., Confectioner, 108 Meeting St.
Reynolds, Ann, Mrs., Widow, Henrietta St., Neck
Reynolds, George N., Coach Maker, 117 Meeting St.
Reynolds, William, Dr., 117 Meeting St.
Rhodes, Elizabeth, Widow, Chalmers St., near Church St.
Rice, William, Attorney, 76 Broad St.
Rich, Charles T., State Constable, 11 Price's Al.
Rich, J., Chair Maker, 202 Meeting St.
Richard, J. B., Confectioner, 251 King St.
Richardson, C. Y., Bell Hanger & Engineer, 99 Meeting St,
Richardson, Louisa, Seamstress, John St., Neck, F.P.C.

Richardson, Robert, Bell Hanger & Engineer, 99 Meeting St.
Richardson, Seaborn, Church St., near Amen St.
Riecke, Claus, Grocer, 20 Meeting St.
Riecke, George, Grocer, 346 King St.
Riecke, Gerd, Grocer, cr. E. Bay & Pinckney Sts.
Riecke, Gerd, Grocer, cr. King & Vanderhorst St., Neck
Rieser, Frederick, Tailor, 6 West St.
Riggs, John S., Saddler & Harness Maker, 189 Meeting St.
Righton, Joseph, Cooper, Water St.
Riley, M. A., Miss, 14 Mazyck St.
Riley, William, Book Seller & Printer, 110 Church St.
Ring, D. A., Paint Store, 113 E. Bay St., res. 133 Queen St.
Ring, George E., 3 College St.
Ripley, N. F., Ship Chandler, 3 Vendue Range
Ripley, N. F., Turpentine Distillery, Judith St., Neck
Ripley, S. P., 15 George St.
Ripley, Tilson, Judith St., Neck
Rivers, George, Mrs., Widow, w. end Montague St.
Rivers, Joseph, Charlotte St., Neck
Rivers, W. H., Printer, 133 Wentworth St.
Rivers, William, Planter, w. end Savage St.
Riviere, J. P., Fancy Store, 181 King St.
Roach, Edward, City Treasurer, 19 Society St.
Roach, William, Clerk of Council, 21 Montague St.
Robb, James, Grocery & Liquor Store, 190 King St.
Robbins & Conner, Hardware Merchants, 310 King St.
Roberts, George, Dry Goods Store, n.w. cr. King & Berresford Sts.
Roberts, William, Custom House, res. 32 Wall St.
Robertson, Adam, Painter, 5 State St.
Robertson, Alexander, Factor, res. 89 Tradd St.
Robertson, George, Accountant, res. 48 Meeting St.
Robertson, James, Merchant, 76 E. Bay St., res. 27 E. Bay St.
Robertson, John T., Secretary, Railroad Co., res. 48 Meeting St.
Robertson, William, Mrs., Widow, 86 Tradd St.
Robini, ----- & Co., Madam, Dyers
Robins, A. A., Fruit Store, 3 Market St.
Robinson, Alexander, Secretary, Fire & Marine Insurance Co., res. 23 E. Bay St.
Robinson, James K., Factor, res. Judith St., Wraggborough, Neck
Robinson, John & Sons, Factors, Edmondston's Whf., res. Judith St., Wraggborough
Robinson, John, Factor, res. Judith St., Wraggborough, Neck
Robinson, Murray, Judith St., Wraggborough, Neck
Robinson, Randall, Teller, Bank of U. S., res. w. side Pinkney St., Neck
Robinson, S. T., Planter, Radcliffborough, near Duncan St., Neck
Robinson, Samuel, Judith St., Wraggborough, Neck
Robinson, William, Attorney, 8 Waring's Row
Robinson, William, Attorney, Judith St., Wraggborough, Neck
Robinson, William, Blacksmith, 24 Wall St.
Robiou, Elizabeth, Widow, 104 Market St.

Roche, E. L., Tailor & Draper, 36 Broad St.
Roche, Henry, Grocer, cr. King & Ann Sts., Neck
Rock, John, Grocer, 1 New St.
Roddy, Martin, Grocery Store, 15 & 17 Queen St.
Rodgers, John B., 38 Pitt St.
Rodgers, John R., Capt. of the Guard, 7 Lynch St.
Rodgers, T. L., Clerk, w. end Beaufain St.
Rodrigues, B. A., Surgeon Dentist, cr. Meeting & Hasell Sts.
Rodrigues, S., Mattress Store, 77 Queen St.
Roe, James, Professor of Music, 125 Church St.
Roger, Thomas, Merchant, res. 95 Meeting St.
Rogers, Charles, Custom House, res. 6 Orange St.
Rogers, Charles, Tailor, 5 Coming St., F.P.C.
Rogers, Lewis, State Constable, 16 Burns Ln.
Rogers, S. B., Comb & Jewellery Store, 175 King St.
Rogers, William, Clerk, Reading Room, 47 Tradd St.
Rogge, Conrad, Grocer, 3 Tradd St.
Rolando, F. G., Cooper, 14 Champney St.
Rolando, Isabella, Mrs., 71 Tradd St.
Roorbach, O. A., 296 King St.
Roper, B. D., Jr., Attorney, St. Michael's Al., 4 Gibbes St.
Roper, B. D., Planter, 4 Gibbes St.
Roper, R. W., Planter, 5 Legare St.
Rose, Arthur G., Bank of U. S., res. Elizabeth St., Mazyckborough, Neck
Rose, Diall & Co., Bakers, cr. Washington & Boundary Sts.
Rose, James, Planter, 292 E. Bay St.
Rose, John, w. side Cannon St., Neck
Rosenbohm, J. H., Grocer, 88 Meeting St.
Ross, David, Coal Measurer, 4 Motte St.
Ross, David M., 42 Anson St.
Ross, James L., King St., op. Citadel, Neck
Ross, James, Merchant, 167 E. Bay St.
Ross, John, Millwright, 5 Society St.
Rotureau, Charles, 84 King St.
Rotureau, P. R., Accountant, 84 King St.
Roulain, A., Blacksmith, 49 Wentworth St.
Roumillat, A., Confectioner, 69 Meeting St.
Roumillat, Eugene, Niagara Garden, Meeting St., near Wolf St., Neck
Roumillat, G. W., Widow, 69 Meeting St.
Roumillat, Ulysses, Confectioner, 52 Broad St.
Roupell, Mary, Mrs., Widow, 102 Tradd St.
Roupell, Mary, Widow, 51 George St.
Rouse, C., Bricklayer, Mary St., btw. King & Meeting Sts., Neck
Rouse, William, Silver Smith, Mary St., btw. King & Meeting Sts., Neck
Rousseau, J., Coffee House, 3 Vendue Range
Route, Catharine, Widow, 14 Friend St.
Route, William G., Clerk, U. S. Bank, 14 Friend St.
Roux, Louis, Notary Public, 87 E. Bay St.
Rowan, Samuel, Grocer, 262 King St.
Rowand, Charles E., 93 Meeting St.
Rowand, Robert, 11 Legare St.
Rowand, Thomas, 93 Meeting St.
Rowe, G. R., Shoe Maker, 200 Meeting St.
Roye, Francis, Fruit Store, 92 Market St.

Ruddock, Susanna, Widow, 39 King St.
Rumph, Henry, n. cr. Meeting & Wolf Sts., Neck
Rumple, George H., Grocer, King St., btw. Mary & Ann
   Sts., Neck
Runciman, J., Capt. w. side Cannon St., Neck
Russ, Benjamin, Ship Carpenter, 56 Wentworth St.
Russ, John, Ship Carpenter, 56 Wentworth St.
Russ, Sarah, Widow, 56 Wentworth St.
Russell, J. B., Blacksmith, Mary St., near Meeting St.,
   Neck
Russell, John, Accountant, 172 King St.
Russell, Joseph, Saddler, 342 King St.
Russell, S., Mrs., Widow, 16 Wentworth St.
Russell, Sarah, Mrs., Widow, 11 Lynch St.
Ruthgen, John, Grocer, cr. Nassau & Columbus Sts., Neck
Rutland, Watson, Blacksmith, 19 Laurens St.
Rutledge, Edward, Mrs., Widow, 11 Lamboll St.
Rutledge, Harriet, Mrs., Widow, 117 Tradd St.
Rutledge, J., Mrs., Widow, w. side Pinckney St.,
   Cannonborough, Neck
Rutledge, John, Planter, 292 E. Bay St.
Ryan, Dennis, 95 Church St.
Ryan, James, Boarding House, 31 Elliott St.
Ryan, John, 30 Minority St.
Ryan, Laurence, City Sheriff, 72 Church St.
Ryan, Thomas, Rice Mills, Gadsden's Whf.
Ryan, William, Grocer, cr. Beaufain & St. Philip St.
Rye, Philip, Shoemaker, 58 Broad St.
Ryley, J., Druggist, 16 Broad St.
Salmond, George, Dry Goods Store, 331 King St.
Salomon, Sarah, Widow, 195 E. Bay St.
Salstein, John, 75 Boundary St.
Saltar, T. R., Ship Joiner, Knox's Whf., res. Philadelphia
   St.
Saltus, F. W., 23 Friend St.
Salvo, C., Cabinet Maker, 93 King St.
Salvo, Corrado, Musician, 96 King St.
Sampson, Emanuel, Clerk, 103 Market St.
Sampson, Jane, Widow, 103 Market St.
Sampson, S., Clerk, 169 E. Bay St.
Sanders, Joseph, Bricklayer, cr. Pitt & Vanderhorst St.,
   Neck
Sanders, William, Carpenter, Neck
Santini, Philip, Fruit Store, 35 Market St.
Sargent, John, Attorney, King St., near Vanderhorst St.,
   Neck
Sargent, Mary Ann, Mrs., 265 E. Bay St.
Sarzedas, David, Dr., 107 Queen St.
Sasportas, Joseph, Butcher, Line St., Hampstead, F.P.C.,
   Neck
Sass, E. G., Clerk, Weights & Measurers, 79 Queen St.
Sass, Jacob, Col., 79 Queen St.
Sassard, John, Capt., cr. Laurens & Washington Sts.
Sauerhoff, George, Grocer, 8 Champney St.
Saunders, Simon, Hair Dresser, 43 Broad St.
Savage, Sarah, cr. Broad & Savage Sts.
Sawyer, William, Dry Goods Store, 361 King St., cr.
   Boundary St.
Saylor, Samuel S., 131 Church St.
Schaffner, Fred, Grocery Stores, cr. Queen & State Sts. &

9 Pinckney St.
Scharenberg, C., Grocer, 10 Rutledge St.
Schirer, Mary C., Boarding House, 72 Queen St.
Schirmer, J. F., Cooper, Boyce & Co. Whf., res. 79
   Queen St.
Schirmer, William, Cooper, 79 Queen St.
Schmidt, John W., Dr., 53 Church St.
Schmidt, Lewis, Vinegar Distiller, cr. St. Philip &
   Morris Sts., Neck
Schnieder, C., Clerk, 12 Middle St.
Schnierle, Frederick, 13 Friend St.
Schnierle, John, Attorney, 55 Meeting St., 13 Friend St.
Schnierle, John M., Carpenter, 13 Friend St.
Schouboe, F. L., Grocery, cr. Elliott St. & Bedon's Al.
Schrage, D., Grocer, e. side Elliott St., Cannonborough,
   Neck
Schriber, J., 33 Society St.
Schriener, John H., Merchant, 18 Magwood's Whf., res.
   257 E. Bay St.
Schroder, Jacob, Grocer, cr. Church & Market Sts.
Schroder, John, 14 Wentworth St.
Schroder, M., Millinery, 257 King St.
Schroder, William T., 79 E. Bay St., res. 257 King St.
Schulte, Henry, Grocer, 117 Broad St.
Schulte, J. H., Grocer, cr. King & Queen Sts., res. 101
   Market St.
Schulz, John, Mrs., Widow, 299 E. Bay St.
Schutte, John, Grocer, 18 Archdale St.
Scott, Charles, Furniture Ware Room, 167 King St.
Scott, Jane, Mrs., Widow, 4 Magazine St.
Scott, M. B., Mrs., Widow, 26 Horlbeck's Al.
Scott, Margaret, Widow, 7 Pinckney St.
Scott, -----, Miss, Teacher, Free School, Pinckney St.
Scott, Morgan, 12 Smith's Ln.
Scott, Rebecca, Mrs., Widow, cr. St. Philip &
   Vanderhorst Sts., Neck
Scott, William, Hair Dresser, 185 King St.
Screven, Rebecca, Mrs., 19 Lynch St.
Seabrook, Thomas B., Planter, 16 Rutledge St.
Sebring & Edgerton, Drapers & Tailors, 32 Broad St.
Seeber, William & Co., Grocers, 43 St. Philip St.
Seigness, Charles, Coachmaker, 78 Anson St.
Seigness, John, 14 Cumberland St.
Seixas, -----, Mrs., Widow, 48 Broad St.
Selin, Peter, Fruit Store, 59 Market St.
Selvy, C., Carter, n. Boundary St., Neck, F.P.C.
Seyle, John H., Carpenter, 149 Meeting St.
Seyle, Samuel, Masonic Hall, 220 King St.
Seymour, Ann, Mrs., 57 King St.
Seymour, R. W., Attorney, 57 Meeting St., res. Back St.
Seymour, William W., 155 Queen St., F.P.C.
Shachte, John, Grocer, cr. Radcliffborough & Radcliff
   Sts., Neck
Shackelford, Eliza, Mrs., Widow, 12 Society St.
Shackelford, J. M., Wholesale Grocer, 161 & 163 E. Bay
   St.
Shackelford, William F., Clerk, 161 E. Bay St.
Shaffer, C. G., Printer, 115 Broad St.
Shaffer, Frederick, Carpenter, cr. Pitt & Boundary Sts.,
   Neck

59

Shalac, Harriet, Widow, King St., near Broad St.
Shanks, Charles, Boot & Shoe Maker, 91 E. Bay St.
Shannon, John, Dry Goods Store, 102 Church St.
Shea, Brown, Shoe Maker, 38 State St.
Shea, F., Mrs., Grocery, Henrietta St., Neck
Shecut, J. L. E. W., Dr., 108 Wentworth St.
Shegog, John, Grocer, 65 Market St.
Sheppard, James, Saddler, 26 Coming St.
Sheppard, John, 24 Coming St.
Sheppard, Thomas, Collector, n. Boundary St., Neck
Shields, Mary, Mantuamaker, Anson St., near Hasell St.
Shievely, C. G., Paint & Oil Store, 238 Meeting St.
Shievely, Mary Ann, Widow, 240 Meeting St.
Shinie, John H., 257 E. Bay St.
Shirer, Alfred, Carpenter, 12 Archdale St.
Shirer, Harriet, Widow, 12 Archdale St.
Shirer, M., Merchant, e. side King St., Neck
Shoolbred, James, Planter, 34 Montague St.
Shoolbred, John, Dr., w. end Boundary St., Neck
Shrewsbury, Edward, Carpenter, Charlotte St.,
   Mazyckborough, Neck
Shroudy, W. B. T., 17 Archdale St.
Sibley, George B. R., Iron Monger, 6 Amen St.
Siddons, J., Furniture Ware Room, 127 Meeting St.
Siegling, John, Pianoforte & Music Warehouse, 233 King
   St.
Siemer, Herman, Grocer, cr. St. Philip & Wentworth
   Sts.
Sifly & Mintzing, Lumber Mill, w. end Queen St.
Sifly, Henry, 24 Friend St.
Sifly, John, Carpenter, 82 Market St.
Sigwald, John C., Carpenter, 100 Boundary St.
Sigwald, Mary Ann, Widow, 6 Burns Ln.
Sikes, Walter G., Maiden Ln.
Silliman, Eliza, Boarding House, 7 Liberty St.
Silver, William F., Lucas St., Cannonborough, Neck
Simmons, J. M., Boarding House, 33 Broad St.
Simmons, J. W., Mrs., 296 E. Bay St.
Simmons, Stephen, Capt., 3 Water St.
Simmons, W. N., Accountant, 33 Broad St.
Simms, William G., King St., near John St., Neck
Simonds, Elvira, Mrs., cr. Radcliffborough & Cannon Sts.,
   Neck
Simonds, J. W., Apothecary, 357 King St.
Simons & Barnwell, Factors, Hamilton & Co. N. Whf.
Simons, Ann, Mrs., Widow, 18 Lynch St.
Simons, Benjamin B., Dr., 301 E. Bay St., office Middle
   St.
Simons, Charles, Engraver, 268 King St.
Simons, Edward, Planter, cr. Broad & Mazyck Sts.
Simons, Eliza, Mrs., Widow, 21 Laurens St.
Simons, Eliza, Nurse, Henrietta St., Neck, F.P.C.
Simons, Harris, Planter, Alexander St., Wraggborough,
   Neck
Simons, James, Alexander St., Wraggborough, Neck
Simons, James, Attorney, 50 Broad St.
Simons, John A., Planter, Meeting St., near Mary St.,
   Neck
Simons, John C., Painter, 189 King St.
Simons, K. L., Mrs., Widow, n.w. end Radcliffborough,
   Neck
Simons, Mary, 4 Burns Ln.
Simons, Thomas G., Planter, w. end Bull St.
Simons, Thomas Y., Dr., 71 Church St.
Simons, W. F. & Co., Painters, 69 Queen St.
Simons, William, Alexander St., Wraggborough, Neck
Simonson, W., Planter, 1 Middle St.
Simonton, C. S., Factor, Price's Whf., res. 22 Society St.
Simpson, J. W., Dry Goods Store, 191 King St.
Simpson, Jane, Mrs., Widow, 43 Society St.
Simpson, Lydia, Mrs., Widow, 11 Smith's Ln.
Simpson, Thomas W., Surgeon Dentist, 191 King St.
Sinclair, Alex, Factor, Boyce & Co. Whf., res. 81 Broad
   St.
Singleton, Michael, Shoe Maker, 38 Wentworth St., F.P.C.
Sires, J. P., Accountant, Warren St., Radcliffborough,
   Neck
Sitler, H. H., American Hotel, 99 E. Bay St.
Skirving, Bethia, Mrs., cr. Coming & Bull Sts.
Slatter, Thomas H., Baker, 186 Meeting St.
Slattery, M., Dry Goods Store, 197 King St.
Slawson, D., Bakery, 195 King St.
Sleigh, John W., Butcher, Amherst St., Hampstead, Neck
Slowman, Eliza, Mrs., 48 Montague St.
Sluter, Jacob, Dry Goods Store, 349 King St.
Smallwood, Martha, Widow, 33 Pinckney St.
Smith & M'Leish, Blacksmiths, Gadsden's Whf.
Smith, A. C., Discount & Transfer Clerk, Union Bank
Smith, B. B., Mrs., Widow, 304 E. Bay St.
Smith, B. R., Merchant, 122 E. Bay St., res. Warren St.,
   Radcliffborough
Smith, Benjamin B., Dr., 16 Coming St.
Smith, Benjamin F., Clerk, 13 E. Bay St.
Smith, Benjamin S., Clerk, 10 Coming St.
Smith, Benjamin, Ship Chandlery & Paint Store, back of
   Exchange, res. 13 E. Bay St.
Smith, Charles, Blacksmith, Gadsden's Whf.
Smith, Daniel E., Printer, Price's Al.
Smith, E. M., Capt., 3 Minority St.
Smith, Elizabeth, Mrs., Amherst St., Hampstead, Neck
Smith, Francis, Tailor, John St., Neck, F.P.C.
Smith, H. W., Sail Maker, 9 Champney St.
Smith, Hugh, Mrs., Widow, 7 Rutledge St.
Smith, J. A., Miss, Boarding House, 69 Broad St.
Smith, J. M., Boarding House, 20 Queen St.
Smith, J. M., Carpenter, 4 Mazyck St.
Smith, James, Clerk, 18 Beaufain St.
Smith, James E., Teller, State Bank, res. 8 Back St.
Smith, James, General Store, cr. State & Chalmers Sts.
Smith, James H. & Malone, Attorneys, 72 Broad St.
Smith, James H., Attorney, Mary St., Hampstead, Neck
Smith, Jane, Grocery, 17 Lynch St.
Smith, John, 23 Hasell St.
Smith, John, 40 George St.
Smith, John, Capt., 18 Smith St.
Smith, John, Clerk, St. Philip's Church, 14 Magazine St.
Smith, John R., w. side Pinckney St., near Lines, Neck
Smith, Martha, Mrs., Widow, 9 College St.
Smith, Mary G., Mrs., Widow, 76 Broad St.
Smith, Mary, Miss, cr. St. Philip & Radcliff Sts., Neck

Smith, Oliver M., Attorney, Hunt's Range
Smith, P. F., English & Classical High School, 190 King St.
Smith, Patrick, Grocer, cr. Anson & Wentworth Sts.
Smith, Q. H., Mrs., Washington St., Mazyckborough, Neck
Smith, R. B. & E., Attorneys, 104 Church St.
Smith, R. B., Attorney General, 104, res. 18 Church St.
Smith, R. P., Accountant, Society St., near King St.
Smith, Richard, Cabinet Maker, 90 Queen St.
Smith, Robert, Planter, 16 Legare St.
Smith, Samuel, Mrs., Widow, 73 Broad St.
Smith, Theodore L., Magistrate, Hampstead, Neck
Smith, Thomas, Rev., King St., near Spring St.
Smith, W. J., Custom House, res. e. end Hampstead, Neck
Smith, Whiteford, Factor, Holmes' Whf., res. cr. Beaufain & Archdale Sts.
Smith, William, Jr., Ship Wright & Wharf Owner, Smith's Whf., Neck
Smith, William M., Planter, 22 Meeting St.
Smith, William S., Clerk of Court of Common Pleas, res. 71 Broad St.
Smith, William W., Planter, 185 E. Bay St.
Smylie, Andrew, w. end Beaufain St.
Smyzer, Henry, Carpenter, 4 Hard Al.
Snow, Ann, Milliner, Henrietta St., Neck, F.P.C.
Snowden, William E., Factor, 9 Fitzsimons' Whf., res. 291 E. Bay St.
Sollee, Harriet, Mrs., Widow, 97 Church St.
Sollee, Henry, Teller, Union Bank, res. 97 Church St.
Solomon, Alexander, 34 Hasell St.
Solomon, S., Dry Goods Store, 91 Market St.
Solomons, Israel, Mrs., Widow, 79 Boundary St.
Solomons, L., Carpenter, 79 Boundary St.
Solomons, M., Clerk, 79 Boundary St.
Solomons, M., Confectionary, 309 King St.
Sommer, Henry, Turner, 61 Market St.
Sparing, David, Painter, King St., near Warren St., F.P.C., Neck
Sparnock, Henry, Custom House, res. 21 Wall St.
Spears, Archibald, Clerk, Planters & Mechanics Bank, res. 204 Meeting St.
Speissiger, L. P. & S. L., Repairer of Musical Instruments, 180 King St.
Speissiger, Samuel L., Engraver, 10 Anson St.
Spencer, Ann, Seamstress, Henrietta St., Neck, F.P.C.
Spencer, Catharine, Dry Goods Store, 196 King St.
Spencer, Maria, Widow, 5 Guignard St.
Spidle, John G., 14 Archdale St.
Spofford, Haseltine & Co., Wholesale Shoe Store, 280 King St.
Sprecks, Claus, Grocer, 17 Market St.
Springer, S. C., Merchant, res. 57 King St.
Squires, Lanson, Blacksmith & Boiler Maker, 3 Pinckney St., res. 252 E. Bay St.
St. Amand, J. P., Clerk, 203 Meeting St.
St. Amand, John A., Coachmaker, 203 Meeting St.
St. Mark, John, Hair Dresser, 12 Queen St., F.P.C.
St. Mark, Sarah, Seamstress, 12 Meeting St., F.P.C.

Stall, Frederick, Butcher, Thomas St., Cannonborough, Neck
Stanley, Elias, 46 Beaufain St.
Stapleton, Mary, Meeting St., near Spring St., Neck
Starke, Charles, Grocer, w. end. Laurens St.
Steed, James, Dr., Lucas St., Cannonborough, Neck
Steedman, C. J., Custom House, res. Washington St., Mazyckborough, Neck
Steedman, Thomas, Jr., Custom House, res. Charlotte St., Mazeykborough, Neck
Steedman, Thomas, Sr., n. side Boundary St., Neck
Steele, J. A., Planters & Mechanics Bank, res. Smith St., near Cannon Bridge, Neck
Steele, William G., Lumber Factor, w. end. Beaufain St.
Steele, Williiam, Warren St., near Coming St., Neck
Steike, John, Dry Goods Store, 59 Market St.
Steinmetz, B., Drayman, n. Boundary St., Neck, F.P.C.
Steinmeyer, F., Carpenter, n. side Boundary St., Neck
Steinmeyer, John, Carpenter, 2 Back St.
Stent, John, Carpenter, w. end Queen St., res. 37 King St.
Stenton, Elizabeth, Grocery, 30 King St.
Stephens, Thomas B., Printer, res. Union Bank, upstairs
Stephens, Thomas T., Teller, Union Bank, res. upstairs
Stevens, Henderson & Adger, Importers of Hardware, 110 & 112 E. Bay St.
Stevens, J. R., 136 King St.
Stevens, Joseph L., Dr., 10 Lamboll St.
Stevens, Samuel N., Factor, res. w. end Magazine St.
Stewart, A., Mrs., Widow, 9 Wentworth St.
Stewart, Angus, Carolina Hotel, 56 Broad St.
Stewart, Jane, 11 Greenhill St.
Stewart, R. L., U. S. Bank, res. Pitt St.
Stewart, Robert, Carpenter, 15 Burns Ln.
Stillman, James, Clerk, 215 King St.
Stock, John Y., Broker & Auctioneer, 9 State St., res. 25 Friend St.
Stocker, James M., Merchant, res. 12 Society St.
Stocker, Rebecca, Mrs., Widow, e. end Laurens St.
Stockfleet, John, Grocer, cr. Henrietta & Elizabeth Sts., Neck
Stoddard, Birch & Co., Merchants, 272 King St.
Stoddard, E. B., Wholesale & Retail Shoe Store, 325 & 327 King St.
Stoll, Justinus, Warren St., near King St., Neck
Stoll, William J., 38 Mazyck St.
Stone, William, Carpenter, cr. College & Boundary Sts.
Stoney, John, Merchant, 190 res. 293 E. Bay St.
Stoppelbein, Elizabeth, Widow, 44 Coming St.
Stoppelbein, Jacob, Tailor, 34 State St.
Storm, J. G., Merchant Tailor, 227 King St.
Storm, P., Mrs., Artificial Florist, 153 King St.
Stow, F. H., Accountant, 270, res. 241 King St.
Street & Boinest, Merchants, 126 E. Bay St.
Street, Angelique, Mrs., Widow, 50 Queen St.
Street, Joseph, Wheelwright, E. Bay St., near Market St.
Strobel, Benjamin B., Dr., 80 Broad St., res. 29 Mazyck St.
Strobel, John, 29 Mazyck St.
Strobel, Martin, Attorney, 102 Meeting St.

Strobel, -----, Misses, Seminary, 29 Mazyck St.
Strobel, Sarah, Mrs., Widow, 14 Back St.
Strobel, William D., Accountant, 102 Meeting St.
Strohecker, Charles C., Attorney, 53 Meeting St.
Strohecker, Henry F., Clerk, res. 20 Horlbeck's Al.
Strohecker, John, Hardware Store, 163 Meeting St., res. 20 Horlbeck's Al.
Stroub, Jacob, Carpenter, 14 Burns Ln.
Stuardi, John, Printer, 102 Market St.
Stuart, John A., Editor of Mercury, 14 Coming St.
Sturgis, Mary, Mrs., Widow, 24 S. Bay St.
Sturken, Henry, King St., near Lines, Neck
Suares, Abraham, Clerk, 199 King St.
Suares, B. C., Merchant Tailor, 199 King St.
Suares, J., Mrs., Widow, 199 King St.
Suder, P. J., Clerk, Steam Mill, E. Bay St.
Sullivan, Mary, Mrs., Widow, 76 Anson St.
Sully, W. C., Capt., 2 State St.
Summers, P., Mrs., Boarding House, 26 Elliott St.
Surau, Francis, Shoe Maker, King St., above Radcliff St., Neck
Surtis, Thomas, Pilot, 3 Longitude Ln.
Sutcliffe, J. H., Baker, 83 Queen St.
Sutton, R. E., Bricklayer, 335 King St.
Sutton, R., Mrs., 212 Meeting St.
Sweegan, Matthew, Grocer, 7 Market St.
Sweeny, James, Merchant, 9 George St.
Swift, Thomas B., State Constable, 75 Tradd St.
Swinton, Eliza, Miss, 21 Archdale St.
Symme, John T., Tailor, 16 Middle St.
Symmes, Thomas, Dry Goods Store, 253 King St.
Symmons, E. L., Glass Cutter, 116 Meeting St.
Syphan, Sophia, s. side Cannon St., Neck
Taber, William R., Accountant, cr. Smith & Montague Sts.
Talle, Charles, Grocer, King St., near Lines, Neck
Talley, N., Rev., Radcliffborough, near Vanderhorst St., Neck
Talvande, A., Mrs., Academy, 24 Legare St.
Talvande, R., Mrs., Widow, 98 Tradd St.
Tamplett, J., 183 Meeting St.
Tanswell, William N., Locksmith & Bell Hanger, 54 Queen St.
Taveau, Augustus, Planter, 154 Wentworth St.
Taylor, C., Mrs., Mantuamaker, 5 Beaufain St.
Taylor, Isaac, Tailor, 3 Beaufain St., F.P.C.
Taylor, J. H., Merchant, res. 76 Queen St.
Taylor, Joshia, Factor, res. 3 Lamboll St.
Taylor, Mary, Seamstress, cr. Church & Water Sts., F.P.C.
Taylor, Mary, Seamstress, Middle St., F.P.C.
Taylor, R., Shoe Store, 359 King St.
Taylor, Robert R., Clerk, 3 Lamboll St.
Taylor, William, Shoe Store, 249 King St.
Teasdale, R., Factor, Chisholm's N. Whf., res. 1 Orange St.
Telfer, Robert, Gauger, 123 King St.
Tennant & Legare, Factors, Williams' Whf.
Tennant, Charles, Bricklayer, 60 Anson St.
Tennant, E., Mrs., Widow, Tradd St.
Tennant, J., Mrs., 1 Minority St.

Tew, Eleanor, Mrs., Widow, 80 Wentworth St.
Tew, Henry S., Ship Chandler, 177 E. Bay St.
Tharin, D. & T., Wheelwrights, King St., btw. Mary & Ann Sts., Neck
Tharin, Edward C., Accountant, Reid St., near Meeting St., Neck
Thayer, C. S., Mrs., Widow, 106 Tradd St.
Thayer, E., Bookseller, Teacher of Free School, 79 Broad St.
Thayer, Edward, 106 Tradd St.
Thayer, T. H., Broker & Auctioneer, 9 State St., res. 9 Lynch St.
Thayer, Thomas W., Clerk, 25 Queen St.
Thayer, W. H., Accountant, 106 Tradd St.
Thee, John H., Grocer, 18 Market St.
Thetford, Andrew, Carpenter, Mazyckborough, near Boundary St., Neck
Thomas, Isabella M., Coming St.
Thomas, Morris, 305 King St.
Thomas, S. J., 325 King St.
Thomas, Stephen, Jr., 117 E. Bay St.
Thomas, Stephen, Judith St., Wraggborough, Neck
Thompson, Adeline, Mrs., Vernon St.
Thompson, Ann, 9 Burns Ln.
Thompson, Ann, Mrs., Widow, Court House Sq.
Thompson, ---, Attorney, Hunt's Range, res. 10 New St.
Thompson, George, Bricklayer, 32 Hasell St.
Thompson, George, Carpenter, 99 King St.
Thompson, Henry, Mariner, 2 Elliott St.
Thompson, James, Blacksmith, 226 E. Bay St.
Thompson, John, Blacksmith, 11 Market St.
Thompson, Joseph, Saddler, cr. Broad & Church Sts.
Thompson, Mary C., Widow, 25 State St.
Thompson, William, Boarding House, 109 Meeting St.
Thompson, William, Boarding House, 13 Elliott St.
Thompson, William, Grocer, 9 Legare St.
Thomson, D. L., Dry Goods Store, 151 King St.
Thomson, F., Mrs., Midwife, 85 King St.
Thomson, Henry, King St., near John St., e. side, Neck
Thorn, Rebecca, Mantuamaker, Boundary St., op. Elizabeth St., F.P.C.
Thrane, J. W., 22 Market St.
Thurston, Robert, Factor, Vanderhorst's Whf., res. Wentworth St.
Thwing, Edward, Broker & Auctioneer, 10 State St.
Tidyman, Hester, Mrs., Widow, 5 Rutledge St.
Tidyman, Philip, Dr., Planter, 3 Ladson's Court
Tileston, William M., 280 King St.
Timmons, George, 6 Smith's Ln.
Timmons, William & Sons, Hardware Merchants, 165 E. Bay St.
Timrod, William H., Bookbinder & Stationer, 115 E. Bay St.
Tinken, John, Grocer, 43 Beaufain St.
Tobias, A., Auctioneer, 22 Vendue Range, res. 52 Tradd St.
Tobias, Isaac, Jailer, Magazine St.
Tobias, Joseph, Mariner, 3 Whim Court
Todd, J. W., Wood Factor, Price's Whf.
Todd, James, Tailor, 26 Pinckney St.

Tolck, C. H., Grocer, n.e. cr. State & Market Sts.
Tolck, John D., Grocer, 93 E. Bay St.
Tomatis, Eugene, Painter, Chalmers St., near State St.
Toomer, Anthony, Dr., Chapel St., Neck
Toomer, H. B., Jr., Merchant, Price's Whf., res. 11 Green St.
Toomer, Henry B., City Assessor, cr. St. Philip & Boundary Sts.
Toomer, Joshua W., Attorney, St. Michael's Al., res. cr. Ann & Meeting Sts.
Toomer, Joshua W., Attorney, cr. Ann & Meeting Sts., Neck
Toomer, Mary, Mrs., w. end Boundary St., Neck
Toppan, Edward, Wholesale Dry Goods, 273 King St.
Tornland, Andrew, Grocer, cr. Elizabeth & Mary Sts., Neck
Torre, Ann, Mrs., Widow, 18 New St.
Torrington, George, Grocer, 17 E. Bay St.
Touchstone, F., Planter, St. Philip St., near Orphan House, Neck
Toussegar, Eliza, Miss, 11 Water St.
Toutain, Adeline, Tailoress, John St., Neck, F.P.C.
Tovey, Henry C., Pump Makers, 176, res. 282 E. Bay St.
Townsend, Mary, Mrs., Widow, 5 Clifford St.
Townsend, T. J., Clerk, 5 Clifford St.
Trapier, Benjamin, Planter, Pinckney St., Cannonborough, Neck
Trapier, Richard, U. S. Navy, 6 Short St.
Trapier, Sarah, Mrs., 6 Short St.
Trapmann, L., Merchant, Prussian Consul, 79 E. Bay St., res. w. end Broad St.
Trenholm, Charles, 2 Friend St.
Trenholm, Edward, Accountant, 2 Friend St.
Trenholm, George A., Factor, 2 Friend St.
Trescot, Caroline, Mrs., Widow, 48 Beaufain St.
Trescot, Henry, Mrs., Widow, Coming St., near Boundary St., Neck
Trescot, Henry, U. S. Bank, 97 Meeting St.
Trescot, -----, Mrs., Seminary, 97 Meeting St.
Trott, J. W., Grocer, 110 King St.
Trouche, A. P., Accountant, 73 Church St.
Troude, Victor, Upholsterer, 91 Queen St.
Trout, Thomas, Merchant, res. 63 Meeting St.
Trout, William, Pilot, 8 Lynch St.
Truesdell, David, Oyster House, 30 Queen St.
Tucker, John H., Planter, n.e. side Hampstead, Neck
Tucker, Mary, Mrs., Widow, 69 Church St.
Tunis, C. H., Factor, res. 54 E. Bay St.
Tunno, Sarah, Mrs., Widow, 8 New St.
Tupper, Tristam, Merchant, Dewees Whf., res. 30 Tradd St.
Turnbull, J., 5 Water St.
Turnbull, Joseph, 37 Guignard St.
Turnbull, R. J., Mrs., Widow, 12 Logan St.
Turnbull, William A., Merchant, 5 Water St.
Turner, George R., Capt., Doughty St., Cannonborough, Neck
Turner, John, Wood Dealer, Charlotte St., Neck, F.P.C.
Tyler, Joseph & Co., Merchants, 138 E. Bay St.
Tyson, C., Hair Dresser, 1 Tradd St., F.P.C.

Ulmo, M. A., Apothecary, 88 King St.
Ummensetter, Dorothea, Mrs., Widow, 55 Beaufain St.
Uttermahl, L. W., Accountant & Collector, 115 E. Bay St.
Valentine, Samuel, Merchant, 229, res. 117 King St.
Valk, J. L., res. 122 Church St.
Valk, J. R., State Bank, res. 122 Church St.
Vanbrunt, E. J., Bookbindery, 121 E. Bay St., res. 339 King St.
Vanbrunt, R., Bookbinder, 121 E. Bay St., res. 339 King St.
Vance, Francis, Mrs., Widow, 7 Green St.
Vanderhorst, E., Hair Dresser, 1 Tradd St., F.P.C.
Vanderhorst, Elias, Wharf Owner, John St., Neck
Vanderhorst, Richard, Mrs., Widow, Charlotte St., Mazyckborough, Neck
Vandine, Jane, cr. Beaufain & Coming Sts.
Vanhagen, Mary, 10 Burns Ln.
Vanhorn, Abner, Brass Founder, 206 E. Bay St., res. 237 E. Bay St.
VanRhyn, J. M., 22 Broad St.
Vanwilson, William, Wheelwright, 48 St. Philip St.
Vanwinkle, J., 276 King St.
Vardell, John, Bricklayer, Vanderhorst St., near St. Paul's Church, Neck
Vardell, T. A., Mrs., Widow, Vanderhorst St., near St. Paul's Church., Neck
Varden & Fabian, Painters, 55 Queen St.
Varner, Henry, 3 West St.
Varney, N., Boarding House, Bedon's Al.
Vaughn, -----, Mrs., Widow, 20 Pinckney St.
Vause, John T., 27 Mazyck St.
Veitch, William, Apothecary, 223 King St.
Venning, J. M., Factor, Charlotte St., Mazyckborough, Neck
Venning, J. M., Lumber Yard, Gadsden's Whf.
Veronee, Samuel, Baker, cr. Hanover & Reid Sts., Neck
Verree, John, Carpenter, 3 Pitt St., F.P.C.
Vidal, James, Marine & Commercial Hotel, 129 E. Bay St.
Villaneau, J. B., Tailor, 44 Anson St.
Vincent, H. E., Ship Chandler, 83 E. Bay St.
Vincent, William J., Exchange Office, 107 E. Bay St., Res. 134 Church St.
Vinro, J. W., Accountant, Boyce & Co. Whf.
Vinro, Sarah, Mrs., Midwife, 44 Wentworth St.
Vinyard, John, America St., Hampstead, Neck
Vogel & Salvo, Cabinet Makers, 93 King St.
Vonglahn, Claus, Grocer, Radcliffborough, near St. Paul's Church, Neck
Vose Carsten, Grocer, cr. Pinckney & Cannon Sts., Neck
Wade, Alexander, Clerk, 29 Society St.
Wagner, Ann, Mrs., Widow, 52 St. Philip St.
Wagner, Effingham, Planter, 3 New St.
Wagner, George, 17 Legare St.
Wagner, Jacob, Mariner, Nassau St., Neck
Wagner, John, Dr., cr. Meeting & Queen Sts.
Wagner, Peter, Grocer, 66 Church St.
Wagner, S. J., Custom House, res. 118 Queen St.
Waldo, Catherine, Mrs., Widow, 43 Tradd St.
Walker & M'Kensie, Dry Goods Store, cr. King & Liberty Sts.

Walker, Alexander, Merchant, res. 15 Friend St.
Walker, Henry D., Carpenter, 24 Magazine St.
Walker, J. M., Attorney, 25 St. Michael's Al., res. 34
Meeting St.
Walker, James E., 145 Meeting St.
Walker, John C., Bookbinder & Stationer, 101 E. Bay St.
Walker, John, Capt., 15 Guignard St.
Walker, John F., Boyce & Co. Whf., res. 306 E. Bay St.
Walker, John, Planter, 56 Broad St.
Walker, M., Mantuamaker, Ann St., near Meeting St.,
Neck, F.P.C.
Walker, Mary, Widow, Lucas St., Cannonborough, Neck
Walker, Thomas & Sons, Stone Cutters, 145 Meeting St.
Walker, William, 86 Market St.
Wall, Richard, 22 State St.
Wallace, Andrew, Ship Owner, n. cr. Church & Chalmers
Sts.
Wallace, Ann, Miss, 89 Church St.
Wallace, Elizabeth, Mrs., Widow, 20 Society St.
Wallace, S., Mrs., Chalmers St., near Church St.
Wallace, Thomas, Dry Goods Store, 360 King St.
Wallace, William N., Carpenter, Columbus St., Neck
Waller, William, Saddler, 41 Broad St.
Walling, John, Hampstead, Neck
Wallis, J. C., Veterinary Surgeon, Market St., op. State St.
Walpole, Horace, Planter, 1 Lamboll St.
Walsh, M. P., Factor, 2 Edmondston's Whf.
Walsh, M. P., Merchant, e. side King St., near Lines,
res. Spring St., Neck
Walter, E. W., Factor, res. 61 Meeting St.
Walter, Jerry, Auctioneer, 8 Vendue Range, res. 65
Meeting St.
Walton, A. Y., Res, 23 George St.
Walton, Elizabeth, Mrs., Widow, 46 St. Philip St.
Walton, J. W. Y., Hardware Merchant, 314 King St.
Ward, F. S., Clerk, City Court, 22 Wall St.
Ward, George, Planter, e. side Hampstead, Neck
Ward, John, 92 Tradd St.
Ward, Mary, Ready Made Linen Store, 42 Broad St.
Ward, Sarah, Mrs., 7 Water St.
Waring, D. J., Mrs., Widow, 4 George St.
Waring, Francis M., Factor, 2 Hasell St.
Waring, Horatio S., Dr., 81 Wentworth St.
Waring, Morton A., Planter, w. side St. Philip St., near
Cannon St., Neck
Waring, Morton, Sr., w. side St. Philip St., near Cannon
St., Neck
Waring, Thomas, w. end Montague St.
Warley, C. & Co., Wine Merchants & Factors, 35 Broad
St.
Warley, C., Vanderhorst's Row
Warley, Mary, Miss, 30 Hasell St.
Warner, Penelope, Mrs., Widow, 43 Tradd St.
Warren, Elizabeth, 9 West St.
Warren, Henrietta, 44 State St.
Warren, Susanna, Mrs., Widow, 18 Guignard St.
Warrington, Isaac, Shoe Maker, 6 Minority St.
Washington, William, Planter, 289 E. Bay St.
Waters, William, Clerk of Market, cr. King & Society Sts.
Watson, Henry, Grocer, 47 Market St.

Watson, S. & J., Merchants, 74 E. Bay St., res. 7
Archdale St.
Waugh, A. C., Clerk, 204 Meeting St.
Webb, D. C., Factor, w. side Pinckney St.,
Cannonborough, Neck
Webb, Samuel, Capt., 1 Hard Al.
Webb, Thomas L., Planter, e. side Pinckney St., near
Lines, Neck
Webster, John, Clerk, 277 King St.
Weed & Benedict, Hat Warehouse, 313 King St.
Wehmon, Martin, Grocer, cr. Anson & Hasell Sts.
Weissinger, Charles, King St., near Wolf St., Neck
Weissinger, Leonard, King St., near Wolf St., Neck
Welch, Mary, Coming St., near Vanderhorst St., Neck
Welling & Ballantine, Harness Makers, 119 Meeting St.
Welling, John B., Turner, 119 Meeting St.
Wells, Catharine, Henrietta St., Neck, F.P.C.
Wells, J. T., Commission Merchant, 162 E. Bay St.
Wells, Sarah, Chalmers St., near Meeting St.
Welsh, Peter, Ironmonger, 236 E. Bay St.
Welsman, J., Capt., 88 Church St.
Welsman, J. T., Accountant, 88 Church St.
Wenger, John, Painter, 26 State St.
Wesner, Frederick, Master, Work House, n.w. cr. Queen
& Mazyck Sts.
West, C. H., Ship Chandler, 79 E. Bay St., res. 9 Church
St.
West, C. L., U. S. Appraiser, back of Exchange, res. 79
E. Bay St.
West, Thomas, Painter, 121 Meeting St.
Westcoate, M. A., 6 Swinton's Ln.
Westendorff, C. P. L., Collector, Courier Office, res. 21
Horlbeck's Al.
Weston, Anthony, Wheelwright, n. Boundary St., Neck,
F.P.C.
Weston, P., Dr., Planter, e. side Hampstead, Neck
Weston, Samuel, Tailor, 104 Queen St., F.P.C.
Weyman, Dedrick, Grocer, cr. St. Philip & Vanderhorst
Sts., Neck
Weyman, Francis, Grocer, cr. Church St. & Lightwood's
Al.
Weyman, Mary R., 2 Wall St.
Whaley, William S., Planter, e. end Cannon St.,
Cannonborough, Neck
Wharton, Jane, Mrs., Seminary, Reid St., Neck
Whilden, Joseph, 22 Magazine St.
Whitaker, Daniel K., Attorney, 19 St. Michael's Al.
Whitaker, William, Grocer, cr. Elizabeth & Henrietta Sts.,
Neck
White, Alonzo J., 20 Broad St.
White, Edward, 270 King St., res. cr. King & Society
Sts.
White, Fred, 270 King St., res. s.w. cr. King & George
Sts.
White, George K., Factor, Anson St., near Pinckney St.
White, James, Grocer, Gadsden's Whf.
White, John, 216 Meeting St.
White, John B., Attorney, 6 Friend St.
White, John, Planter, 303 E. Bay St.
White, John, Stone Cutter, 131 Meeting St.

White, Thomas, Grocer, cr. Meeting & Mary Sts., Neck
White, William H., Grocer, n.e. cr. Church & Market Sts.
Whitesides, T. J., Shoe Maker, 22 Washington St.
Whiting, E. M., Turner, 189 Meeting St.
Whitney, Archibald, Collector, 9 Cumberland St.
Whitney, Mary, Boarding House, cr. E. Bay & Tradd Sts.
Whitney, Octavius L., Dry Goods Store, 350 King St.
Whitridge, J. B., Dr., 10 Montague St.
Whitsel, Frederick, w. side Vanderhorst St., Neck
Whittemore & Bigelow, Tallow Chandlers, cr.
   Vanderhorst & Warren Sts., Neck
Whittemore, Cephas, St. Philip St., near Radcliff St.,
   Neck
Whitty, Edward, Grocer, 234 E. Bay St.
Wicks, -----, Capt., cr. State & Queen Sts.
Wienges, Conrad, Grocer, cr. Church & Linguard Sts.
Wienges, Everhard, Lamboll St.
Wienges, J. H., 25 Mazyck St.
Wienges, Jacob, Grocer, cr. Pitt & Montague Sts.
Wienges, Rebecca, Widow, 18 Burns Ln.
Wigfall, Paul, Bricklayer, 61 Beaufain St.
Wigfall, Thomas, Planter, Washington St.,
   Mazyckborough, Neck
Wightman, J. T., Turner, 116 Meeting St.
Wightman, John W., Painter, 118 King St
Wightman, William, Painter, 199 Meeting St.
Wilbur, William W., Comb & Fancy Store, 166 King St.
Wilcox, S. W., Wharfinger, Fraser & Co. Whf.
Wildman, N. H. & Co., Hat Warehouse, 279 King St.
Wiley, Lerroy M., Merchant, 265 King St.
Wiley, Mary, Nurse, Church St., near Linguard St.
Wiley, Parish & Co, Wholesale Dry Goods Store, 265
   King St.
Wiley, William, 20 Lynch St.
Wilken, Jurgen, Grocer, cr. George & Coming Sts.
Wilken, Jurgin, Grocer, cr. Charlotte St., Mazyckborough,
   Neck
Wilken, Peter, Grocer, 105 Church St.
Wilkes & Middleton, Factors, 9 Hamilton & Co. Whf.
Wilkes, John, 15 Meeting St.
Wilkie, George, 7 Lynch St.
Wilkie, W. & George W., Hardware Store, 61 E. Bay St.
Wilkie, William B., Cashier, Union Bank, res. 8 Liberty St.
Wilkie, William, Planter, 122 Meeting St.
Wilkins, M. L., Planter, Charlotte St., Mazyckborough,
   Neck
Wilkinson, John, Tallow Chandler, King St., btw. Radcliff
   & Morris Sts., Neck
Wilkinson, Willis, Dr., Planter, 20 Lynch St.
Will, Robert, Bricklayer, 220 King St.
Williams, Catharine, 89 Queen St.
Williams, Catharine, Widow, 107 Church St.
Williams, E. H., Factor, 5 Gibbes St.
Williams, Frances, 2 Green St.
Williams, H. H., 321 King St.
Williams, John, Coachmaker, 41 Hasell St.
Williams, John, Mariner, 8 Wentworth St.
Williams, Paris, Barber, 53 Society St., F.P.C.
Williams, Samuel, Printer, George St.
Williams, Simpson, Capt., 27 Mazyck St.

Williams, Thomas P., Merchant, 45 E. Bay St., res. 256
   Wentworth St.
Williamson, Elizabeth, Milliner, 107 Meeting St.
Williman, Elizabeth, Mrs., w. end Boundary St., Neck
Willington, A. S. & Co., Courier Office, 107 E. Bay St.
Willis, Henry, Carpenter, Line St., Hampstead, Neck
Willman, Sarah, Mrs., Boarding House, 7 State St.
Wilson, Abraham, Planter, s.w. cr. John & Meeting Sts.,
   Neck
Wilson, Alexander B., Planter, w. end Radcliffborough,
   Neck
Wilson, Andrew, 132 Church St.
Wilson, George, Butcher, Amherst St., Hampstead, F.P.C.,
   Neck
Wilson, George, Pilot, Church St.
Wilson, Hugh, Planter, cr. Pinckney & Bridge Sts., Neck
Wilson, James, Seed Store, 236 King St.
Wilson, John, cr. Church & Chalmers Sts.
Wilson, John L., Attorney, 45 Beaufain St.
Wilson, Joshua, Butcher, Nassau St., Neck, F.P.C.
Wilson, Robert, Boarding Officer, Custom House, res. 16
   Hasell St.
Wilson, Samuel, Dr., 7 New St.
Wilson, Susan, 22 Pinckney St.
Wilson, William H., Col., 100 Meeting St.
Winslow, Edward, Merchant, Hamilton & Co. N. Whf.
Winthrop, A., Clerk, U. S. Bank, res. 115 Tradd St.
Winthrop, F. & C., Merchants, 7 Champney St., res. 113
   Tradd St.
Winthrop, Henry, M. D., 36 Society St., res. 113 Tradd
   St.
Winthrop, J. A., Factor, S. Bay St., res. 115 Meeting St.
Winthrop, Joseph A., Factor, 7 Hamilton & Co. Whf., res.
   115 Tradd St
Winthrop, William, res. 115 Tradd St.
Wise, Catharine, Mrs., Widow, Coming St.
Wise, Edward, Boarding House, 43 Elliott St.
Wish, Richard S., City Marshal, w. end Queen St.
Wiss, Emanuel, Coach Trimmer, 111 Boundary St.
Withers, Francis, Planter, Cannon St., near Radcliff St.,
   Neck
Withers, William, Bricklayer, Reid St., Hampstead, Neck
Witter, Benjamin, Mrs., Widow, 37 Meeting St.
Witter, Eliza S., Mrs., Widow, 29 Tradd St.
Wolf, Rachel, Mrs., Widow, 8 Orange St.
Wolff, F. A., Saddler, 198 Meeting St.
Wolff, James, Magazine St., near Jail
Wolker, Betsy, Pastry Cook, 239 King St., F.P.C.
Wolter, E. H., Boarding House, 61 Market St.
Wood & Co., Grocers, 210 King St.
Wood, Daniel, Hampstead, Neck
Wood, E., Mrs., e. side Spring St., Neck
Wood, Edward, State Constable, 52 Elliott St.
Wood, Francis, 9 Magazine St.
Wood, George, Custom House, res. Lodge Al.
Wood, George, Grocer, 132 Meeting St.
Wood, H. C., Clerk, 16 Broad St.
Wood, James, Butcher, w. side Cannon St., Neck
Woolett, Thomas, Boarding House, 13 Bedon's Al.
Wooley, Charles, Boat Builder, 10 Champney St., res. 2

65

Stoll's Al.

Woolf, Isaac, Clothing Store, 360 King St.

Woolf, R., Clothing Store, 135 E. Bay St.

Woolf, Sarah, Clothing Store, 360 King St.

Wotherspoon, Robert, Accountant, 79 E. Bay St., res. 4 Orange St.

Wottton, Catherine, Widow, e. side Coming St., Neck

Wragg, Heroit & Simons, Factors, 13 Hamilton & Co. Whf.

Wragg, Samuel, Cashier, State Bank, Alexander St., Mazyckborough, Neck

Wragg, William T., Dr., cr. King & John Sts., Neck

Wright, Alexander, Mrs., Widow, 10 Queen St.

Wright, John J., w. end Cannonborough, Neck

Wright, R., Mrs., Dry Goods Store, 174 King St.

Wright, Robert, Steward, Orphan House, Neck

Wrinich, John, Academy, 95 Market St.

Wulff, Jacob, Vice Consul of Hamburgh, Union Insurance Office

Wurdemann, C. D., Mrs., Dry Goods Store, 218 King St.

Wurdemann, J. G. H., Dr., 149 Meeting St.

Wyatt, John R., State St., op. Lodge Al.

Wynn, Robert, Saddler, 83 Broad St.

Yates & M'Intyre, Lottery Office, 26 Broad St.

Yates, David S., Accountant, 89 Broad St.

Yates, Deborah, Mrs., Widow, 80 Broad St.

Yates, J. A., U. S. Appraiser, 22 Church St.

Yates, J. H., Carpenter, 51 Queen St.

Yates, James L., Accountant, 161 E. Bay St.

Yates, Jane, Mrs., Widow, Baptist Town

Yates, Jeremiah D., Attorney, 89 Broad St.

Yates, Seth, Cooper, w. end Bull St.

Yeadon & M'Beth, Attorneys, St. Michael's Al.

Yeadon, Richard, Jr., 96 Wentworth St.

Yeadon, Richard, Sr., 35 King St.

Yeadon, William, Col., Superintendant, Arsenal at Citadel, Neck

You, John C., Academy, 4 Archdale St.

You, Thomas C., 115 Queen St.

Young, James, Rigger, 5 Cumberland St.

Young, Joseph, Capt., 283 E. Bay St.

Young, Martha, Seamstress, 22 Laurens St., F.P.C.

Young, Thomas, Rigger, 5 Motte St.

Zealy, A. C., Mrs., Midwife, 63 King St.

Zealy, Joseph, Accountant, 108 Wentworth St.

Zealy, W. E., Accountant, 63 King St.

Zerbst, F., Grocer, cr. Wentworth & Rutledge Sts.

Zerbst, F., Grocer, s. side Cannon St., Neck

Zylks, Thomas, 14 Bull St.

Zylstra, John P., Lumber Measurer, 149 E. Bay St.

Zylstra, P. C., 149 E. Bay St.

The 1836 Supplement

Daniel J. Dowling issued the *Supplement to Charleston Directory, Containing the Removals, New Firms, Public Officers, and Changes, Taken Place from September [1835] to July, 1836 to Which is Added a Calendar for 1886 [sic]* (Charleston: Dowling, 1836). Thus the 1835-36 directory must have appeared during the summer of 1835. The reception of that volume by some people thoroughly irked Dowling. He stated that "inviduous remarks have been made, as to its general correctness." He challenged his critics to compare his work with all the directories that had appeared in Charleston and other cities previously. Furthermore, he stated only two mistakes in the entire work had been pointed out, and the "hyper-critics" had been asked to indicate others. But they only came up with "miserable subterfuges" stating they did not have the time and such. Most of them, he remarked, had no even patronized the work. His critics must have been right because he issued this volume. This directory, according to Dowling, became necessary because "in a city like ours, where changes are daily, almost hourly . . . it is impossible to attain any thing like perfection." The directory has 378 entries. As usual white residents of the city were listed first, then whites in the Neck, followed by free persons of color in business in the city, and free persons of color in the Neck.

The advertisements in the directory give some idea of life in the city. For example, the soda water fount operated by J. B. Nixon at 260 King Street sold coffee in the "French style, and soda water, with a variety of syrups" and William B. Purvis worked not only as a cabinet maker and upholsterer but also as an undertaker. The Charleston Hotel at 67 Market Street "offered hot coffee and other refreshment, at all hours of the day" and served dinner "on the table exactly at 2 o'clock." This habit of taking the main meal of the day at 2 p.m. lasted well into the second half of the 20th century. The hotel also had a "spacious nine pin alley" attached to it. Dowling also advertised that he had begun the serial republication of Dr. David Ramsay's *History of South-Carolina*, published in 1809, in 80 to 100 page sections in order that the ordinary person might be able to purchase it. The work was being reissued because he "could find but one complete copy in the City--this copy belonged to the Charleston Library Society."

Aimar & Durham, Hat & Shoe Store, 97 E. Bay St.
Aitken, John, Telegraph Coffee House, 119 E. Bay St.
Allen, N. G., Bricklayer, St. Philip St., near George St.
Allen, T. P., Academy, St. Philip St., near George St.
Allen, William, Painter & Glazier, 118 Meeting St.
Allens & Paddock, 6 Broad St.
Andrews, L. F. W., Rev., 1st Universalist Society, 84 Market St.
Arnold, William, Railroad, 245 E. Bay St.
Astle, George, Shoemaker, 4 Tradd St.
Bacot & Gibbes, Merchants, 138 E. Bay St.
Ball, John, Mrs., Widow, 292 E. Bay St.
Ball, John, Rev., 77 Queen St.
Barber, F. C., Merchant, Fitzsimons' Whf.

Barker, Samuel G., Auctioneer, 17 Vendue Range
Barksdale, Thomas, Planter, cr. Broad & Logan Sts.
Battersby, Joseph, Merchant, Hamilton & Co. Whf.
Becaise, B. P., Gunsmith, 24 State St.
Becker, Daniel & Co., Grocery, cr. Bull & Coming Sts.
Bee, J. M., Teller, State Bank, 78 Queen St.
Benson, W. G., Auctioneer, 31 Broad St.
Berney, James, M. D., 96 Church St.
Berney, William, Broker, 5 State St.
Bird, J. S., Military & Fancy Store, 231 King St.
Birlke, C., Commission Merchant, Boyce & Co. Whf.
Birnie & Ogilvie, Merchants, 21 Broad St.
Bishop, S. N., Merchant, Fitzsimons' Whf., res. 33 Broad St.
Black, Francis C. & Co., Edmonston's Whf., 40 Society St.
Blair, Hugh & Co., 77 E. Bay St.
Boag, S. W., King St., op. Society St.
Bordenhave, John, Hairdresser, 6 Queen St.
Bourdoc, John, 6 Guignard St.
Brase, Peter, Grocer, s.e. cr. King & Broad Sts.
Brenton, Archibald, Classical Teacher, 25 Broad St.
Brewster, Charles & Co., Grocery, cr. Market & State Sts.
Bringloe, R., Mrs., Dyer & Scourer, 42 Tradd St.
Bringloe, Richard, Boat Builder, 42 Tradd St.
Broops, J. P., Capt., Steamer Santee. 45 Anson St.
Broughton, Mary, Widow, s.w. cr. E. Bay & Laurens Sts.
Brown. Mary, Mrs., Widow, 60 Tradd St.
Browneil, E., Draper & Tailor, 33 Broad St.
Bruce, Mary, Widow, Fancy Store, 188 King St.
Bruning, Henry, Grocery, cr. State & Anson Sts.
Bruns, H. M., Professor of Languages, 6 Bull St.
Bryan, Jon, Dry Goods Store, 263 King St.
Buist, George, Classical & English Seminary, 223 Meeting St.
Bullwinkle, George, cr. Beaufain & Mazyck Sts.
Burges & Honor, Booksellers & Stationers, 18 Broad St.
Burke, John H., Pilot, 21 Church St.
Burns, S. A., Tutor, 6 Bull St.
Capers, L. G., Merchant, 224 Meeting St.
Cardozo, I., Weigher, Custom House, res. formerly Hunt's Law Range
Cardozo, J. N., Editor, Southern Patriot, res. formerly Hunt's Law Range
Carey, Eugene M., Apothecary, 34 Broad St.
Carroll & Porter, Attorneys, 63 Broad St.
Carson & Hamilton, Wholesale Grocers, 118 E. Bay St.
Carter, Robert, Grocery, 246 E. Bay St.
Casey, T. E., Justice of Peace & City Marshal, 96 Meeting St.
Chafee, Otis J., Cordial, Wine & Spirit Merchant, 14 Vendue Range
Chandler, Marvin & Co., Fancy Store, 306 King St.
Chapman, William, Factor, 69 E. Bay St.
Charier, F. M., Dress Maker, 190 King St.
Cheesborough, J. W., Merchant, 224 Meeting St.
Chitty, J. W., Boarding House, 34 Queen St.
Chreitzberg, George, Baker, cr. Queen & Mazyck Sts.
Clapp, J. B., Teacher, 17 Burns Lane, res. 359 King St.
Cleary, N. G., Planter, 284 E. Bay St.
Cohen, J. H., Broker & Auctioneer, 6 Gillon St.

Cohen, J., Jr. & Co., Factors, Edmondston's Whf.
Conway, W. D., M. D., 7 Queen St.
Cooke, George, Portrait Painter, 204 King St.
Cooper, George W., Magistrate, 84 E. Bay St.
Cormack, Thomas, Factor, 17 Vanderhorst's Whf.
Corzier, William, Grocery, 241 E. Bay St.
Craft, G. J., Attorney, 22 St. Michael's Al.
Crawford, J., Mrs., Widow, 39 Tradd St.
Crawford, William, 39 Tradd St.
Crouch, H. W., M. D., 6 Cumberland St.
Cuddy, Edward, Professor of Music, 39 Tradd St.
Curtis, R. J., Portrait Painter, 118 King St.
Davis, Francis, Fruit Store, Market St., near Anson St.
Dawson, Charles P., Planter 48 Broad St.
DeAlvigny, Noel, Physician & Dentist, 151 King St.
Deas, C. D., Factor, 21 Vanderhorst's Whf.
Deas, Henry, Jr., Accountant, Tradd St., cr. Council St.
Denny, T. W., Dr., 88 Queen St.
Depras & Carter, Boot & Shoe Store, cr. King & Hasell Sts.
Desaussure, C. A., Factor, 10 Hamilton & Co. Whf.
Devreux, T. E., Teacher, 34 Coming St.
Dick, James, Auctioneer, Vendue Range, res. 28 Broad St.
Dingwall, Fordyce William, 72 E. Bay St., res. 69 Broad St.
Donegan, James, Grocery, e. cr. Wall & Boundary Sts.
Douglas, J., Tailor, Chalmers St., op. City Sq.
Douglas, J., Tailor, Chalmers St., op. City Sq.
Dowling, Daniel J., Printer & Publisher, 83 Broad St.
Drummond, Gracy, Midwife, 38 Anson St.
Drummond, James, 38 Anson St.
Duffus, J. A., Dry Goods Store, 72 King St.
Duke, J. H., Asst. Secretary, Union Insurance Co., 83 Broad St.
Dupont, Francis, Paper Hanger, 151 King St.
Durand, Victor, Merchant, 73 E. Bay St.
Eaton, A., Boarding House, 8 Queen St.
Eckhard, G. B., Attorney, 6 St. Michael's Al.
Elfe, Edward, M. D., 122 Meeting St.
Elford & LaRoche, Conductors of the Marine Telegraph, back of Custom House
Elliott & Condy, Brokers, 25 Broad St.
Elsford, J. M., Mathematician, back of Custom House
Enslow, F., Professor of Music, 205 King St.
Esdra, J., Fancy Store, 214 King St.
Fabian, L., Mrs., Widow, Boarding House, 115 Queen St.
Fairchild, H. C., Clerk, 240 King St.
Feugas, H. P., French Tutor, Wentworth St., s. side, near King St.
Finley & Phin, Druggists, 31 Broad St.
Finley, J. E., Dr., res. Fort St.
Forrest, John, Rev., Pastor, 12 Church St.
Fourgeaud, A., Bakery, 197 E. Bay St.
Francis, George, Pilot, 4 Tradd St.
Francois, Samuel & Co., Cigar Manufacturers, 231 E. Bay St.
Fraser, Luke H., Hat Store, 9 Broad St.
Friedlander, J. M., Grocery, cr. Bull & Rutledge Sts.
Frisbie, R., Capt., 34 Tradd St.
Frost, Henry R., M. D., off. 80 Broad St., res. 80 Broad St.

Gager, James H., Hardware, 293 King St.
Gantt & Mortimer, Brokers, 6 State St.
Garrison, Isaac, Clothing Store, 105 E. Bay St.
Geldsnaur, H., Grocer, cr. Queen & Mazyck Sts.
Gerretts, Henry, Grocer, n.e. cr. Anson & Wentworth Sts.
Gibbes, C., Widow, 89 Tradd St.
Gibbes, John R., Bank of Charleston, res. 2 State St.
Gibbes, S. W., Attorney, 1 Court House Sq.
Gibbes, Waring & Johnston, Factors, 16 Hamilton & Co. Whf.
Gibbon, G. & J., Merchants, 8 Gillon St.
Gibbs, M. G., Broker, 29 Broad St., res. 51 Meeting St.
Gillespie & Hamilton, Mechanic's Retreat, 2 Queen St.
Gilman, Samuel, Rev., 66 Tradd St.
Gleize, William, M. D., 226 King St.
Gnech, M. E., Dry Goods Store, 193 King St.
Goff, E., Mrs., Millinery, 156 King St., upstairs
Goodwin, S. E., Dressmaker, 300 King St.
Gourdin, Theodore, M. D., off. 34 Meeting St., 48 Queen St.
Gowan & Caw, Watch Makers, 78 Meeting St.
Graddick, C. C., cr. Boundary & Middle Sts.
Gray, J. B., Teacher, 70 Queen St., res. 220 E. Bay St.
Green, C. F., Grocery, s.e. cr. King St. & Burns Ln.
Grencker, Mary, Dry Goods Store, cr. State & Amen Sts.
Gridland, T. W., Looking Glass Manufacturer, 155 King St.
Groustine, J., Professor of Music, n.w. cr. Church & Chalmers Sts.
Guinebault, M. T. C., Professor of French, 66 Tradd St.
Gundermann, Anton, Grocery, n.w. cr. Church & Chalmers Sts.
Guy, T. B., Merchant, E. Bay St., res. 5 St. Michael's Al.
Gyles, John A., Attorney, Court House Sq.
Hall, George, Mrs., Fancy Store, 180 King St.
Hardie, T., English & Classical Seminary, 97 Church St.
Harris, T. M., Boarding House, 4 Champney St.
Harrison, W. N., Book Agent, 123 Church St.
Hase, John, Grocery, cr. Anson & Society Sts.
Haviland, Harrill & Allen, Druggists, 304 King St.
Hayden, N., Jewelry & Fancy Store, 267 King St.
Heide, H. C., Grocery, cr. Queen & State Sts.
Heimsath, Frederick, Grocery, n.w. cr. Church & Water Sts.
Hennington, William, Turner, 61 Market St.
Henry, Edward, Grocery, s.w. cr. E. Bay & Wentworth Sts.
Henry, Philip J., Joiner, 91 Church St.
Henry, S. W., Furniture Warehouse, 171 Meeting St.
Heriot, R., Notary Public, 71 E. Bay St.
Hersman, J., Dry Goods Store, 188 King St.
Hewson, C. P., 119 E. Bay St.
Hillman, J., 224 Meeting St.
Hilzeim, H. & P., Grocery, 128 Meeting St.
Hilzeim, P. S., cr. Anson & Laurens Sts.
Hite, G. H., Miniature Painter, 151 King St.
Hobson, A., Boot & Shoe Store, 111 E. Bay St.
Holcombe, J. C., Factor, 53 Beaufain St.
Holland, Jane, Widow, 89 Tradd St.
Holmes, F. S., 4 Vanderhorst's Whf.

Holmes, James V., Gunsmith, 70 Queen St.
Hood, William, Merchant, 87 E. Bay St.
Horlbeck, Daniel, Magistrate & Attorney, 1 Court House Sq.
Hough, S., Charleston Hotel, 67 Market St.
Howard, John, Mrs., Boarding House, 2 Pinckney St.
Howland & Townsend, Dry Goods Store, near King & Market Sts.
Hughes, Thomas, Furniture Broker, 155 Meeting St.
Hull, Townsend & Knevals, Clothing Store, 287 King St.
Hyams, David, Store Keeper, cr. Queen & Philadelphia Sts.
Hyams, M. D., Rice Dealer, 81 E. Bay St.
James, Robert, Printer, King St., op. Whim Court
James, W. H., Ship Carpenter, King St., op. Whim Court
Jeanerett, J. C., Wharfinger, Boyce & Co. Whf.
Jervey, E., Painter, St. Philip St.
Jewett & Hamilton, Dry Goods Store, 294 King St.
Johns, Joel, Painter, 248 E. Bay St.
Johnson, C., Hat & Cap Store, 254 King St.
Johnson, David, M. D., off. 88 Queen St., res. 99 Queen St.
Joshua, P. & J. W. Thrase, Grocers, cr. Anson & Market Sts.
Kalb, Jacob H., Baker, 40 Elliott St.
Keeby, Thomas M., Dry Goods Store, 344 King St.
Keenan, William, Engraver, 86 Broad St.
Kennedy, S., Blacksmith, Chalmers St., s. side, near State St.
Keogh, Eliza, Mrs., Milliner, cr. Beaufain & Coming Sts.
Kerregan, J. H., Tailor, 4 Queen St.
Kilkenny, T. T. W., cr King & Tradd Sts.
King W. A., Blacksmith, Chalmers St., s. side, near State St.
King, W. D., Mr. & Mrs., Young Ladies Seminary, 287 King St.
King, W. P., Assistant Editor, Courier, 63 Broad St.
King, William & Co., 10 Hamilton & Co. Whf.
Kinloch, George, Grain Merchant, 253 E. Bay St.
Kittleband, Susan, Widow, Boarding House, 39 Tradd St.
Klink, F. N., Grocery, cr. Boundary & Washington Sts.
Knepley, S., Blacksmith, res. 94 Meeting St.
Knowles, E., Corset & Stock Maker, 278 King St.
Knox, William P. & Son, Shipwrights, Knox's Whf.
Kohncke, C. F., Grocery, 37 State St.
Lafitte, Augustus, Commission Merchant, Fitzsimons' Whf.
Lamb, James, Merchant, Magwood's N. Whf.
Lance, William, Attorney, 79 Broad St., res. Wentworth St., near St. Philip St.
LaRoche, John G., Notary Public, back of Custom House
Laroussaliere, E., Wharfinger, Lynch St.
Lassen, H., Grocery, cr. Bull & Pitt Sts.
Laumonnier, Julia, Ladies Seminary, cr. Archdale & Clifford Sts.
Lazarus, B. D. & Co., Hardware Store, 127 E. Bay St.
Lebby, Benjamin F., 63 Church St.
Legare, J. B., Attorney, 79 Broad St.
Leitner, Edward F., M. D., 28½ Tradd St.
Lenox & Reid, Bar Room, 268 King St.

Lilenthal, Henry, Grocery, cr. St. Philip & George Sts.
Lining, Thomas, Dr., off. 50 Broad St., res. 17 Legare St.
Livingston, Jane, Widow, Anson St., near Pinckney St.
Lloyd, William, Auctioneer, 5 Broad St., res. 7 State St.
Lloyd, William, Venetian Blind Maker, 159 Meeting St.
Locke, G. B., Merchant, 126 E. Bay St.
Logan, C., Broker & Auctioneer, 26 State St.
Logan, W. D., Ship Chandler, 181 E. Bay St., res. cr. Minority & State Sts.
Lowden, John, Merchant, 27 E. Bay St., res. 54 Meeting St.
Lusher, J. O., Dr. 84 Queen St.
Magrath, A. G., Attorney, 63 Meeting St., res. 197 Meeting St.
Magrath, John, Factor, Fitzsimons' Whf., res. 197 Meeting St.
Maguire, L., Grocer, 10 Tradd St.
Maguire, P., Clerk, 10 Tradd St.
Maguire, P. H., Merchant Tailor, 187 King St.
Mann, G. & Co., Confectioners, 4 Tradd St.
Markley & Clark, Coach Maker, 124 Meeting St.
Marsh, William, Wholesale Grocer, 173 E. Bay St.
Martens, J., Grocery, s.e. cr. Meeting & Society Sts.
Martin & Walker, Factors, 3 Boyce & Co. Whf.
Mathewes, E., Factor, Hamilton & Co. Whf.
Matthews, J. P., Druggist, Meeting St., 1 door from Market St.
Mazyck, Gaillard & Mazyck, Factors, 20 Vanderhorst's Whf.
McClelland & Brownlee, Dry Goods Store, 355 King St.
Michel, John F., Goldsmith & Jeweller, 246 King St.
Michel, William, M. D., 78 Queen St.
Millar, William, Teacher, 222 King St.
Miller, Robert, Merchant, 60 E. Bay St.
Milliken & Walton, Wholesale Grocers, 180 E. Bay St.
Moise, A., Attorney, formerly Hunt's Law Range
Moisson, John, Gun & Locksmith, 16 State St., res. 52 Broad St.
Molyneaux, T. B., Commission Merchant, Magwoods N. Whf.
Monefeldt, W. G., Surgeon Dentist, 152 King St.
Monroe, Robert, Seed Store, 262 King St.
Moore, W. B., Hay & Corn Store, 239 King St.
Moorhead & M'Kean, Grocers, 226 King St.
Morris, Edward, Merchant, Vanderhorst's Whf.
Morris, Henry, Notary, Planters & Mechanics Bank, res. Court House Sq.
Morris, James, Merchant, 136 E. Bay St.
Moses, M. J. & Co., Commission Merchants, 14 Vendue Range
Moses, Perry, Dry Goods Store, 160 King St.
Murphy, W. A., Dry Goods Store, 222 King St.
Myers, F., Boot & Shoe Maker, 26 Queen St.
M'Cormick, T. & C., Dry Goods Store, 60 King St.
M'Culloch, Hugh & Co., French Coffee House, 141 E. Bay St.
M'Donald & Shannon, 1 Boyce & Co. Whf.
M'Feeters, Andrew, Saddler, 227 King St.
M'Gruber, Charles M., Black & White Smith, 4 Chalmers St.

M'Hugh, F. Q., Attorney, Court House Sq.

M'Leish & Smith, Engineers & Blacksmiths, Gadsden's Whf.

M'Millan, John, Commission Merchant, Edmondston's Whf.

Nabb., J., Shipping Office, 81 E. Bay St., res. Church St.

Napier, T. & Co., Rice Mills, Gadsden's Whf., res. 69 E. Bay St.

Newton, Susan, Nurse, 22 Queen St.

Nixon, J. B., Coffee & Soda Water Fount, 260 King St.

Olsher, C., Grocery, 108 Tradd St.

Otis & Roulain, Coach Makers, 203 Meeting St.

O'Sullivan, J., Dry Goods Store, 353 King St.

O'Sullivan, Pat, Printer, Mercury Office, Legare St.

Page, J. W., Collector, 25 Broad St.

Parker, Orien, Capt., 3 Stoll's Al.

Parmly, J., Dentist, 109 Meeting St.

Payne & White, Carriage Spring Makers, 49 Wentworth St.

Pearson, Thomas, Clock & Watchmaker, 349 King St.

Pecare, Samuel, Clothing Store, 86 Meeting St.

Pepoon, B. F., Clerk, Sheriff's Office, res. 10 Broad St.

Peronneau, Mazyck & Finley, Attorneys, Court House Sq.

Perry, S., Attorney, 79 Broad St.

Phillips, John, Capt., 4 Lynch St.

Picault, F. D., Merchant, 155 E. Bay St., res. 6 State St.

Pitray, Viel & Co., Merchants, Magwood's N. Whf.

Plumeau, J. F., Agent, Northern Stage, 6 Broad St., res. 94 King St.

Poirier, P., Mrs., Fancy Store, 9 Queen St.

Porcher, Peter, Dr., 57 Tradd St.

Pregnall, Henry, House Carpenter, 14 Tradd St.

Purves, William B., Cabinet Maker, 153 Meeting St.

Ralston, Sarah, Widow, Boarding House, 66 Tradd St.

Recli, C., Coffee House, 3 Vendue Range

Rice, William, Attorney, Court House Sq.

Riggs, J. S., Mrs., Boarding House, 53 Wentworth St.

Robinson, George, Cotton Broker, Edmondston's Whf.

Roger & Bunting, Emporium, 338 King St.

Root & Taylor, Dry Goods Store, cr. King & Boundary Sts.

Rose, A. G., Cashier, Charleston Bank, res. Mazyckborough

Rose, G. H., Boarding House, cr. Tradd St. & Beadons Al.

Rose, James, Planter, 293 E. Bay St.

Ruggles, N., Boot & Shoe Store, 299 King St.

Runver, Jacob, Grocery, 57 Market St.

Ryan, H. K., Chalmers St., near Church St.

Sahlman, R., Grocery, cr. State St. & Unity Al.

Sancker, J., Grocery, s.w. cr. Boundary & St. Philip St.

Scheriff, Frederick, cr. Broad & New Sts.

Schmidt, Theodore, Professor of Music, 117 Queen St.

Schreiner, J. H., Provision Merchant, Edmondston's Whf.

Schroder, W. T., Merchant, 74 E. Bay St., res. 257 King St.

Simonton, C. S., Factor, 12 Hamilton & Co. Whf.

Smith, B. & Son, Ship Chandlery, back of the Exchange

Smith, B. F., Merchant, 13 E. Bay St.

Smith, C. B., Mrs., 17 West St.

Smith Fowler & Co., Shoe Store, 147 King St.

Smith, James, General Agent, 83 Broad St.

Smith, Manly, Fruit Store, 193 King St.

Smith, Patrick, Grocery, s.w. cr. Anson & Wentworth Sts.

Smith, S. M., Button Warehouse, 329 King St.

Smith, William, Boot & Shoe Store, 191 King St.

Somons, C., Engraver, 233 King St., res. op. Tivoli

Speissager, J. D., Music Teacher, Church St., near Market St.

Speissager, L. P., Piano & Organ Tuner, Church St., near Market St.

Squires & Petsch, Ship Blacksmiths, e. end Pinckney St.

Squires & Rogers, Hardware Store, 300 King St.

Stevens, G. R., Clothing Store, 286 King St.

Stigin, Henry, Grocery, n.e. cr. E. Bay & Market Sts

Stoppfelbein, Jacob, Tailor & Draper, 21 Queen St.

Street & Boinest, Merchants, 3 Boyce & Co. Whf.

Strobel, B. B., Dr., State St., few doors below Market St.

Suder, Peter, House Carpenter, 49 Wentworth St.

Sweeney, T., Tailor, Meeting St., near Market St.

Taylor, J. A., Auctioneer, 32 Vendue Range, res. 76 Queen St.

Taylor, Lawton & Co., Factors, Roper's Whf.

Thayer, T. H., Broker & Auctioneer, 7 State St.

Thompson, J. B., Attorney, Court House Squre, res. 10 New St.

Tilton, R. T., Mrs., Boarding House, 81 Market St.

Tobias, A. & Co., Auctioneers, cr. Vendue Range & E. Bay St.

Torre, D. A., Merchant, 182 E. Bay St., res. 65 Broad St.

Trescott, H., State Bank, res. 97 Meeeting St.

Turnbull, Andrew, Planter, 110 Broad St.

Valentine, S., Dry Goods Store, 117 King St.

Vanwinkle, J., 306 King St.

Vardell, Thomas, Bricklayer, 282 E. Bay St.

Vogel & Salvo, Cabinet Makers, 225 King St.

Walker, Alexander, Merchant, res. 15 Friend St.

Walker, James E., Stone Cutter, 66 Queen St.

Walker, W. S. & R. D., Stone Cutters, 145 Meeting St.

Wallmann, W. J. H., Grocery, cr. Archdale & Berresford Sts.

Welling, William, Boarding House, 47 State St

Wells, J. G., Clerk, 240 King St.

Whitney, O. L., Dry Goods Store, 340 King St.

Whitney, T. A., Dry Goods Store, 352 King St.

Wilken, Daniel, Grocery, cr. George & Coming Sts.

Wilkes & Yates, Ship Chandlers, 61 E. Bay St.

Wilkie, Susan, Mrs., Widow, Farmers Hotel, 226 King St.

Williams, J. & T. P., Merchants, 45 E. Bay St., res. 256 Coming St.

Williams, M. E. H., Lumber Merchant, res. 6 Cumberland St.

Wilmans, A. F. & Co., Hardware Merchants, 244 King St.

Wilson, George, Pilot, Zig Zag Al.

Wilson, J. L., Attorney, 4 St. Michael's Al., res. cr. Beaufain & Mazyck Sts.

Winslow, E., Merchant, 49 E. Bay St.

Wise, E., Boarding House, cr. Elliott & Gadsdens Al.

Wood, George, Grocery, cr. Meeting & Market Sts.

Wurdemann, J. G. H., Dr., 218 King St.

Yates, J. D., Sheriff, off. Court House
Yates, J. H., House Carpenter & Ship Joiner, 13 Tradd St.
Yeadon & McBeth, Attorneys, off. 5 Broad St.

Zeyffert, Andrew, Cabinet Maker, res. 34 Queen St.

The Directory for 1837-38

True to his word D. J. Dowling issued the next directory for the city known as *Dowling's Charleston Directory, and Annual Register for 1837 and 1838. Containing: Names of Person in Business, Heads of Families, List of the Streets, Lanes, Alleys and Courts, Hotels, Taverns, Boarding Houses, Churches, Public Buildings, Packets, Insurance Companies, Banks, Pilots, Officers of the United States, State, and City Government &c. And Embellished with a Plan of the City of Charleston* (Charleston: D. J. Dowling, 1837). The directory contains 2,496 records which is 1,101 less than the 1835-36 volume. At the end of the directory, Dowling stated that "the preceding list of names collected during the summer months of June and July, at which period several of the inhabitants are always absent, may contain a few ommissions or errors -- in FOUR THOUSAND NAMES these *must* occur sometimes. He promised another supplement in October "if information sufficient offers -- and any names should be found wanting." He also said the volume appeared late due to the difficulty of obtaining paper for the map. This directory has quite a number of people listed more than once, but with different addresses.

Abrahams, A. H., Merchant, 14 Vendue Range, res. 122, King St.
Abrahams, E., 41 Society St.
Abrahams, H., Mrs., Dry Goods & Clothing Store, 207 King St.
Ackis, J., Bricklayer, 28 Pinckney St.
Adams, Essell, Accountant, 122 Queen St.
Adams, Jasper, Rev., Cannon St., Neck
Adams, Mary, Widow, 43 Coming St.
Adams, Thomas, Capt., Mariner, 37 Meeting St.
Addison, Frances, Widow, 12 Coming St.
Addison, George, Watchmaker, 254 King St.
Addison, Joseph, Ship Carpenter, 6 Wentworth St.
Addison, Thomas, Merchant, 14 Coming St.
Adger, James & Co., Hamilton & Co. Whf., res. King St., near Spring St., Neck
Adger, Robert, Merchant, Hamilton & Co. Whf., res. King St., near Spring St., Neck
Adkins, Simpson, Pilot, 17 Church St.
Aiken, William, Planter, Judith St., Neck
Aikin, Thomas, Dr., 150 Meeting St.
Aimar, Sebastian, Boot & Shoe Store, 183 E. Bay St.
Aimar, Thomas, Hat & Boot Store, 81 E. Bay St.
Ainger, Joseph, Cooper, Vanderhorst's Whf.
Airs, Thomas, Boat Builder, 156 E. Bay St.
Aldrich, J. T., Bookkeeper, Commercial N. Whf.
Aldrich, Robert, Wharfinger, Commercial Whf., res. 15 Tradd St.
Alexander, David, President, Union Insurance Co., res. 7 Logan St.
Alexander, H., Dr., 7 Legare St.
Alexander, J. J., Secretary, Union Insurance Co., 80 Queen St.
Alexander, Samuel, Harbor Master, off. Champney St. near E. Bay St., res. 85 Queen St.

Allan, Richard, Dr., 48 Tradd St.
Allbright, Susan, 22 Berresford St.
Allen, H. C., Coffee House, 45 Market St.
Allen, James, Boarding House, 50 King St.
Allen, William, Teacher, 32 St. Philip St.
Allender, Benjamin & Co., Bookbinders, res. 44 Queen St.
Allender, William, Bookbinder, Philadelphia St.
Allens, L., Grocer, 18 State St.
Allens, Paddock & Carter, Stock Exchange Dealer, 6 Broad St.
Allerding, H., Grocer, cr. Anson & Wentworth Sts.
Alston, Charles, Planter, 7 Fort St.
Alston, G., Mrs., Widow, 49 Bull St.
Alston, William Ashe, Attorney, 48 Broad St.
Alston, William, Col., Planter, 11 King St.
Aman, N., Blacksmith, 40 Bull St.
Ancrum, Jane, Widow, 11 Bull St.
Anderson, E. K., Factor, Edmondston's Whf.
Anderson, John, Capt., Mariner, 17 Church St.
Anderson, N. E., Mrs., Millinery, 353 King St.
Anderson, Thomas, Merchant, 353 King St.
Andrea, Francis N., Tailor, Philadelphia St.
Andrews, Moses, Mrs., 27 Hasell St.
Anthony, A. T., Widow, 180 E. Bay St.
Anthony, Jane, Widow, King St., near Mary St., Neck
Anthony, Sarah, Cannon St., Neck
Antonio, Aires, Globe Tavern, 203 King St.
Apples, Henry, Grocer, 71 Tradd St.
Arkest, John E., Bricklayer, n. side Boundary St.
Arms, Eliza, 18 George St.
Arms, S. C., 18 George St.
Arnold, J. W. B., Merchant Tailor, 111 King St.
Artman, John, Coach Maker, 5 Archdale St.
Artope, George, Engineer, 186 King St.
Ashton, A. E., Bookkeeper, res. Mary St., Neck
Astle, George, Boot Maker, 8 Tradd St.
Atkinson, C., Merchant, 116 King St.
Atwell, George E., Jewelry & Variety Store, 242 King St.
Aubin, Joseph, Wine Merchant, res. 2 West St.
Auld, -----, Misses, Seminary, 8 George St.
Aveille, P. A., Merchant, 165 E. Bay St.
Aveille, R., Miss, 16 Horlbeck's Al.
Axson, Jacob, City Recorder, 17 Meeting St.
Axson, John, Planter, Charlotte St., Cannonborough, Neck
Axson, S., Mrs., Boarding House, 15 Cumberland St.
Azevado, R. D., Widow, 97 King St.
Babcock, S. & Co., Booksellers & Stationers, 290 King St.
Babcock, William, Bookseller, res. 290 King St.
Babson, Ann R., 175 King St.
Bachman, John, Rev., Cannon St., Neck
Backhouse, William, 5 Lynch St.
Bacot, Andrew, 11 Archdale St.
Bacot, -----, Assistant Postmaster, 68 King St.
Bacot, O. D., Factor, res. S. Bay St.
Bacot, R. Wainwright, Clerk, 68 King St.
Bacot, T. W., Widow, 68 King St.
Badger, James, Clerk, Planters & Mechanics Bank, Res. Washington St., Mazyckborough

72

Bailey, & Dawson, Attorneys, 69 Meeting St.
Bailey, A., Watchmaker, 235 King St.
Bailey, Henry, Attorney General, 69 Meeting St.
Bailey, J. S., Grain Merchant, 31 E. Bay St.
Bailey, Josiah E., Printer, E. Bay St., near Broad St.
Bailey, Mary, 115 Queen St.
Bailey, Samuel, Merchant, Hamilton & Co. Whf.
Bailey, W. J., Merchant, Central Whf.
Baker, B., Widow, 74 King St.
Baker, R. L., Druggist, s.e. cr. Broad & E. Bay Sts.
Baker, R. S., Rev., cr. Broad & Friend Sts.
Baker, Sproulls & Co., Hat Store, 286 King St.
Baldwin, John, Attorney, res. 11 Market St.
Ball, Elias, Planter, 21 Lynch St.
Ball, John, Boarding House, Elliott St.
Ball, John, Mrs., Widow, Alexander St., Neck
Ball, William, Boarding House, Elliott St.
Ballantine, A., Harness Maker, Market & Beaufain Sts.
Ballund, A. & Co., Grocers, 21 Market St.
Balwinkle, John, King St., Neck
Bamphield, C., Cabinet Maker, 71 Meeting St., F.P.C.
Bancroft, J. & Co., Merchants, 94 E. Bay St.
Bankershaw, -----, Mrs., Widow, 24 St. Philip St.
Banks, H. C., Mrs., Seminary, 373 King St.
Banks, Hugh, Merchant, 16 Liberty St.
Bann, Eliza, Widow, 3 Clifford St.
Barber, F. C., Merchant, Fitzsimons' Whf.
Barbot, A., Merchant, 29 E. Bay St.
Barbot, P. J., Accountant, 22 E. Bay St.
Barguet, Barbara, Umbrella Maker, 113 Meeting St.,
    F.P.C.
Bark, John W., Carpenter, 11 Middle St., F.P.C.
Barker, H., Accountant, 285 King St.
Barker, J., Merchant, 64 King St.
Barker, J. S., 22 Society St.
Barksdale, Mary, Miss, 48 Wentworth St.
Barksdale, Thomas, Planter, 125 Broad St.
Barnes, Charles, Accountant, Thomas St., Neck
Barnes, W. B., Accountant, Thomas St., Neck
Barnes, W. B., Custom Inspector, Charlotte St., Neck
Barnwell, William H., Rev., 15 Logan St.
Baron, Eliza, Widow, 103 Broad St.
Baron, Esther, Miss, 32 Society St.
Barre, John, Wine Store, 25 Market St.
Barrett, Jacob, 109 Broad St.
Barrett, Rachel, Widow, cr. King & Boundary Sts.
Bartless, Mary, Widow, 10 Middle St.
Bartlett, F. M., Boot & Shoe Maker, 199 King St.
Bartlett, William, cr. Boundary & Elizabeth Sts.
Barton, & Pregnal, Sashmakers, 16 Tradd St.
Barton, Jane, 9 Pitt St.
Bascom, -----, Mrs., Widow, Boarding House, 9 Bull St.
Battersby, Joseph, Merchant, Commercial Whf.
Battiste, John, Grocer, 21 Market St.
Bauxbaum, Eliza, Widow, 120 Queen St.
Baxter, Amos, Carpenter, n. side, Boundary St., F.P.C.
Bay, E. H., Hon., Judge, 52 Meeting St.
Beaufort, F., Butcher, Hampstead, Neck
Becker, Daniel, Grocer, cr. Bull & Pitt Sts.
Becker, E., Grocer, 25 St. Philip St.

Becker, Hans, Grocer, 16 St. Philip St.
Bee, James F., Teller, State Bank, res. 100 Queen St.
Bee, Joseph, Planter, Cannon St., Neck
Bee, Robert R., Cooper, Hamilton & Co. Whf.
Bee, Smith R., Widow, 3 Friend St.
Bee, W. C., Merchant, 56 Wentworth St.
Bee, William R., 3 Friend St.
Beekman, F., Accountant, res. 17 St. Philip St.
Beekman, J., Painter, res. 17 St. Philip St.
Behling, L., Grocer, cr. E. Bay & Market Sts.
Beile, John P., Bookseller & Stationer, 20 King St.
Belin, A. H., Planter, 13 Archdale St.
Bell, David, Jr., Accountant, 25 Society St.
Bell, David, Sr., Accountant, 25 Society St.
Bell, John, Cooper, 1 Clifford St.
Bell, -----, Miss, Seminary, 45 George St.
Bell, Richard, Dry Goods Store, 310 King St.
Bell, William, Mason, 48 Society St.
Bellinger, John, Dr., cr. Green & College Sts.
Bemar, Eliza, Widow, 3 Green St.
Benjamin, Philip, Fruiterer, 16 St. Philip St.
Benjamin, S. A., Clothing Store, 48 E. Bay St.
Bennett, Christopher, Printer, 41 State St.
Bennett, E. S., Dr., 139 Meeting St., res. 21 Rutledge St.
Bennett, Isaac, Mrs., Widow, Charlotte St., Neck
Bennett, Peter B., Grocer, 60 Elliott St.
Benoist, A., Baker, cr. King & Reid Sts., Neck
Benson, William & Crafts Grocery, cr. Prioleau & Cordes
    Sts.
Benson, William G., Auctioneer, 38 Broad St.
Bentham, R. & Holmes, Attorneys, St. Michael's Al.
Bentham, Robert, Attorney, Smith St., Neck
Beringer, William, Planter, 281 E. Bay St.
Berney, William, Broker & Auctioneer, 5 State St.
Berrett, William H., Bookseller, cr. Broad & State Sts.
Berry, Benjamin, Accountant, 9 Smith St.
Berry, Mary, Widow, res. 6 Friend St.
Bessent & Miller, Dry Goods Store, 21 King St.
Besser, Charles, Tailor, 156 King St.
Bettison, Sarah, Widow, 17 Savage St.
Beusse, John H., Dry Goods Store, 197 E. Bay St.
Bevin, Daniel, Grocer, cr. Lines & King St.
Bigelow, -----, Mrs., Widow, cr. Vanderhorst & St. Philip
    Sts.
Biggs, -----, Mrs., Widow, 11 St. Philip St.
Biglow & Dorrance, Merchants, 90 E. Bay St.
Bileins, William, Accountant, res. 3 Lynch St.
Birch, Edward, Factor, 13 Back St.
Birch, Edward, Factor, 3 Dawes' & Co. Whf.
Bird, J. S., Military & Fancy Store, 223 King St.
Bird, William, Ship Carpenter, 7 Lynch St.
Birnie & Ogilvie, Hardware Store, 21 Broad St.
Bischoff, A., Grocer, cr. Anson & Laurens Sts.
Bishop, S. N., Merchant, 7 State St.
Bitchman, H., Grocer, 18 S. Bay St.
Bitchman, J., Grocer, Thomas St., Neck
Black, A. W., Notary Public, 71 E. Bay St.
Black, Alexander, 97 Wentworth St.
Black, Francis C., Merchant, 11 Champney St.
Black, James, Factor, Magwood's Whf.

Black, W. P., Baker, 183 King St.
Blackwood, John, Accountant, 24 Pitt St.
Blackwood, John, Mrs., 24 Pitt St.
Blain, Andrew, Wheelwright, Meeting St., Neck
Blain, William S., Schoolmaster, 26 State St.
Blair, Hugh & Co., Wholesale Grocers, 79 E. Bay St.
Blake, Charles, Merchant, 4 Vendue Range
Blake, Edward, Teller, Bank of S. C., 10 Water St.
Blake, -----, Misses, 8 King St.
Blanchard, Sarah, Widow, 182 E. Bay St.
Blum & Cobia, Auctioneers, 30 Vendue Range
Blum, Andrew, Free School, Hampstead, Neck
Blum, F., Accountant, 1 Lynch St.
Blum, J. Charles, Auctioneer, res. King St., Neck
Boag, William S., Wholesale Druggist, 281 King St.
Bohles, L. E., Grocer, cr. Archdale St. & Swinton's Ln.
Boinest, Daniel, Merchant, res. 12 State St.
Bolchoz, Sophia, Milliner, 227 King St.
Bolchoz, Sophia, Widow, Millinery, 277 King St.
Bolles, A., Teacher, Green St.
Bonneau, Charlotte, Widow, 10 King St.
Bonneau, D., Coming St., Neck
Bonneau, I. E., Factor, Hamilton's Whf., res. 15 Church St.
Bonneau, Martha, Coming St., Neck
Bonnell, John, Capt., Mariner, 4 Lynch St.
Bonner, Eliza, 108 King St.
Bordenave, John, Hair Dresser, 2 Queen St.
Bornes, Joseph, Tailor, 119 Church St.
Bosch, T. H., Grocer, cr. Wolf & Nassau Sts., Neck
Bossett, Vincent, Confectioner, King St., Neck
Boucheir, J. & Co., Grocers, 134 King St.
Boudo, H., Jewelry & Fancy Store, 146 King St.
Boulger, C., Grocer, 32 King St.
Bounetheau, D., Watchmaker, St. Philip St., Neck
Bounetheau, E. W., Magistrate, St. Philip St., Neck
Bourdon, Jane S., Tailoress, 1 Chalmers St.
Bours, Luke, Bookkeeper, 62 Church St.
Boutan, Peter B., Baker, King St., near John St., Neck
Bowen, -----, Rt. Rev., Bishop, Coming St., Neck
Bowers, John E., Gunsmith, 67 Boundary St.
Bowman, M. H., Miss, cr. St. Philip & Beaufain Sts.
Bowman, -----, Mrs., Widow, 16 Beaufain St.
Boyce, John, Jr., Merchant, 45 E. Bay St.
Boyce, Ker & Co., Factors, Boyce & Co. Whf.
Boyd, William, Painter, Thomas St., Neck
Boyden, Mary E., Widow, 9 Laurens St.
Boykin, Samuel, Mrs., Widow, 9 Laurens St.
Boylston, Henry, Dr., 358 King St., near the Citadel
Bradford, William, Ship Carpenter, 16 Vernon St.
Bradley, Margaret, Widow, 31 Anson St.
Brady, John, Mrs., Widow, 16 Anson St.
Brailsford, B., Mrs., 32 S. Bay St.
Brailsford, E., Widow, 1 Lamboll St.
Brailsford, -----, Misses, 14 Hasell St.
Brailsford, W. R., Factor, 1 Dawes & Co. Whf.
Brailsford, William, Factor, res. 54 King St.
Branson, Ware, Sail Maker, 32 E. Bay St., res. 7 Lynch St.
Branton, Philip, Mrs., Widow, 161 E. Bay St.

Brase, Peter, Grocer, 121 Broad St.
Bremar, K., Mrs., 12 Logan St.
Brenan, Charles, Factor, Fitzsimons' Whf., res. 3 Society St.
Bressac, Edward, Merchant, 38 Queen St.
Brewster, C. R., Attorney, res. Radcliffborough, op. Duncan St.
Brewster, Charles, Bookkeeper, Coming St., Neck
Bridges, John, Capt., Mariner, 313 King St.
Bridgett, John, Boarding House, 19 George St.
Bringloe, Richard, Custom House, res. 17 Church St.
Brisbane, Mary, Widow, 29 Meeting St.
Britton, E., Printer, 39 Wentworth St.
Britton, E., Widow, 38 Coming St.
Brocklebank, William, Bricklayer, Meeting St., Neck
Brodie, R. H., Foundry, 41 Coming St.
Broughton, Alexander, 53 Wentworth St.
Broughton, Mary M., Widow, 74 Anson St.
Brow, C. F., Planter, 49 Anson St.
Brow, Mary, Widow, Teacher, 62 Tradd St.
Brown & Welsman, Factors, Dawes & Co. Whf.
Brown, Albert, Painter, King St., Neck, F.P.C.
Brown, Alexander H., Magistrate, 55 Meeting St.
Brown, Alexander, Merchant, King St., Neck
Brown, Ann, Widow, 41 Tradd St.
Brown, E. H., Block & Pump Maker, 3 Liberty St.
Brown, E. H., Pump & Block Maker, 164 E. Bay St.
Brown, Eliza J., Fruit Store, 48 King St.
Brown, George W., Livery Stables, 102 Church St.
Brown, George, Wholesale Grocer, 47 Broad St.
Brown, Harriet, Teacher, 41 Tradd St.
Brown, J. B. & L., Hat Store, 17 Broad St.
Brown, J. S., Hair Dresser, 124 Meeting St., F.P.C.
Brown, James, Butcher, Hampstead, F.P.C.
Brown, James W., Accountant, 5 Fort St.
Brown, John, Accountant, King St., near Broad St.
Brown, John, D., Keeper, City Burial Ground, Cannon St.
Brown, Lavinia, Mantuamaker, 7 Friend St., F.P.C.
Brown, Magdaline, 94 Market St.
Brown, Malcolm, Shoe Maker, 35 Anson St., F.P.C.
Brown, Malcolm, Shoe Maker, St. Philip St., Neck, F.P.C.
Brown, Neil, Planter, King St., Neck
Brown, P. W., Tinner, King St., near John St., Neck
Brown, R. E., 61 Tradd St.
Brown, Richard, House Carpenter, 29 St. Philip St.
Brown, W. D., House Carpenter, 3 Liberty St.
Browne, Robert, Factor, 51 Church St.
Brownell, Edmund, Clothing Store, 33 Broad St.
Bruce, Mary, Mrs., Dry Goods Store, 180 King St.
Brunning, Henry, Grocer, cr. State & Amen Sts.
Brunton, A., Tin Plate Worker & Plumber, 13 Tradd St.
Bryan, Charles, Wharfinger, res. 4 Orange St.
Bryan, George S., Attorney, 9 Waring's Row.
Bryan, John, Col., 22 Hasell St.
Bryan, Jonathan, Dry Goods Store, 259 King St.
Bryan, L., Mrs., Widow, 22 Hasell St.
Bryant, Charles H., Wharfinger, Magwood's Whf.
Bryant, W., Merchant, res. 18 Broad St.
Buckner, Jackson, Bricklayer, 89 Market St.

Budd, Thomas S., Capt., Mariner, 24 Church St.
Buist, A., Rev., 3 Church St.
Buist, George, 106 Wentworth St.
Buist, Mary, Widow, 5 Church St.
Bulger, Henry, Cabinet Maker, 12 Rutledge St.
Bulow, J. J., Planter, cr. King & Cannon Sts., Neck
Bultman, C. F., Grocer, 14 King St.
Bundreck, Charles, Grocer, 5 King St.
Burchmyer, John C., Commission Merchant, 80 E. Bay St., res. 30 Society St.
Burckmyer, C., Commission Merchant, 64 E. Bay St.
Burckmyer, C., Merchant, 64 E. Bay St., res. 12 New St.
Burdell, Mary Ann, Widow, 39 Wall St.
Burden, Kinsey, Planter, 10 Logan St.
Burger, Samuel, Tax Collector, 51 Queen St.
Burges, James S., Printer & Bookseller, 55 Broad St.
Burgher, Nicholas, Grocer, 9 Mazyck St., cr. Magazine St.
Burie, John, House Carpenter, 6 Pitt St.
Burk, Martin, Dry Goods Store, 209 King St.
Burke, A. James, Printer, res. n. side Boundary St.
Burke, Samuel, Boat Builder, Williams' Whf.
Burke, William, 192 Broad St., cr. Friend St.
Burnham & Solomons, Druggists, 347 King St.
Burns, James, Cutler, 100 King St.
Burns, -----, Mrs., Widow, 3 St. Philip St.
Burrill, Samuel, Shoe Maker, 15 Archdale St.
Burrill, William, Grocer, cr. Bull & Smith Sts.
Burrows & Cordry, Joiners, Knox's Whf.
Burrows, Frederick, Pilot, 4 Gillon St.
Busing, Mary, Widow, 19 Montague St.
Bussacker, Charles, 299 King St.
Butler, C. P., Jeweller, 109 King St.
Byrne, Jacob, Bricklayer, 39 Coming St.
Bythewood, M., 227 E. Bay St.
Calder, Alexander, Planters Hotel, Church & Queen Sts.
Calder, J., Cabinet Ware Room, 8 Meeting St.
Calder, James, Merchant, Chisolm's Whf., res. 21 Meeting St.
Calder, William (Moffett & Calder), res. 18 George St.
Caldwell, J. M., Factor, Edmondston's Whf., res. 20 Society St.
Caldwell, R. & J., Factors, Magwood's S. Whf.
Caldwell, William A. & Sons, Auctioneers & Commission Merchants, 23, 25 & 27 Vendue Range
Calvert, Thomas, Blacksmith, 122 Church St.
Cambridge, St. John, Printer, 9 Minoritiy St.
Cameron, G. S., 218 King St.
Cammeron, Samuel, Sail Loft, Fitzsimons' Whf.
Camoult, Ann, 16 Beaufain St.
Campbell, A. W., Factor, 18 New St.
Campbell, A. W., Factor, Vanderhorst's Whf.
Campbell, Ann, L., 99 Broad St.
Campbell, Frederick, Hair Dresser, 101 Market St., F.P.C.
Campbell, I. M., Dr., 99 Broad St.
Campbell, J. B., Attorney, 9 State St.
Campbell, -----, Mrs., Midwife, 50 Beaufain St.
Cannon, George, Dry Goods Store, King St.
Canter, Rebecca, Widow, School, 134 King St.
Cantor, Emanuel, Grocer, 97 Market St.
Capdeville, Mary, Miss, 68 Church St.

Capers, L. G., Merchant, 162 Meeting St.
Capers, M. E., Widow, Hampstead, Neck
Capers, William, Rev., Boundary St., Neck
Carbery, John, Bookkeeper, Charleston Neck
Cardozo, J. N., Editor of Patriot, 56 E. Bay St.
Carew, Edward, Meeting St., near Ann St., Neck
Carlisle, Margaret, Widow, 6 Anson St.
Carmand, F., Woolen Draper & Mercer, 86 Queen St.
Carnochan, Richard, Merchant, 18 Hamilton & Co. Whf.
Carpenter, C., Carver & Gilder, 18 Queen St.
Carpenter, James, Butcher, Butchertown, Neck
Carr, C. D., Tailor, 30 Broad St.
Carr, Robert, Druggist, Coming St., Neck
Carran, Daniel, Wheelwright, 124 Church St.
Carrere, William G., Wharf Agent, Hamilton & Co. Whf.
Carrier, William, Accomptant, Radcliffborough
Carroll, & Porter, Attorneys, 66 Broad St.
Carroll, B. R., Lucas St., Neck
Carroll, J. L., Wholesale & Retail Boot & Shoe Store, 327 King St.
Carroll, John S., Dry Goods Store, 327 King St.
Carson & Hamilton, Merchants, 143 & 145 E. Bay St., Res. 11 Laurens St.
Carson, Elisha, Merchant, Magwood's S. Whf.
Carson, Eliza, Widow, 90 Tradd St.
Carson, William A., Planter, 90 Tradd St.
Carsten, Edward, 36 Society St.
Carsten, Elizabeth, Widow, 36 Society St.
Carsten, Robert, Grocer, 152 E. Bay St.
Carswell, J., 211 E. Bay St.
Cart, Francis, Accomptant, Boundary St., Neck
Cart, John, Bookkeeper, Planters & Mechanics Bank, Boundary St., Neck
Cart, John, Measurer of Wood & Coal, 28 Bull St.
Cart, John, Measurer of Lumber, 28 Bull St.
Carter, O., Factor, Gadsen's Whf.
Carter, William, Broker, 10 New St.
Carvalho, S. N., Dry Goods Store, 143 King St.
Carvalho, S. N., Dry Goods Store, 175 King St.
Caskins, Robert W., Clerk, 218 King St.
Cason, -----, Coal Measurer, 2 Lynch St.
Cassady, P., Livery Stables, fronting Church, Chalmers, & Queen Sts.
Cassin, F., Grocer, 7 S. Bay St.
Cassin, James, Factor, Gadsden's Whf.
Castion, Eugene, Cigar Maker, n. side, Boundary St., F.P.C.
Catherwood, J. J., Watchmaker, 63 Broad St.
Caulier, George, 39 Broad St.
Caveldaly, Adolph, 19 King St.
Cay, J. C., Merchant, E. Bay St.
Cay, ------, Madame, 35 Wall St.
Chadwick, S., & Co., Merchants, cr. Magwood's Whf. & E. Bay St., res. 11 Meeting St.
Chaffee, Otis J., Cordial, Wine, & Spirit Merchant, 76 E. Bay St.
Chambers, Margaret, Widow, 184 Meeting St.
Champlin, Jackson, Bricklayer, 89 Market St.
Champlin, Oliver, Collector, 6 Magazine St.
Chandler, -----, Mrs., Widow, Boundary St., Neck

Channing, John, Dry Goods Store, 84 Church St.
Chapeau, John B., 116 Church St.
Chapman, C. C. P., Writing Academy, 178 King St.
Chapman, James, Factor, Edmondston's Whf., res. Water St.
Chapman, Thomas, Cashier, State Bank, res. 26 Pitt St.
Chapman, W. & Co., Dry Goods Store, 206 King St., Res.18 Pitt St.
Chapman, William, Merchant, res. 18 Pitt St.
Chase, P. S., Shoe Store, 132 King St.
Chastean, Charles, M. D., 6 State St.
Chaurre, E. G., Tailor, 128 Archdale St.
Chazal, E. C., Widow, 48 Anson St.
Cheesborough, J. W., Merchant, 21 E. Bay St.
Cheney, E., (Joye & Cheney), Grocer, 43 E. Bay St.
Chew, Thomas R., Blacksmith, Lucas St., Neck
Chicest, Thomas, Tailor, Butchertown, F.P.C.
Chichester, J., Cabinet Maker, Coming St., F.P.C.
Childs, Robert, Hudson St., near King St., Neck
Chirslon, William C., Tailor, 16 Middle St., F.P.C.
Chisolm, George, Factor, 23 Legare St.
Chisolm, George, Factor, Commercial Whf.
Chisolm, George, Mrs., Widow, 13 E. Bay St.
Chisolm, Octavius, 13 E. Bay St.
Chitty, John W., Dry Goods Store, 102 King St.
Chrietzburg, George, Grocer, 133 King St.
Chrietzburg, -----, Mrs., Widow, 19 Beaufain St.
Chrietzburg, Reyly, Baker, 111 Queen St.
Christophel, George, Grocer, 132 King St.
Christopherson, C., Grocer, 192 King St.
Chupein, Louis Y., Fancy Dry Goods Store, King St.
Chupein, Louis Y., Mineral Water Fountain, 95 E. Bay St.
Chupein, T. L., China & Fancy Store, 162 King St.
Chupein, Theodore, Bookkeeper, res. 159 King St.
Church, Margaret, Umbrella Maker, 23 St. Philip St.
Church, R. L., Salesman, 307 King St.
Clancy, John, Grocer, King St., Neck
Clancy, William, Rt. Rev., Bishop, 92 Broad St.
Clark, B. & Co., Dry Goods Store, 137 King St.
Clark, B., Dry Goods Store, 137 King St.
Clark, Charles, Wharfinger, res. 10 Friend St.
Clark, Henry, 67 Queen St.
Clark, John, Wagon Yard, King St., Neck
Clark, Mary, Widow, 67 Queen St.
Clark, Richard, Planter, 21 Church St.
Clark, William, Grocer, 101 Queen St.
Clark, William, Grocer, s.e. cr. Anson & Wentworth Sts.
Clarke, Charles, Grocer, 49 E. Bay St.
Clarkin, John, Dry Goods Store, 135 King St.
Clarkson, E., Widow, 2 Bull St.
Clarkson, John, Planter, 2 Bull St.
Clarkson, William, Planter, 2 Bull St.
Clastra, Stephen, House Carpenter, Coming St., Neck
Clayborn, James, Planter, 5 Rutledge St.
Clayton, David, Factor, King St., Neck
Cleapor, J. W., Sail Maker, Price's Whf., res. 9 Wall St.
Cleary, Susan M., Mrs., 259 E. Bay St.
Clement, Nicholas, Grocer, 52 State St.
Clements, R., Accountant, 367 King St.
Clements, William, Wood Factor, St. Philip St.

Cleveland, John, Laborer, 8 Water St.
Clifford, Henry, Factor, Holmes' Whf., res. 12 Middle St.
Clifford, L. C., Bookkeeper, 4 E. Bay St.
Clissoy, R., Bandbox Manufacturer, 82 King St.
Clough, J. B. & Co., Merchants, 116 E. Bay St.
Clyde, Thomas M., Tanner, cr. Wolf & Hanover Sts.
Cobia, Ann, 18 Montague St.
Cobia, F. J., Reid St., Neck
Cobia, Henry, Auctioneer, res. 2 Wall St.
Cobia, Nicholas, Planter, 112 Wentworth St.
Cobie, John, Grocer, 9 Back St.
Coche, Joseph, Confectioner, 64 State St.
Cochran, C. B., Teacher, 108 Wentworth St.
Cochran, John, Blacksmith, Cumberland St.
Cochran, Samuel, Tailor, 341 King St., F.P.C.
Cochran, Sarah, Widow, Butchertown, Neck
Coffin, E., Dr., 269 E. Bay St.
Coffin, Thomas A., 269 E. Bay St.
Cogdell, John S., Col., President, Bank of S. C., res. cr. Tradd & Meeting Sts.
Cohen, A. N., Dry Goods & Clothing Store, 244 King St.
Cohen, D. D., 103 Broad St.
Cohen, H., Merchant, 75 Boundary St.
Cohen, Hyam, City Inquirer & Assessor, res. 79 Broad St.
Cohen, J., 9 Rutledge St.
Cohen, J. Hays, Accountant, 79 Broad St.
Cohen, J., Jr., & Co., Merchants, Edmondston's Whf.
Cohen, Jacob, Jr., res. 371 King St.
Cohen, Jacob, Sr., res. 371 King St.
Cohen, Marks, 103 Broad St.
Cohen, Mordecai, res. 103 Broad St.
Cohen, Nathan A., Tailor & Clothing Store, 151 E. Bay St.
Cohen, P. M., & Co., Druggists, 61 Broad St.
Cohen, Rachel, 96 Tradd St.
Cohen, S. J., & Son, Dry Goods Store, 340 King St.
Cohen, Solomon, res. 371 King St.
Cohrs, H. A., Dry Goods Store, 308 King St.
Colburn, B. P. & Co., Dry Goods Store, 226 King St.
Colburn, J. S., Dry Goods Store, 78 Broad St.
Colcock, C. J., President, State Bank of S. C., res. 2 Orange St.
Colcock, John, Factor, Commercial Whf.
Coleman, John, Accountant, 19 St. Philip St.
Collins, James B., Boarding House, 6 Elliott St.
Collins, Peter, Fruit Store, 265 King St.
Colston, Jacob, Grocer, 132 Coming St.
Condy & Elliott, Broker & Auctioneer, 22 Broad St.
Condy, Thomas D., U. S. Marshall, res. Cannon St., Neck
Conner, H. W., Hardware Store, 294 King St., Res.29 Society St.
Conner, Samuel, Capt., 29 Hasell St.
Conyers, Mary, Tailoress, 21 Boundary St.
Cook, Daniel, Factor, Edmondston's Whf.
Cook, J. C., Printing Office, 63 Wentworth St.
Cook, John A., Grocer, e. end Boundary Sts.
Cook, Motte & Co., Lumber Merchants, Edmondston's Whf.
Cook, -----, Mrs., Boarding House, 30 St. Philip St.
Cook, Otto, Grocer, cr. Tradd & E. Bay Sts.
Cooler, Archibald, 22 Mazyck St.

Cooper, George W., Magistrate, res. 8 Short St.
Cooper, J. J., Boot Maker, 110 King St., F.P.C.
Cooper, N., Shoe Store, cr. King & Queen Sts., res. 64 Anson St.
Cooper, Parris, Tailor, 39 Coming St., F.P.C.
Copes, James, Pilot, 14 Water St.
Coppery, Francis, House Carpenter, Butchertown, F.P.C.
Corano, C., Widow, 41 George St.
Corbett, Eliza, Widow, 3 Rutledge St.
Corbett, James, Dry Goods Store, 316 King St.
Corbett, Thomas, Jr., Planter, 19 Lynch St.
Corby, John, Blacksmith, cr. Vernon & Washington Sts.
Cordes, A., Baker, 44 King St.
Cordes, A., Cabinet Maker, 44 King St.
Cordes, Thomas, Mrs., Charlotte St., Neck
Corimick, Thomas, Factor, 17 Vanderhorst's Whf.
Cornisky, Eliza, Grocery, 8 Tradd St.
Cornwall, E. S., Accountant, 375 King St.
Corrie, Samuel, Wheelwright, King St., near John St., Neck
Cortea, H. C., Stevedore, n. side Boundary St.
Cotchett, George, res. 22 Church St.
Courtney, -----, Mrs., Boarding House, 38 Broad St.
Cowan, John, Cabinet Maker, 151 Meeting St.
Cowan, Maria, Widow, 10 Clifford St.
Cowperthwaite, E. H., Furniture Store, 163 King St.
Cox, Rodolph, Sail Maker, 5 Champney St., res. 114 King St.
Cox, William, Bookkeeper, 46 E. Bay St.
Coy, George W., Merchant, Dewees' Whf.
Craft, George, Planter, 112 Tradd St.
Crafts, G. J., Attorney, 16 St. Michael's Al.
Cramer, G. W., Merchant, 56 Queen St.
Cranmer, John, Carpenter, 11 Wall St.
Cranston, Edward, res. 27 Mazyck St.
Cranston, Harrall, 27 Mazyck St.
Cranston, Horatio, res. 27 Mazyck St.
Crawford, Ann, Widow, 3 Mazyck St.
Crawford, John, Wharfinger, 1 Rutledge St.
Crawford, Susan, Widow, 3 Elliott St.
Cregare, Ann, Widow, 3 Clifford St.
Creighton, James, Planter, Charlotte St., Neck
Cremon, John, Mariner, 62 State St.
Crew, E. B., Accountant, 52 Wentworth St.
Crews, A. J., 117 Queen St.
Cripps, -----, Misses, 45 Meeting St.
Crocker, D., & Co., Merchants, 68 E. Bay St.
Crole, George, Capt., Mariner, 16 Pinckney St.
Cromwell, E., Miss, Seminary, 24 Horlbeck's Al.
Croom, Bryan, 19 E. Bay St.
Crosby, Mary, Widow, Hampstead, Neck
Crosier, William, Grocer, 315 E. Bay St.
Cross, C. W., Mrs., Widow, cr. Meeting & Tradd Sts.
Cross, William, Bricklayer, 8 Beaufain St.
Crouch, Charles, Attorney, 8 Coming St.
Crovat, G. F., Ship Carpenter, 156 E. Bay St.
Crovat, Lewis, Grocer, res. 265 King St.
Crovat, Peter, Ship Carpenter, 156 E. Bay St.
Crovat, Peter, Sr., Paint & Oil Store, 265 King St.
Crozier, William, Grocery, 21 E. Bay St.

Cruickshank, Mary, Widow, King St., near John St., Neck
Cudworth, John, Printer, Horlbeck's Al.
Cunningham, A., House Carpenter, 8 Beaufain St.
Curry, James, Capt., Mariner, 3 Fort St.
Curtis, Ann, 51 Coming St.
Curtis, E., House Carpenter, 1 Broad St.
Curtis, Joseph, Carpenter, 2 Inspection St.
D'Alvigne, Noel, Jr., Surgeon & Dentist, 162 King St.
D'Orval, -----, Madame, Boarding School, John St., Neck
Daley, William, Grocer, Meeting & Market Sts.
Dalton, Francis, 100 Meeting St.
Daniels, Moses E., Trader, 29 Wentworth St.
Daniels, Stephen, Tailor, 128 Meeting St.
Daniels, W. M., Watchmaker, cr. Meeting & Chalmers Sts.
Dantazler, A., Grocer, 283 King St., Neck
Darby, George, 1 Gibbes St.
Darby, R., Mrs., Widow, 126 Queen St.
Dart, Benjamin S., Factor, Davis & Co. Whf.
Daufresne, Peter, French Teacher, 128 Queen st.
Davega, Grace, Widow, 87 Boundary St.
Davega, M., Merchant, 221 King St.
Davenne, Edmond, Merchant, 12 Hamilton & Co. Whf.
David, R. P., Sausage Maker, 24 Market St.
Davidson, James, Painter, 42 Tradd St.
Davidson, Thomas, Lumber Measurer, 9 S. Bay St.
Davidson, William, cr. E. Bay St. & Crafts' Whf., res. 192 E. Bay St.
Davis, Edward, Boarding House, 67 Church St.
Davis, Eliza, Tailoress, 3 Wentworth St.
Davis, G. Y., Factor, res. 10 Wentworth St.
Davis, George A., Mrs., Widow, 38 Tradd St.
Davis, George S., Merchant, 16 E. Bay St.
Davis, J. A., Merchant, 16 E. Bay St.
Davis, John, Bookkeeper, 104 King St.
Davis, John, Capt., Mariner, 24 E. Bay St.
Davis, John, Coming St., Neck
Davis, Martha, Widow, 1 Coming St.
Davis, Mary, Widow, 11 Tradd St.
Davis, T. P., Merchant, 4 E. Bay St.
Davis, Thomas, Capt., Mariner, 33 Tradd St.
Davison, Mary, 107 Wentworth St.
Dawson, Caroline, Widow, 7 Hasell St.
Dawson, J. L., Dr., 43 Church St.
Dawson, O., State Bank, res. 11 Bull St.
Dawson, W. H., Broker, 26 Montague St.
Dawson, W. H., Broker & Auctioneer, 27 Broad St.
Day, E., Clothing Store, 337 King St.
Day, F., Fancy & Millinery Store, cr. George & King Sts.
Day, Michael, Merchant, 152 E. Bay St.
Day, Z., Carriage Warehouse, Wentworth St.
Dean, H., 218 King St.
Deas & Broun, Factors, 21 Vanderhorst's Whf.
Deas, C. D., Factor, Vanderhorst's Whf.
Deas, C., Merchant, res. 54 Wentworth St.
Deas, E. Horry, Dr., off., 12 Society St.
Deas, Henry, Dr., 1 Friend St.
Deas, -----, Miss, Millinery, 59 King St.
Deas, S., Planter, 54 Wentworth St.
Deas, Thomas H., Planter, 2 Hasell St.
Deasel, C. H., Dr., Planter, Pitt St., Neck

Debow, John, Chair Maker, n.e. cr. King & Anson Sts.
Decamp, James, Bandbox Maker, 73 King St.
DeChoiseul, -----, Count, French Consul, E. Bay St.
Decottes, A. C., Bookkeeper, 100 Tradd St.
Decottes, E. A., Bookkeeper, 100 Tradd St.
Decottes, L., Mrs., Widow, 100 Tradd St.
Deery, James, Shoe Maker, 27 Church St.
Dehon, Sarah, Widow, 11 Meeting St.
Deickman, H., Grocer, 43 Queen St.
Dela, Richbourg, Planter, Hampstead
Delaney, John B., 6 Archdale St.
Delano, E. & J. B., Merchants, cr. E. Bay & Vendue Sts., Res. 16 George St.
Delany, M., Capt., Mariner, Church St.
Deliessline, F. A., 11 Smith St.
Della Torre, A., Merchant, res. 67 Broad St.
Dellinger, John, A., Crockery Store, 273 King St.
Deming & Bulkley, Pianofortes & Furniture, 197 King St.
Dempsey, Thomas, 105 Queen St.
Dennehy, J., Printer, cr. State & Amen Sts.
Dennis, N., Tailor, res. 130 Friend St.
Denny, T. S., Dr., 88 Queen St.
Depras & Carter, Shoe Store, s. cr. King & Hasell Sts.
Dereef, R. E., Wood Factor, Hampstead, F.P.C.
Desaussure, Henry, A., Attorney, 39 Broad St.
Desir, Joseph, 7 Berresford St.
Deveaux, J. P., n. side, Boundary St.
Deveaux, Martha, Widow, 32 Tradd St.
Devencau, Elizabeth, 102 King St.
Dewar, William S., Merchant, Hamilton & Co. Whf.
Dewar, William S., Merchant, 34 E. Bay St.
Dewees, John, Merchant, 32 E. Bay St.
Dewees, Mary, Widow, Alexander St., Neck
Dewees, William, Factor, Dewees & Co. Whf.
Dexter, Mercy, 11 Bedon's Al.
Dibble, A. C., Hat Store, 35 Broad St.
Dick & Holmes, Auctioneers, 17 Vendue Range
Dick, James, Auctioneer, res. 26 Broad St.
Dickman, T. W., & Co., Dry Goods Store, 306 King St.
Dicks, Henry, Butcher, cr. E. Bay & Boundary Sts.
Dickson & Jervey, Drs., cr. Meeting & Hudson Sts.
Dickson, S. & I., Grocers, 185 E. Bay St.
Dickson, S. Henry, Dr., res. cr. Meeting & Hudson Sts.
Dile, Jane, Dry Goods Store, 18 King St.
Dinkins, L. J., Factor, Fitzsimons' Whf.
Disher, Robert, Meeting St., Neck
Divenu, S., 7 Clifford St.
Divver, James, Academy, 7 Burns Lane
Dixon, John, Soap & Candle Manufactory, King St.
Dobson, O. L., State Assessor, res. 2 Water St.
Doggett, S. W., Female Academy, Meeting St., op. Burns Ln.
Donegan, J., Grocer, cr. Wall & Boundary Sts.
Doner, George, Bookkeeper, 62 E. Bay St.
Donmall, Charles, Professor of the Flute, 204 King St.
Dorrance & Bigelow, Merchants, 90 E. Bay St.
Dorrance, Benjamin, Merchant, 90 E. Bay St.
Dorrell, John, Carpenter, 12 Laurens St.
Dorrell, Robert, Factor, res. 11 Lynch St.
Dors, U. P., Merchant, 24 King St.

Dotterer, Thomas, Iron Foundary, 17 Wentworth St.
Doucin, M., Painter, 94 King St.
Doucin, Philip M., Wharfinger, Boyce & Co. Whf.
Dougherty, J., Wood Factor, 15 S. Bay St.
Douglas, A., Bookkeeper, res. n.e. cr. Queen & Church Sts.
Douglas, Campbell, Grocer, cr. Meeting & Market Sts.
Douglas, Joseph, Tailor, 36 Chalmers St.
Douglas, William, Clerk, 69 E. Bay St.
Dowling, D. J., Printer & Stationer, 107 E. Bay St.
Downey, Peter, Dry Goods Store, 12 Horlbeck's Al.
Downie, Robert, Tin Plate Worker, 59 Broad St.
Doyle, Andrew, Rev., cr. Broad & Friend Sts.
Doyle, James, Tailor, 40 King St.
Drayton, William, Dr., 2 Montague St.
Drege, P. & Co., Clothing Store, 139 E. Bay St.
Drew, James, Factor, Gadsen's Whf.
Drummond, John, Boot Maker, 57 Broad St.
Dubois, -----, Mrs., Widow, res. Queen St.
Duc, F., Grocer, King St., Neck
Duc, H. A., Tin Plate Worker, King St., Neck
Duckworth, A. H., Merchant, Commercial Whf.
Duffus & Taylor, Dry Goods Store, 224 King St.
Duffus, James, 120 King St.
Duffus, John, Notary Public, 69 E. Bay St., res. 103 King St.
Duffus, John, Notary Public, 103 King St.
Duffy, John, 20 S. Bay St.
Duggan, Thomas, Bricklayer, 48 Broad St.
Duggin, Gregory, cr. Broad & Friend Sts.
DuJarday, Heny, Madame, Seminary, 70 Queen St.
Duke, John H., Union Insurance Co., res. 1 Amen St.
Dukes, W. C. & Co., Factor, Edmondston's Whf.,
Dukes, William C., Factor, res. King St., Neck
Duncan & Brewster, Attorneys, 67 Meeting St.
Dunkin, B. E., Attorney, Radcliffborough, Neck
Dunlap, James, Clothing Store, 276 King St.
Dunlap, William, Accountant, 223 King St.
Dunn, George, 8 Beaufain St.
Dunn, William, Dry Goods Store, cr. Meeting & Market Sts.
Dupont, F., Upholsterer & Paper Hanger, 127 King St.
Dupony, A., Factor, Fitzsimons' Whf.
Dupree, A., Mrs., Widow, Tradd St.
Dupree, Francis, Pilot, 34 Church St.
Dupree, James, Carpenter, 25 Wall St.
Dupree, James, Lumber Measurer, 25 Wall St.
Duquercron, F., Merchant, Frazer & Co. Whf., res. 10 Tradd St.
Durand, V., Merchant, 29 E. Bay St.
Durand, Victor, Merchant, 93 King St.
Durban, E. J., Accountant, 29 Horlbeck's Al.
Durbee, E. & Co., Clothing Store, 220 King St.
Durieux, C., Baker, 67 E. Bay St.
Durkes, H., Grocer, Cannon St., Neck
Duryea, Jacob, Boarding House, Church St.
Dutreau, D., Fruit Store, 329 King St.
Duval, John, Tin Plate Worker, 2 Queen St.
Dymore, Jane, 9 Bank St.
Eager, William M., Accountant, 30 Tradd St.

Early, Jane, Widow, 47 King St.
Earnest, Catherine, Widow, 54 Vanderhorst St., Neck
Eason & Dotterer, Foundry, Eason's Whf.
Eason, Robert, 21 Anson St.
Easterby, Jane M., Boarding House, cr. Queen & Church Sts.
Eaton, A., Mariner, 4 Champney St.
Eccles, Thomas J., Printer, res. 238 King St.
Eckhard, G. B., Attorney, 19 George St.
Eckhard, George B., Attorney, 4 St. Michael's Al.
Eckhard, M. E., Widow, 33 Society St.
Eckhard,-----, Mrs., Widow, 19 George St.
Edgerton, E. W., Merchant Tailor, 32 Broad St.
Edmondston, C. & Co., Factors, Edmondston's Whf.
Edmondston, Charles, res. 3 Battery St.
Edmondston, S. A., Clerk, 3 E. Bay St.
Edwards, E., Accountant, 373 King St.
Edwards, Edward H., Col., Planter, 9 Meeting St.
Edwards, George, Planter, cr. King & Ann Sts.
Edwards, J. J., Accountant, 373 King St.
Edwards, James, Planter, 26 Wall St.
Egleston & Frost, Attorneys, 50 Broad St.
Egleston, G. W., Attorney, Radcliffborough
Ehney, P. M., Custom House, res. 10 Pinckney St.
Elder, James, Tanner, John St., Neck
Eleston, James, Clerk, Edmondston's Whf.
Elfe, Albert, House Carpenter, 89 George St.
Elfe, Edward, Dr., res. 98 Meeting St.
Elfe, Eleanor, 96 Wentworth St.
Elfe, Robert, Attorney, res. 98 Meeting St.
Elfe, Thomas, House Carpenter, 89 George St.
Elfe, William, 91 Boundary St.
Elford, Frederick, Wharfinger, Vanderhorst's Whf.
Elford, James, Nautical Establishment, Gillon St.
Elliott & Condy, Brokers, 22 Broad St.
Elliott, J. S., Widow, 10 George St.
Elliott, Thomas O., Attorney, 105 King St.
Elliott, W. S., Broker, 22 Broad St.
Ellis, Mary, Widow, 172 E. Bay St.
Elmore, Amelia, Tailoress, 18 Vernon St.
Elsworth, John T., U. S. Gauger, 11 Boundary St.
England, Alexander, Planter, 54 Tradd St.
England, John, Rt. Rev., Catholic Bishop, Broad & Friend Sts.
English, James, Ship Carpenter, 13 King St.
Enslow, Joseph L., Cooper, 44 E. Bay St., res. 44 Wentworth St.
Enston, William, Furniture Ware Room, 163 King St.
Entz, John F., Merchant, Central Whf.
Esdra, J., Mattress Maker, 85 Market St.
Estill, William, Bookbinder, 17 Queen St.
Eude, Louis, French Coffee House, 125 E. Bay St.
Evans, Charles, Turner, 141 Meeting St.
Evans, J. W., Accountant, 159 E. Bay St.
Evans, L., Cutler, 17 St. Michael's Al.
Evans, William, Capt., Watchmaker, 85 Boundary St.
Eveleigh,-----, Dr., 24 Montague St.
Ewart, Williams & Co., Factors, Magwood's S. Whf.
Fabian, Louisa, Widow, 91 Queen St.
Fabian,-----, Mrs., Boarding House, Queen St., op.

Archdale St.
Fabian, William, Painter, res. Queen St., op. Archdale St.
Fair, Margaret, 117 Queen St.
Fairchild, R., Tavern, 260 King St.
Fanning & Weed, Merchant, res. 3 George St.
Farley, John, Teacher, 3 Bull St.
Farrar & Robinson, Merchants, 96 E. Bay St.
Farrar, S. S., Merchant, 96 E. Bay St.
Fasbender, J. H., Watchmaker, Meeting St., near Cumberland St.
Fasbender,-----, Mrs., Grocery, Meeting St., near Cumberland St.
Fash, Leonard, Jr., Engineer, 26 Vernon St.
Fash, Leonard, Sr., Grocery, cr. Meeting & Hasell Sts.
Fay, James, Boarding House, 27 King St.
Fayolle, Theodore B., Music Master, 86 King St.
Fehrenbeck, F., Dry Goods Store, King St., Neck
Fell, Thomas D., Tin Plate Worker, 100 Market St.
Fell, W., Mrs., 76 Broad St.
Fenn, M. B., Dry Goods Store, 212 Meeting St.
Ferguson, Eliza, Widow, 10 Orange St.
Ferrett, John F., Fruit Store, 43 Market St.
Ferretta, Josephine, Miss, 134 Meeting St.
Feugas, H. P., French & English Institution, Wentworth St.
Field, Nathaniel, Sail Maker, Hasell St.
Fields, Rebecca, Widow, Ann St., Neck
Fife, James, Merchant, 53 E. Bay St., res. 5 E. Bay St.
Fillette, A., Mrs., Dry Goods Store, 133 King St.
Finagin, John, Draper & Tailor, 40 Broad St.
Fink, Frederick, Grocer, 123 E. Bay St.
Fink, J. P., Grocery, 39 Beaufain St.
Finklea, James, Saddler, 14 Wentworth St.
Finley & Phin, Druggists, 31 Broad St.
Fisher, John, Factor, Fitzsimons' Whf.
Fisher, Rebecca, Widow, 21 Coming St.
Fisk, Horace, 293 King St.
Fisk, Theophilus, Rev., 64 Wentworth St.
Fitzgibbon, P. S., Bookseller, 5 Wentworth St.
Fitzsimons, Elizabeth, Widow, 26 Hasell St.
Flagg,-----, Mrs., Widow, 25 Beaufain St.
Flagg, Rachel, 120 Queen St.
Flemming, P., Grocer, 144 Pinckney St., cr. E. Bay St.
Flemming, Ross & Co., Merchants, 149 E. Bay St.
Flemming, T., Merchant, 301 King St.
Flynn, William, Accomptant, 26 Mazyck St.
Fogartie, Edward, Bricklayer, 21 Wall St.
Fogartie, F., Fruit Store, 37 Anson St.
Folger, Edward, Accomptant, 5 West St.
Folker, Lawrence H., Accountant, Horlbeck's Al.
Folker, Thomas, Rev., John St., Neck
Foot, Catherine, Mrs., 1 Berreford St.
Forbes, John B., Tin Plate Worker, 106 King St.
Forbes, William P., Tin Plate Worker, 23 Tradd St.
Fordham, Richard, Blacksmith, Pump & Block Maker, cr. Exchange & E. Bay Sts., res. 9 Society St.
Fordyce, William Dingwall, Consul for Uruguay, Res. Broad St.
Fort, Townsend & Co., Wholesale Dry Goods Store, 284 King St.
Fourgeaud, Arnold, Baker, 181 E. Bay St.

Fox, Ann, Mrs., Beaufain St.
Fox, R. W., Capt., Mariner, 2 Chalmers St.
Francis, David, Tailor, St. Philip St., F.P.C.
Francis, Henry, Rigger, 168 E. Bay St.
Francis, James, Barber, St. Philip St., F.P.C.
Francis, John, Hair Dresser, 298 King St., F.P.C.
Francis, Samuel, Tobacconist, 201 E. Bay St.
Francisco,-----, Mrs., Widow, 19 George St.
Fraser, Charles, Attorney, 39 King St.
Fraser, Charles, Portrait Painter, 93 Tradd St.
Fraser, Frederick, Planter, 93 Tradd St.
Fraser, Frederick, Rigger, 9 Chalmers St.
Fraser, J. & Co., Merchants, Central Whf.
Fraser, John, Factor, 119 Queen St.
Fraser, John, Planter, 4 Short St.
Fraser, L. H., Hat Store, 9 Broad St.
Frazer, J. L., Wood Factor, cr. Vernon & Wharf Sts.
Freer, E. H., House Carpenter, 65 Beaufain St.
Freymuth, Charles, Apothecary, cr. Church & Elliott Sts.
Friend, James, Carpenter, Boundary St.
Frost & Egleston, Attorneys, 50 Broad St.
Frost, H. R., Dr., 74 Broad St.
Fuller, Oliver, Capt., res. Meeting St.
Furman, C. M., Cashier, Bank of S. C., res. Ladson's Court.
Gadsden, Alexander E., Dr., cr. Church St. & Elliott St.
Gadsden, C., Mrs., Widow, cr. S. Bay & King Sts.
Gadsden, Christopher, Rev., Alexander St., Neck
Gadsden, Fisher, res. Charlotte St., Neck
Gadsden, J. W., Factor, Chisolm's Whf., res. 5 Meeting St.
Gadsden, Thomas N., Broker & Auctioneer, 12 State St., Res. 13 Church St.
Gager, James H., Hardware Store, 287 King St.
Gaillard & Mazyck, Factors, Commercial Whf.
Gaillard, A. T., Factor, Commercial Whf.
Gaillard, C., Widow, 58 Wentworth St.
Gaillard, D. S., Widow, 7 Court House Sq.
Gaillard, E., 218 King St.
Gaillard, Theodore, Accomptant, 77 Wentworth St.
Galliott, Alexis, Tobacconist, 105 E. Bay St.
Gantt & Mortimer, Brokers, 6 State St.
Gantt, T. J., Register in Equity, 56 King St.
Garcia, James, Professor of Music, Butchertown, Neck
Gardner, J., Planter, Cannon St., Neck
Garrett, Ann, Widow, Meeting St.
Garritson, Isaac, Clothing Store, 105 E. Bay St.
Gates, Thomas, Butcher, Butchertown, Neck
Gatewood, William C., Lottery Office, 26 Broad St.
Gauthier, F., French Language Teacher, 29 Coming St.
Gefkin, Henry, Carpenter, 38 Anson St.
George, John, Fruit Store, 39 Market St.
Gerard, Elizabeth, Mrs., 17 Church St.
Gerard, Peter G., Merchant Tailor, 29 Broad St.
Gerdts, Henry, Grocer, Hasell & Anson Sts.
Geyer, John S., Planter, Charlotte St., Neck
Geyer, Mary, Mrs., 16 Lynch St.
Geyer, R. C., Clerk, 16 Lynch St.
Geyer, W. J., Coach Maker, 52 Wentworth St.
Gianini, Jacob, Fruit Store, 65 Market St.
Gibbes, C. & J., Merchants, 10 Vendue Range

Gibbes, George, Mrs., Widow, 4 State St.
Gibbes, John B., Clerk, 2 State St.
Gibbes, John R., Charleston Bank Porter, 2 State St.
Gibbes, Waring & Johnson, 6 Dawes & Co. Whf.
Gibbon, George & John, Merchants, 6 Gibbes St.
Gibbs & Williams, Wood Factors, 3 Gibbes St.
Gibbs, Benjamin, Factor, John St., Neck
Gibbs, Catharine, Widow, 74 Church St.
Gibbs, Elizabeth, Widow, 74 Church St.
Gibbs, Ellen, Widow, 77 Tradd St.
Gibbs, Mary P., Widow, 111 Broad St.
Gibbs, Samuel, Attorney, 111 Broad St.
Gibbs, Sarah, Miss, Cannon St., Neck
Gibson, Alexander, Merchant, 59 Coming St.
Gibson, David C., Attorney, 170 Meeting St.
Gibson, Elizabeth, Widow, 170 Meeting St.
Gibson, William, Bookkeeper, Dawes & Co. Whf.
Gidiere, J., Fancy Store, btw. 320 & 322 King St.
Gidiere, Joseph, Dry Goods Store, 220 King St.
Gidiere, M., Dry Goods Store, 220 King St.
Giese, Charles, Grocer, cr. Meeting St. & Horlbeck's Al.
Gifflin, Alexander, Accountant, 30 Chalmers St.
Gilchrist, John, Shoe Maker, John St., Neck
Gilchrist, Robert, B., Attorney, 253 E. Bay St.
Gildersleve, B., Rev., Editor of Observer, 40 Chalmers St.
Gilliland, W. H. & Co., Wholesale Dry Goods Store, 307 King St.
Gilliland, William H., 20 George St.
Gilman, Samuel, Rev., 7 Orange St.
Gilmore, W. S., Accomptant, 307 King St.
Gitsinger, B. R., Printer, res. 6 Broad St.
Gleason, H. B., Crockery Store, 250 King St., res. King St., near Hudson St., Neck
Glen, John, cr. Reid & Meeting Sts., Neck
Glenn, Daniel L., House Carpenter, 91 Tradd St.
Glenn, James, Planter, 91 Tradd St.
Glenn, John, Mrs., Widow, 91 Tradd St.
Glenn, John, Ship Carpenter, 91 Tradd St.
Glenn, Margaret, Widow, 91 Tradd St.
Glenn, Thomas C., House Carpenter, 91 Tradd St.
Glover, William, Boot & Shoe Maker, 37 Wentworth St.
Gnech, -----, Mrs., Dry Goods Store, King St.
Godard, Rene, President, Union Bank, res. 161 King St.
Goff, E., Mrs., Milliner, 146 King St.
Goldsmith, Henry, Clerk, w. end Magazine St.
Goldsmith, Morris, w. end Magazine St.
Gonfraville, Theodore, Tivoli Garden, Meeting St., Neck
Gonzalez, B., Merchant, 15 Champney St., res. 4 George St.
Gonzalez, John, Grocer, 12 E. Bay St.
Goodrich, Ann, Widow, Butchertown, Neck
Goodwin, E. M., Widow, 275 & 277 King St.
Gordon, Alexander & M'Cartney, 15 Broad St.
Gordon, C. P., Bank Officer, 15 Smith St.
Gordon, John, Mrs., Widow, 158 Meeting St.
Gorman, Henry, Tailor, King St., Neck
Gospray, F., Carpenter, Coming St., Neck
Gottlib, John, Tailor, 48 Elliott St.
Gould, Mary, 19 Chalmers St.
Gouldsmith, Richard, Cabinet Maker, 191 King St.

Gourdin & Smith, Factors, Commercial N. Whf.
Gourdin, H., Factor, Commercial N. Whf., res. 6 Meeting St.
Gowan, Peter, Watchmaker, cr. Meeting & Chalmers Sts.
Gradick, C. C., Grocer, cr. Boundary & Middle Sts.
Gradick, John N., Carpenter, 6 Laurens St.
Grand, -----, Miss, 39 Queen St.
Granniss, White & Co., Merchants, 256 King St.
Grant, Ellen, Widow, 7 Montague St.
Graves, D. D., Dr., 50 Broad St., res. cr. Meeting & Wentworth Sts.
Gray, Alexander, Grocer, 174 E. Bay St.
Gray, Henry, Attorney, 136 E. Bay St.
Gray, James W., Commissioner in Equity, res. 136 E. Bay St.
Gray, John B., Teacher, 136 E. Bay St.
Gready, A. T., Variety Store, 172 King St.
Green, Aaron, Butcher, 19 Pitt St., F.P.C.
Green, James, Merchant, Commercial Whf.
Green, John, House Carpenter, 37 Pitt St.
Green, M., Seamstress, 96 King St., F.P.C.
Green, T. F., Merchant, Charlotte St., Neck
Green, Thomas P., Druggist, 169 E. Bay St., Res. Washington St., Neck
Greenhill, Mary, Widow, 5 Adams St.
Greenland, A., Bricklayer, John St., Neck
Greenland, Elizabeth, Widow, 76 Tradd St.
Greer, John M., Bookseller, 135 King St.
Greer, W., 260 King St.
Gregg, Alexander, Grocery, 147 E. Bay St.
Gregorie, J. Ladson, Lt., Magazine Guard at Citadel
Greig, H. L., Teacher, 33 Society St.
Grierson, George, 163 Wentworth St.
Grimball, J. B., Planter, 4 S. Bay St.
Grimball, Paul, Planter, 7 Smith St.
Grimke, Henry, Attorney, 64 Broad St.
Grimke, Mary, Widow, 273 E. Bay St.
Groaning, Lewis, Accomptant, Radcliffborough
Groaning, M. L., Widow, Radcliffborough
Gross, John F., 181 Meeting St.
Groves, -----, Mrs., Milliner, 248 King St.
Guenver, John M., Scourer, 248 King St.
Guerin, -----, Mrs., Widow, Coming St., Neck
Guerry, Grandison, Bookkeeper, 23 Society St.
Guerry, P., Shoe Store, 114 King St.
Guillilman, Peter, Seed Store, King St., Neck
Gullatt, Helen, Archdale St., op. Bottle Al.
Guy, John, Bricklayer, 7 Middle St.
Guy, Joseph, Carpenter, n. side Boundary St.
Guy, Theodore B., Merchant, 112 E. Bay St.
Gyles, J. A., Attorney, Court House Sq.
Hahnbaun, E. R., Widow, 168 Meeting St.
Haig, Margaret, Widow, 144 Meeting St.
Haley, John, Dry Goods Store, 58 State St.
Hall, Daniel, Mrs., Widow, Court House Sq.
Hall, J., Fancy Dry Goods Store, 176 King St.
Hall, William, Dr., 271 E. Bay St.
Hamill, Thomas, Wheelwright, 120 Church St.
Hamilton, James, Capt., Seaman's Boarding House, 19 Queen St.

Hamilton, James, Hon., State Senator, President, Charleston Bank, res. 190 E. Bay St.
Hamilton, John R., & Carson, Merchant, res. 8 Society St.
Hamilton, John, Ship Carpenter, 3 Hasell St.
Hamilton, William, 173 E. Bay St.
Hammett, Ripley, Wharfinger, Fitzsimons' Whf.
Hammond, Ogden, Planter, 12 S. Bay St.
Hamye, C. H., Marion Coffee House, res. 153 E. Bay St.
Hanahan, D., Grocer, cr. Minority & Wall Sts.
Hanckel, C., Rev., 115 Boundary St.
Hankel, Stewart, 115 Boundary St.
Happoldt, Albert, Butcher, Butchertown, Neck
Happoldt, C. L., Coach Maker, 16 Wall St.
Happoldt, John M., Gunsmith, 117 Meeting St.
Harbers, G. H., Grocery, cr. Meeting & Boundary Sts.
Harby, H. J., Blacksmith, 125 Church St., res. 12 Pinckney St.
Harckley, Henrietta, 162 E. Bay St.
Hard, Benjamin F., Planter, 52 Society St.
Hardie, Thomas, School, 256 King St., res. 218 King St.
Harkamp, John, Grocer, 97 Broad St.
Harleston, -----, Dr., Commissioner of Cross Roads, Ratcliffborough
Harper, James, 196 Tradd St.
Harper, James, Baker, 69 King St.
Harper, James, Merchant, Gibbes' Whf.
Harper, W. W., Chemist & Apothecary, 196 King St.
Harral, Wright & Co., Saddlery Warehouse, 289 King St.
Harris & Roosevelt, Hardware Store, 285 King St.
Harris, Abraham, Clothing Store, 41 State St.
Harris, Isaac, Fruiterer, 41 Market St.
Harris, L., Clothing Store, 187 E. Bay St.
Harris, Rebecca, Fruiterer, 114 King St.
Harrison, D. W., Depository, Chalmers St.
Harrison, J., Tavern, 16 Queen St.
Hart, N. & Son, Hardware Store, cr. Market & King Sts.
Hart, Richard, Wharfinger, Edmondston's Whf.
Hartge, Henry, Grocer, cr. Alexander & Boundary Sts.
Harvey, Edward, Dyer & Scourer, 82 Queen St.
Harvey, James E., Bookkeeper, res. 82 Queen St.
Harwood & Co., Dry Goods Store, 255 King St.
Hase, John, Grocer, cr. Society & Anson Sts.
Hasell, Hannah, Widow, 18 Meeting St.
Hasell, Thomas M., Merchant, 21 Society St.
Hasghell, -----, Mrs., Widow, 7 Montague St.
Haslett, John, President, Fire & Marine Insurance Co., Res. 50 Church St.
Haslop, Frederick, Grocer, 203 E. Bay St.
Hatch, A. M. & Co., Boot & Shoe Store, 301 King St.
Hatch, L. M., Merchant, 301 King St.
Hatch, William, Ship Carpenter, 34 Hasell St.
Hatcher, Thomas, Broker & Auctioneer, 109 Church St.
Hattier, William, Fruiterer, 75 Market St.
Hauschildt, Peter, American Hotel, 83 E. Bay St.
Haviland, Harral & Allen, Druggists, 286 & 288 King St.
Hawie, Sarah, 37 State St.
Hayden, Joseph, Barber, 49 King St.
Hayden, Joseph, Hair Dresser, 140 E. Bay St., F.P.C.
Hayden, Nathaniel, Military & Fancy Goods Store, 263

King St.

Hayden, Thomas A., Printer, res. 11 Mazyck St.

Hayford, -----, Mrs., Dry Goods Store, 109 King St.

Hayne, Elizabeth, Sr., Widow, 27 Meeting St.

Hayne, R. Y., Hon., Mayor of City, res. 24 King St.

Hayne, William A., Teller, Bank of S. C., res. St. Philip St., Neck

Hayne, William E., State Treasurer, Fireproof Building

Hazlehurst, G. A., Factor, Holmes & Co. Whf.

Healy, John, Dry Goods Store, 58 State St.

Heath, Thomas H., Planter, 9 Boundary St.

Hedderly, John, Accountant, 17 King St.

Heffernon, E., Mrs., Dry Goods Store, 161 King St.

Heide, H. C., Grocer, 14 Queen St.

Heilbron, James, Apothecary, res. 62 Church St.

Heimsath, F., Grocer, cr. Church & Water Sts.

Heins, John H., Grocer, Judith St., Neck

Helfer, M., Shoe Maker, King St., near John St., Neck

Henry, Edward, Grocer, cr. Wentworth & E. Bay Sts.

Henry, George, Factor, Boyce & Co. Whf., res. 47 Anson St.

Henry, Joel, Cabinet Maker, cr. Wentworth & Meeting Sts.

Henry, P. S., Mattress Store, 37 Queen St.

Henry, R. F., Merchant, 149 E. Bay St., res. cr. Smith & Wentworth Sts.

Henry, S. W., Furniture Stores, 68 & 185 Meeting St.

Herbert, M., Boarding House, 47 State St.

Herck, John, Grocer, 89 Tradd St.

Herckenrath & Lowndes, Merchants, 4 Hamilton's Whf.

Heriot, B. D., Navy Agent, 16 Vanderhorst's Whf.

Heriot, O. B., Accountant, 39 E. Bay St.

Heriot, R. & Son, Notary Publics, 39 E. Bay St.

Heriot, W. B., 39 E. Bay St.

Hersman, J., Dry Goods Store, 178 King St.

Hertz, H. M., Wood Factor, res. King St., near Hudson St.

Hertz, Isaac E., Accountant, 97 King St.

Hertz, Jacob E., Dry Goods Store, 97 King St.

Hervey, George, Merchant, Hamilton & Co. Whf.

Heyward, Arthur, Planter, Charlotte St., Neck

Heyward, Nathaniel, Planter, 351 E. Bay St.

Hichborn, W. C., Merchant, 44 Tradd St.

Higham, Fife & Co., Merchants, 55 E. Bay St.

Hilgen, Frederick, Grocer, 62 Anson St.

Hill, Ann, Widow, Lucas St., Neck

Hillard & Thomas, Grocery, 5 & 7 Vendue Range

Hillard & Wade, Grocers, 185 E. Bay St.

Hillard, O. B., Grocer, res. 118 King St.

Hillard, W. H., Grocer, 5 & 7 Vendue Range

Hilman, Ann, Boarding House, 51 E. Bay St.

Hines, Thomas, Accountant, 103 Broad St.

Hitchborn, W. C., Merchant, 68 E. Bay St.

Hobson, A., Bootmaker, 97 E. Bay St.

Hobson, A., Shoe Store, 187 King St.

Hobson, A., Shoe Store, 97 E. Bay St.

Hodges, George, Boarding House, Queen St.

Hodgson, William, Baker, Gadsden's Whf.

Hoff, John C., Printer, 10 Broad St.

Hoff, John, Mrs., Widow, 9 George St.

Hoff, Philip, Bookseller & Stationer, 10 Broad St.

Hokestupe, F., Grocer, Thomas St., Neck

Holbrook & Ogier, Drs., 1 State St.

Holbrook, Edward, Dr., 25 Legare St.

Holbrook, J. Edwards, Dr., 1 State St.

Holcombe, Peck & Co., Merchants, Central Whf.

Holland, Jane, Widow, 77 Tradd St.

Holmes, C. R., Factor, Holmes & Co. Whf.

Holmes, Henry, 29 Church St.

Holmes, I. E., Attorney, 1 E. Bay St.

Holmes, John V., Gunsmith, 68 Queen St.

Holmes, Sandiford & Dick, res. 35 E. Bay St.

Holton, M. S., 19 Cumberland St., F.P.C.

Holwell, T. W., Accountant, 70 Church St.

Honour, John, Rev., Bookkeeper, Courier Office.

Honour, Thomas & Sweeny, Bookbinders, back of Court House

Hood, E., Mrs., Dry Goods Store, 8 King St.

Hopkins, J. A., Cooper, Boyce & Co. Whf.

Horlbeck, Daniel, Attorney, 3 Court House Sq.

Horlbeck, Edward, Bricklayer, 29 Horlbeck's Al.

Horlbeck, Elias, M.D., 174 King St.

Horlbeck, Henry, Bricklayer, 29 Horlbeck's Al.

Horlbeck, Henry, Jr., Bricklayer, 29 Horlbeck's Al.

Horlbeck, John, Bricklayer, cr. Meeting & Boundary Sts.

Horry, Ann Julia, Miss, 32 Meeting St.

Horry, Mary S., Widow, cr. Meeting & Tradd Sts.

Horsey, Thomas J., Teller, Planters & Mechanics Bank, res. 79 Boundary St.

Hough, S., Charleston Hotel, 71 Market St.

Howard, A. G., Dr., City Inspector, 89 Church St.

Howard, James, Capt., Hard Al.

Howard, R., Mrs., Widow, Washington St., Neck

Howard, Richard, Cooper, Cordes & E. Bay Sts.

Howard, Robert, Custom House, res. 28 Hasell St.

Howard, Robert, Wood Factor, 80 Anson St., F.P.C.

Howard, S., Druggist, 34 Broad St.

Howard, S. M., Botanic Garden, St. Philip St., Neck

Howe, Samuel, Boot Store, 87 Tradd St.

Howland, B. J., Merchant, 135 E. Bay St.

Howland, Ward & Taft, Merchants, 135 E. Bay St.

Howland, William, Dry Goods Store, n.e. cr. King & Meeting Sts.

Hubert, C., Merchant, 75 Tradd St.

Hudson, J. M., Dry Goods Store, 338 King St.

Huger, Alfred, Postmaster, 114 Broad St.

Huger, Benjamin, Dr., 110 Broad St.

Huger, D., 5 Coming St.

Huger, D. E., Hon., 28 Meeting St.

Huger, John, Planter, 3 Meeting St.

Huggins, E., Miss, 26 Vernon St.

Hughes, George, Stove Maker, 40 King St.

Hughes, T., Furniture Store, 145 Meeting St.

Hull, Townsend & Knevals, Merchant Tailors, 283 King St.

Hume, John, Planter, 117 Wentworth St.

Humphreys, Joseph P., 88 Market St.

Hunt, B. F., Attorney, 2 Court House Sq.

Hunt, N., Stove Store, cr. King & Queen Sts.

Hurst, W. A., Blacksmith, E. Bay St., op. Hasell St.

Hurst, C. W., Blacksmith, 15 Hasell St.

Huryman, J., Dry Goods Store, 3 Coming St.

Husman, H., Grocer, cr. Water & Meeting Sts.
Hussey, B. B., Bookseller, 237 King St.
Hyam, Daniel, 28 Queen St.
Hyams, Henry, Clothing Store, 315 King St.
Hyams, Moses D., Rice Merchant, 63 E. Bay St.
Hyams, Solomon, 186 King St.
Hyatt, M'Burney & Co., Wholesale Dry Goods Store
Hyde, Joseph, Architect, 115 Church St.
Inglesby, James, Dr., 39 Tradd St.
Inglesby, Mary, Mrs., Widow, 5 Orange St.
Inglesby, W. H., Attorney, 5 Orange St.
Ingraham, George H., Factor, Central Whf., res. 18 Laurens St.
Ingraham, Louisa, Widow, 10 King St.
Irving, J. B., Dr., Factor, 10 Hamilton & Co. Whf.
Irwing, -----, Mrs., Millinery, 331 King St.
Israel, N. H., Dry Goods Store, 186 King St.
Ithier, C., Boarding House, 28 State St.
Izard, H., Mrs., Widow, 27 Legare St.
Jackson & Co., Drapers, 282 King St.
Jackson, George, Wholesale & Retail Tin Ware, 279 King St.
Jackson, J., Miniature Painter, 253 King St.
Jackson, John, Farmer, Meeting St., Neck
Jackson, M. A., Millinery, 171 King St.
Jackson, R. S., Pianaforte Warehouse, 321 King St.
Jacob, M., Boarding House, 15 Market St.
Jacobs, M., Planter, 81 Boundary St.
Jacoby, George, Grocer, 55 Church St.
Jager, F., Grocer, 17 Elliott St.
James, R., Printer, 7 Tradd St.
James, Susan, Mantuamaker, 15 Orange St., F.P.C.
Javain, H. J., Jeweller, 151 King St.
Jeannerette, C., Accountant, 94 E. Bay St.
Jeannerette, J. C., 54 Church St.
Jeannerette, James, Merchant, 96 E. Bay St.
Jeffords, John, Grocer, 13 Middle St.
Jeffords, John H., Sail Maker, Gibbes' Whf
Jenney, R., Saddler, 326 King St.
Jervey, James, Clerk, U. S. Court, 13 Laurens St.
Jervey, Thomas H., Mariner, 25 Church St.
Jervey, Waring & White, Brokers, 20 Broad St.
Jesup, Z. R., Boot & Shoe Store, 158 King St.
Jeuido, Ann, Widow, 3 Gibbes St.
Jeuido, Eliza, Widow, Boundary St.
Jewett & Hamilton, Wholesale Dry Goods Store, 228 King St.
Jewett, Eliza, 32 State St.
Jinkins, James, Hair Dresser, 49 Society St., F.P.C.
Johnson, A. A., Hotel, 69 Broad St., F.P.C.
Johnson, Benjamin, Umbrella Manufactory, 240 King St.
Johnson, C., Hat & Cap Store, 246 King St.
Johnson, James L., Grist Mill, 22 Market St.
Johnson, John, Mrs., Widow, 51 Anson St.
Johnson, Joseph, Dr., Druggist, 11 Broad St.
Johnson, Sally, Pastry Cook, 87 Wentworth St., F.P.C.
Johnson, William, Shoe Maker, 40 State St.
Johnston, Alex, Boot Maker, 23 Broad St.
Johnston, Elizabeth, Widow, 69 King St.
Johnston, G. A., Millwright, 69 King St.

Johnston, H. & L., Boot & Shoe Stores, 103 E. Bay St., 222 King St. & cr. Market & Meeting Sts.
Johnston, J., Planter, 19 Pitt St.
Johnston, James S., Corn Store, res. 95 Wentworth St.
Johnston, Jane, Miss, 328 King St.
Johnston, M'Kewn, Machinist, Hasell St. Cont'd.
Johnston, T. W., Tavern, King St.
Jones, C., Dry Goods Store, 77 Market St.
Jones, Catharine, Midwife, 38 Society St.
Jones, Edward, House Carpenter, St. Philip St., Neck
Jones, Elias, Wood Factor, St. Philip St., Neck
Jones, John S., Hardware Store, 129 E. Bay St.
Jones, -----, Misses, 1 Guignard St.
Jones, Paul, House Carpenter, St. Philip St., Neck
Jones, R., Mrs., Widow, 15 Coming St., Neck
Jones, W. H., Watchmaker, 234 King St.
Jones, W. L., Apothecary, 253 King St.
Jones, William, Druggist, St. Philip St., Neck
Jones, Wiswall, Merchant, 82 E. Bay St.
Jordan, A., Fruiterer, 247 King St.
Jordan, Edward, Sail Maker, Cordes St.
Joshua, Peter, Grocer, 35 Market St.
Joye & Cheney, Grocers, 55 E. Bay St.
Joye, D. G., Grocers, 57 E. Bay St.
Judge, James, Dry Goods Store, 42 King St.
Kalb, J. H., Baker, 44 Elliott St.
Kanapaux, William, Jeweller, 84 Market St.
Kane, Christopher, Bricklayer, 154 E. Bay St.
Keast, John, Shoe Maker, King St., near Broad St.
Keckeley, Ann, Widow, King St., Neck
Keckeley, E. C., Dr., Apothecary, King St., Neck
Keckeley, George, Dr., Meeting St., Neck
Keckeley, John, Iron Mongery, 17 Beaufain St.
Keckeley, Thomas, House Carpenter, King St., Neck
Keels, George, House Carpenter, Boundary St., Neck
Keenan, William, Engraver, 51 Broad St.
Keith, S., Merchant, cr. Dewees' Whf. & Napier's Range
Kelly, Ann Y., Widow, 144 E. Bay St.
Kelly, John A., Boat Builder, 65 Church St.
Kelly, Silcox & Co., Furniture Warehouse, 166 King St.
Kelsey, C. & G. H., & Halstead, Dry Goods Store, 271 King St.
Kennedy, A. J., Watchmaker, 59 Broad St.
Kennedy, Ann, Fruit Store, 73 Market St.
Ker, John C., Merchant, 197 Meeting St.
Kerr, Andrew, Hair Dresser, 205 King St.
Kerr, Thomas J., Factor, Edmondston's Whf., res. 20 Laurens St.
Kerrison, C. & E. L., Dry Goods Store, 201 King St.
Kershaw, Charles, Mrs., Widow, 5 Rutledge St.
Ketchum, Joel & Co., Dry Goods Store, 233 King St.
Kiddell, Charles, Broker. 35 Broad St.
Kilkenny, Timothy, Grocery, 53 Tradd St.
King & Walker, Attorneys, 9 St. Michael's Al.
King, George W., Merchant, 16 Vendue Range
King, Mitchell, Attorney, 9 St. Michael's Al., res. cr. Meeting & George Sts.
King, W. & Co., Merchant, Hamilton & Co. Whf.
King, W. D., Professor of Elocution, Agent for Periodicals, Etc., off. 91 Church St.

King, William, A., Blacksmith, 11 Chalmers St.
King, William S., Editor of Courier, res. 6 Broad St.
Kinloch & Mordecai, Grain Merchants, cr. Commercial
  Whf. & E. Bay St.
Kinloch, George, Grain Dealer, res. 223 E. Bay St.
Kinsey, A., Mrs., Dry Goods Store, 239 King St.
Kirk, John, Watchmaker, 22 Horlbeck's Al.
Kirk, Mary, 22 Horlbeck's Al.
Kirk, William, Watchmaker, 22 Horlbeck's Al.
Kirkland, Mary, Widow, St. Philip St.
Kirkpatrick, John & Co., Factors, Edmondston's Whf.
Kirkwood, William, Ship Builder, 5 Middle St.
Kittleband, George, Bookkeeper, St. Philip St.
Klinck, N., Grocer, Gadsden's Whf.
Klink, John, Grocery Store, cr. Boundary & Coming Sts.
Knepley, Solomon, Blacksmith, 74 & 82 Meeting St.
Knowles, -----, Miss, Fancy Dry Goods Store, 264 King St.
Knox, William, Ship Carpenter, 225 E. Bay St.
Kohlman, B. F., Clerk, 63 Tradd St.
Kohlman, J. H., Grocer, 63 Tradd St.
Kohnke, C. F., Distillery, 31 State St.
Kornahrens, John N., Grocer, 59 Market St.
Kunhardt, William, Factor, Edmondston's Whf.
Labat, Isaac C., Auctioneer, 53 Broad St.
Laborde, Francis, Merchant, 9 Vendue Range
Labruce, Catharine, Widow, Hampstead, Neck
Lacassaigne, Edward, Hair Dresser, 144 King St.
Lacoste, A., Rigger, 19 Middle St.
Lacoste, C. G. A., Mrs., Fancy Store, 127 King St.
Lacoste, -----, Mrs., Widow, Radcliff St., Neck
Ladey, A., Boot Maker., Meeting St., Neck
Ladey, William, Grocer, cr. Meeting & Mary Sts., Neck
Ladson, James H. & Co., Merchant, Hamilton's Whf.
Lafar, B. D., Cooper, 18 Vendue Range
Laffiteau, S. M., Accountant, Commercial Whf.
Lafitte, A. & Brother, Merchants, Central Whf.
Lafitte, Edward, Merchant, Central Whf.
Lafrentz, F. C., Grocer, cr. Bull & Coming Sts.
Laken, Henry, Grocer, cr. St. Philip St. & Butchertown
Lamb, James, Merchant, Magwood's Whf., res. 199
  Meeting St.
Lambert, Catharine, Widow, 92 Laurens St.
Lambert, W. C., Mattress Store, 41 Queen St.
Lamotte, James, 21 Beaufain St.
Lance, Francis, Broker & Auctioneer, 4 State St.
Lance, Francis, Broker, res. 15 Logan St.
Lance, M. H., Rev., Charlotte St., Neck
Lance, William, Attorney, 81 Broad St.
Landershine, David, Ship Carpenter, Middle St.
Landreth, Robert, 233 King St.
Lane, Samuel, Tailor, 48 Broad St.
Langley, J. R., Mrs., 39 Queen St.
Lanneau, Bazil, Merchant, 102 E. Bay St., res. 43 Tradd
  St.
Lanneau, Fleetwood, Merchant, 26 Society St.
Lanneau, Peter, Accountant, 69 King St.
Laroche, Ann, Widow, Lucas St., Neck
Laroche, J. G., Notary Public, E. Bay St.
Larronde, Emile, Merchant, Magwood's N. Whf.
Lassen, Hans, Confectionery, 4 Wall St.

LaTourrette, James & Co., Hat & Cap Store, 297 King St.
Launay, N., Hat Store, 322 King St.
Laurens, Henry, Mrs., cr. Laurens & E. Bay Sts.
Laval, William, Comptroller General, res. 15 Beaufain St.
Lawrence, Robert, Accountant, 35 King St.
Lawton, J. & C., Merchants, 40 E. Bay St.
Lawton, R. B., Franklin Hotel, 21 King St.
Lazarus, Benjamin, Merchant, 83 Tradd St.
Lazarus, Joshua, 202 E. Bay St.
Lazarus, Levy & Lopez, Hardware Store, 113 E. Bay St.
Lea, John, C., Pilot, 28 Lightwood's Al.
Lea, W. P., Capt., Mariner, 28 Lightwood's Al.
Lebleux, -----, Mrs., Dry Goods Store, 84 King St.
LeCaron, Charles, Merchant, Edmondston's Whf.
Leckie, David, Merchant, 173 E. Bay St.
Lee, E., Hair Dresser, 65 Broad St., F.P.C.
Lee, E., Milliner, 103 Wentworth St., F.P.C.
Lee, J., Pastry Cook, 8 Tradd St., F.P.C.
Lee, James, Capt., Mariner, 36 State St.
Lee, William, Teller, State Bank of S. C., res. Alexander
  St., Mazyckborough
Legare, Hugh S., Hon., U.S. Congressman, res. 80 Bull
  St.
Legare, J. B., Attorney, res. 195 E. Bay St.
Legare, J. D., 45 Anson St.
Legare, James, Factor, Radcliffborough
Legare, James, Mrs., Widow, 57 King St.
Legare, O'Hear & Legare, Factors, Commercial Whf.
Legare, Solomon, Planter, 107 Tradd St.
Legare, Thomas, Wood Factor, Williams' Whf.
Lege, J. M., Dancing Master, 60 Queen St.
Legg, William, Shoe Maker, 45 Coming St., F.P.C.
Lehre, Ann, Mrs., Widow, cr. Meeting & Society Sts.
Lehre, Thomas, Ordinary, res. 56 King St.
Leland, Brothers & Co., Merchants, Commercial Whf.
Leland, D. W., Merchant, Commercial Whf.
Leland, Dexter, Academy, Philadelphia St.
Lepenne, J. J., Gardener, King St., near Mary St., Neck
Leprince, A., Fancy Store, 197 King St.
LeSeigneur, -----, Dr., 40 Church St.
Lesesne, Henry D., Attorney, 4 Green St.
Lesesne, -----, Misses, Teachers, 35 Society St.
Lesesne, W. J., 35 Society St.
Levy, Barnard, Printer, res. 97 King St.
Levy, D. C., (Tobias & Co.), Auctioneer, cr. E. Bay St. &
  Vendue Range
Levy, Elias, Gauger, res. 70 Broad St.
Levy, Jacob C., Champney St., res. 255 E. Bay St.
Levy, Levine L., Clothing Store, 189 E. Bay St.
Levy, M. C., 207 King St.
Levy, Moses, State Constable, 3 Berresford St.
Levy, Reuben, Merchant, cr. West & Mazyck Sts.
Lewis & Robertson, Merchants, 18 E. Bay St.
Lewis, John, Factor, res. 12 Meeting St.
Lieure, Peter, Clothing Store, 87 E. Bay St.
Lightbourn, Eliza B., Widow, 13 Pinckney St.
Lindergreen, Charles, Custom House, 4 Hard Al.
Lindsay, Lewis, Butcher, Butchertown
Lindsay, William, Merchant, 155 E. Bay St.
Ling, Philip, Carriage Maker, 76 Market St.

Lipman, R., Clothing Store, 73 E. Bay St.
Litle, James, Cotton Gin Maker, 153 Meeting St.
Little, Robert, Charlotte St., Neck
Livingston, Jane, Widow, 12 Anson St.
Livingston, Philip P., 6 Water St.
Lloyd, Joseph, Jr., Accountant, Boundary St., Neck
Lloyd, Joseph, Sr., Accountant, Boundary St., Neck
Lloyd, Martin, Druggist, 13 Bull St.
Lloyd, William, Broker, res. 16 State St.
Lloyd, William, Venetian Blind Maker, 149 Meeting St.
Logan, Christian, Millwright, Lucas St., Neck
Logan, G. C., Millwright, Holmes & Co. Whf.
Logan, George, Dr., 37 Coming St.
Logan, George W., Attorney, 44 Chalmers St.
Long, C. C., Bookkeeper, 143 E. Bay St.
Long, Robert, (Cohen & Co.), Merchant, Edmondston's Whf.
Lopez, -----, Dr., 12 Hasell St.
Lord, Archibald, Custom House, res. 39 Church St.
Lord, Richard, Wood Factor, Dawes & Co. Whf.
Lord, Samuel & Stocker, Merchants, cr. Gibbes Whf. & E. Bay St.
Lost, Sarah, 31 Coming St.
Lovegreen, A. A., Dry Goods Store, 312 King St.
Lowden, John, Merchant, Hamilton & Co. Whf.
Lowndes, James, 14 Meeting St.
Lowndes, William, 81 Wentworth St.
Lowther, Thomas, House Carpenter, 113 King St.
Lubet, Mary, 50 Society St.
Lubkin, L., Grocer, cr. Anson & Boundary Sts.
Lucas, John, House Carpenter, 3 Logan St.
Lucas, Jonathan, Jr., Merchant, Vanderhorst's Whf.
Lucas, William, Planter, Coming St., Neck
Lunquest, John, Jeweller, 5 Market St.
Lusher, O., Dr., 84 Queen St.
Lyle, William, Grocer, 83 Market St.
Lynah, James, Planter, 194 E. Bay St.
Lynch, C., Mrs., Millinery, 315 King St.
Lynch, F. C., Tailor, 315 King St.
Lynch, John S., Painter, 1 King St.
Lyndershine, Catharine, Coming St., Neck
Lyon, George, Watchmaker, 127 E. Bay St.
Lytle, J. S., U. S. A. District Postmaster, 79 Broad St.
Macauley, George, Planter, 76 Church St.
Macbeth, James, Merchant, Hamilton's Whf.
Macbeth, Robert, Attorney, 9 Legare St.
Mackay, Albert, Dr., 89 Market St.
Mackay, E., Miss, Seminary, King St., near Ann St.
Mackey, Mary, Widow, 134 Church St.
Mackie, James, Clerk, 79 Broad St.
Magness, Sarah, Widow, 135 Church St.
Magrath, Alexander G., Attorney, 65 Meeting St.
Magrath, John, Factor, Fitzsimons' Whf.
Magwood, Charles & Patterson, Merchant, Magwoods' Whf.
Main, W. B., Shipwright, 15 Wall St.
Maine, Alexander, Merchant, 44 Anson St.
Mairs, L., Merchant, 147 King St.
Malcolm, J. M., Accountant, 343 King St.
Mallery, -----, Mrs., Boarding House, 33 Broad St.

Manigault, Henry, Mrs., Widow, 16 Meeting St.
Manly, B., Rev., Editor, Southern Watchman, 28 King St.
Mann, George, Confectioner, King St., Neck
Mann, John, Mason, 37 Boundary St.
Manson, George, Shipwright, 2 Marsh St.
Marienhoff, J. M., Grocer, 7 Elliott St.
Marion, M., Widow, King St., near John St., Neck
Markley, B. A., Attorney, Cannonborough
Marks, Joseph, Grocer, 8 Queen St.
Marsh, James, Shipwright, 138 E. Bay St.
Marsh, Jeremiah, Shipwright, 138 E. Bay St.
Marsh, William, Wholesale Grocer, 171 E. Bay St.
Marshall, James, Engraver, Radcliff St., Neck
Marshall, James, Grocery, cr. King & George Sts.
Marshall, John, Accountant, 101 Broad St.
Marshall, John T., Baker, 61 Tradd St.
Marshall, John, Wood Factor, Gadsden's Whf.
Martigniat, J., Tobacconist, 126 Meeting St.
Martin, Ann, Boarding House, 22 Elliott St.
Martin, J. N., Bricklayer, cr. King & Wolf Sts.
Martin, Jacob, Blacksmith, 60 Wentworth St.
Martin, Jacob, Blacksmith, 7 Coming St.
Martin, Robert, & Walker, Factors, Boyce & Co. Whf.
Martin, T. B., Shoe Store, 334 King St.
Martin, Thomas D., Magistrate, res. 4 Cumberland St.
Mason, George, Clerk, Union Bank, 22 Lynch St.
Massott, H., Watchmaker, 5 Queen St.
Massroln, John P., Dry Goods Store, 57 State St.
Mathews & Bonneau, Factors, Hamilton's Whf.
Mathews, David, Shoe Maker, n. side Boundary St.
Mathews, Edward W., Factors, 10 Hamilton's Whf.
Mathey, Charles, Watchmaker, 153 King St.
Mathiessen & Poirier, Clothier, cr. Queen & E. Bay Sts.
Mathiessen, C. F., Fancy Goods Store, 157 King St.
Mathiessen, -----, Mrs., Widow, S Laurens St.
Matthews, J. P., Druggist, 129 Meeting St.
Matthews, William, Planter, Charlotte St., Neck
Maxcy, Virgil, 1 Lynch St.
Maxey, Flora, Seamstress, 5 Cumberland St., F.P.C.
Maxton, John, Baker, 17 Tradd St.
Maxwell, H. E., Widow, res. 89 Meeting St.
Maxwell, James, House Carpenter, Lucas St., Neck
Maxwell, William R., Planter, 89 Meeting St.
May, John, Cabinet Maker, 66 Queen St.
May, Margaret, Mrs., Vanderhorst St., Neck
Maynard, Ann, Mrs., Grocery, cr. Meeting & Wentworth Sts.
Mazyck, Alexander H., Attorney, res. 175 Meeting St.
Mazyck, Catharine, Miss, 177 Meeting St.
Mazyck, N. B., Widow, 175 Meeting St.
Mazyck, William & Gaillard & Mazyck, William, Jr., Factors, Commercial Whf.
Mazyck, Y. F., Planter, res. 175 Meeting St.
Meacher, Thomas, Grain Merchant, 31 Queen St.
Mead, Alfred, Grocer, 2 Boyce & Co. Whf.
Meeker, Samuel, Carriage Repository, 132 Meeting St.
Meislahn, Hans, Grocer, cr. Middle & Laurens Sts.
Memminger & Jervey, Attorneys, Meeting St.
Memminger, C. G., Attorney, res. 168 Wentworth St.
Merchant, P. M., House Carpenter, St. Philip St., Neck,

F.P.C.
Meyer, J., Grocer, cr. Coming & Boundary Sts., Neck
Meyer, -----, Mrs., Corset Maker, 81 King St.
Meyers, D., Grocer, King St., Neck
Meyers, F., Grocer, cr. Smith & Boundary Sts., Neck
Meyers, John, Grocer, cr. St. Philip St. & Butchertown
Meyers, Louda, Grocer, cr. King St. & Butchertown
Michel, Francis, District Coroner, 54 E. Bay St., Res.
Coming St., Neck
Michel, J. C., Watchmaker, 238 King St.
Michel, John, Quorum Unis, Broker, Notary Publice etc.,
E. Bay St., res. St. Philip St., Neck
Michel, William, Dr., 78 Queen St.
Michell, Francis, Confectioner, 87 Market St.
Michell, Mary, Widow, 4 Society St.
Middleton, G. G., cr. Smith & Boundary Sts., Neck
Middleton, H., cr. Smith & Boundary Sts., Neck
Middleton, T., Factor, Hamilton & Co. Whf., res. 10
Meeting St.
Mignot, R., Confectioner, 160 King St.
Miles, Ann, Mrs., Widow, cr. Radcliff & St. Philip Sts.
Miles, C. G., 21 Smith St.
Miles, Smith, Accountant, cr. Radcliff & St. Philip Sts.
Miles, Thomas, House Carpenter, 133 Smith St.
Miller, A. E., Bookseller & Printer, 4 Broad St.
Miller, Hannah, Baker, 135 Meeting St.
Miller, J. C., Factor, 1 Edmondston's Whf.
Miller, John, Grocer, 115 King St.
Miller, John, Ropewalk, Radcliffborough
Miller, M., Jewelry Store, 14 King St.
Miller, R. S., Baker, 123 Church St.
Miller, Ripley & Co., Wholesale Dry Goods Store, 268
King St.
Miller, Robert, Merchant, 22 E. Bay St.
Miller, Samuel Stent, Printer, 84 E. Bay St.
Miller, Stephen, Ropewalk, Radcliffborough
Millers, -----, Miss, School, 1 Chalmers St.
Milligan, William, Iron Mongery, St. Philip St.
Milliken & Walton, Wholesale Grocers, 108 E. Bay St.
Milliken, Thomas, Planter, 80 Church St.
Milliken, William, Wholesale Grocer, 108 E. Bay St.
Mills & Beach, 26 Vendue Range
Mills, F. D., Academy, 43 Queen St.
Mills, O. & S. & Co., Grain Dealers, cr. Dawes' Whf. & E.
Bay St.
Mills, S. S., Hay & Corn Merchant, 19 Pitt St.
Mishaw, J., Boot Maker, 55 Queen St., F.P.C.
Missroon, James, Nautical Store, 51 E. Bay St.
Missroon, -----, Mrs., Widow, 2 Battery
Mitchell, Margaret, Mrs., Widow, 50 Meeting St.
Mitchell, -----, Miss, Fancy Store, 165 King St.
Mitchell, Nelson, Attorney, St. Philip St., Neck
Mitchell, Rebecca, 2 Washington St., Neck
Moffett & Calder, Dry Goods Store, 230 King St.
Moffett, George, Merchant, 9 Burns Ln.
Moise, Abraham, Attorney, 1 Court House Sq.
Molyneux, T. B., Merchant, Magwood's Whf.
Monefeldt, W. S., Surgeon Dentist, 142 King St.
Monk, Stephen, Academy, 35 Tradd St.
Monpoey, H., Wood Factor, 41 Bull St.

Monroe, Robert, Seed Store, 257 King St.
Montague, Catharine, Widow, 54 State St.
Montgomery & Cheesborough, Factors, Hamilton & Co.
Whf.
Montgomery, Alexander, Watchmaker, 296 King St.
Mood, E. M., Pump & Block Maker, 178 E. Bay St.
Mood, J. & P., Jewelry Wholesale & Retail, 257 King St.
Mooney, James E., British Consul, St. Philip St., Neck
Mooney, M., Mrs., Dry Goods Store, King St., Neck
Moore, Ellen, Widow, Vanderhorst St., Neck
Moore, George H., Gunsmith, 47 Queen St.
Moore, J. N., Rev., Academy, 4 Wentworth St.
Moore, Richard, Painter, St. Philip St., Neck
Moorhead, J. G., cr. Wentworth & Meeting Sts.
Morang, B., Tailoress, 58 King St.
Mordecai, B., Miss, 52 King St.
Mordecai, M. C., Merchant, 24 Vendue Range
Mordecai, Thomas W., Merchant, 11 S. Bay St.
Moreland, A., Lumber Yard, 8 S. Bay St.
Morgan, Benjamin, Capt., Mariner, 20 Middle St.
Morriatti, -----, Mrs., Dry Goods Store, 203 King St.
Morris & M'Kensie, Wheelwrights, King St., Neck, F.P.C.
Morris, Christopher G., Merchant, cr. Wentworth & E. Bay
Sts.
Morris, Edward, Merchant, 72 E. Bay St.
Morris, James, Merchant, 76 E. Bay St.
Morrison, Jane D., Widow, 9 Market St.
Morrison, S., Cabinet Maker, 95 Market St.
Mortimer, Julia, 23 Hasell St.
Mortimer, Samuel H., (Gantt & Mortimer), Broker, res. 9
Bull St.
Mortimer, Thomas, Coming St., Neck
Moses, J., Dry Goods Store, 188 King St.
Moses, Levy, 158 King St.
Moses, Perry, Dry Goods Store, 150 King St.
Moses, R. I., Dry Goods Store, 248 King St.
Moses, Reuben, 203 King St.
Moss, Joseph & Co., Clothing Store, 303 King St.
Motta, L. A., Dry Goods Store, 114 King St.
Motte, Isaac, Mrs., Widow, 24 Meeting St.
Motte, Joseph, Shoe Maker, Charlotte St., Neck, F.P.C.
Mouzon, Henry, Accountant, cr. Anson & Boundary Sts.
Mowry, Smith, Jr., Merchant, cr. E. Bay St. & Dewees
Whf.
Muggridge, -----, Mrs., Boarding House, 204 King St.
Muir, Jane, Widow, 82 Church St.
Muir, Robert, Merchant, 18 Hamilton's Whf.
Mullins, C. P., 5 Lamboll St.
Munds, Israel, Rev., Teacher, 41 State St.
Munn, B. S., Printer, 182 King St.
Munro, M. E., Grain Store, 16 E. Bay St., res. 3 Bedon's
Al.
Munro, M., Widow, 53 Church St.
Murden, Eliza, Mrs., Seminary, 54 Society St.
Murden, Jeremiah, Merchant, 15 Vendue Range
Murphy, E., Widow, 125 Meeting St.
Murphy, William A., Dry Goods Store, 214 King St.
Murphy, William, Collector, Coming St., Neck
Murray, H. C., Accountant, 13 Rutledge St.
Murray, W. C., Merchant, 13 Rutledge St.

Murrell, John C., 21 Middle St.
Mushington, E., Pastry Cook, 126 King St., F.P.C.
Mushington, William, Hair Dresser, 112 Church St., F.P.C.
Musterho, John C., Collector, 13 Rutledge St.
Musterho, W. D., Collector, 13 Rutledge St.
Myers, David, 158 E. Bay St.
Myrne, John, Bricklayer, 13 Rutledge St.
M'Anally, Elizabeth, Widow, 174 Meeting St.
M'Bride, Mary, Widow, 46 Church St.
M'Bride, P., Dry Goods Store, 332 King St.
M'Burney, J. R., Dry Goods & Grocery, King St., Neck
M'Burney, John, Factor, King St., Neck
M'Call, Mary, Widow, 60 Broad St.
M'Call, Susan, Widow, 7 Legare St.
M'Carter, J. J., Book Store, 292 King St.
M'Cartney & Gordon, Hardware Store, 15 Broad St.
M'Cartney, Samuel, 15 Broad St.
M'Clintick, R., Tin Plate Work, 336 King St.
M'Clough, James, 2 Chalmers St.
M'Cormick, T. & C., Dry Goods Store, 62 King St.
M'Cormick, Thomas, Merchant, Vanderhorst's Whf.
M'Crea, John & Co., Dry Goods Store, 323 King St.
M'Cready, Edward, Attorney, res. 20 Anson St.
M'Cready, James, Accountant, 171 King St.
M'Cready, Jane, Widow, 4 Anson St.
M'Cready, William, Accountant, 171 King St.
M'Culloch, Hugh, U. S. Coffee House, 115 E. Bay St.
M'Cully, F., Commission Merchant, Fitzsimons' Whf.
M'Donald, Alexander, Grocery, 302 King St.
M'Donald, J. C. W., Dr., 98 Church St.
M'Donald, Sarah, City Hotel, 173 E. Bay St.
M'Dowall, A. & Co., Dry Goods Store, 121 King St.
M'Dowall, Andrew & Co., Merchants, 20 E. Bay St.
M'Dowall, Shannon & Co., Factors, Boyce's Whf.
M'Hugh, Francis Q., Attorney, 55 Meeting St.
M'Infuss, Ann, 1 Montague St.
M'Intosh, -----, Dry Goods & Hardware, King St., Neck
M'Intyre, M., Dry Goods Store, 97 King St.
M'Intyre, P., Tavern, 94 King St.
M'Kee, Abel, Joiner, 20 Pinckney St.
M'Kee, John, Merchant, 2 Vendue Range, res. 15 George St.
M'Kenzie, A., Vanderhorst St., Neck
M'Kenzie, Archibald, Saddler, 105 Church St.
M'Kenzie, G. T., Saddler, 105 Church St.
M'Kenzie, Richard, Saddler, 252 King St.
M'Kewn, J. S., Accountant, res. 43 George St.
M'Kewn, Mary, Widow, cr. E. Bay & Boundary Sts.
M'Kewn, S. W., Shipwright, res. 43 George St.
M'Kewn, William, Bricklayer, res. 43 George St.
M'Kinlay, William, Tailor, 130 King St., F.P.C.
M'Kinley, Peter, Carpenter, 11 Water St.
M'Kinney, -----, Mrs., Dry Goods Store, 138 King St.
M'Lane, John, Butcher, Butchertown, Neck
M'Lean, James, Billiard Room, 69 Church St.
M'Master, John, Dry Goods & Millinery, 343 King St.
M'Millan, -----, House Carpenter, Butchertown, Neck
M'Millan, John & Co., Factors, Magwood's N. Whf.
M'Millan, John, Merchant, 10 Vendue Range

M'Namee, James, Boarding House, 20 Queen St.
M'Neil, John, John St., Neck
M'Neil, Mary, Widow, 111 Tradd St.
M'Neil, -----, Miss, 27 King St.
M'Neil, Sarah, Widow, 111 Tradd St.
M'Neill & Blair, Grocers, 44 Broad St.
M'Nellage, John, Sail Maker, Gillon St., res. 1 Reaper's Al.
M'Nicol & Davidson, Factors, cr. Crafts' Whf. & E. Bay St.
M'Pherson, Elizabeth, Widow, 289 E. Bay St.
M'Pherson, James, Planter, 289 E. Bay St.
Nardin & Wood, Botanic Physicians, 367 King St.
Nathans, E., Mrs., Widow, 3 Beaufain St.
Nathans, M., Clothing Store, 143 Church St.
Nathans, N. & Co., Dry Goods Store, King St., Neck
Nayel, Vincent, Baker, 46 Queen St.
Neagles, E., Mrs., Widow, 39 King St.
Nedderman, Fred, Oil Store, 84 Market St.
Nelne, John, 9 Wentworth St.
Neufville, Ann, Widow, 86 Anson St.
Neve, William, 19 Wall St.
Neville, A., Cabinet Maker, 57 Wentworth St.
Neville, Eliza, Widow, 217 E. Bay St.
Newbold, Samuel, Grocer, 33 E. Bay St.
Newhall, Edward, Dry Goods Store, 128 King St.
Newton, William, Capt., Merchant, Butchertown, Neck
Newton, William M., Butchertown, Neck
Niche, A., Grocer, cr. Meeting & Henrietta Sts.
Nopie, William, Dyer, 159 Meeting St.
Norman, G. A., Dry Goods Store, 25 Tradd St.
Norris, James C., Magistrate, King St., res. Hampstead
Norris, James, Hotel, cr. George & King Sts.
North, E. W., Dr., off. 60 Meeting St.
Northrop, C. B., Attorney, 1 Court House Sq.
Nunan, Eliza, Widow, 18 George St.
O'Brien, Thomas, 101 Church St.
O'Connor, E., Boarding House, 17 Chalmers St.
O'Hanlon, Charles, 117 E. Bay St.
O'Hanlon, T., Fruit Store, 71 King St.
O'Hear, James, Factor, Radcliffborough, Neck
O'Hear, Joseph, Planter, Radcliffborough, Neck
O'Neale, Charles, Factor, King St., Neck
O'Neale, John, Butcher, Butchertown
O'Neill, F., Merchant, 133 E. Bay St.
O'Neill, Richard, Boot Maker, 30 State St.
O'Neill, Thomas, Boot Maker, 7 Queen St.
O'Reilly, J. T., (Cock & Co.), Merchants, Edmondston's Whf.
Oakley, R. S., Druggist, 144 King St.
Oakley, W. C., Wholesale & Retail Fancy Dry Goods Store, 295 King St.
Oatsmile, James, Grocer, 117 Broad St.
Obenhasser, John, Apothecary, 137 Church St.
Odena, J. E. S., Saddlery, 219 King St.
Ogier, J. L., Dr., 1 State St.
Ogilby, William, British Consul, 88 E. Bay St.
Ogilvie & Bernie, Hardware Store, Broad St.
Oliphant, David, Painter, cr. Meeting & Society Sts.
Oliver, J. H., Carver & Gilder, 124 King St.

Oliver, Sarah, Mantuamaker, 3 Montague St., F.P.C.
Olney, G. W., Merchant, 11 & 13 Vendue Range
Oppenheim, H. W., cr. King & Hudson Sts., Neck
Osterndorf, L. H., Grocer, 21 State St.
Otis & Roulain, Carriage Makers, 193 Meeting St.
Ottolengui, Abraham, Holmes & Co. Whf.
Owens, -----, Butcher, John St., Neck
Owens, Jacob, Wood Factor, 17 Lynch St.
Oxlade, T. C., Watchmaker, 58 Broad St.
Oxlade, Thomas, Painter, 6 State St.
Page, Eliza, St. Philip St., Neck
Page, John, 7 Bull St.
Palmer, Justus, Grocer, 9 E. Bay St.
Parisot, John, cr. Queen & Archdale Sts.
Parker, Eliza, Miss, 31 Church St.
Parker, Samuel, Mrs., Widow, 6 George St.
Parker, William, Mrs., 1 Legare St.
Parkerson, J., Bell Hanger & Engineer, 90 Meeting St.
Pasnauski, G., 97 King St.
Pasnauski, G., Rev., King St., near John St.
Pasnauski, H., 97 King St.
Passalaigue, L., Baker, cr. Wall & Boundary Sts.
Patrick, C., Merchant, 58 E. Bay St., res. 3 Middle St.
Patten, George, Cabinet Maker, 103 Meeting St.
Patterson & Magwood, Factors, Magwood's Whf.
Pattini, Joseph, Fruit Store, 19 Market St.
Patton, William, Factor, 6 Fitzsimons' Whf.
Paul & Brown, Grocers, 47 Broad St.
Payne, J. S., Broker & Auctioneer, 10 State St.
Payne, J. S., Widow, 48 Wentworth St.
Payne, R. K., Surveyor, Blake St., Neck
Pearson, Thomas, Watchmaker, 339 King St.
Pecari, R., Mrs., Clothing Store, 4 Meeting St.
Pelsu, Ann, Mrs., Widow, 7 Coming St.
Pemberton, G. O., Draper & Tailor, 4 Tradd St.
Pemble, David, Dry Goods Store, 143 Church St.
Pennal, Robert, Grocer, cr. King & Boundary Sts.
Pepoon, B. F., Attorney, 10 Broad St.
Perdy, William, 43 Society St.
Pereira, Domingo, Store Keeper, 14 Market St.
Peronneau, Henry, Attorney, 95 Tradd St.
Peronneau, James F., Dr., cr. Church & Elliott Sts.
Peronneau, Mazyck, & Finley, Attorneys, 4 Court House
    Sq.
Perry, Edward, Mrs., Widow, Coming St., Neck
Perry, Julia, Miss, 33 Coming St.
Perry, S., Attorney, 81 Broad St.
Perry, W. H., Capt., Mariner, 18 Tradd St.
Petigru & Lesesne, Attorneys, 12 St. Michael's Al.
Petigru, James L., Attorney, res. 15 Friend St.
Petit, Charles P., Saddler, King St., Neck
Petit, F., Confectioner, 130 Meeting St.
Petit, N. F., Tin Plate Worker, 80 Market St.
Petsch, William, Blacksmith, cr. Middle & Minority Sts.
Pezant, John L. & Co., Merchants, 162 E. Bay St.
Phelan, Margaret, Widow, 66 Meeting St.
Phillips, Eliza, Mantuamaker, 13 Coming St., F.P.C.
Phillips, John, Attorney, 90 Church St.
Phillips, John, Capt., 4 Lynch St.
Phin & Finley, Druggists, 31 Broad St.

Picault, F. D., & Co., Clothiers & Tailors, 131 E. Bay St.
Picault, -----, Mrs., Boarding House, 12 Queen St.
Pillans, John C., House Carpenter, 29 King St.
Pinckney, H. L., 176 King St.
Pinckney, -----, Misses, 193 E. Bay St.
Pinckney, Thomas, Mrs., Widow, 9 King St.
Pindaris, Ann, Widow, King St., near Lines
Pindaris, Jacob, House Carpenter, King St., near Lines
Pindaris, John, Engineer, King St., near Lines
Pitray, Viel & Co., Merchant, Magwood's N. Whf.
Place, H., Capt., Mariner, 54 State St.
Plane, Willam, Custom House, res. 36 Church St.
Plurnet, Mary, Mantuamaker, 15 Orange St., F.P.C.
Poincignon, E., Tin Plate Worker, 15 Queen St.
Poincignon, John, Tin Plate Worker, 28 Wentworth St.
Poirier & Matthiessen, Clothing Store, cr. E. Bay & Queen
    Sts.
Poirier, P., Fancy China Store, 2 Queen St.
Poland, Oliver, 40 Elliott St.
Police, Francis, Clothing Store, 161 E. Bay St.
Pool, William, Rev., Boundary St., Neck
Poole, William L., Maj., U.S. Ordnance Department,
    Cannon St., Neck
Poole, William, Maj., Coming St., Neck
Porcher, Francis Y., Dr., cr. Church & Cumberland Sts.
Porcher, Peter, Dr., cr. Tradd & Meeting Sts.
Porcher, Thomas, Planter, 198 E. Bay St.
Porter, Isabella, Dry Goods Store, 32 Tradd St.
Porter, W. L. & Son, Grocers, 35 Queen St.
Post, R., Rev., 26 Meeting St.
Postell, Sarah, Widow, Alexander St., Neck
Potter, Jane, Mrs., Widow, Bull St., Neck
Poulton, R., Widow, 42 Church St.
Pratt, Charles, Drayman, 22 West St., F.P.C.
Pratt, E., Widow, 5 Laurens St.
Prentice, E., Miss, 34 Society St.
Preslau, Moses, Clothing Store, 63 Queen St.
Pressly, M. G., Miss, 31 George St.
Preston, James, Merchant, 157 E. Bay St.
Preston, John, Grocery, 103 Church St.
Prevost, G. A., Merchant, Magwood's N. Whf.
Price, Maria, Mantuamaker, 25 Montague St., F.P.C.
Price, Thomas, Bookkeeper, 5 Society St.
Prince, A., Cooper, Pitt St., Neck
Prince, Edwin, Bricklayer, Coming St., Neck
Prince, Eliza, Widow, John St., Neck
Pringle, George, Merchant, Magwood's Whf., res. King
    St., Neck
Pringle, J. A., (Adger & Co.), Merchant, res. 2 Orange St.
Pringle, James R., Customs Collector, res. 2 Orange St.
Pringle, -----, Misses, 156 Meeting St.
Prioleau, F. C., Accountant, 80 E. Bay St.
Prioleau, James, Custom House, res. 3 Orange St.
Prioleau, Philip, Dr., 160 Meeting St.
Prioleau, T. G. & Baron, Drs., 127 Meeting St.
Prioleau, Thomas G., Dr., res. cr. Washington & Charlotte
    Sts., Neck
Pritchard, C. C., Dr., 233 E. Bay St.
Pritchard, Paul, Shipwright, 6 Hasell St.
Proctor, William, Bookkeeper, 18 Horlbeck's Al.

Purcington, G. P. & Co., Painters, 140 Meeting St.
Purse, Henry W., Accountant, 15 King St.
Purse, Thomas, Accountant, 15 King St.
Purse, Thomas, Accountant, John St., Neck
Purse, William, Watchmaker, John St., Neck
Purves, William B., Cabinet Maker, 143 Meeting St.
Pyatt, M. H., Widow, cr. Meeting & Charlotte Sts., Neck
Quash, Albert, Sr., Hair Dresser, 2 Anson St., F.P.C.
Quash, F. D., Planter, 83 Boundary St., Neck
Quash, Matthew, Pastry Cook, 13 Pitt St., F.P.C.
Quash, Robert H., Factor, 18 Vanderhorst's Whf.
Query, H., Mrs., Widow, 22 George St.
Quimby, J., Carpenter, res. 45 George St.
Quinby, E., Mrs., Widow, 45 George St.
Quinby, Joseph, Ship Joiner, 35 Wall St.
Quinby, Thomas, Grocery, 8 Minority St.
Quinlan, John, 27 King St.
Quinnan, -----, Mrs., Wooden Ware Store, 251 King St.
Ralston, Robert, Planter, 70 Tradd St.
Rame, C., Confectioner, 147 Meeting St.
Ramsay, E., Widow, 11 Meeting St.
Ramsay, -----, Misses, School, 66 Broad St.
Ramsay, W. G., Dr., 52 E. Bay St.
Ramsay, William, Printer, res. 66 Broad St.
Rantin, Alexander, Carpenter, John St., Neck
Ravenel, C., Widow, 60 Broad St.
Ravenel, Daniel, President, Planters & Mechanics Bank, Res. 11 George St.
Ravenel, E., Miss, 60 Broad St.
Ravenel, Edmund, Dr., 42 Meeting St.
Ravenel, James, Accountant, 12 Commercial N. Whf.
Ravenel, Stevens & Co., Factors, 12 Commercial N. Whf.
Ravenna, J. D., Professor of Languages, State St.
Recli, Carlo, Ferry Coffee House, 3 Vendue Range
Redfern, J., Boot & Shoe Maker, 9 Tradd St.
Redmond, W. & R., Factors, Central Whf.
Reeder, Oswell, Merchant, King St., Neck
Reedy, James, Carpenter, 93 Church St.
Reedy, -----, Mrs., Boarding House, 93 Church St.
Reeves, Mathew S., Professor of Music, St. Philip St., Neck
Reid, Andrew, Auctioneer, Vendue Range, res. 107 King St.
Reid, Elizabeth, 21 Cumberland St.
Reid, George, Bank of South Carolina, res. 11 Logan St.
Reid, Sarah, Dry Goods Store, cr. Anson & Society Sts.
Reilly, Thomas, Bookkeeper, Commercial N. Whf.
Reinhart, J. F., Boarding House, King St., Neck
Rembert, J., Factor, 237 E. Bay St.
Remington, Thomas, Guilder, 101 Meeting St.
Remley, P., Bricklayer, Boundary St., Neck
Requier, A., Confectioner, 84 Meeting St.
Reynolds, Clark, (Reynolds & Reynolds), Coach Makers, 117 Meeting St.
Reynolds, George, 117 Meeting St.
Reynolds, George N., 117 Meeting St.
Reynolds, -----, Mrs., 367 Meeting St.
Rice, William, Attorney, 1 Court House Sq., res. 68 Broad St.
Richards & Sandford, 132 E. Bay St.

Richardson, C. Y., Bell Hanger & Engineer, 97 Meeting St.
Richardson, Robert, Bell Hanger & Engineer, 97 Meeting St.
Riecke, Claus, Grocer, 20 Meeting St.
Riecke, George, Grocer, cr. King & Mary Sts., Neck
Riecke, Gerd, Grocer, 228 King St.
Riggs, John S., Harness Maker, 179 Meeting St.
Righton, Joseph, Cooper, 5 Water St.
Riley, Joseph, Wharfinger, Commercial Whf.
Riley, William, Bookseller & Printer, 92 Church St.
Ring, D. A., Oil and Color Store, 41 E. Bay St., res. 4 Church St.
Ripley, N. F., Merchant, 6 Vendue Range
Ripley, S. P., (Miller, R. & Co.), Merchant, res. 7 George St.
Rippon, W. H., 48 King St.
Rivers, Mary, G., Widow, 7 Wentworth St.
Rivers, T. F., Comb Manufactory, 154 King St.
Rivers, William, Printer, 115 Wentworth St.
Riviere, J. P., Dry Goods Store, 149 King St., Neck
Roach, N., Planter, North St., Neck
Robb, James, Grocer, 132 King St.
Roberts, George, Dry Goods Store, 71 Church St.
Roberts, Mary Ann, 5 Elliott St.
Robertson, George, res. 48 Meeting St.
Robertson, James, Merchant, 12 Hamilton & Co. Whf., Res. 17 E. Bay St.
Robins, A., Fruit Store, 1 Market St.
Robinson, Alex, Secretary, Fire & Marine Insurance Co., Res. 11 E. Bay St.
Robinson, Randal, Bank Officer, Thomas St.
Robinson, S. T., Cashier, Planters & Mechanics Bank, Res. Judith St., Neck
Robinson & Caldwell, Factors, Commercial Whf.
Roche, Edward, City Treasurer, res. 13 Society St.
Rock, John, Grocer, cr. Boundary & St. Philip Sts., Neck
Roddy, M., Grocer, 13 Queen St.
Rodgers, C., Tailor, 9 Coming St.
Rodgers, John, R., Capt., City Guard, res. 2 Church St.
Rodgers, S. B., Comb Manufactory, 155 King St.
Rodgers, William, Bookkeeper, 9 Middle St.
Rodrigues, B. A., Surgeon Dentist, cr. Meeting & Hasell Sts.
Rodrigues, S., Mattress Store, 45 Queen St.
Roger, Thomas J., Merchant, Magwoods N. Whf.
Rogers, Lewis, Wheelwright, 14 Burns Ln.
Rolando, F. G., Cooper, 13 Champney St.
Root, J. B. & Taylor, Dry Goods Store.
Roper, B. D., Attorney, St. Michael's Al.
Roper, William, Planter, 3 Logan St.
Rose, A. C., Cashier, Charleston Bank, Elizabeth St., Neck
Rose, Eliza, Widow, Butchertown, Neck
Rose, Hugh, Planter, 267 E. Bay St.
Rose, James, Planter, 267 E. Bay St.
Rose, John, Grocer, cr. Meeting & Wolf Sts., Neck
Ross, D. M., Carpenter, 38 Anson St.
Ross, David, 4 Motte St.
Ross, J. L., Contractor for Railroads, 377 King St.
Ross, James, Merchant, 149 E. Bay St.

Ross, John, Engineer, 6 Society St.
Ross, Sarah, Widow, 39 Wentworth St.
Roumillat, C., Niagara Garden, Meeting St., Neck
Roumillat, U., Confectionary, 50 Broad St.
Roundey, J. W., Bookkeeper, 1 Society St.
Rout, William G., Clerk, Charleston Bank, res. 14 Friend St.
Rove, Francis, Fruit Store, 86 Market St.
Rowand, Charles, 17 Logan St.
Rowand, Robert, Wood Factor, 7 S. Bay St.
Rowe, Henry, Painter, 6 Middle St.
Ruby, John, Capt., 53 Coming St.
Ruggles, N., Shoe Store, 366 King St.
Rumph, G. H., Blacksmith, Wolf St., Neck
Russell & Sass, Auctioneers & Commercial Merchants, Vendue Range
Rust, John, Grocer, cr. John & St. Philip Sts., Neck
Rustant, A., 3 Queen St.
Rutland, Mary Ann, 15 Wentworth St.
Rutledge, Frederick, Mrs., Widow, 117 Tradd St.
Rutledge, H., Widow, 2 Hasell St.
Rutledge, John, Planter, St. Philip St., Neck
Ryan, Ann, Boarding House, 21 Elliott St.
Ryan, John, Carpenter, 70 King St.
Ryan, Laurence, City Sheriff, 72 Church St.
Ryan, William, Grocer, cr. State & Chalmers Sts.
Ryley, Honoria, Widow, Coming St., Neck
Salter, T. R., Ship Joiner, 229 E. Bay St.
Salvo, Corrado, Fruit Store, 92 King St.
Sampson, S., Sr. & Co., Merchant Tailors, 262 King St.
Sargent, John, Attorney, King St., Neck
Sass, E. G., 57 Queen St.
Saunders, S., Hair Dresser, 43 Broad St.
Sawyer, William, Dry Goods Store, 348 King St.
Schaffer, Fred, House Carpenter, cr. Boundary & Pitt Sts.
Schaffner, J., Widow, 11 Pinckney St.
Schirmer, Jacob F., Cooper, 59 Queen St.
Schmidt, A., 103 Broad St.
Schmidt, James, King St., Neck
Schmidt, John W., Dr., 27 Church St.
Schnieder, Christian, Clerk, 18 Middle St.
Schnierle, Fred, House Carpenter, 11 Friend St.
Schnierle, John, Col., res. 11 Friend St.
Schnierle, John M., House Carpenter, 11 Friend St.
Schnierle, William, Carpenter, res. 11 Friend St.
Schoolbred, John, Planter, Boundary St., Neck
Schooner, C., Miss, 11 Wentworth St.
Schriber, J., Mrs., 31 Society St.
Schriener, John H., Merchant, cr. Edmondston's Whf.
Schroder, J., Grocer, 49 Market St.
Schroder, John, Sugar Refiner, 12 Wentworth St.
Schultz, Louisa, Widow, 60 Tradd St.
Schultz, Susan, Widow, 275 E. Bay St.
Scott, Ann, Widow, cr. Vanderhorst & St. Philip Sts., Neck
Scott, C., Cabinet Maker, 141 King St.
Scott, -----, Dr., 369 King St.
Scott, E. C., Accountant, 96 Meeting St.
Scott, M. B., Mrs., Seminary, 96 Meeting St.
Scott, William, Hair Dresser, 169 King St.

Seabrook, William, Planter, 11 New St.
Sebeck, C., Grocer, cr. Radcliff & St. Philip Sts.
Sebring & Edgerton, Drapers & Tailors, 32 Broad St.
Seigness, C., Coach Maker, 346 King St.
Seigness, John, 8 Cumberland St.
Selin, Peter, Fruit Store, 57 Market St.
Seymour, Ann, Widow, 41 King St.
Seymour, R. W., Attorney, 57 Meeting St.
Shackelford, Boag & Co., Merchants, 114 E. Bay St.
Shackelford, W., Mrs., 14 Society St.
Shanks, C., Boot Maker, 75 E. Bay St.
Shecut, -----, Dr., Botanical Apothecary, 115 King St.
Shegog, J., Grocer, 69 Market St.
Sheing, Alex, School Teacher, 99 Wentworth St.
Shelton, Samuel, Merchants Hotel, cr. Society & King Sts.
Shemson, John, Accomptant, St. Philip St., Neck
Sheppard, Thomas C., Accountant, Boundary St., Neck
Shievely, C. G., Paint & Oil Store, 182 Meeting St.
Shiner, M., Merchant, King St., Neck
Shinie, William, House Carpenter, 49 Coming St.
Shirtliff, Elizabeth, n. side Boundary St.
Short, J. & Co., Merchants, Magwoods Whf.
Shrewsborough, Edward, Charlotte St., Neck
Shroudy, W. B., 1 Fort St.
Shultze, Charles, Shoe Maker, 24 Queen St.
Siddons, Joseph, Furniture Ware Room, 78 Market St.
Siegling, John, Music Warehouse, 225 King St.
Sigwald, Mary, Widow, 4 Burns Ln.
Simmons, William, Accountant, 20 Horlbeck's Al.
Simonds, J. W., Dr., Druggist, 347 King St.
Simons & Barnwell, Factor, Hamilton & Co. Whf.
Simons & Phillips, Paint Store, 49 Queen St.
Simons, Benjamin B., Dr., res. E. Bay St., off. 14 Middle St.
Simons, Eliza, Widow, 3 Lynch St.
Simons, J. C., Oil & Paint Store, 193 King St.
Simons, John, Rigger, 144 E. Bay St.
Simons, -----, Mrs., n. side Boundary St.
Simons, Thomas Y., Dr., off. 43 Church St., res. 45 Church St.
Simonton, C. S., 28 Society St.
Simpson, Jane, Widow, 39 Society St.
Sinclair, Alex, Merchant, Boyce & Co. Whf.
Singee, John, King St., Neck
Skeen, W., Wharfinger, 36 Tradd St.
Slattery, G., Dry Goods Store, 341 King St.
Sloken, H., Cabinet Maker, King St., Neck
Sloman, Eliza, Widow, 27 Montague St.
Sluken, John, Accomptant, John St., Neck
Sluter, Jacob, Dry Goods Store, 339 King St.
Smith & Malone, Attorneys, 64 Broad St.
Smith, A. C., 14 State St.
Smith, Albert, Shoe Maker, Cannon St., F.P.C.
Smith, Ann, Q., Washington St., Neck
Smith, Benjamin & Son, Paint & Oil Store, rear of Exchange
Smith, Benjamin, R., Merchant, 62 E. Bay St.
Smith, Benjamin R., Merchant, res. Radcliffborough
Smith, E. M., Capt., Mariner, 3 Minority St.
Smith, F., Commercial Whf.

Smith, Fowler, Fancy Shoe Store, 123 King St.
Smith, George, Mariner, 15 Boundary St.
Smith, H., Mrs., Widow, 15 Bull St.
Smith, H. W. & Co., Sail Makers, 5 Champney St.
Smith, Hugh, Mrs., Widow, 15 Rutledge St.
Smith, J. H., Attorney, Mary St., Hampstead
Smith, J., Miss, Boarding House, 71 Broad St.
Smith, J., Mrs., Widow, 13 Montague St.
Smith, John, Attorney, 15 Bull St.
Smith, John, Carpenter, 25 Hasell St.
Smith, O. M., Attorney, 3 Court St. Sq.
Smith, P., cr. Wentworth & Anson Sts.
Smith, R. B. & E. Smith, Attorneys, cr. Elliott & Church Sts.
Smith, R. P., (Trenholm & M'Cormick), Auctioneers, Vendue Range
Smith, Richard, Paper Store, 90 Queen St.
Smith, Samuel, Mrs., Widow, 75 Broad St.
Smith, W., Factor, Holmes Whf.
Smith, W., Grocer, 19 Montague St.
Smith, W. W., Planter, 167 E. Bay St.
Smith, William, Boot & Shoe Maker, 177 King St.
Smith, William M., Planter, 22 Meeting St.
Smith, William, Merchant, 107 Meeting St.
Smith, William S., 73 Broad St.
Smith, William, Shipwright, Washington St., Neck
Socredo, John, Tailor, 3 Lamboll St., F.P.C.
Sollee, Henry, Teller, Union Bank
Sollee, T., Mrs., 73 Church St.
Solomon, A., Widow, 101 Market St.
Solomons, A., Druggist, res. 341 King St.
Solomons, Israel, Mrs., res. 341 King St.
Solomons, L., Carpenter, res. 341 King St.
Sourhoff, George, Grocer, 20 State St.
Spainger, S., 41 King St.
Sparing, David, Painter, King St., Neck, F.P.C.
Sparnock, H., Custom House, res. 25 Queen St.
Spears, J., Bookkeeper, Radcliffborough, Neck
Speissiger, L. P., Pianoforte Tuner, 137 Church St.
Speissiger, Thomas, Grocer, 11 Pinckney St.
Spell, John, Accomptant, Radcliffborough, Neck
Spencer, -----, Mrs., Dry Goods Store, 329 King St.
Spofford, Haseltine & Co., Wholesale Shoe Store, 266 King St.
Sproulls, Baker & Co., Hat Warehouse, 272 King St.
St. Amand, J. A., Livery Stable, Society St., near King St.
St .Mark, William, Drayman, 28 Middle St., F.P.C.
Starke, Charles, Grocer, 8 Laurens St.
Steedman, Charles, Col., Custom House, Washington St., Neck
Steedman, Thomas, Custom House, res. Charlotte St., Neck
Steedman, William B., Accountant, Washington St., Neck
Steele, John, Bank Officer, North St., Neck
Steinmyer, F., House Carpenter, Boundary St.
Stent, John, House Carpenter, 23 King St.
Stetting, John, Grocer, cr. Market & State Sts.
Stevens, A., Capt., Mariner, 6 Minority St.
Stevens, Henderson & Adger, Importers of Hardware, 54 E. Bay St.

Stevents, J. R., Clothing Store, 270 King St.
Stewart, Angus, Carolina Hotel, 54 Broad St.
Stewart, Jane, Widow, 7 Adams St.
Stewart, Robert, Carpenter, 3 Burns Ln.
Stewart, Sarah, Widow, Wentworth St., Neck
Stickly, Fred, Engineer, St. Philip St., Neck
Stickman, J., cr. King & Radcliff Sts., Neck
Stiles, Copeland, 301 King St.
Stillman, James, Bookkeeper, 164 Meeting St.
Stock, John Y., Broker & Auctioneer, 4 State St.
Stocker, J. N., Merchant, res. 12 Society St.
Stockins, J. H., Grocer, 31 King St.
Stoddard, E. B., Wholesale & Retail Boot & Shoe Store, 317 King St.
Stoddard, Miller & Co., Merchants, 254 King St.
Stoll, Stephen, St. Philip St., Neck
Stoney, J., off. 118 E. Bay St., res. 24 Hasell St.
Storm, J. G., Merchant Tailor, 217 King St.
Storm, -----, Mrs., Artificial Florist, 129 King St.
Stoutland, E., Accomptant, 301 King St.
Stowe, Robert, Veterinarian, Butchertown, Neck
Straus, John, Boot & Shoe Store, King St., Neck
Street & Boinest, Merchants, 6 Boyce & Co. Whf.
Street, H. G. & Son, Grocers, cr. Church St. & St. Michael's Al.
Street, James, Boarding House, 6 Bedon's Al.
Strobel, Benjamin B., Dr., 74 Meeting St.
Strobel, Martin, 78 Meeting St.
Strohecker, George, 156 Meeting St.
Strohecker, Henry, 156 Meeting St.
Strohecker, J., Hardware Store, 156 Meeting St.
Strohecker, Louis, Wood Factor, Montague St.
Stuart, J. A., Editor of Mercury, res. Ann St., Neck
Suares, A., Accomptant, 139 King St.
Suares, B. C., Merchant Tailor, 139 King St.
Suares, Judith, Mrs., Widow, 189 King St.
Suder, Peter J., Carpenter, 17 Society St.
Sullivan, John, House Carpenter, John St., Neck
Sullivan, Mary, Widow, 72 Anson St.
Sullivan, P., Dry Goods, 190 King St.
Surtis, Thomas, Capt., Mariner, 30 Church St.
Sutcliffe, J. H., Baker
Sweegan, M., Grocer, 7 Market St.
Sweeny & Honour, Bookbinders, rear of Exchange
Swift, T. B., State Constable, 75 Tradd St.
Symmes, Thomas, Dry Goods Store, 245 King St.
Tabor, R. W., Bookkeeper, Radcliffborough, Neck
Taft, A. R., (Howland, Ward & Taft), res. 7 Laurens St.
Tally, R. Nicholas, Coming St., Neck
Tanswell, W. N., Bell Hanger, 53 Meeting St.
Tavel, Louis, Boundary St., n. side
Taylor, E. W., Dry Goods Store, 350 King St.
Taylor, George T., Attorney, 11 St. Michael's Al.
Taylor, J. H., Auctioneer, 28 Vendue Range
Taylor, T. R., Boot & Shoe Store, 241 King St.
Taylor, William S., Coach Maker, 13 Church St.
Teague, -----, Mrs., Boarding House, 335 King St.
Teasdale, A., Planter, 7 Orange St.
Teithew, J., Grocer, cr. Radcliff & Coming Sts.
Teitken, Hammond, Grocer, Butchertown

Telfer, Robert, Gauger, 99 King St.
Tennant, Charles, Planter, 60 Anson St.
Tew, Henry S., Ship Chandler, 159 E. Bay St.
Tharin, T. C., Wheelwright, cr. Mary & King Sts., Neck
Thayer, Ebenezer, Book Store, 81 Broad St.
Thayer, H., 10 Lynch St.
Thayer, John D., Clerk, 63 E. Bay St.
Thayer, T. H., Broker & Auctioneer, 7 State St.
Thee, H. M., Grocer, Gadsden's Whf.
Thee, John H., Grocer, 10 Market St.
Thomas, E., Boot Maker, 56 State St.
Thomas, Isabella, 1 Coming St.
Thomas, M., Merchant, 297 King St.
Thomas, Mary D., 45 Coming St.
Thomas, Stephen, (Gaillard & Thomas), res. 19 Pinckney St.
Thompson, Ann, Widow, 1 Burns Ln.
Thompson, Eliza, Dry Goods Store, 12 King St.
Thompson, F., Mrs., Midwife, 65 King St.
Thompson, George, Mason, 38 Tradd St.
Thompson, J. B., Attorney, 2 Court House Sq.
Thompson, J. B., Attorney, 9 New St.
Thompson, J., Saddler, 45 Broad St.
Thompson, James, Dry Goods Store, 142 E. Bay St.
Thompson, John, Grocer, 1 Bull St.
Thompson, John, Whitesmith, 51 State St.
Thompson, W., 40 Meeting St.
Thrane, J. W., Grocer, 28 Market St.
Thurston, R., Merchant, 23 Vanderhorst's Whf.
Thursty, T. H., 18 Hasell St.
Thwing, Edward, Broker & Auctioneer, 17 State St.
Tilton, Henry, Engineer, John St.
Tilton, Nathaniel H., Boarding House, 91 Market St.
Timmons, G. P., 147 E. Bay St.
Timmons, George, Clerk, Union Bank
Timmons, W. L., 147 E. Bay St.
Timmons, William & Son, Hardware Store, 147 E. Bay St.
Timrod, William H., Bookbinder, 10 Broad St.
Tobias, Abraham & Co., Auctioneers, cr. Vendue Range & E. Bay St.
Tobias, I., Jail Keeper, Magazine St.
Tolck, J. D., Grocer, 77 E. Bay St.
Toomer, Joshua W., Attorney, cr. Ann & Meeting Sts., Neck
Toomer, T. V., Dr., off. s.e. cr. Ann & Meeting Sts., Neck
Torrington, M., Grocery, 5 E. Bay St.
Tousseger, Eliza, Miss, 20 Water St.
Tovey, H. & Son, Pump & Block Makers, E. Bay St.
Townsend, Mary, 23 Middle St.
Trapier, B., Planter, Coming St.
Trapier, Paul, Rev., 41 Meeting St.
Trapmann, L., Merchant, 58 E. Bay St.
Trenholm & Holmes, Dry Goods Store, 162 King St.
Trenholm, Smith & M'Cormick, Auctioneers, 19 & 21 Vendue Range
Trescott, E., Mrs., Widow, Coming St., Neck
Trescott, Edward, Engineer, Coming St., Neck
Trescott, Henry, State Bank, res. 4 Anson St.
Trotte, -----, Mrs., Widow, 79 King St.
Trouche, A., Merchant, Vanderhorst's Whf., res. 47 Church St.

Trout, T., Merchant, N. Commercial Whf., res. 55 Meeting St.
Truesdell, David, Oyster House, 30 Queen St.
Trumbull, Ann, Widow, 1 Logan St.
Trumbull, William, Planter, 22 Water St.
Tunis, C. H., Miss, cr. Vanderhorst's Whf. & E. Bay St.
Tunno, S. C., Widow, 74 Tradd St.
Tupper, T., Merchant, cr. Napier's Range & Gibbes' Whf.
Turley, M. H., Accountant, 45 E. Bay St.
Tweed, Ellen, Widow, School, Charlotte St., Neck
Tydgenau, M., Grocer, 5 Montague St.
Underwood, Thomas C., Tailor, 75 Meeting St.
Uttermahl, Mary O., Burns Ln.
Vage, George W., Accountant, 22 Queen St.
Valentine, Samuel, Dry Goods Store, 147 King St.
Valentine, Samuel, Merchant, 38 Wentworth St.
Vance, Francis, Mrs., Lynch St.
Vance, William, Planter, Butchertown, Neck
Vancooth, J. A., 4 Hamilton & Co. Whf.
Vanderhorst, Elias, Planter, John St., Neck
Vangan, Ann, Widow, cr. Motte & Pinckney Sts.
Van Rhyn, J. M., Planter, Hampstead, Neck
Vanwinkle & Sparks, Variety Store, 290 King St.
Vardell, E., Mrs., Widow, 37 Bull St.
Vardell, John, Bricklayer, Vanderhorst St., Neck
Vardell, -----, Mrs., Widow, Vanderhorst St., Neck
Vardell, Thomas R., Bricklayer, 261 E. Bay St.
Varden, J. A., Painter, Tradd St., near E. Bay St.
Veitch, William, Apothecary, 213 King St.
Venberg, Benjamin, Grocer, 3 South Bay St.
Vent, Eugene, Accountant, 36 Hasell St.
Vere, Susan, Confectionary, 73 Tradd St., F.P.C.
Vernon, W. T., Merchant, Commercial Whf.
Verre, Robert, 20 Water St.
Vidal, James, (Picault & Co.), Clothing Store, 131 E. Bay St.
Villaneuve, Margaret, Widow, 40 Anson St.
Vincent, H. E., Jr., Clerk, 65 E. Bay St.
Vincent, J. B., Clerk, 65 E. Bay St.
Vincent, T. E., Ship Chandler, 65 E. Bay St.
Vincent, William, Broker, 114 Church St.
Vinro, -----, Mrs., Midwife, 36 Wentworth St.
Vogel & Salvo, Furniture Warehouse, 216 King St.
Wagner, Charles, Collector, cr. Butchertown & St. Philip St.
Wagner, George, Grocer, cr. Butchertown & St. Philip St.
Wagner, J., Dr., 75 Meeting St.
Wagner, Jacob, Engineer, Meeting St., Neck
Wagner, John A., Grocer, cr. E. Bay & Pinckney Sts.
Wagner, Peter, Grocer, 50 Church St.
Walker, Alex, Bookkeeper, 13 Friend St.
Walker, J. C., Bookbinder and Stationer, 85 E. Bay St.
Walker, J. E., Stone Cutter, 64 Queen St.
Walker, John F., Merchant, Boyce & Co. Whf., res. 204 E. Bay St.
Walker, Joseph, Accountant, 85 E. Bay St.
Walker, W., Stone Cutter, 137 Meeting St.
Wall, R., 22 State St.

Wallace, Thomas, Dry Goods Store, 344 King St.
Walter, C. H., Grocer, 61 Market St.
Walter, E. W., Factor, Boyce & Co. Whf.
Walter, J., Auctioneer, 8 Vendue Range
Walton, A. Y., 17 George St.
Walton, J. W. S., Hardware Store, 300 King St.
Walton, John M., (Milliken & Walton), 108 E. Bay St.
Wanderpool, John, 7 Bull St.
Wanless, A., Saddle & Harness Maker, 91 King St.
Ward, Francis S., Clerk of City Court.
Ward, J. G., Merchant, 135 E. Bay St.
Ward, Mary, Widow, 42 Broad St.
Ward, T., Miss, 7 Water St.
Ware, Mary, Butchertown, Neck
Waring, C., Mrs., Widow, 2 George St.
Waring, Frances, Factor, Cannon St., Neck
Waring, Morton A., Broker, St. Philip St.
Waring, Thomas, Merchant, 3 Lynch St.
Waring, Thomas R., Factor, Vanderhorst's Whf.
Warley, Ann, Mrs., Widow, 79 Tradd St.
Warley, Thomas, Accountant, 79 Tradd St.
Warren, Susan, 46 Elliott St.
Warrington, J., Boot Maker, 219 E. Bay St.
Watson, S. & J., Merchants, 28 E. Bay St.
Webb & Son, Factors, Commercial Whf.
Webb, D. C., Merchant, cr. Butchertown & Cannon St.
Webb, John, Factor, Commercial Whf.
Webb, T. L., Factor, Commercial Whf.
Webb, Thomas C., Merchant, cr. Butchertown & Cannon St.
Webber, Sarah, Widow, Market St.
Weed & Benedict, Hat Warehouse, 305 King St.
Weed, Henry, Accountant, 285 King St.
Welling, William, Jr., Blacksmith, 125 Meeting St.
Welling, William, Sr., Boarding House, 43 State St.
Wells, T. T., Widow, cr. E. Bay St. & Vendue Range
Welsh, J., Painter, Radcliff St., Neck
Welsh, John, Carpenter, Reid St., Neck
Welsh, Peter, Variety Store, 146 E. Bay St.
Welsman, James, Capt., 72 Church St.
Wen, J. D. O., Mrs., Fancy & Staple Dry Goods, 136 King St.
Wen, L., Dr., Surgeon Dentist, 136 King St.
Wenner, Charles J., Blacksmith, 49 State St.
Wescott, J., Butcher, Hampstead, Neck
Wesner, Frederick, Master of Work House, 13 Magazine St.
West, C. L., U. S. Appraiser, rear of Exchange
West, Charles H., Merchant, 61 E. Bay St., res. 11 Church St.
Westendorff, Charles, Grain Dealer, cr. E. Bay & Market Sts.
Weston, Jacob, St. Philip St., Neck
Weston, Jacob, Tailor, Coming St., F.P.C.
Weston, T., Miss, Hampstead, Neck
Weyman, A. C., Widow, cr. Church St. & Lightwood Al.
Weyman, Mary R., Miss, 50 Wentworth St.
Whaley, W., Planter, Butchertown
Whitaker, D. K., Attorney, 7 St. Michael's Al.
White, John, Planter, 279 E. Bay St.

White, John, Stone Cutter, 123 Meeting St.
White, William, Engineer, Coming St., Neck
White, William H., Grocer, cr. Market & Church Sts.
Whitemore, C., Soap & Candle Manufactory, Radcliff St.
Whitney, Archibald, Broker & Notary, 11 Cumberland St.
Whitney, E. M., Turner, 179 Meeting St.
Whitney, O. L., Dry Goods Store, 224 King St.
Whitridge, J. B., Dr., 9 Montague St.
Whitsinger, Charles, Planter, King St., Neck
Whitsinger, Daniel, Planter, King St., Neck
Widhall, James, Trader, 34 Chalmers St.
Wiehman, John F., Grocer, Meeting St., Neck
Wienges, Rebecca, Widow, 18 Burns Ln.
Wight & Wescott, Furnishing Warehouse, 193 King St.
Wightman, John, Turner, 192 Meeting St.
Wightman, William, Grocer, cr. Meeting & Society Sts.
Wilbur, W. W., Comb Manufactory, 156 King St.
Wilcox, Ann, John St., Neck
Wilcox, Mary, Widow, 26 Laurens St.
Wiley, L. M., (Parish & Co.), Wholesale Dry Goods Store, 261 King St.
Wiley, Mary, Widow, 138 Church St.
Wiley, W. J., Collector, 353 King St.
Wiley, William, Trader, 20 Lynch St.
Wilkes & Middleton, Factors, Hamilton & Co. Whf.
Wilkes, John, 13 Meeting St.
Wilkie, -----, Mrs., Hotel, 218 King St.
Wilking, M., Planter, 9 Lamboll St.
Williams, John, Capt., Mariner, 8 Wentworth St.
Williams, John, Commercial Merchant, 37 E. Bay St.
Williams, Judith, Mantuamaker, 7 Legare St., F.P.C.
Williams, -----, Mrs., Widow, 23 Beaufain St.
Williams, Thomas, House Carpenter, Coming St.
Williams, W. B., (Ewart & Co.), Factors, Magwood & Co. Whf.
Williamson, John, 7 Cumberland St.
Williman, Barron, res. 103 Broad St.
Williman, Charles, res. 103 Broad St.
Williman, Eliza, Boundary St., Neck
Williman, -----, Miss, res. 103 Broad St.
Willis, H., House Carpenter, cr. Line & Meeting Sts.
Willis, J. G., Accomptant, 232 King St.
Wilmans, A. F. & Co., Hardware Store, 228 King St.
Wilmot, J. & T. T., Jewelry & Fancy Articles, 267 King St.
Wilson, A. B., Radcliffborough, Neck
Wilson, Hugh, Planter, cr. Cannon & Line Sts.
Wilson, J., Accomptant, 111 Broad St.
Wilson, J. L., Accountant, 121 King St.
Wilson, J., Seed Store, 282 King St.
Wilson, John L., Attorney, 2 St. Michael's Al., res. 10 Laurens St.
Wilson, Robert, Capt., Custom House, 13 Hasell St.
Winchester, -----, Mrs., Seminary, John St.
Winger, Jacob, Grocer, cr. Pitt & Montague Sts.
Winger, -----, Mrs., Widow, 18 Burns Ln.
Winthrop & Holmes, Factors, 195 S. Bay St.
Winthrop, Augustus, Bank Officer, 97 Tradd St.
Winthrop, F. & C., Merchants, 5 Champney St.
Winthrop, F., Factor, 97 Tradd St.
Winthrop, H., Dr., off. 42 Society St., res. Tradd St.

Winthrop, Henry, Dr., 97 Tradd St.
Winthrop, J. A., Factor, 6 Hamilton & Co. Whf.
Winthrop, J., Factor, 99 Tradd St.
Wise, Alford, Painter, 36 Elliott St.
Wise, Edward, Clothing Store, 32 Elliott St.
Wish, Richard, City Marshal, 25 Broad St.
Witherspoon, Robert, Merchant, Coming St., Neck
Witsell, F., Planter, Radcliffborough, Neck
Witter, E. S., Widow, 30 Tradd St.
Wolff, F. A., Harness Maker, 140 Market St.
Wood, Daniel, Butcher, Hampstead, Neck
Wood, Edward, Constable, 52 Elliott St.
Wood, George, Custom House, 2 Motte St.
Wood, John, Engraver, cr. St. Philip & John Sts.
Wood, Mary, Grocer, 202 King St.
Woolf, Isaac, Dry Goods, cr. King & Boundary Sts.
Woolf, R., Clothing Store, 121 E. Bay St.
Woolf, Sarah, Dry Goods, cr. King & Boundary Sts.
Wotton, E., Mrs., Nurse, 58 King St.
Wragg, Simons & Co., Factors, Hamilton & Co. Whf.
Wragg, W. T., Dr., King St., 1 door n. of John St., Neck
Wright, Ann, Mantuamaker, 9 Rutledge St., F.P.C.
Wright, H., Fancy Dry Goods Store, 164 King St.
Wurdemann, J. G. H., Dr., 210 King St.

Wurdemann, -----, Mrs., Widow, 210 King St.
Wyatt, J., Accountant, 23 Montague St.
Yates & M'Intyre, Lottery Office, 26 Broad St.
Yates, D., Widow, 6 Church St.
Yates, Francis, 58 Church St.
Yates, J. A., U. S. Appraiser, rear of Custom House
Yates, J. D., Sheriff, 81 Tradd St.
Yates, J. L., Merchant, 5 Water St.
Yates, John, Carpenter, 28 Tradd St.
Yates, -----, Mrs., Widow, 81 Tradd St.
Yeadon, Richard, Bank Officer, 21 King St.
Yeadon, Richard, Jr., Editor of Courier, res. 96
    Wentworth St.
You, John C., Custom House, res. 4 Archdale St.
Young, J., 59 Queen St.
Young, James, Rigger, Cumberland St.
Young, William, Baker, 44 Church St.
Young, William M., Accountant, 222 King St.
Zealy, C., Mrs., Midwife, 47 King St.
Zealy, Joseph, Accountant, 45 E. Bay St.
Zealy, Joseph T., Carpenter, 3 Inspection St.
Zealy, W. E., Bank Officer, 47 King St.
Zerbst, F., Grocer, King St., Neck

The Directory for 1840-41

This seems to be the next directory after Dowling's 1837-38 edition. It was published by T. C. Fay, with the title of *Charleston Directory, and Strangers' Guide, for 1840 and 1841, Embracing Names of Heads of Families - - Firms, and the Individuals Composing Them; Together with All Persons in Business, and Their Residences, Alphabetically Arranged. Also, Each Street and Numbers Where Practicable, with the Names of the Occupants Respectively Noted -- Thereby Answering the Purpose of a Cross Index* (Charleston: T. C. Fay, 1840). Fay states that "It is matter of surprise, that a work so much required has not been more regularly performed, and .... the fear of the expense exceeding the patronage, has probably been the cause of its neglect." Therefore, it is possibly that most directories are in existence. Fay summarily deals with the confusing nature of street numbers in the city. He states, "As the houses in several streets are numbered alike, I have, in most cases put them as they should be -- *in order.* No 89, on the corner of Meeting and Queen, is correct, and the same number on Reynolds and Son [he is referring to the firm of Reynolds and Son], is wrong." Apparently the firm used No. 89, but he lists them as 93 and 95 King St. "The odd numbers on King street run regularly to Messrs. Wilmot's, 209; the number on the next door above is 225, and continue so to Liberty-street; but I have put them down in proper order, leaving it for the owners or other authorities to reconcile these matters." As a result many of the numbers have little meaning. A house or business with one number on King Street in another directory may be the same as a different number in this one. The listing of streets and the occupants on them in the cross index gives an idea of the varied nature of housing in the city. The cross index is not included here. Fay includes the free person of color with the whites but indicates them with a "+" sign. In this list, the "+" has been replaced by "F.P.C." which appears at the end of the listing. No distinction was made by Fay between the city and the Neck. The directory has 3,765 entries. Often names were listed under the heading of a firm and did not appear elsewhere. Here they have been alphabetized with the rest of the entries. This directory lists a number of doctors as "Thomsonians." According to Peter McCandless, *Moonlight and Madness* (Chapel Hill, 1996), these belonged to a botanical medical sect led by a guru named Samuel Thomson that sold "family rights" to practice medicine. In South Carolina and many other states they succeeded in getting medical licensing laws repealed.

Abbott, Simon B., Dr., Thomsonian, 367 King St., res., Charlotte St.
Abrahams, A. H., cr. Boundary & Washington Sts.
Abrahams, Ann, Mrs., 48 E. Bay St., cr. Hamilton's Whf.
Abrahams, Elias, 3 Burns Ln.
Abrahams, J., 14 Clifford St.
Ackis, John, Bricklayer, res. n. St. Philip St.
Adams, A., Capt., 29 King St.
Adams, E. L., 62 King St.
Adams, Mary A., 43 Coming St.

Adams, Mary Jane, Mrs., 8 Middle St.
Adams, P. C., Firm of Burckmyer & Co., Merchants, 76 E. Bay St., res. King St.
Adams,-----, Wheelwright, 19 Back St.
Addison, Edward, Cabinet Maker, 14 Pitt St.
Addison, Joseph, Cabinet Maker, 14 Pitt St.
Addison, Joseph, Firm of Addison & Ulmo, Shipwrights, S. Bay St., res. 9 Lynch St.
Adger, James, Firm of James Adger & Co., Commercial Merchants, Hamilton's Whf., res. 80 n. King St.
Adger, Robert, Firm of James Adger & Co., Commercial Merchants, res. 76 Queen St.
Adger, Robert S., n. Spring St.
Adger, William, Hardware, 54 E. Bay St., res. 80 n. King St.
Affenassieffe, Daniel, Paints & Oil, 33 Coming St.
Agrell, Charles, Grocer, 59 Market St.
Ahrens, John, Grocer, 16 Market St.
Aiken, Bella, 55 Boundary St., F.P.C.
Aiken, Louisa, 30 Pitt St., F.P.C.
Aiken, Thomas, Dr., 150 Meeting St.
Aiken, William, Planter, America St.
Aimar, Sebastain, Mrs., 44 State St.
Aimar, Thomas, Accountant, 16 Vernon St.
Alderson, John, Firm of Alderson & Pregnell, Blind Makers, 16 Tradd St.
Aldret, S., Pilot, 7 Stoll's Al.
Aldrich, Robert, Wharfinger, res. 15 Tradd St.
Alexander, John J., res. 80 Queen St.
Alexander, Samuel, Harbor Master, 15 Exchange St., res. 85 Queen St.
Allen, A., Capt., 88 Queen St.
Allen, Ellen, 6 Burns Ln., F.P.C.
Allen, H. C., Tavern, 8 Tradd St.
Allen, Phoebe A., Mrs., Boarding, 6 Exchange St.
Allen, Richard, Dr., 2 Legare St.
Allen, Samuel L., Firm of Haviland, Harral & Co., Drugs, res. 286 King St.
Allen, Thomas P., Firm of James J. McCarter & Co., Bookstore, 112 Meeting St., res. 32 St. Philip St.
Allen, William, Firm of Allen & Davids, Painters, res. 94 Meeting St.
Allender, Benjamin, 38 Bull St.
Allender, W. N., Mrs., Boarding, 110 Meeting St.
Alley, John, Cabinet Maker, 207 E. Bay St.
Alsguth, C. B., 12 Archdale St.
Alson, Tom, 18 King St., F.P.C.
Alston, Charles, Planter, 3 E. Bay St.
Alston, Grace A., 4 Minority St., F.P.C.
Alvigney, N. D., Dr., Dentist, 74 Queen St.
Amand, P., Cigar Maker, n. Coming St.
Amesbury, Mary Ann, Mrs., Dry Goods, 138 Church St.
Amey, Augustus, Firm of Entz & Amey, Commission Merchants, Central Whf., res. 116 E. Bay St.
Amey, John W., Officer of Customs, 17 Mazyck St.
Ancker, G. V., Firm of Levy & Ancker, Clothing, res. 189 E. Bay St.
Ancrum, Hasell, Planter, cr. Church & S. Bay Sts.
Ancrum, Jane, Mrs., 2 S. Bay St.
Ancrum, John, Firm of Ancrum & Oliver, Tailors, 209 E.

Bay St.
Andersen, N. E., Mrs., 351 King St.
Andersen, Robert, Merchant, 28 King St.
Anderson, E. R, Firm of John Kirkpatrick & Co, Factors,
Exchange Whf., res. Cannonborough
Andrews, A. O., Capt., Hasell St., near St. Mary's Church
Anger, John, Mary St.
Anger, Joseph, Cooper, res. Linguard St.
Anger, Matha, Mrs., 126 Tradd St.
Annelly, Mrs., 162 King St.
Anthony, Hannah, 1 Motte's Ln., F.P.C.
Anthony, Jane, Mrs., n. King St.
Anthony, -----, Mrs., 56 n. King St.
Antonio, A., Mrs., Tailoress, 35 State St.
Antonio, Aries, Exchange Coffee House, 107 E. Bay St.
Arms, Elizabeth, Mrs., 18 George St.
Arms, William, Jailor, Charleston District
Armstrong, Archibald, Mrs., 17 Middle St.
Armstrong, William, Mrs., 108 Wentworth St.
Arndt, Henry, n. Meeting St.
Arnold, J. W. B., Tailor, 111 King St.
Arnold, Louisa, cr. Archdale & Berresford St.
Artman, John, 5 Archdale St.
Artopie, George, Bennett's Mills, E. Bay St.
Astle, George, Bootmaker, 28 Tradd St.
Atkinson, C., Firm of J. B. Clough & Co., Commission
Merchants, Central Whf., res. 67 Church St.
Atwell, Mary, Mrs., 131 King St.
Aubin, Joseph, Real Estate Broker, 23 Broad St.
Auld, Emeline, Miss, Teacher, 8 George St.
Aveilhe, P. A., Firm of John L. Pezant & Co., Merchants,
165 E. Bay St., res. 2 Boundary St.
Axson, Ann, Mrs., Boarding, 15 Cumberland St.
Axson, Jacob, Hon., Recorder, City Court, City Hall, res.
17 Meeting St.
Axson, John, Planter, Cannonsborough
Babcock, Sidney, Firm of Babcock & Co., Booksellers,
276 King St., res. New Haven
Babcock, William R., Firm of Babcock & Co.,
Booksellers, 276 King St., res. 4 Green St.
Bachman, John, Rev., Cannonborough
Bacot, T. W., Assistant Post Master, res. 68 King St.
Badger, Mary, Mrs., Boarding, 1 Hasell St.
Bail, John, Mariner, 46 Elliot St.
Bailey, Henry, Firm of Bailey & Brewster, Attorneys, 69
Meeting St., res. 85 Meeting St.
Bailey, Isaac S., Firm of O. Mills & Co., Grain & Hay, 10
E. Bay St., res. 82 Tradd St.
Baker, Barnard E., 57 King St.
Baker, Fisher, Plasterer, 17 S. Bay St.
Baker, John M. S., Firm of Baker & Jefferys, Sash &
Blinds, cr. Church & Amen Sts.
Baker, L. B., Firm of Baker & Goodsell, Hatters, 274 King
St., res. cr. Society & Meeting Sts.
Baker, -----, Mrs., Boarders, 79 Boundary St.
Baker, R. S., Rev., Catholic Seminary, 92 Broad St.
Baker, Robert L., 5 St. Michael's Al.
Baldwin, W. H., Attorney, res. 24 Beaufain St.
Ball, Elias O., 21 Lynch St.
Ball, Isaac, Mrs., cr. E. Bay & Vernon Sts.

Ball, John, Mrs., 21 E. Bay St.
Ball, Keating, Planter, 21 E. Bay St.
Ball, -----, Mrs., 99 Queen St.
Ballantine, John, Saddler, Mary St.
Ballard, Joseph, 83 King St.
Ballund, Alex, Grocer, 61 Market St.
Bampfield, George, Cabinet Maker, 30 Tradd St.
Bancroft, James, Firm of Bancroft & Co., Merchants, 94 &
96 E. Bay St., res. 197 Meeting St.
Banks, H. L., Mrs., School, n. King St.
Banks, Hugh R., Firm of Wiley, Lane & Co., Wholesale
Dry Goods, 3 Hayne St., res. 16 Liberty St.
Banks, -----, Mrs., 6 n. King St.
Bannister, William, Firm of Bannister & Lanneau, Dry
Goods, 2 Hayne St., res., New Hotel
Baptist, John, Clothing, 27 Market St.
Barber, F. C., Acountant, 10 Bull St.
Barbot, A., Merchant, 29 E. Bay St.
Barginann, B., Grocer, Cannon St.
Barinds, E., Dr., 97 King St.
Barker, S. G., Firm of Harris, Roosevelt & Baker,
Merchants, 17 Hayne St., res. 90 Wentworth St.
Barker, Sandford, 20 Montague St.
Barksdale, Thomas, Planter, 10 New St.
Barnes, Thomas, President St.
Barnett, W. N., Bookseller, 159 Meeting St.
Barnwell, Edward, Jr., Firm of Simons, Barnwell & Co.,
Factors, 2 Southern Whf., res. 16 Meeting St.
Barnwell, W., Rev., 8 Logan St.
Baron, Alexander L., Dr., Firm of Prioleau & Baron,
Meeeting St., res. 108 Queen St.
Barquet, Barbary, 2 Beadon's Al., F.P.C.
Barr, -----, 12 King St.
Barre, John, Wine & Liquors, cr. Market & State St.
Barreau, Mary Jane, w. end Beaufain St.
Barrett, Jacob, Wentworth St., near Meeting St.
Barrett, Lucy, Mrs., 67 Boundary St.
Barron & Prioleau, Drs., 108 Queen St.
Barron, A. J., Miss, 103 Broad St.
Bartless, W. H., Acountant, 1 Laurens St.
Bartlett, Franklin M., Shoes, 203 King St.
Bartlett, William, Boundary St.
Bass, Margaret, 49 Meeting St., F.P.C.
Bateman, Christian, Miller, 30 George St.
Battersby, Joseph, Firm of Battersby & Nephew,
Commercial Merchants, 38 E. Bay St., res. Church St.
Baty, Ann, 9 Burns Ln.
Bauxbaum, Eliza, 120 Queen St.
Baxter, Phoebe, Dress Maker, 4 Wall St., F.P.C.
Bay, Elihu H., Mrs., 52 Meeting St.
Beach, E. M., Firm of O. Mills & Co., Grain & Hay, 10 E.
Bay St.
Beach, J. S., Firm of Beach, Power & Boyce, Shoe Store,
10 Hayne St.
Beasley, John, Tailor, 25 King St.
Beaufort, Fred, Butcher, Hanover St.
Beckley, John, Vanderhorst St.
Beckman, Adolph, 17 St. Philip St.
Beckman, C. J., Grain Store, 63 Market St.
Bedford, Colman, Livery Stables, 102 Meeting St.

Bee, Frances, Mrs., 3 Friend St.
Bee, James M., Assistant Teller, State Bank, res. 79 Wentworth St.
Bee, Joseph F., Planter, Cannonborough
Bee, Robert H., Cooper, Hamilton's Whf., res. 72 Tradd St.
Bee, W. R., 3 Friend St.
Bee, William C., Firm of Ladson & Bee, res. 116 Tradd St.
Beecher, Fred, Dry Goods, 292 King St.
Behing, Ernest, Grocer, 130 E. Bay St.
Behing, Luder, Grocer, cr. Market & E. Bay Sts.
Behlin, A., 15 Archdale St.
Behlin, Hester, Mrs., 15 Archdale St.
Behrman, John, Grocer, cr. Wall & Minority Sts.
Beil, John P., Bookseller, 280 King St.
Bell, David, Jr., Accountant, 1 Hasell St.
Bell, David, Sr.
Bell, John L., 6 Laurens St.
Bell, Richard, Merchant, 310 King St.
Bell, William, Planter, 48 Society St.
Bellanton, Fillet, Seamstress, 27 State St., F.P.C.
Bellenger, John, Dr., 11 College St.
Belzer, Mary, Mrs., 70 n. King St.
Bement, William, 14 Orange St.
Benjamin, Philip, Fruits, 29 Beaufain St.
Benjamin, S. A., Clothing, 99 E. Bay St.
Bennett, Charles, Printer, 15 Orange St.
Bennett, Edward, Mrs., Boarding, 30 Pinckney St.
Bennett, Elias S., Dr., Market St., near King St., res. 81 Rutledge St.
Bennett, Thomas, Gov., Cannonborough
Bennett, W. S., Silk Store, 110 Meeting St., cr. Hayne St.
Benoist, Achille, Baker, 38 n. King St.
Benson, Lawrence, 26 George St.
Benson, William, 19 State St.
Benson, William G., Auctioneer, 23 Broad St., res. 4 King St.
Benter, C., Grocer, 50 Church St., cr. Stoll's Al.
Bentham, Emeline, Pastry Cook, 184 Meeting St., F.P.C.
Bentham, Robert, Firm of Bentham & Hunt, Attorneys, 2 St. Micheal's Al., res. Vanderhorst St.
Berbant, -----, Mrs., 369 King St.
Berbant, Samuel J., Accountant, 13 College St.
Bernard, Laura, cr. George & St. Philip St., F.P.C.
Berney, Mary, Mrs., 41 Tradd St.
Berney, William, Broker, State St., res. 41 Tradd St.
Berrett, W. H., Bookseller, 36 Broad St.
Berringer, Mary, Warren St.
Berry, Benjamin, Carpenter, 47 George St., F.P.C.
Berry, John, 6 Cumberland St.
Berry, Maria, Mrs., 6 Friend St.
Bessent, Peter, Accountant, Archdale St.
Besser, Charles, Tailor, Market St., res. n. Meeting St.
Beteman, George, 3 S. Bay St.
Betson, William, Bricklayer, 16 Orange St.
Betteman, H., Grocer, Judith St.
Betterson, Elizabeth, Mantuamaker, 16 Orange St.
Beusse, D., Accountant, 197 E. Bay St.
Bevan, Mary, Mrs., Hotel, cr. King & Line Sts.
Bevin, J. H., res. over Planters & Mechanics Bank, E. Bay St.

Bicaise, Frederick, Carpenter, 26 State St.
Bicaise, Peter Paul, 26 State St.
Bicause, B. P., Gunsmith, 26 State St.
Biglow, L., Wholesale Grocer, 100 E. Bay St.
Billins, Daniel, 3 Lynch St.
Binge, H., Tailor, 28 Green St.
Bingly, Charles W., Accountant, 22 Middle St.
Bingly, Selina, Mrs., 22 Middle St.
Bird, John S., Fancy Store, 231 King St.
Bird, Jonas, Dry Goods, 99 King St., F.P.C.
Bird, -----, Mrs., 64 Church St., cr. Longitude Ln.
Bird, William, Ship Carpenter, 7 Lynch St.
Birkle, Constant, Firm of Hopley & Birkle, Merchants, Exchange Whf.
Birnie, George, Firm of Birnie & Ogilvie, Hardware, 21 Broad St., res. Scotland
Birnie, W., Firm of Birnie & Ogilvie, Hardware, 21 Broad St., res. 3 Smith St.
Bisbee, William, Engineer, Steam Saw Mill, S. Bay St.
Bishoff, Albert, Grocer, n. St. Philip St.
Bissell, Henry C., Firm of Miller, Ripley & Co., 270 King St.
Bize, Johanna, Mrs., 11 Pitt St.
Black, Alexander, 97 Wentworth St.
Black, Alexander W., Shipping Master, 71 E. Bay St., res. Savage St.
Black, Elizabeth, Mrs. 8 King St.
Black, F. C., Commission Merchant, 13 Exchange St., res. 46 Society St.
Black, William P., Baker, 181 King St.
Blacklock, J. F., Firm of James Calder & Co., Importers, Commercial Whf., res. 87 Meeting St.
Blackwood, Thomas, Mrs., 24 Pitt St.
Blain, Andrew, Wheelwright, n. Meeting St.
Blair, Hugh, Firm of Blair Hugh & Co., Wine Merchant, 59 E. Bay St., res. 29 E. Bay St.
Blair, Neil, Firm of Blair Hugh & Co., Wine Merchant, res. 44 Broad St.
Blair, William, Firm of McNeill & Blair, Wine Merchant, 44 Broad St., res. cr. Broad & Church Sts.
Blake, Charles, Port Warden
Blake, Edward, Teller, Bank of S. C., res. 10 Water St.
Blakely, John, Firm of Blakely & Rogers, Merchants, 99 N. King St.
Blakely, W. J., 70 n. King St.
Blamon, J., Carpenter, 75 Church St.
Blamyer, -----, Maj., Ann St.
Blamyer, William, Planter, 281 E. Bay St.
Blanch, Jacob, Boarding, 13 Elliot St.
Blanch, Sarah, Seamstress, 4 Zig Zag Al., F.P.C.
Blanchard, Ed, Carpenter, 5 Clifford St.
Blanchard, S., Carpenter, 80 Tradd St.
Bland, Frances, Mantuamaker, 13 Mazyck St., F.P.C.
Bland, James, 13 Mazyck St., F.P.C.
Blum, Andrew, School, Hampstead
Blum, J. Charles, Firm of Blum & Cobia, Auctioneers, 30 Vendue Range, res. 72 n. King St.
Blum, Mary, Mrs., 73 n. King St.
Blumenthal, Charles E., Teacher, 81 Wentworth St.
Bochilhoff, Peter C., Grocer, 130 Tradd St.

Boesch, J. J., 84 King St.
Boesche, J. U., Coppersmith, Amen St., cr. Church St.
Bogle, James, Potrait Painter, 190 King St.
Bohles, L. E., Grocer, 20 Archdale St. cr. Princess St.
Boinest, Daniel, Firm of Street & Boinest, Commission Merchants, 6 Boyce's Whf., res. 21 State St.
Bolger, Christian, 32 King St.
Bolger, Henry H., Cabinet Maker, 14 Smith St.
Bolles, A., Teacher, 7 College St.
Bonneau, Catharine, Mrs., 9 Smith's Ln.
Bonneau, John E., Firm of Mathews & Bonneau, Factors, Hamilton's Whf., res. 15 Church St.
Bonneau, Martha, Mrs., N Coming St.
Bonneau, Thomas, Mrs., 34 Coming St.
Bonnell, John, Capt., 14 Atlantic St.
Bonnell, John, Jr., Firm of Hall & Bonnell, Merchants, 4 E. Bay St., 14 Atlantic St.
Bonnell, Thomas, Accountant, 14 Atlantic St.
Bonner, Eliza, Mrs., 30 Middle St.
Bonney, Joel, Capt., 21 Tradd St.
Boon, W. J., Bricklayer
Booth, William, Capt., 12 Magazine St.
Bordenave, John, Barber, 4 Queen St.
Boree, Charlotte, 82 Anson St., F.P.C.
Boroughs, Samuel, Pilot, 11 Broad St.
Borton, Amasa, Doughty St.
Boryles, John H., Grocer, 13 Pitt St.
Bosker, Henry, Cabinet Maker, 27 n. King St.
Bottger, John, Reid St.
Boucher, John, Grocer, 162 King St.
Bounetheau, David, Watch Maker, n. St. Philip St.
Bounetheau, E. W., Magistrate, n. St. Philip St.
Bounetheau, H. B., Firm of James Hamilton & Co., Factors, 24 E. Bay St., res. Commercial House
Bourdon, Maria, Mrs., Tailoress, 59 King St.
Bourne, N. G., Accountant, Vendue Range
Bours, Luke, 69 E. Bay St., res. 62 Church St.
Bowers, John E., Gunsmith, 21 St. Philip St.
Bowie, James S., Firm of S. & L. Bowie, Dry Goods, 15 Hayne St., res. 3 George St.
Bowie, L., Firm of S. & L. Bowie, Dry Goods, 15 Hayne St., res. New Hotel
Bowman, Mary Ann, Mrs., 2 Hard Al.
Bowman, Mary, Miss, 16 Beaufain St.
Boyce, Ker, President, Commercial Bank, res. 16 George St.
Boyce, Samuel, Firm of Beach, Power & Boyce, Shoe Store, 10 Hayne St., res. 16 George St.
Boyd, J. D., Boyd's Hotel, 311 King St., cr. George St.
Boyd, William, Vanderhorst St.
Boyden, Mary E., Mrs., 172 Meeting St.
Boyes, Henry, Grocer, cr. Charlotte & Washington Sts.
Boylton, Henry, Dr., 368 King St.
Bradford, William, Blacksmith, 4 Gillon St.
Bradly, John C., 4 Mile House
Bradly, Margaret, Mrs., 15 Water St.
Brady, -----, 127 Queen St.
Brady, Catharine, Mrs., 16 Anson St.
Brady, Edward, 50 King St.
Brady, Edward, Mrs., 5 Motte's Ln.

Brady, John, 113 King St.
Brady, John, Grocer, 20 State St., cr. Unity Al.
Brailsford, E., Miss, 32 S. Bay St.
Brailsford, Elizabeth, Mrs., 122 Queen St.
Brailsford, W. R., Factor, 23 Vanderhorst Whf., res. Orange St.
Brailsford, William, 2 Friend St.
Brandreth, Benjamin, Pills, 70 Meeting St.
Brandt, John, 5 King St.
Brantly, W. T., Rev., 1 College St.
Brase, Peter, cr. King & Broad Sts.
Brediert, H., 5 St. Philip St.
Brennan, Charles, Factor, Fitzsimmons' Whf., res. Stewart's
Brennen, Peter S., Shoe Maker, 89 Queen St.
Brewer, Peter, Grocer, Smith's Ln.
Brewster, C. R., Firm of Bailey & Brewster, Attorneys, 69 Meeting St., res. Cannonborough
Bridgeman, C. C., Printer, 12 E. Bay St.
Bridgeman, Catharine, cr. Columbus & Nassau Sts.
Briggs, H. S., 33 Society St.
Bright, Robert, Druggist, 11 Broad St.
Bringlow, Richard, Boat Builder, 17 Church St.
Brisbane, Mary, Mrs., 29 Meeting St.
Bristol, Timothy, Firm of Smith & Bristol, Shoe Store, 214 King St.
Bristol, William B., Shoe Store, 175 King St.
Britton, Edward H., Printer, 8 Cliffford St.
Britton, Thomas J., Shoe Maker, 16 Philadelphia St.
Brockelbank, William, Plasterer, n. Meeting St.
Brodie, R. H., 41 Coming St.
Brodie, Robert H., 55 Church St.
Brogan, Alfred, n. St. Philip St.
Broughton, Daniel, Mrs., 4 King St.
Broughton, Philip, Mrs., 261 E. Bay St.
Brow, Harriet, Mrs., Teacher, 5 St. Micheal's Al.
Brower, Ann, Mrs., 12 Anson St.
Brown, -----, 2 Coming St.
Brown, Alexander, Factor, Price's Whf., res. 75 n. King St.
Brown, Alexander H., Sheriff, res. Tradd St.
Brown, Alexander, Merchant, 87 n. King St.
Brown, Ann, w. end Wentworth St.
Brown, Benjamin, Firm of Brown & Oliphant, 287 King St.
Brown, Charles, Painter, 49 Anson St.
Brown, Eliza, Mrs., 17 Short St.
Brown, Eliza, Mrs., 96 Broad St.
Brown, Elizabeth, Mrs., 48 King St.
Brown, G. B., 240 King St., res. Society St.
Brown, G. W., Merchant, Gibbes' Whf., res. 10 Montague St.
Brown, George, Firm of Paul & Brown, Grocers, 47 Broad St.
Brown, Ira, Firm of Curtis & Brown, House Carpenters, 12 Laurens St., res. cr. Meeting & Hasell Sts.
Brown, J. D., 29 St. Philip St.
Brown, James H., Accountant, 51 Meeting St.
Brown, James, Mrs., Society St., Burnt District
Brown, James, Mrs., Washington St.

Brown, James, Planter, Charlotte St.
Brown, James W., Linguard St.
Brown, John B. & Lawrence, Hatters, 29 Broad St.
Brown, Mary, Mrs., 14 New St.
Brown, -----, Mrs., 21 Coming St.
Brown, -----, Mrs., Court House Yard.
Brown, P. W., Radcliff St.
Brown, Peter, Barber, 1 Price's Al., F.P.C.
Brown, R. E., Firm of Brown & Wellsman, Factors, 14 Southern Whf., res. 22 Church St.
Brown, Robert, Firm of Brown & Wellsman, Factors, 14 Southern Whf., res. 22 Church St.
Brown, S. K., Carpenter, 28 Laurens St.
Brown, W. W., Carpenter, Mary St.
Browne, Ann, Mrs., Linguard St.
Browne, E. H., Pump Maker, 29 St. Philip St.
Browne, Elizabeth, Mrs., 29 St. Philip St.
Brownell, Edward, Clothing, 33 Broad St.
Brownell, Rodolphus, Accountant, 33 Broad St.
Browning, Jenkins, Dr., 367 King St.
Brownlee, Elijah, Shoes, 359 King St.
Bruce, George, Boots & Shoes, 81 Market St.
Bruce, Mary, Mrs., Fancy Store, 104 Meeting St.
Bruen, John W., Teacher, German School, 17 Archdale St.
Bruning, H., Grocer, cr. State & Amen Sts.
Bryan, Elizabeth, Mrs., 32 Beaufain St.
Bryan, Jonathan, Jr., Firm of Jonathan Bryan & Son, Merchants, 227 King St.
Bryan, Jonathan, Sr. Firm of Jonathan Bryan & Son, Merchants, 227 King St.
Bryan, Lydia, Mrs., 8 Wall St.
Bryant, C. H., Farmer, Neck
Bryce, James, Firm of Smith & Bryce, Hardware, 268 King St.
Buckheister, John H., State Constable, res. Marsh St.
Budd, Thomas, Capt., 82 Tradd St.
Buist, Arthur, Rev., 62 Church St.
Buist, George, 106 Wentworth St.
Buist, George, Mrs., 99 Wentworth St.
Bulkley, Erastus, Firm of Deming, Bulkley & Co., Cabinet Ware, 241 King St., res. 43 King St.
Bulkley, Erastus, Marble Agent, 49 Broad St.
Bull, Edward [Edmond?], Firm of Clark & Bull, Brass Founders, 132 E. Bay St., res. cr. Meeting & Market Sts.
Bull, W. J., Planter, 120 Tradd St.
Bullen, Richard, Capt., 52 Church St.
Bullwinkle, Henry, Grocer, cr. Charlotte & Elizabeth Sts.
Bulow, John J., Planter, n. King St.
Bunch, Dennis, Butcher, 10 Market St.
Bunch, Silas, n. Meeting St.
Bundrock, John, Grocer, 1 Tradd St.
Burch, Edward C., Merchant, 4 E. Bay St., res. 14 Savage St.
Burckmyer, C., Firm of Burckmyer & Co., Merchants, 76 E. Bay St., res. 12 New St.
Burckmyer, John C., Merchant, 60 E. Bay St., res. Society St.
Burdell, Emma, Mrs., n. St. Philip St.
Burdell, Robert, Accountant, 17 Cumberland St.
Burdgess, William B., Engineer, 28 Tradd St.

Burger, N. H., Grocer, 9 Mazyck St.
Burger, Samuel, Tax Collector, 51 Queen St.
Burgess, James, Firm of Burgess & Walker, Stationers, 85 E. Bay St., res. 116 King St.
Burgess, James W., Firm of Burgess & James, Printing Office, 44 Queen St., res., 114 King St.
Burie, Daniel, Blacksmith, n. Meeting St.
Burke, John H., Pilot, 17 Church St.
Burke, Samuel, Boat Builder, William's Whf., res. Boundary St.
Burke, Sarah, Mrs., 17 Church St.
Burke, W. L., Rev., 78 Wentworth St., cr. St Philip St.
Burner, Frederick, Boundary St.
Burnham, R. R., Boundary St.
Burnham, R. W., Drugs, 241 King St.
Burnham, William, Locksmith, 6 Laurens St.
Burnie, William, 29 George St.
Burnie, William, 3 Smith St.
Burns, Henry, Cannonborough
Burns, Henry M., Teacher, High School, 2 Burns Ln.
Burns, Jacob, Bricklayer, 65 Anson St.
Burns, James, Pilot, 7 Atlantic St.
Burns, Mary Ann, 5 Short St.
Burns, William, Cannon St.
Burrell, William, Mrs., 11 Smith St.
Bush, T., Firm of A. G. Crane & Co., Importers, 147 Meeting St.
Bush, William, Rev., 18 Archdale St.
Bussacker, Charles, Dry Goods, 297 King St.
Butler, C. P., Jeweller, 109 King St.
Butler, Robert, Capt., Mary St.
Butler, Thomas, Capt., Hanover St.
Butt, J. F., Grocer, 1 Market St.
Cahallan, Timothy, 22 Elliott St.
Caie, Julia, Madame, 33 Wall St.
Cain, John, Fisherman, 16 Church St., F.P.C.
Cain, W. D., Shoes, n. King St.
Calder, J., Cabinet Ware Room, 80 Meeting St.
Calder, James, Firm of James Calder & Co., Importers, Commercial Whf.
Calder, William, Firm of Moffett & Calder, Merchants, 230 King St., res. 13 George St.
Caldwell, J., Firm of R. & J. Caldwell, Factors, Magwood's Whf.
Caldwell, James M., Firm of Robinson & Caldwell, Factors, Magwood's Whf., res. Judith St.
Caldwell, John, Mill, Beaufain St., res. Neck
Caldwell, John, Firm of W. A. Caldwell & Sons, Auctioneers, 23 Vendue Range, res. 101 Meeting St.
Caldwell, R., Firm of R. & J. Caldwell, Factors, Magwood's Whf., res. Planters Hotel
Caldwell, Richard, Firm of W. A. Caldwell & Sons, Auctioneers, 23 Vendue Range, res. 101 Meeting St.
Caldwell, W. A., Firm of W. A. Caldwell & Sons, Auctioneers, 23 Vendue Range, res. 101 Meeting St.
Caldwell, W. S., Firm of McCready & Caldwell, Attorneys, 87 Meeting St., res. 101 Meeting St.
Callahan, William, Boarding, 86 Meeting St.
Calvit, Mary Ann, Linguard St.
Calvit, Mortimer, Bricklayer, Henrietta St.

Calvit, Thomas, res. Sullivan's Island.
Calvo, Charles, Printer, 11 Price's Al.
Calvo, Emma, 11 Price's Al.
Calvo, John, Printer, 11 Price's Al.
Cambridge, Ann, Miss, 79 King St.
Cambridge, Martha, Mrs., 9 Minority St.
Cameron, George S., Wholesale Crockery, 21 Hayne St.
Cameron, S. D., Sail Maker, Fitzsimons' Whf., res. 120 E. Bay St.
Cammer, John, Carpenter, 19 Rutledge St.
Cammer, Peter, Farmer, back of Race Course
Camonade, Henry D., Deputy City Sheriff, res. 45 Coming St.
Campana, Mary, Fruits, 62 State St.
Campbell, Caroline, 22 Laurens St.
Campbell, Isaac, Dr., 99 Broad St.
Campbell, J., Shoes & Boots, 142 E. Bay St.
Campbell, James B., Firm of Campbell & Dukes, Attorneys, 40 Broad St., res. Cannonborough
Campbell, James B., Firm of H. B. Gleason & Co., Wholesale Crockery, 14 Hayne St., res. Cannonborough
Campbell, Martha, 50 Beaufain St.
Canaday, James, Grocer, 110 E. Bay St.
Canal, Joseph, Fruits, 343 King St.
Cannaday, Edward, 59 Coming St.
Cannon, George, Jr., Merchant, 318 King St.
Canter, Rebecca, Mrs., 12 Clifford St.
Cantwell, Patrick, Officer of Customs, res. Marsh St.
Capdevielle, -----, Miss, 64 Church St.
Capers, Legrand G., Boundary St., btw. Pitt & Coming Sts.
Capers, Thomas F., Firm of Capers & Huger, Auctioneers, 6 State St., res. 107 Tradd St.
Capers, William, Rev., Boundary St., near Pitt St.
Caravella, Teressa, Pastry, 61 Coming St., F. P. C.
Cardlay, John, Collector, Charlotte St.
Cardozo, J. N., Editor, Southern Patriot, res. 4 Court House Sq.
Cardozo, Jacob, Custon House Officer, res. 4 Court House Sq.
Cardozo, Sarah N., 4 Court House Sq.
Carew, Edward, n. Meeting St.
Carey, E. M., Druggist, 34 Broad St.
Carlisle, Margaret, 6 Anson St.
Carmand, Francis, Merchant Tailor, 86 Queen St.
Carnochan, B. P., Butcher, Cannon St.
Carnochan, John, Pilot, 8 Stoll's Al.
Carnochan, Richard, Merchant, 18 Hamilton's Whf.
Carpenter, James, Butcher, Cannon St.
Carr, Charles D., Merchant Tailor, 30 Broad St.
Carr, Felix, Catholic Seminary, 92 Broad St.
Carrier, William, Agent, Hamilton's Whf.
Carriere, M. E., Dr., Radcliffborough
Carrington, William, Jeweler, 189 King St.
Carrol, B. R., Thomas St.
Carrol, Bernard, 22 State St.
Carrol, D. G., 306 King St.
Carrol, J. L., 361 King st.
Carson, Elisha, Wholesale Grocer, 145 E. Bay St., res. 11 Laurens St.
Carson, Elizaberh, Mrs., 90 Tradd St.

Carson, R. H., Firm of Chambers & Carson, res. 3 Liberty St.
Carson, W. A., Planter, 90 Tradd St.
Carsten, E., Mrs., 36 Society St.
Carsten, Frederick, Grocer, cr. Anson & Boundary Sts.
Carsten, W. F., 5 Wall St.
Carstrillon, Diego, Fruits, 87 King St.
Cart, John, 28 Bull St.
Cart, John, Jr., Discount Clerk, Planters & Mechanics Bank, res. Boundary St., near Pitt St.
Carter, Caroline, 5 Coming St., F.P.C.
Carter, John B., Shoes, 89 E. Bay St., res. 6 Broad St.
Carter, Orlando, Mrs., Gadsden's Whf.
Carter, William, Firm of Carter, Lloyd & Stock, Brokers, 6 Broad St., res. Ladson's Court
Carvallo, E. N., 241 King St.
Cary, Jacob, Accountant, 51 E. Bay St.
Casey, Mary, Mrs., Boarding, 8 Anson St.
Cashin, John, Carpenter, Charlotte St.
Cason, Ann L., 37 George St.
Cassidy, Patrick, 103 Church St.
Caswell, -----, Mrs., Boarding, 211 E. Bay St.
Catherwood, J. J., Watch Maker, 65 Broad St.
Cattel William, Planter, Pinckney St.
Caulier, George, Dr., 74 Anson St.
Causse, Adolph, Cannonborough
Caw, Peter, Firm of Gowan & Caw, Watchmakers, cr. Meeting & Chalmers St., res. 6 S. Bay St.
Cay, John C., Firm of J. L. Pezant & Co., Merchants, 165 E. Bay St.
Cay, John E., Firm of John L. Pezant & Co., Merchants, res. 165 E. Bay St.
Cay, Nancy, 32 Pitt St., F.P.C.
Chadwick, Samuel, Firm of S. Chadwick & Co., Merchants, 70 E. Bay St., res. 11 Meeting St.
Chafee, Otis, Wine Merchant, 141 E. Bay St.
Chalsner, Thomas D., Firm of Chalsner & French, Carpenters, 33 Queen St.
Chamberlain, Charles V., Firm of Miller, Ripley & Co., Wholesale Dry Goods, 270 King St.
Chambers, J. S., res. 3 Liberty St.
Chambers, John, Gadsen's Whf.
Chamlatte, Harriet, 36 State St.
Champlin, A. J., Bricklayer, 26 Magazine St.
Champlin, O. P., City Lamp Lighter, res. 26 Magazine St.
Champlin, Samuel, Custom House, res. Planters Hotel
Chapeau, John B., 106 Church St.
Chapman, C. C. P., Writing Master, cr. King & Clifford Sts.
Chapman, Henry, 27 Beaufain St.
Chapman, James, Commission Merchant, 13 Exchange St., res. 4 Water St.
Chapman, Samuel, Agent, Exchange St., res. 26 Pitt St.
Chapman, Samuel, Pilot
Chapman, Thomas, Cashier, Bank of State of S. C., res. 26 Pitt St.
Charles, -----, Madame, 99 Broad St.
Charlon, Francis, Grocer & Distiller, n. King St.
Chase, P. S. 132 King St.
Chatteau, M. M., Mrs., Dry Goods, 51 State St.

Chazal, Caroline, 48 Anson St.
Chazal, J. P., Dr., 48 Anson St.
Cheeny, E., Jr., Firm of Joye, Lawton & Co., Grocers, 57 E. Bay St., res. 2 Pinckney St.
Cheeseborough, John, Factor, 1 Vanderhorst's Whf., res. 109 Broad St.
Cheney, E., Jr., Firm of Joyce, Lawton & Co., res. 2 Pinckney St.
Cheupein, L. Y., Soda Water, 95 E. Bay St.
Cheupein, T. L., Fancy Store, 152 King St.
Chew, Thomas R., Blacksmith, Cannonborough
Childs, Jane, Vanderhorst St.
Chisolm, George, Factor, 26 S. Bay St.
Chisolm, John M., Planter, 14 Rutledge St.
Chisolm, Octavius, Mrs., 24 King St.
Chisolm, Octavius, w. end Tradd St.
Chisolm, Robert, 12 Legare St.
Chitty, E., Mrs., Wolf St.
Chitty, J. W., Grocer, 77 Market St.
Chitty, Joseph, Bar Keeper, 119 E. Bay St.
Chors, H. A., Mrs., 13 Coming St.
Chrietzburg, Clara, 19 Beaufain St.
Chrietzburg, George, 111 Queen St., cr. Mazyck St.
Chrietzburg, -----, Mrs. 8 Mazyck St.
Christeansen, Jasper, Grocer, 138 Meeting St.
Christeansen, Jasper, 43 n. King St.
Christian, J., Grocer, n. King St.
Christie, David F. Savage St.
Christopher, George, 13 King St.
Christopher, John, Belvidere Mill
Church, M., Mrs., Umbrella Maker, 23 St. Philip St.
Church, T. G., 15 St. Philip St.
Claggett, Thomas, Firm of Silcox, Brother & Co., 166 King St.
Clancy, Mary A., Mrs., 17 n. King St.
Claper, Harman, Boundary St.
Clark, Aaron, King St. Rd.
Clark, Charles, Firm of Clark & Bull, Brass Founders, 132 E. Bay St., res. 2 Motte's Ln.
Clark, Charles, Grocer, 49 E. Bay St., cr. Tradd St.
Clark, John, Lumber Merchant, w. end Beaufain St.
Clark, John, Store & Tavern, n. King St.
Clark, Richard, Capt., Pilot, 21 Church St.
Clark, Thomas S., Tavern, New Theatre
Clark, William, 21 College St., F.P C.
Clarken, John, Merchant, 216 King St.
Clarkson, John, 2 Bull St.
Clarkson, T. B., Planter, 6 Smith St.
Clarkson, William, Planter, 2 Bull St.
Clastriera, Stephen, Carpenter, Vanderhorst St.
Clawson, John C., Spring St.
Clayton, David, Boarders, 369 King St.
Clayton, Robert, Firm of Humphries, Dupree & Co., Dry Goods, 12 Hayne St., res. 241 King St.
Cleapor, John W., Firm of Cleapor & Fields, Sail Makers, Price's Whf., res. 58 Anson St.
Cleary, Catharine, Mrs.,13 Short St.
Clements, Edward, Mrs., Cannon St.
Clemmens, Nicholas, Grocer, 52 State St.
Cleveland, J. F., Firm of Collins & Cleveland, Factors, 5

Boyce's Whf., res. 89 Meeting St.
Cleveland, John, 18 Water St.
Cleveland, John, 39 Church St.
Cleveland, John A., Dentist, 207 King St.
Clifford, Henry, Factor, Holmes' Whf., res. 12 Middle St.
Clifford, L. C., Merchant, 118 E. Bay St., res. 275 E. Bay St.
Clough, J. B., Firm of J. B. Clough & Co., Commission Merchants, Central Whf.
Clyde, Mary, Mrs., 1 George St.
Clyde, Thomas N., cr. Wolf & Hanover Sts.
Coates, Charles, 86 Wentworth St.
Cobia, Francis J., Reid St.
Cobia, Henry, Firm of Blum & Cobia, Auctioneers, 30 Vendue Range, res. 112 Wentworth St.
Cobia, -----, Misses, 18 Montague St.
Coburn, Peter, Carpenter, res. Neck
Cochran, J. C., Southwestern Railroad Bank, res. Islington
Cockfield, Benjamin, 10 Washington St.
Coffin, A., Dr., 72 Tradd St.
Coffin, C., Mrs., cr. Rutledge & Wentworth Sts.
Coffin, George, 96 Broad St.
Coffin, Thomas A., Planter, 5 Rutledge St.
Cogdell, John S., President, S. C. Bank, res. Meeting St., cr. Tradd St.
Cogdell, R. W., Teller, Bank of the State
Cohen, Augustus, Accountant, 39 Tradd St.
Cohen, Casper, 83 Wentworth St.
Cohen, D. D., 50 Society St.
Cohen, H., Radcliff St.
Cohen, H. S., Clothing, 179 E. Bay St.
Cohen, Hyam, City Assessor, res. 39 Tradd St.
Cohen, J., Jr., Merchant, Exchage St., res. 63 Meeting St.
Cohen, Jacob, 271 King St.
Cohen, L. L., Dr., Firm of P. M. Cohen & Co., Druggists, 167 Meeting St., res. 39 Tradd St.
Cohen, Mordecai, 107 Broad St.
Cohen, N. A., Clothing, 151 E. Bay St.
Cohen, N. A., Merchant, 308 King St.
Cohen, P. M., Dr., Firm of P. M. Cohen & Co., Druggists, 167 Meeting St., res. 39 Tradd St.
Cohen, S., Merchant, 329 King St.
Colburn, B. P., Firm of B. P. Colburn & Co., Dry Goods, 216 King St., res. Charlotte St.
Colburn, J. S., Dry Goods, 78 Broad St., cr. King St.
Colcock, Charles, Carpenter, 2 Orange St.
Colcock, John, Carpenter, 2 Orange St.
Colcock, John, Factor, Commercial Whf., res. 2 Orange St.
Cole, E., Mrs., Hanover St.
Collins, Charles, Firm of Humphries, Dupree & Co., Dry Goods, 12 Hayne St.
Collins, J. B., Boarding, 3 Elliott St.
Collins, Robert, Firm of Collins & Cleveland, Factors, 5 Boyce's Whf., res. 89 Meeting St.
Colson, Charles, Tailor, 6 Middle St.
Condict, S. H., Firm of Condict & Co., Saddlery, 265 King St.
Condy, T. D., Firm of Elliott, Condy & Dawes, Auctioneers, 1 Broad St., res. Cannonborough
Condy, Thomas D., District Marshal, U.S. Court House,

Queen & Meeting Sts.

Condy, Thomas D., Firm Elliott, Condy & Daws, res. Cannonborough

Confo, Elizabeth, 160 King St.

Connor, H. W., Firm of H. W. Connor & Co., Hardware, 8 Hayne St., res. cr. Meeting & Queen Sts.

Conway, William B., Farmer, n. King St.

Cook, Daniel, Lumber Merchant, 1 Lynch St.

Cook, John A., Grocer, Boundary St.

Cook, Otto, Firm of Cook & Seaman, Grocers, cr. E. Bay & Tradd Sts.

Cooler, Nancy, 68 Beaufain St., F.P.C.

Cooper, G. W., Attorney, 1 Court House Sq., res. 8 Short St.

Cooper, George, 59 Boundary St., F.P.C.

Cooper, N., Jr., 64 Anson St.

Cooper, Nathan, Sr., Firm of Cooper & Hunt, Shoe Store, cr. King & Queen Sts., res. 64 Anson St.

Cooper, Thomas J., 20 n. King St., F.P.C.

Cooper, William, Shoe Maker, 64 King St.

Copes, James, Capt., Pilot, 12 E. Bay St.

Coram, Charlotte, Mrs., 51 George St.

Corbette, Elizabeth, Mrs., 2 Rutledge St.

Corbette, James, 316 King St.

Corby, John, Jr., Firm of Corby & Son, Ship Smiths, Knox's Whf., res. Washington St.

Corby, John, Sr., Firm of Corby & Son, Ship Smiths, Knox's Whf., res. Vernon St.

Cordes, R., Mrs., Charlotte St.

Cordes, Theodore, Dry Goods, 65 Market St.

Cordray, Thomas, Carpenter, Pritchard St., res. Boundary St.

Cormier, Francis, Ship Carpenter, 16 Washington St.

Cormier, Theodore, Blacksmith, 16 Washington St.

Cornwell, Amelia, Mantumaker, 76 Broad St., F.P.C.

Corrie, Samuel, Wheelwright, 22 King St.

Corse, A., Baker, 77 Boundary St.

Cotchett, George, Factor, Commercial Whf., res. 2 Orange St.

Cotto, Alice, Mrs., 6 St. Philip St.

Cotton, Edward, Tailor, 10 Stoll's Al., F.P.C.

Course, John, 1 King st.

Courtenay, D., Mrs., Widow, 127 Boundary St.

Courtenay, E., Mrs., Boarding, 38 Broad St.

Courtenay, E. S., Custom House, res. 127 Boundary St.

Cowan, Joseph R., Carpenter, 3 Whim Court

Cowan, Maria, 10 Clifford St.

Cowperthwait, E. P., Cabinet Ware, King St., cr. Clifford St.

Cox, James M., Accountant, cr. E. Bay St. & Vanderhorst's Whf.

Cox, Julia, Pastry Cook, 73 Boundary St., F.P.C.

Cox, Rodolph, Firm of Smith & Cox, Sail Makers, Little's Whf., res. Little's Whf.

Cox, William H., 4 Hard Al.

Craft, Edward, Accountant, res. 73 Church St.

Craft, Thomas, Accountant, 21 Broad St.

Crafts, George J., Attorney, 94 Church St.

Crafts, Margaret, 77 Tradd St.

Cramer, George W., 62 Queen St.

Cramer, John, Tavern, 30 Queen St.

Crandel, Ann, 30 Beaufain St.

Crane, A. G., Firm of A. G. Crane & Co., Importers, 147 Meeting St., res. Victoria Hotel

Crawford, John, 2 Rutledge St.

Craych, Robert, Tailor, Boundary St.

Crews, A. J., Firm of Watson, Crews & Co., Merchants, 28 E. Bay St., res. 21 Friend St.

Crews, Edward, 10 Princess St.

Crimmel, Margaret, Gadsen's Whf., F.P.C.

Cripps, Ann, Miss, 45 Meeting St.

Crocker, D., Firm of D. Crocker & Co., Commission Merchants, 68 E. Bay St.,

Cross, Adeline, Mantuamaker, 16 Chalmers St., F.P.C.

Cross, G. W., Mrs., cr. Meeting & Tradd Sts.

Cross, Henry, Bricklayer, 1 Smith St.

Cross, Matthew W., Bricklayer, 1 Smith St.

Crouch, Charles, 6 Coming St.

Crovat, Gibb F., Carpenter

Crovat, Louis J., Grocer, 320 King St.

Crovat, Peter, Carpenter.

Crow, Harriet, Mrs., Marsh St.

Cruickshank, Mary, Mrs., 12 King St., cr. John St.

Cruickshank, Samuel, Col., Tanner, 22 Queen St.

Cubie, John, Grocer, 19 Back St.

Cudworth, John, Printer, 88 Tradd St.

Culbert, James, n. King St.

Cunningham, Andrew, Carpenter, 4 St. Philip St.

Cunningham, Richard, Henrietta St.

Curran, Daniel, Grocer, 113 n. King St.

Currie, John, Wheelwright, 25 n. King St.

Curtis, Ann, 54 King St.

Curtis, Ephraim, Carpenter, 1 Pitt St.

Curtis, Francis, Dr., 12 Smith St.

Curtis, James M., Carpenter, 8 Archdale St.

Curtis, Joseph, Carpenter, Inspection St.

Curtis, Philander, Firm of Curtis & Brown, House Carpenters, 12 Laurens St., res. cr. Meeting & Hasell Sts.

Cuthbert, James, 89 n. King St.

Cuthbert, James, Mrs., 118 Tradd St.

Dacoster William P., Machinist, 112 Queen St., F.P.C.

Daggett, Sheppard, Carpenter, 180 E. Bay St.

Daggett, William, Painter, 36 Broad St., res. 181 E. Bay St.

Daly, John T., Shoes, 293 King St.

Daly, W. & J., Merchants, 369 King St.

Daly, William, cr. Meeting & Market Sts.

Dangerfield, Richard, Carpenter, 55 Tradd St.

Danna, -----, Carpenter, n. St. Philip St.

Danna, Stephen, Tailor, Cannonborough

Dart, B. S., 47 Tradd St.

Daufrene, Alexander, 128 Queen St.

Davenne, E., Commission Merchant, 12 Hamilton's Whf.

Davids, Francis, Tailor, 12 John St., F.P.C.

Davids, Isaac A., Firm of Allen & Davids, Painters, 94 Meeting St., res. 74 Meeting St.

Davidson, James, Painter, 46 Tradd St.

Davis, Eliza, 17 Berresford St.

Davis, G. Y., Firm of G. Y. Davis & Co., Merchants,

Hamilton's Whf., res. New Hotel
Davis, Henry, Auctioneer, 45 Market St.
Davis, J. M., Mrs., Cannonborough
Davis, Jane, Mrs., Boarding, 67 Church St.
Davis, Martha, 14 Pinckney St.
Davis, Martha, John St.
Davis, Mary, 26 Mazyck St.
Davis, Mary A., 38 Tradd St.
Dawes, Hugh P., Firm of Elliott, Condy & Dawes, Auctioneers, 1 Broad St., res. King St.
Dawson, A. V., Attorney, 69 Meeting St.
Dawson, Ann, Ann St.
Dawson, C. L., Mrs., 36 Broad St.
Dawson, Caroline L., 2 George St.
Dawson, Charles P., 106 Broad St.
Dawson, Charlotte, Mrs., cr. Rutledge & Bull Sts.
Dawson, J. L., Dr., 48 Tradd St.
Dawson, John, Carpenter, 17 Back St.
Dawson, -----, Miss, 34 Bull St., cr. Rutledge St.
Dawson, Octavus, 11 Bull St.
Day, Fisher, Merchant, 304 king St., cr. George St.
Deas, E. H., Dr., Shirras Dispensary, 42 Society St.
DeCamp, James, 73 King St.
DeCottes, Edward, Mrs., 100 Tradd St.
Decottes, E. A., Firm of Decottes & Brothers, Hay & Grain Store, cr. E. Bay & Market Sts., res. Queen St.
Decottes. A. C., Firm of Decottes & Brothers, Hay & Grain Store, cr. E. Bay & Market Sts., res. Queen St.
Deevy, Ann, Mrs., Dry Goods, 77 Church St.
DeHaans, H., Clothing, 21 Market St.
Dehon, Sarah, Mrs., 39 Meeting St.
Delage, Mary, Seamstress, 219 E. Bay St.
Delamotte, Jacob, Dr., 80 Broad St., res. 11 Logan St.
Delange, Leonard, Accountant, 29 State St.
Delange, Martha L., Mrs., 29 State St.
Delany, Frances, 48 Church St.
DeLaroy, John, 6 Archdale St.
DeLatorre, A., E. Bay St.
Delatre, Adel, 22 Wall St., F.P.C.
DeLaumont, R., Broker, 96 E. Bay St., res. Mary St.
Delesseline, Jacob, Gunsmith, 10 Burns Ln.
Delius, Edward, Firm of Winslow & Delius, Commission Merchants, Hamilton's Whf., res, New Hotel
Deming & Thayer, Bonnets, 299 King St.
Deming, Barzilia, Firm of Deming, Bulkley & Co., Cabinet Ware, 241 King St.
Dempsey, D., Mrs., 105 Queen St.
Deneaux, A., Mrs., Dry Goods, Market St., near King St.
Deneaux, -----, res. Market St., near King St.
Dener, C., Mrs., 27 Mazyck St.
Denniss, N., Constable, res. Jail, Mazyck St.
Denny, T. S., Dr., 88 Queen St.
Depras, C., Shoes & Trunks, 113 E. Bay St.
Derhoh, Charles, Engineer, 88 n. King St.
Dessaussure, Charles A., Firm of King & Desaussure, Factors & Commission Merchants, Hamilton's Whf., res. 30 Meeting St.
Dessaussure, Henry A., Attorney, 39 Broad St., res. 35 Meeting St.
Dessaussure, Henry S., Dr., 76 Broad St., res. 35 Meeting

St.
DesVarney, Peter, Drayman, 26 John St., F.P.C.
Detmauldt, C., Surveyor, 44 Bull St.
Deveaux, J. P., Accountant, Wharf St.
Deveaux, Mary, Mrs., 32 Tradd St.
Deveaux, Thomas E., n. King St.
Devineaux, Emily, Dry Goods, 89 King St.
Dewar, W. S., Commission Merchant, 6 Fitzsimons' Whf.
Dewees, John, Rice Merchant, 72 E. Bay St., res. Mary St.
Dewees, William, Factor, Dewees' Whf., res. 29 Broad St.
Dewing, L. C., Straw Bonnets, 171 Meeting St.
Dezell, Charles, Dr., Pitt St.
Dibble, A. C., Hat Store, 37 Broad St., res. 7 Burns Ln.
Dibble, P. V., Firm of Wildman & Dibble, Hat Store, 169 Meeting St., res. Burns Ln.
Dick, James, Firm of Dick & Holmes, Auctioneers & Commission Merchants, 17 Vendue Range, res. 28 Broad St.
Dick John, 25 King St.
Dickenson, Henry, Capt., 21 Coming St.
Dickinson, L., Mrs., Boarding, cr. Meeting & Cumberland St.
Dickinson, Samuel, Livery Stables, 40 Society St.
Dickinson, Townsend, Firm of Dickinson, Sebring & Statham, Importers, 149 Meeting St., res. New Hotel
Dickman, Carsten, Grocer, Mary St.
Dickson, Samuel H., Dr., Firm of Dickson & Jervey, 22 George St., res. cr. Meeting & Hudson Sts.
Dinkins, L. J., Commission Merchant, 8 Fitzsimons' Whf.
Disher, E., Mrs., Mary St.
Disher, Robert, Cannon St.
Diver, James, School, 114 Wentworth St.
Dixon, John, Chandler, n. King St.
Dixon, Thomas, 23 Montague St.
Dixon, Thomas, Cannon St.
Dobson, O. L., State Assessor, 8 Water St.
Dollason, Anrew, 40 Beaufain St.
Dorell, John W., Carpenter, 10 Laurens St.
Dorr, Mary, Bridge St., Neck
Dorrance, B., Commission Merchant, 92 E. Bay St.
Dorrell, Edwin R., Surveyor, Hampstead
Dotterer, Thomas, Engineer, Charlotte St.
Doty, Andrew, Coachmaker, w. end Queen St.
Doucin, P. M., Wharfinger, res. Tradd St.
Dougherty, John, Factor, 15 S. Bay St., res. 85 Tradd St.
Dougherty, Joseph, Plasterer, 117 Church St.
Dought, Andrew, Painter, 100 Queen St.
Douglas, -----, Mrs., Milliner, 116 Wentworth St.
Douglas, Robert, Tailor, 58 Elliott St., F.P.C.
Douglass, Benjamin, Commission Merchant, 78 E. Bay St.
Douglass, C., Wine & Liquors, cr. Meeting & Market Sts.
Douglass, Elizabeth, 4 Lamboll St., F.P.C.
Douglass, John, Nassau St.
Douglass, Joseph, Tailor, 5 State St.
Downe, Peter A., Accountant, 63 Church St.
Downie, Robert, Tinner, 59 Broad St.
Doyle, Edward, cr. State & Cumberland Sts.
Doyle, J., Mrs., 71 King St.
Doyle, M., 3 Motte's Ln.
Doyle, William, 62 King St.

Drayton, Alfred, Southwestern Railroad Bank, res. 7 Water St.
Drayton, Charles, 19 S. Bay St.
Drayton, Emma, 65 King St.
Drayton, John, Mrs., w. end Bull St.
Drayton, Sarah, Fruits, 55 Anson St., F.P.C.
Drege, Peter, Firm of Peter Drege & Co., Clothing, res. 139 E. Bay St.
Drummond, James, Shoemaker, 63 n. King St., F.P.C.
Drummond, John, Shoemaker, 57 Broad St.
Drummond, Moses, Shoe Maker, 5 College St., F.P.C.
Dubois, Eleanor, Mrs., 25 Archdale St.
Dubose, M., Mrs., Warren St.
Ducksworth, H. A., Firm of Battersby & Nephew, Commercial Merchants, 38 E. Bay St., res. Church St.
Due, Francis, Grocer, cr. King & Columbus Sts.
Due, Henry A., Tinner, cr. King & Spring Sts.
Duffus, James, Firm of Duffus & Taylor, Dry Goods Merchants, 303 King St., res. 18 Pitt St.
Duffus, John, Notary Public, 69 E. Bay St., res. St. Andrews Hall
Duffus, -----, Mrs., Matron, St. Andrews Hall, 88 Broad St.
Duggan, Mary, Mrs., Boarders, 126 Church St.
Duggan, Thomas, Bricklayer, 126 Church St.
Duke, John H., Accountant, Amen St.
Duke, William, Printer, 119 Church St.
Dukes, Joseph H., Firm of Campbell & Dukes, Attorneys, 40 Broad St., res. 40 n. King St.
Dukes, W. C., Factor, Exchange Whf., res. n. King St.
Duncan, Resett, Dry Goods, 99 King St.
Dunkin, B. F., Hon., Warren St.
Dunlap, James. Merchant Tailor, 278 King St.
Dunlap, William, 132 Tradd St.
Dunlap, William, 59 Boundary St.
Dunn, George, Lumber Merchant, 115 Wentworth St.
Dunn, John, 80 Tradd St.
Dunn, John E., Accountant, 28 Chalmers St.
Dunn, William, Dry Goods, 371 King St.
Dunmovant, John, Dr., 15 George St.
Dunovant, John, Firm of John Dunovant & Co., Factors, Fitzsimmons' Whf., res. 15 George St.
Dupignac, Ebenezer, 263 King St.
Dupont, F., Paper Hanger, 127 King St.
Dupont, Mary, 80 Beaufain St., F.P.C.
Dupont, -----, Mrs., Boarders, 40 Hasell St.
Dupre, Abigail, Mrs., Society St, near E. Bay St.
Dupre, Francis, Pilot, 34 Church St.
Dupre, James, Measurer of Lumber, res. Wall St.
Dupree, Ira, Firm of Humphries, Dupree & Co., Dry Goods, 12 Hayne St.
Duquercron, F., 19 Tradd St.
Durand, Victor, Merchant, 137 E. Bay St.
Dursse, E., Mrs., 129 Queen St.
Dutrieux, C., Baker, 67 E. Bay St.
Duval, John B., Tinner, Market St., near King St., res. Laurens & E. Bay Sts.
Duval, -----, Madame, School, Hudson St.
Duval, W. E., Tobacconist, 2 Queen St.
Dwight, Caroline, Pastry Cook, 76 King St., F.P.C.
Eager, William, Warren St.

Eahman, Henry, n. King St.
Eason, -----, Charlotte St.
Eason, -----, Mrs., Boarders, 253 King St.
Eason, R. J., Commission Merchant, 8 Vendue Range, res. cr. King & Wentworth Sts.
Easterby, Jane M., Commercial House, cr. Queen & Church Sts.
Eccles, Thomas J., Editor of the Bulletin, 75 E. Bay St.
Eckhard, George B., City Attorney, 94 Church St., res. 19 George St.
Eckhard, M. E., Mrs., 33 Society St.
Edmonston, Charles, Commission Merchant, Central Whf., res. 6 Legare St.
Edmonston, Charles, Jr., 27 Friend St.
Edwards, E. H., Gen., 9 Meeting St.
Edwards, George, Planter, n. King St.
Edwards, Joseph, Carpenter, 51 Anson St.
Edwards, -----, Mrs., 44 St. Philip St.
Edwards, P. J., Dr., 53 Boundary St., res. 26 Wall St.
Egan, Henry J., Printer, Gadsden's Whf.
Egerton, E. W., Firm of Sebring, Egerton & Richards, Tailors & Drapers, res. 32 Broad St.
Egleston, George W., Firm of Egleston & Frost, Attorneys, 97 Church St., res. cr. Thomas & Warren Sts.
Ehney, Elisha W., Carpenter, 227 E. Bay St.
Ehney, P. M., Officer of Customs, res. Pinckney St.
Elbridge, James, Conductor, Rail Road, res. Boundary St.
Elder, James, Tanner, John St., cr. n. Meeting St.
Elfe, Albert, Carpenter, 39 George St.
Elfe, Edward, Dr., 98 Meeting St.
Elfe, -----, Misses, 96 Wentworth St.
Elfe, Robert, Attorney, res. 98 Meeting St.
Elfe, William, 91 Boundary St.
Elford, Ann, 66 State St., F.P.C.
Elford, Frederick P., Wharfinger, Vanderhorst's Whf., res. 15 Anson St.
Elford, John R., Wharfinger, Boyce's Whf., res. King cr. Tradd Sts.
Ellard, Julia, 24 St. Philip St.
Ellard, Mary Ann, 24 St. Philip St.
Elliott, Amelia, Seamstress, 58 State St., F.P.C.
Elliott, Barnard S., 10 George St.
Elliott, Eliza, 40 St. Philip St.
Elliott, Gibbs, Dr., 10 George St.
Elliott, T. O., Attorney, Court House Sq., res. n. King St.
Elliott, William S., Firm of Elliott, Condy & Dawes, Auctioneers, 1 Broad St., res. 10 Legare St.
Elsworth, Foster, 11 Boundary St.
Elsworth, J. T., U. S. Gauger, 11 Boundary St.
Emery, J. R., Clerk, 2 Unity Al.
Emery, Jonathan E., 2 Unity Al.
Emmerly, William, Drayman, 5 Price's Al., F.P.C.
England, Alexander, Planter, 46 Tradd St.
England, John, Rt. Rev., Bishop, Catholic Seminary, 92 Broad St
English, James, 13 S. Bay St.
Enslow, Joseph L., Cooper, 44 E. Bay St., res. 36 Tradd St.
Enston, William, 145 King St.
Entz, John F., Firm of Entz & Amey, Commission Merchants, Central Whf., res. 116 E. Bay St.

Ernest, Catharine, Vanderhorst St.
Ernest, Harman G., Grocer, 1 New St.
Esdra, Z., Mrs., Mattress Maker, 36 Queen St.
Esnard, Jane, Pastry, 25 St. Philip St., F.P.C.
Esnard, Peter, 44 King St.
Estill, William, Bookbinder, 4 Broad St.
Evans, Charles, Turner, Market St., near King St.
Evans, George, Accountant, 68 Church St.
Evans, George, Shoes, Market St.
Evans, Leacraft, Razor Straps, 61 Queen St.
Evans, Robert, 40 Coming St.
Evans, Robert, Turner, 17 Back St.
Evans, Susan, Mrs., 28 Pitt St.
Eveleigh, Thomas, Dr., Thomsonian, 8 Smith St.
Evringham, Rebecca, 91 Queen St.
Ewan, John, Silversmith, 140 King St.
Faber, Eliza C. Mrs., 65 Tradd St.
Faber, Henry, Mrs., 273 E. Bay St.
Faber, -----, Mrs., Alexander St.
Faber, W. W., Hampstead
Fabian, L., Mrs., 91 Queen St.
Fairchild, Daniel, Factor, Williams' Whf., res. 11 Lynch St., F.P.C.
Fairchild, Rufus, Tavern, 264 King St.
Fairchild, Samuel W., Agent, Dupignac, 263 King St.
Fanning, Frederick D., Firm of Hatch & Co., 7 Hayne St.
Farley, John, Teacher, 1 Bull St.
Farrar, S. S., Firm of Farrar & Hayes, Wholesale Grocers, 23 Hayne St., res. 149 E. Bay St.
Fashbender, J., Fancy Store, 88 Meeting St.
Fay, James, Tavern, 27 Queen St.
Fay, Mary, Mrs., 34 King St.
Fay, T. C., Printer, 91 Queen St.
Fayolle, -----, Madame, 86 King St.
Fazer, J. L., Washington St.
Fean, J. W., S. Bay St.
Fehrenback, N., Mrs., Dry Goods, cr. Church & Tradd Sts.
Fehrenback, N., Watch Maker, cr. Church & Tradd Sts.
Felepe, Antonio, Tavern, 21 Market St.
Felix, Peter, Distiller, Mary St.
Fell, Thomas D., Tinner, Market St., near King St.
Fell, W. W., Mrs., 2 Beaufain St.
Fendal, J. L., Firm of Deming, Bulkley & Co., Cabinet Ware, 241 King St., res. New York
Fenelon, Eugene, Milliner, 108 King St.
Fenwick, William, 20 Archdale St.
Ferguson, James, 5 Mazyck St., F.P.C.
Ferguson, -----, Mrs., Widow, 10 Orange St.
Ferrett, Adaline, 2 Smith's Ln.
Ferrett, Charles, 42 Coming St.
Ferrett, Jane, Pastry Cook, 19 Boundary St., F.P.C.
Ferrett, John F., Fruiterer, 43 Market St.
Ferris, Albert G., Capt., 9 Wharf St.
Ficken, John, Grocer, Cannon St.
Fields, Nathan, Firm of Cleapor & Fields, Sail Makers, Price's Whf., res. cr. Hamilton's Whf.
Fieldt, Rebecca, Ann St.
Fife, J. F., Firm of Higham, Fife & Co., Foreign Merchants, 55 E. Bay St., res. Cannonborough
Figeroux, -----, Madame, Milliner, 103 King St.

Fillette, A., Mrs., 133 King St.
Finagin, John, Merchant Tailor, 40 Broad St.
Finagin, -----, Miss, 6 Clifford's Al.
Fink, J. P., Grocer, 39 Beaufain St.
Finklea, James, Saddler, 2 Wharf St.
Finley, Mary, 15 Meeting St.
Finley, William P., Firm of Peronneau, Mazyck & Finley, Attorneys, 4 Court House Sq., res. 15 Meeting St.
Finn, Alex C., Drugs, 31 Broad St.
Finney, Walter, Accountant, 29 Queen St.
Fish, Horace, 18 Cumberland St.
Fisher, John F., Grocer, 41 Archdale St.
Fisher, Samuel, Milliner, 188 King St.
Fisher, Susan, Society St., near Anson St.
Fitsimons, Christopher, Mrs., 24 Hasell St.
Fitts, William, Blacksmith, 14 John St.
Fitzgibbon, P. T., Hats & Caps, cr. State & Linguard Sts.
Flagg, Silvia, 4 Minority St., F.P.C.
Flaish, George, Jeweller, 115 King St.
Flemming, Daniel, 3 Maiden Ln.
Flemming, Eliza, 178 Meeting St.
Flemming, J. H., Carpenter, John St.
Flemming, Patrick, Grocer, 144 E. Bay St., cr. Pinckney St.
Flemming, Stephen, n. King St.
Fles, Michael, Firm of Fles & Levy, Importers, 190 King St.
Flory, William, Carpenter, Ann St.
Floyd, -----, Mrs., 30 Mazyck St.
Flynn, John T., Tailor, 38 Broad St., res. State St.
Fogartie, A., Firm of Harwood & Fogartie, Dry Goods, 112 King St.
Fogartie, Ann, Miss, Teacher, Free School, 21 Wall St.
Fogartie, Edward, Bricklayer, 22 Smith St.
Fogartie, Samuel, Accountant, 21 Wall St.
Foley, David, Carpenter, 4 Whim Court
Folger, Edward, Crockery Ware Packer, 152 E. Bay St.
Folker, -----, Misses, 23 John St.
Folker, P. H., Rev., John St.
Follin, Augustus, 127 King St.
Follin, F. F., Middle St.
Follin, Joseph, Tobacconist, 29 Boundary St.
Fontenay, Louis, Silversmith, Market St., near Meeting St.
Forbes, J. G., City Tinner, res. 33 Coming St.
Forbes, R., Tinner, 23 Tradd St.
Forbes, William P., Tinner, 23 Tradd St.
Ford, Benjamin, Assistant Agent, Southern Methodist Book Room, Hayne St., res. Ann St.
Ford, Frederick A., Planter, Thomas St.
Ford, Louis, Dry Goods, 98 King St.
Ford, Margaret, 19 Church St., F.P.C.
Ford, Perry, Ann St.
Fordham, Richard, Blacksmith, Exchange St., res. 89 Church St.
Forgartie, A., Firm of Harwood & Fogartie, 246 King St.
Forrest, John, Rev., 6 Water St.
Fort, R. W., Firm of Fort, Townsend & Mendenhall, Dry Goods, 1 Hayne St., Deceased
Foster, Godfrey, Fruiterer, 43 n. King St.
Foster, Henry, Butcher, Hampstead

Foster, W. B., Discount Clerk, Bank of State of S.C.
Fourgeaud, A., Baker, 181 E. Bay St.
Fourgeaud, Eugene, Confectioner, 239 & 256 King St.
Fox, Ann, 4 Orange St.
Fox, Mary, 20 Magazine St.
Fox, Richard, Capt., Mariner, 11 Longitude Ln.
Fox, Susan, 41 St. Philip St., F.P.C.
Fox, William, Mrs., n. Coming St.
Francis, Henry, 32 Coming St., F.P.C.
Francis, John, Barber, 296 King St., F.P.C.
Francis, Margaret, Philadelphia St., F.P.C.
Francis, -----, Mrs., 365 King St.
Fraser, Charles, 39 King St.
Fraser, Frederick, Mrs., 93 Tradd St.
Fraser, John, Firm of John Fraser & Co., Commission
  Merchants, Central Whf., res. 4 Short St.
Fraser, -----, Mrs., 19 John St.
Frazer, C. P., Victoria Hotel, cr. Princess & King Sts.
Freeman, Mary, 59 Boundary St., F.P.C.
Freeman, William, Capt., Mariner, 74 Church St.
French, E. P., Firm of Chaloner & French, Carpenters, 33
  Queen St.
Friand, Lewis, Firm of Gouvegniere & Friand, 47 Queen
  St.
Friday, Christian, Grocer, 64 n. King St.
Friend, James, Carpenter, 14 Bull St.
Friend, John, Carpenter, n. Pitt St.
Fritz, Valentine, Farmer, Neck
Frost, Edward, Firm of Egleston & Frost, Attorneys, 97
  Church St., res. 27 Archdale St.
Frost, Henry R., Dr., 72 Broad St., res. 27 Archdale St.
Frost, Nathan, Bricklayer, Ann St.
Fryer, George, 103 Church St.
Fuegas, H. P., Linguist, 74 King St.
Fuegas, -----, Mrs., Dancing Academy, 74 King St.
Fuller, Benjamin, Planter, n. St. Philip St.
Fuller, Oliver, Capt., Mariner, 105 Meeting St.
Fuller, S., Chandler, n. St. Philip St.
Fulmor, John, Wolf St.
Furst, Daniel, w. end Broad St.
Gabeau, Elizabeth, 10 Vernon St.
Gadsden, Alexander E., Dr., 13 Cumberland St.
Gadsden, Benjamin, 11 Coming St.
Gadsden, Charles E., Rt. Rev., Bishop, cr. Charlotte &
  Alexander Sts.
Gadsden, Fisher, Charlotte St.
Gadsden, J. W., 11 Coming St.
Gadsden, Thomas, Attorney, 20 Church St.
Gadsden, Thomas N., Broker & Auctioneer, cr. Chalmers
  & State Sts.
Gaillard, -----, 1st Lieut., Citadel, n. of Boundary St.
Gaillard, Cornelia, Mrs., 15 Pitt St.
Gaillard, D. C., Accountant, Court House Sq.
Gaillard, D. S., Mrs., Court House Sq.
Gaillard, -----, Mrs., 11 Archdale St.
Gaillard, P. C., Dr., 1 State St.
Gaillard, Theodore, cr. Meeting & Ann Sts.
Gallager, John W., Wood Factor, cr. Lynch & Beaufain
  Sts.
Galliott, Alexis, Tobacconist, 105 E. Bay St.

Galpin, Albert, Cabinet Ware, 284 King St.
Gamage, Edward, 4 Friend St.
Gannon, -----, Guardman, 4 Short St.
Gantt, Thomas J., Firm of Gantt & Mortimer, Auctioneers
  & Brokers, 12 State St., Register in Equity, res. 56 King
  St.
Garcia, James, Music Teacher, 176 E. Bay St.
Gardner, Eliza, Miss, 51 Coming St.
Gardner, James, 35 Society St.
Gardner, Mary Ann, 86 Beaufain St., F.P.C.
Garret, Ann, Mrs., 115 Meeting St.
Garret, G., 58 Broad St.
Garret, George, Boot Maker, 83 Church St.
Gary, J. R., n. King St.
Gates, Thomas, Butcher, Cannon St.
Gatewood, W. C., Lottery Office, 26 Broad St.
Gayer, Nicholas, 3 Longitude Ln.
Gayer, W. J., Carriage Depository, cr. Meeting &
  Wentworth Sts.
Geddes, Gilbert C., Planter, 11 Rutledge St.
Geddings, Eli, Dr., n. Meeting St.
Gefkin, Henry, Firm of Wright & Gefkin, Carpenters, w.
  end Beaufain St.
Gerdts, Carsten, Grocer, cr. Laurens & Anson Sts.
Gerdts, Henry, Grocer, cr. Pitt & Beaufain Sts
German, Augustus, Tallow Chandler, 9 Middle St.
Getty, Jane, 38 Beaufain St.
Geyer, Mary, Mrs., 16 Atlantic St.
Geyer, Rodolph C., Accountant, 16 Atlantic St.
Gibbon, George & John, Merchants, 6 Gillon St.
Gibbs, B. S., Firm of Gibbs & Johnson, Factors, 6
  Southern Whf., res. cr. John & Elizabeth Sts.
Gibbs, Benjamin, Factor, John St.
Gibbs, Benjamin S., Ann St.
Gibbs, C. & Joshua, Commission Merchants, 10 Vendue
  Range
Gibbs, Charlotte, 4 State St.
Gibbs, Eliza, 41 Church St.
Gibbs, Eliza, 43 Church St.
Gibbs, Jane L., 10 George St.
Gibbs, John C., 77 Tradd St.
Gibbs, Joseph S., Firm of Gibbs & Williams, Steam Saw
  Mill, w. end Tradd St., res. cr. Lamboll & Legare Sts.
Gibbs, Robert, Mrs., res. n. Meeting St.
Gibbs, S. W., 81 Broad St.
Gibbs, William, 142 Tradd St.
Giberin, Henry, 111 Wentworth St.
Gibert, Jesse, 3 Coming St.
Gibson, Alexander, Merchant, 2 Boyce's Whf., res. 198 E.
  Bay St.
Gibson, David C., Attorney, 94 Church St., res. 168
  Meeting St.
Gibson, Elizabeth, 168 Meeting St.
Gibson, George, 7 New St.
Gibson, John R., Assistant Clerk, Bank of Charleston, res.
  2 State St.
Gibson, Samuel, Carpenter, Henrietta St.
Gibson, William, Col., Accountant, 1 Back St.
Gibson, William H., Wharfinger, Price's Whf., Res, 166
  Meeting St.

Gidiere, J. M., Firm of Gidiere & Gunther, Grocers, 305 King St.
Gidiere, William M., Dry Goods, 320 King St.
Giese, Charles, Grocer, cr. Meeting & Cumberland Sts.
Gilbert, S. C., Printer, 36 Broad St.
Gilchrist, James, Clerk, Bank of S. C.
Gilchrist, Robert B., Hon., District Judge, U. S. Court House, Queen & Meeting Sts., res. 253 E. Bay St.
Gildersleeve, B., Rev., Editor, Observer, Chalmers St., res. 5 Pitt St.
Giles, John A., Magistrate, Court House Sq., res. Queen St.
Giles, Robert, 2 Gibbes St.
Gilfillen, Alexander, Firm of Robertson & Gilfillen, Factors, Magwood's Whf., res. 30 Chalmers St.
Gilliland, W. D., Firm of Gilliland, Son & Howell, Dry Goods, 114 Meeting St., res. 1 Liberty St.
Gilliland, William H., Firm of Gilliland, Son & Howell, Dry Goods, 114 Meeting St., res. 18 George St.
Gilman, Samuel, Rev., Pastor, Unitarian Church, Archdale St., res. 7 Orange St.
Girardeau, Isaac, 4 Gibbes St.
Girardeau, J. K., 3 Liberty St.
Gissel, Hanke, Grocer, 117 Broad St., res. 18 S. Bay St.
Gitsinger, B. R., Printer, 17 Cumberland St.
Glause, Benjamin, Carpenter, 25 Wall St.
Gleason, H. B., Firm of H. B. Gleason & Co., Wholesale Crockery, 14 Hayne St., res. 273 King St.
Gleason, John N., Crockery, 273 King St.
Glenn, James, 7 Bull St.
Glenn, John, Outdoor Clerk, Planters & Mechanics Bank, res. Reid St.
Glenn, Margaret, Mrs., 91 Tradd St.
Glover, Eliza, 7 Rutledge St.
Glover, G. W., Builder, Wentworth St., near E. Bay St.
Glover, Joseph, Dr., 6 Rutledge St.
Godard, Rene, President, Union Bank, res. 101 King St.
Godet, Ann, 6 S. Bay St.
Godfroy, A. R., Tailor, 55 State St.
Goings, Ann, 15 Clifford's Al., F.P.C.
Goings, Ellen, Seamstress, 25 Coming St., F.P.C.
Goings, Rebecca, 25 Coming St., F.P.C.
Golding, C., Spring St.
Goldsmith, Francis, 62 Broad St.
Goldsmith, Henry, 1 Court House Sq.
Goldsmith, Joseph, 27 Church St.
Goldsmith, M., Merchant, E. Bay St.
Goldsmith, Morris, 22 Beaufain St.
Golfraiville, Theodore, Tivoli Garden.
Gonzales, B., Merchant, 15 Exchange St., res. 4 George St.
Gonzales, John, Shoe Maker, 12 Market St.
Good, Thomas, Mariner, 28 Tradd St.
Goodrich, George, Teacher, 121 E. Bay St.
Goodsell, Nathan C., Firm of Baker & Goodsell, Hatters, 274 King St.
Gordon, C. A., Mrs., n. Meeting St.
Gordon, C. P., Discount Clerk, Bank of Charleston, 15 Smith St.
Gordon, Jane, Mrs., 158 Meeting St.
Gordon, John, News Collector, 8 Stoll's Al.
Gordon, Samuel, Firm of McCartney & Gordon, Hardware

Merchants, 15 Broad St.
Goregan, Thomas, Cigar Maker, n. Meeting St.
Gosprey, Francis, Carpenter, n. Coming St.
Goss, William, late Merchants Hotel, cr. King & Society Sts.
Gough, Emma, 30 S. Bay St.
Gough, John, Bricklayer, 117 Church St.
Gough, Peter, Bricklayer, n. St. Philip St.
Gouldsmith, Richard, Fancy Goods, 199 King St., cr. Market St.
Gourdin, Henry, Firm of Gourdin, Mathiessen & Co., Commission Merchants, Commercial Whf., res. 36 Meeting St.
Gourdin, R. N., Firm of Gourdin, Mathiessen & Co., Commission Merchants, Commercial Whf., res. 36 Meeting St.
Gourdin, Robert, 4 Meeting St.
Gouvegniere, -----, Firm of Gouvegniere & Friand, Cutlers, 47 Queen St.
Gowan, John R., 6 S. Bay St.
Gowan, Peter, Firm of Gowan & Caw, Watchmakers, cr. Meeting & Chalmers St., res. 6 S. Bay St.
Gradick, C. C., Butcher, cr. Middle & Boundary Sts.
Grady, James, Tailor, 92 Queen St.
Graham, Henry, Store, n. King St.
Graham, Sarah, 23 Coming St.
Graham, William C., Dr., 46 Tradd St.
Grant, Alfred, 1 Montague St.
Grant, Ann, 9 Wall St.
Grant, F. W., Merchant, 179 Meeting St., cr. Hasell St.
Graunstein, G., 31 King St.
Gravely, John, Hardware, 35 Broad St., res. New Hotel
Graves, Charles, Planter, cr. Meeting & Wentworth Sts.
Graves, Daniel D., Dr., 62 Tradd St.
Gray, Frances, Mrs., 66 Anson St.
Gray, Henry Y., District Clerk, U.S. Court House, Queen & Meeting Sts., res. 136 E. Bay St.
Gray, James F. Collector, 4 Magazine St.
Gray, James W., Commissioner In Equity, 87 Meeting St., res. 121 Wentworth St.
Gray, -----, Mrs., 136 E. Bay St.
Gray, Ruth, Henrietta St.
Gray, Sarah W., Miss, 4 Magazine St.
Gray, Thomas, Painter, 100 Wentworth St.
Greaday, A. P., Variety Store, 172 King St.
Greaton, John, Insurance Trust Office, 45 Tradd St.
Greely, Catharine, Archdale St.
Green, J. F., Firm of Green & Redmond, Commission Merchants, Central Whf., res. Charlotte St.
Greenhill, Sidney, Mrs., 5 Greenhill
Greenland, J., 24 Archdale St.
Greenland, P., 24 Archdale St.
Greer, John H., Carpenter, Henrietta St.
Greer, John M., Bookseller, 135 King St., res. 181 King St.
Greer, William, Tavern, 264 King St.
Gregg, A., Baker, 44 Elliott St., res. near Bennett's Mills.
Gregg, William, Firm of Hayden, Gregg & Co., Importers of Jewelry, 232 King St., res. Cannonborough
Gregorie, James, Secretary, Port Society
Gregorie, Ladson, Lt., State Guards, Citadel

Griffin, Mary, 2 Archdale St.
Griffith, Ann, Boarding, Wolf St.
Griffith, -----, Capt., Charlotte St.
Griggs, Henry, Teacher, 33 Society St.
Grimkie, Henry, Attorney, 64 Broad St.
Grimkie, John, Dr., 48 St. Philip St.
Grimkie, Sarah, 40 S. Bay St.
Griswold, Julia, Mrs., Dry Goods, Market St., near
  Meeting St.
Groman, Henry, Tailor, 33 King St.
Groning, L., Firm of Smith & Groning, Dry Goods, 19
  Vendue Range, res. John St.
Groning, -----, Mrs., Warren St.
Groover, William, Planter, 14 Liberty St.
Gross, John, Wolf St.
Groves, E., Mrs., Boarding, 3 Queen St.
Gruber, Margaret, cr. Ann & Pinckney Sts.
Guenthier, Charles, Grocer, cr. Meeting & Market Sts.
Guerin, John A., Tailor, 38 Queen St.
Guevian, -----, 58 Broad St.
Guilleman, P., Farmer, cr. Spring & Mary Sts.
Guillet, Ellen, 3 Archdale St.
Guinvier, Morris, 55 Queen St.
Gunboll, Berkley, 4 S. Bay St.
Gunthier, F. W., Firm of Gidiere & Gunther, Grocers, 305
  King St.
Gunthier, F., Teacher of Spanish & French, 29 Coming St.
Guthrey, Peter, 32 State St.
Guy, John, Bricklayer, 24 Middle St.
Guy, T. B., Commission Merchant, 88 E. Bay St., res. 158
  E. Bay St.
Habenich, J. D., Grocer, 6 Tradd St.
Habersham, B. Elliott, Firm of Mathews & Habersham,
  Factors, cr. E. Bay St. & Southern Whf., res. Broad St.
Habersham, Bernard, Miss, 105 Broad St.
Hacker, George, John St.
Hadden, Ann, 1 King St.
Hafer, Julia, Tailoress, 48 Elliott St.
Hagewood, John, Music Teacher, 7 Friend St.
Haig, Alexander, 105 Broad St.
Haig, David, Cooper, 156 E. Bay St.
Haig, Joseph C., Capt., 24 Smith St.
Haig, Margaret, 142 Meeting St.
Haise, Jacob, Columbus St.
Hall, Charlotte, Seamstress, 7 St. Philip St.
Hall, Elizabeth, Boarding, 40 Elliott St.
Hall, Henry T., Firm of Hall & Bonnell, Merchants, 4 E.
  Bay St.
Hall, Jane, 170 King St.
Hall, S., Mrs., Court House Sq.
Hall, William, Dr., 271 E. Bay St.
Halsey, Elisha, Capt., Washington St.
Halsey, John, 13 Anson St.
Halsted, -----, Firm of C. & G. Halsted, Dry Goods, 5
  Hayne St., res. New Hotel
Halsted, J. S., Firm of Kelsey & Halsted, res. New Hotel
Hamett, R. S., Chief Engineer, 6 Longitude Ln.
Hamill, Thomas, Wheelwright, 7 Hard Al.
Hamill, William, 39 E. Bay St.
Hamilton, James, Capt., 19 Queen St.

Hamilton, James, Firm of James Hamilton & Co., Factors,
  24 E. Bay St., res. 90 E. Bay St.
Hamilton, Lucinda, Teacher, cr. Meeting & Chalmers Sts.
Hamilton, Mary, 3 Smith's Ln., F.P.C.
Hamilton, T. Lynch, Firm of James Hamilton & Co.,
  Factors, 24 E. Bay St., res. 90 E. Bay St.
Hampton, Henrietta, 13 Orange St., F.P.C.
Hamye, C. H., Marion Coffee House, 153 E. Bay St.
Hankle, C., Rev., 115 Boundary St.
Hannahan, Hetty, Pastry Cook, 18 Beaufain St., F.P.C.
Hannahan, James, 54 King St.
Hannahan, John, Tradd St.
Hanscomb, Ann, 2 Greenhill St., F.P.C.
Hanson, Christian, 3 Clifford St.
Hantz, C., Tailor & Confectioner, 104 Church St.
Haosman, Charles, Boots & Shoes, 81 E. Bay St.
Happoldt, Albert, Butcher, Cannon St.
Happoldt, Albert, Firm of Weeks & Happoldt, Tavern, 96
  Meeting St., res. Cannon St.
Happoldt, C. D., Butcher, Cannon St.
Happoldt, Charles, Coach Trimmer, 16 Wall St.
Happoldt, John M., Gunsmith, 45 State St.
Happoldt, John, n. St. Philip St.
Harbers, Claus H., Grocer, cr. Meeting & John Sts.
Harbers, John H., Grocer, cr. Wentworth & St. Philip Sts.
Harbey, Martha, 6 Hard Al.
Harby, Henry J., Blacksmith, 125 Church St., res. 12
  Pinckney St.
Hard, Benjamin, 23 Mazyck St.
Hard, Benjamin F., 61 Beaufain St.
Hard, Martha, 61 Beaufain St.
Hardy,-----, School, 5 Burns Ln.
Hare, Robert W., Firm of Harral, Hare & Co., Saddlery, 4
  Hayne St.
Harleston, S., Dr., Thomas St.
Harleston, Sylvia, John St., F.P.C.
Harper, James, Baker, cr. King & Tradd Sts.
Harper, Joseph M., Drugs, 186 King St.
Harral, H. K., Firm of Harral, Hare & Co., Saddlery, 4
  Hayne St.
Harral, James, Firm of Haviland, Harral & Co., Drugs, 286
  King St., res. 286 King St.
Harral, William, Firm of Harral, Hare & Co., Saddlery, 4
  Hayne St., res. 59 Queen St.
Harris, A., Firm of A. & Z. Harris, Clothing Store, 161 E.
  Bay St., res. 187 E. Bay St.
Harris, Abraham, Clothing, 41 State St.
Harris, George, Dyer, 117 Church St.
Harris, Isaac, Fruits, 41 Market St.
Harris, William, Firm of Harris, Roosevelt & Baker,
  Merchants, 17 Hayne St., res. New Hotel
Harris, Z., Firm of A. & Z. Harris, Clothing Store, 161 E.
  Bay St., res. 187 E. Bay St.
Harrison, D. W., Bookseller Depository, Chalmers St.
Harrison, James, Jr., Shoe Maker, 37 Beaufain St., F.P.C.
Harrison, James, Sr., Shoe Maker, 35 Beaufain St., F.P.C.
Harrison, John, Baltimore House, cr. Queen & State Sts.
Harrison, -----, Mrs., 39 Archdale St.
Hart, Daniel, Mrs., 201 Meeting St.
Hart, Mariam, Miss, 117 E. Bay St.

Hart, Nathan & Son, Hardware, 198 King St., res. 154 Meeting St.

Hart, Richard, Wharfinger, Exchange St., res. Radcliffborough

Harvey, Edward, Dyer, 82 Queen St.

Harvey, James E., Accountant, 82 Queen St.

Harwood, W. B., Firm of Harwood & Fogartie, Dry Goods, 112 King St.

Hasell, Hannah, 17 Meeting St.

Hasell, T. M., Merchant, Vanderhorst's Whf., res. 12 Church St.

Haseltine, W. H., Firm of Hoyt & Co., Clothing, 18 Hayne St., res. Boyd's Hotel

Hasham, J., School, 11 Clifford St.

Haskett, Jane, 6 Exchange St.

Hassett, Roger, Amen St.

Hatch, E., Mrs., Millinery & Dry Goods, 348 King St.

Hatch, L. M., Firm of Flemming & Hatch, Merchants. 7 Hayne St.

Hatch, Mary M., 76 Anson St.

Hatch, Prince, Mrs., 136 Church St.

Hatch, W. W., Blacksmith, 141 Church St., res. 49 State St.

Hatch, W. W., Ship Carpenter, res. 348 King St.

Hatcher, Thomas, Broker, 109 Church St.

Hathaway, J. A., U. S. Quartermaster, Victoria Hotel

Hauck, John H., 30 Laurens St.

Haviland, R. B., Firm of Haviland, Harral & Co., Drugs, 286 King St., res. Augusta, Ga.

Hayden, H. Sidney, Firm of Hayden, Gregg & Co., Importers of Jewelry, 232 King St.

Hayden, N., Firm of Hayden, Gregg & Co., Importers of Jewelry, 232 King St.

Hayden, Thomas A., Printer, 11 Mazyck St.

Hayes, John, Grocer, Boundary St.

Hayes, John R., Firm of Farrar & Hayes, Wholesale Grocers, 23 Hayne St., res., 47 Anson St.

Hayne, Arthur P., 27 Meeting St.

Hayne, Robert Y., Mrs., Ladson's Court

Hayne, W. A., Bookkeeper, Bank of S. C., res. St. Philip. St., cr. Vanderhorst.

Hayne, William C., Firm of McDowall, Hayne & Co., Commission Merchants, 30 & 32 E. Bay St., res. 24 Meeting St.

Hayne, William E., Comptroller General, res. 9 Church St.

Hazlehurst, George, Factor, 51 Boundary St.

Headly, John, Mariner, 5 Cumberland St.

Heath, John D., Planter, 17 Bull St.

Heath, Thomas H., 9 Boundary St.

Hebborn, Harriet, 24 Bull St., F.P.C.

Hedley, John L., Firm of Chadwick & Co., Merchants, 70 E. Bay St., res. 15 King St.

Hefferan, E., Dry Goods, 161 King St.

Heilbron, Harriet, 60 Church St.

Heimsath, John, Tavern, cr. Market & E. Bay Sts.

Heissenbottle, C., Boundary St.

Heissenbottle, Henry, Grocer, 20 Meeting St.

Henkin, Deiderick, Grocer, Henrietta St.

Henkin, L., 89 Tradd St.

Henrickson, H., Grocer, 115 King St., cr. Queen St.

Henry, Edward, Grocer, cr. Wentworth & Coming Sts.

Henry, Isaac, Firm of Henry & Sheight, American Hotel, 83 E. Bay St.

Henry, J., 99 Meeting St.

Henry, Joel, 335 King St., res. 28 George St.

Henry, P. J., Mattresses, 37 Queen St.

Henry, R. F., Merchant, 34 State St.

Henry, Samuel W., Furniture, 99 Meeting St.

Henry, W., Grocer, cr. King & Radcliff Sts.

Henry, W. S., 24 Burns Ln.

Henry, William, Carpenter, 326 King St.

Henson, Thomas, 6 Archdale St.

Herbert, Mitchell, Clothing, 57 State St.

Heriot, B. D., Firm of Heriot & Son, Factors, 15 Vanderhorst's Whf., res. 71 Beaufain St.

Heriot, B. G., Firm of Heriot & Son, Factors, 15 Vanderhorst's Whf., res. 71 Beaufain St.

Heriot, D., Mrs., Radcliff St.

Heriot, John, Engineer, 58 Tradd St.

Heriot, Robert, Sr., Planter, Islington

Heriot, Roger, Broker & Notary Public, 43 E. Bay St.

Heriot, W. B., Notary Public, 43 E. Bay St., res. 58 Tradd St.

Herkenrath, Leon, Firm of Herkenrath & Lowndes, Commission Merchants, Hamilton's Whf.

Hernandez, John, Mrs., John St.

Herold, John C., Cabinet Maker, 54 Church St.

Herron, C. C., Carpenter, 43 St. Philip St.

Herron, John H., n. King St.

Herron, William R., Ship Carpenter, 43 St. Philip St.

Hersman, J., Dry Goods, 236 King St.

Hertz, H., Grocer, Alexander St.

Hertz, I. E., Accountant, 75 King St.

Hertz, Jacob, 75 Broad St.

Hertz, James, Dry Goods, 75 King St.

Hertz, Lewis, Clothing, 79 Market St.

Hertz, Margaret C., 63 Beaufain St.

Hertz, William M., n. King St.

Hervey, George, Commission Merchant, Hamilton's Whf.

Herwig, William, Music, 183 King St.

Hewett, Mathew, Mrs., 26 Bull St.

Heyward, Arthur, Planter, Charlotte St.

Heyward, Charles, Planter, Mary St.

Heyward, Elisha, Capt., Washington St.

Heyward, Nathaniel, Planter, 253 E. Bay St.

Hichborn, William C., Firm of D. Crocker & Co., Commission Merchants, 68 E. Bay St., res. 44 Tradd St.

Hickborn, Catharine, Teacher, 44 Tradd St.

Hieronymous, W. T., Firm of Hieronymous & O'Brien, Livery Stables, 100 Church St.

Higgins, Michael, 14 Philadelphia St.

Higham, T., Firm of Higham, Fife & Co., Foreign Merchants, 55 E. Bay St., res. England

Hikell, Lewis, Grocer, cr. Wentworth & St. Philip Sts.

Hilden, F., Grocer, cr. Meeting & John Sts.

Hilgen, Frederick, Grocer, cr. John & Meeting Sts.

Hill, F. C., Portrait Painter, 7 Clifford St.

Hill, Fanny, Charleston Neck, near Race Course, F.P.C.

Hill, James M., Assistant Quarter Master, res. Victoria House.

Hill, -----, Miss, Bridge St., Charleston Neck.
Hill, Nancy, 105 Wentworth St., F.P.C.
Hillard, O. B., 51 Beaufain St.
Hillard, William H., Firm of Hillard & Thomas, Grocers, 7 Vendue Range, res. 31 Pinckney St.
Hillman, Ann, Boarding, 51 E. Bay St.
Hilson, John H., n. Meeting St.
Hinreckson, J. H., Grocer, cr. King & Queen Sts.
Hinson, Elizabeth, 14 Tradd St., F.P.C.
Hislop, Frederick, Grocer, 197 & 203 E. Bay St.
Hislop, Hannah, 4 Middle St.
Hislop, Robert, Cooper, res. 4 Middle St.
Hobson, A., Shoe Maker, 97 E. Bay St.
Hobson, J., Shoes, 97 E. Bay St.
Hodson, William, Mariner, Gadsden's Whf.
Hoff, John C., Printer, 10 Broad St.
Hoff, John, Tailor, 186 Meeting St., F.P.C.
Hoff, Philip, Firm of Hoff & Tucker, Booksellers, res. 10 Broad St.
Hoffman, S., Firm of Solomons & Hoffman, Clothing, 64 Meeting St.
Hogarth, Henry, Firm of Hopkins & Hogarth, Coopers, 4 Longitude Ln., res. 52 Tradd St.
Hogarth, Mary, 18 Wall St.
Holbrook, J. E., Dr., Firm of Holbrook & Ogier, 41 E. Bay St., res. 105 Tradd St.
Holcombe, John C., Commission Merchant, 116 E. Bay St., res. 22 Montague St.
Holland, E. E., cr. Church & Water Sts.
Holland, -----, Mrs., 31 Church St.
Holland, Thomas, Carpenter, 12 Cumberland St.
Holloway,-----, 36 Mazyck St. F.P.C.
Holloway, Mary, 17 College St., F.P.C.
Holloway, Richard, Carpenter, 33 Beaufain St., F.P.C.
Holmes, C. R., Factor, 16 Vanderhorst's Whf., res. 115 Tradd St.
Holmes, Edgar, Collector, 1 E. Bay St.
Holmes, Elizabeth, 3 Price's Al., F.P.C.
Holmes, Emily, 22 Burns Ln.
Holmes, Frances, 54 St. Philip St.
Holmes, H. P., Dr., res. 2 Council St.
Holmes, I. E., Hon., 1 E. Bay St.
Holmes, James, G., Cashier, Southwestern Railroad Bank, res. 1 E. Bay St.
Holmes, James, Mrs., 104 Tradd St.
Holmes, John L., 45 Beaufain St.
Holmes, John V., Gun Smith, 68 Queen St.
Holmes, -----, Mrs., 1 Orange St.
Holmes, Sanford, Firm of Dick & Holmes, Auctioneers & Commission Merchants, 17 Vendue Range, res. 35 E. Bay St.
Holmes, Sarah, 1 Zig Zag Al., F.P.C.
Holmes, Thomas, Tailor, 11 Magazine St., F.P.C.
Holmes, William, 113 Boundary St.
Holst, Charles, Firm of Holst & Ronan, Country Store, 59 N. King St.
Holt, William, Tailor, 92 Meeting St.
Holton, M., 5 St. Philip St.
Holton, Margaret, 19 Cumberland St., F.P.C.
Holwell, T. W., Accountant, 9 E. Bay St.

Homer, Auba, 31 Archdale St., F.P.C.
Homer, -----, Mrs., Boarding, 32 Elliott St.
Honeyhouse, James, 54 King St.
Honour, John H., Rev., 20 Pitt St.
Honour, Thomas M., Accountant, 15 Beaufain St.
Hook, John, Grocer, 33 Church St., cr. Water St.
Hopkins, James A., Firm of Hopkins & Hogarth, Coopers, 4 Longitude Ln., res. 82 Church St.
Hopkins, James A., Wharfinger, Southern Whf., res. 82 Church St.
Hopkins, Mary, 1 Green St., F.P.C.
Hopley, George, Firm of Hopley & Birkle, Merchants, Exchange Whf., res. New Hotel
Hora, William, Clothing, 238 King St.
Horlbeck, Daniel, Magistrate & Attorney, Court House Sq., res. 27 Cumberland St.
Horlbeck, Elias, Dr., 83 Boundary St., 27 Cumberland St.
Horlbeck, Henry, Bricklayer, Etc., 27 Cumberland St.
Horlbeck, John, Bricklayer, cr. Meeting & Boundary Sts.
Horlbeck, John, Carpenter, 27 Cumberland St.
Horlbeck, Maria, 51 Beaufain St.
Horley, John, 13 Anson St.
Horry, Ann, 32 Meeting St.
Horry, Elias, Mrs., cr. Meeting & Tradd Sts.
Horsey, John R., Accountant, 69 Boundary St.
Horsey, Thomas J., Teller, Planters & Mechanics Bank, res. 69 Boundary St.
Horsey, Thomas M., Accountant, 69 Boundary St.
Houschildt, Peter, Capt., 16 n. King St.
Houston, Fanny, 88 Beaufain St., F.P.C.
Houston, R. & T., Tailors, 29 St. Philip St., F.P.C.
Houston, William H., Carpenter, Neck
Howard, A. G., Dr., City Inspector, Health Office, 27 Broad St.
Howard, E., Mrs., 60 Beaufain St.
Howard, Elizabeth, 35 Tradd St.
Howard, Robert, Naval Officer, res. 7 Laurens St.
Howard, Robert T., Rev., res. 7 Laurens St.
Howard, Robert, Wood Factor, William's Whf., res. 80 Anson St., F.P.C.
Howard, T. M., Seedsman, cr. King & Radcliff Sts.
Howard, Thaddeus, Shoes, cr. Queen & Church Sts.
Howe, Philip, 2 King St.
Howe, Silas, 25 Mazyck St.
Howell, S. S., Firm of Gilliland, Son & Howell, Dry Goods, 114 Meeting St., res. 5 Liberty St.
Howes, B. F., Student at Law, Gov. Wilson's, 2 St. Michael Al.
Howland, B. J., Firm of Howland & Taft, Commission Merchants, 135 E. Bay St., res. 45 Anson St.
Howland, Richard G., Firm of Starr & Howland, Steam Plaining, w. end Beaufain St
Howland, William B. Firm of Howland & Caskins, Dry Goods, 200 King St., cr. Market St.
Hoyce, Sarah, Mrs., 37 State St.
Huard, C. P., Mrs., 49 Broad St.
Hubert, Ann, Mrs., 75 Tradd St.
Hubert, C. N., Firm of Higham, Fife & Co., Foreign Merchants, 55 E. Bay St., res. 53 E. Bay St.
Hubert, Charles, 21 Tradd St.

Hubert, -----, Mrs., 53 E. Bay St.
Huchet, Theodore, Firm of Thomas J. Rodger & Co., Commission Merchants, Hamilton's Whf., cr. Anson & Hasell Sts.
Huger, Alfred, Post Master, res. Broad St.
Huger, Daniel, 57 Coming St.
Huger, Daniel E., Firm of Capers & Huger, Auctioneers, 6 State St., res. 107 Tradd St.
Huger, Daniel E., Hon., 28 Meeting St.
Huger, J. Chapman, Commission Merchant, Commercial Whf., res. 110 Broad St.
Huger, John, Planter, 3 Meeting St.
Hughes, B., Mrs., 6 Beaufain St.
Hughes, Thomas, Furniture, 139 Church St.
Hull, A. S., Firm of Hull & Knevals, Merchants, 147 Meeting St., res. 284 King St.
Hulseburg, Aldrich, Grocer, 20 Coming St., cr. George St.
Hume, Robert, 2 Lynch St.
Hume, William, Dr., res. Cannonborough
Hume, William, Planter, res. cr. Smith & Wentworth Sts.
Humphries, Hannah, 6 Mazyck St., F.P.C.
Humphries, James P., Tailor, 113 Meeting St., F.P.C.
Humphries, John, Master, Poor House, 7 Mazyck St.
Humphries, Margaret, 113 Meeting St., F.P.C.
Humphries, William, Firm of Humphries, Dupree & Co., Dry Goods, 12 Hayne St., res. Hasell St.
Huns, Michael, Grocer, 3 S. Bay St.
Hunt, Benjamin F., Firm of Bentham & Hunt, Attorneys, 2 St. Michael's Al., res. 134 Wentworth St.
Hunt, Nathan, Firm of Cooper & Hunt, Shoe Store, cr. King & Queen Sts., res. 19 Coming St.
Hunter, John, Alderman, 22 Pitt St.
Hunting, W. G. & Co., Merchants, 148 King St.
Hurlbut, S. A., Attorney, 12 St. Michael Al., res. 20 Laurens St.
Hurman, H., Tavern, Bedon's Al.
Hurman, Henry, Grocer, Meeting St., res. 17 Water St.
Hurst, C. W., Mrs., Vernon St.
Hurst, Charles, 91 Queen St.
Hurst, James M., Accountant, Planters Hotel
Hussy, Benjamin, Printer, 36 Broad St., res. Roorback's, King St.
Hutchinson, Ann, 22 S. Bay St., F.P.C.
Hutchinson, Mary, 53 Anson St.
Hyams, H., Tailor, 10 Liberty St.
Hyams, James, 13 Price's Al.
Hyams, -----, Misses, 14 Friend St.
Hyams, Moses D., Commission Merchant, 63 E. Bay St.
Hyatt, Edmond, Firm of Hyatt, M'Burney & Co., Dry Goods, 9 Hayne St.
Hyatt, Nathaniel, Firm of Hyatt, M'Burney & Co., Dry Goods, 9 Hayne St., res. New Hotel
Hyde, Henry C., Grocer, cr. Queen & State Sts.
Hyde, L., Grocer, 1 King St.
Hyde, Lewis, Grocer, 335 King St., res. 28 George St.
Hyde, -----, Printer, 25 King St.
Hydrick, John C., n. King St.
Hyer, J., Duncan St.
Ihman, Henry, 88 King St.
Inglesby, Edward, Ship Carpenter, res. 5 New St.

Inglesby, Mary, Mrs., 8 Orange St.
Inglesby, W., Mrs., 37 Tradd St.
Inglesby, William H., Assistant Secretary, Southwestern Railroad, res. 5 New St.
Inglis, M. L., 83 Meeting St., F.P.C.
Ingraham, George H., Firm of Ingraham & Webb, Factors, Central Whf., res. 18 Laurens St.
Ingraham, W. P., Planter, 2 Smith St.
Irvin, Moses, 9 Logan St., F.P.C.
Irvin, Richard, Deputy Register of Mesne Conveyance Office
Irving, John B., Dr., Assistant Cashier, Southwestern Railroad Bank, res. 119 Wentworth St.
Izard, Eliza, 193 E. Bay St.
Izard, Henry, Mrs., 27 Legare St.
Izard, Julia Ann, 13 Water St., F.P.C.
Izard, Tom, 4 Logan St., F.P.C.
Jackson, George, Tin Ware, 167 King St.
Jackson, Joel, Carpenter, Gadsden's Whf.
Jackson, John, Shoe Maker, 22 Chalmers St., F.P.C.
Jackson, M., Mrs., 53 Meeting St.
Jackson, Richard, Milliner, 123 King St.
Jacobs, B. H., Agent, Wilmington Steam Boats, 10 Laurens St.
Jacobs, Cecelia, Fancy Store, 205 E. Bay St.
Jacobs, F., Tailor, 117 Church St.
Jacobs, Matthew, Victualer, 15 Market St.
Jacobs, Myer, Col., Planter, 6 Meeting St.
Jacobs, Philip, 205 E. Bay St.
Jacobs, Simon J., Clothing, 25 State St.
Jacobus, Peter, Firm of Condict & Co., Saddlery, 265 King St.
Jagler, Henry, Grocer, Spring St.
James, Mary, 8 Exchange St., F.P.C.
James, Robert, Firm of Burgess & James, Printing Office, 44 Queen St., res. 17 King St.
James, William, Pilot, 17 King St.
Jaques, George R., 21 Beaufain St.
Jaques, Thomas, Carpenter, Reid St.
Jarke, Nicholas, 2 Pitt St.
Jarvais, Edward, House, Ship & Sign Painter, cr. Linguard & Church Sts.
Javain, Peter, Farmer, Line St.
Jeanerett, Christopher, 197 Meeting St.
Jeanerette, John C., Accountant, 54 Church St.
Jeannerett, J. M., Firm of Bancroft & Co., Merchants, res. 197 Meeting St.
Jefferys, James, Firm of Baker & Jefferys, Sash & Blinds, cr. Church & Amen Sts.
Jeffords, John, Grocer, 13 Middle St.
Jeffords, John H., Sail Maker, 13 Middle St.
Jeffords, William, Carpenter, 13 Wharf St., F.P.C.
Jenkins, Hugh, Blacksmith, n. St. Philip St.
Jenkins, John, Planter, 5 Pinckney St.
Jenkins, -----, Mrs., Lamboll St.
Jennings, Robert, Saddler, 326 King St.
Jervey, James C., Officer of Customs, 34 Church St.
Jervey, James, Dr., Firm of Dickson & Jervey, 22 George St., res. 22 George St.
Jervey, James, Firm of Jervey, Waring & White, Brokers,

18 Broad St., res. 13 Laurens St.

Jervey, James, President, State Bank, 13 Laurens St.

Jervey, Thomas, Capt., Mariner, 25 Church St.

Jervey, Thomas D., Accountant, 26 Lightwood St.

Jervey, William, Attorney, Firm of Memminger & Jervey, res. 13 Laurens St.

Jesup, Zadock, Tinner, 227 King St.

Jeves, Eliza, Boarders, 134 Church St.

Jewell, Daniel, Firm of Jewell & Strong, Cabinet Makers, 45 Society St.

Johnson, A. S., Firm of Watson, Crews & Co., Merchants, 28 E. Bay St.

Johnson, Alexander, Tailor, 76 Broad St., F.P.C.

Johnson, Ann, 24 S. Bay St.

Johnson, B., Umbrella & Cane Maker, Market St., near Meeting St.

Johnson, Clark, 36 Broad St.

Johnson, D. P., Firm of Gibbs & Johnson, Factors, 6 Southern Whf., res. Legare St.

Johnson, David, Dr., 81 Queen St.

Johnson, E. A., 69 Broad St., F.P.C.

Johnson, E., Mrs., 69 King St.

Johnson, Eliza, Jones' Hotel, 67 Broad St., F.P.C.

Johnson, George A., Firm of Lockwood & Johnson, res. 69 King St.

Johnson, H. & Co., Shoes, 222 & 314 King St.

Johnson, H. & L., Shoes, 102 Meeting St.

Johnson, James B., Tailor, 323 King St.

Johnson, James, Chandler, John St.

Johnson, James L., 95 Wentworth St.

Johnson, James, Tailor, 87 King St., F.P.C.

Johnson, James, Tavern, Laurens St., near the Whf.

Johnson, Jane, n. St. Philip St.

Johnson, John, Mrs., 51 Anson St.

Johnson, John, n. Meeting St.

Johnson, Joseph, Dr., Drugs, 11 Broad St., res. 23 Church St.

Johnson, M'Kewn, Machinist, Steam Packet Whf.

Johnson, Mary, Mrs., Midwife, 51 Meeting St.

Johnson, Moultrie, n. St. Philip St.

Johnson, Pinckney D., Firm of Gibbs & Johnson., 6 Southern Whf., res. 25 Legare St.

Johnson, Sally, 91 Wentworth St., F.P.C.

Johnson, T. W., Tavern, 57 n. King St.

Johnson, William, 8 Bull St.

Johnston, George A., Firm of Lockwood & Johnson, Mill Wrights, 4 Hard Al., res. 69 King St.

Jolin, Joel, Painter, 3 Gibbes St.

Jones, Abraham, Steward, Marine Hospital, Back St.

Jones, Ann, 13 Wall St., F.P.C.

Jones, Charlotte, 89 Wentworth St., F.P.C.

Jones, Christina, Dry Goods, 55 State St.

Jones, Elias, cr. n. King & Mary Sts.

Jones, Ellen, 66 Beaufain St., F.P.C.

Jones, Martha, 17 Clifford St., F.P.C.

Jones, Mary, Mrs., n. Meeting St.

Jones, Paul, Carpenter, n. St. Philip St.

Jones, R. V., Secretary, Fire Co., Neck

Jones, Samuel, 8 Bedon's Al.

Jones, Sarah, 6 Zig Zag Al., F.P.C.

Jones, Thomas, Gilder, Victoria Range, 195 King St.

Jones, Thomas S., Deputy Secretary of State, Fireproof Bldg.

Jones, W., Firm of Jones & Smith, Commission Merchants, Dewees Whf., res. 58 Meeting St.

Jones, William, 2 Price's Al.

Jones, William, H., Jeweller, 234 King St.

Jones, William, House Carpenter, 9 Rutledge St.

Jones, William R., Carpenter, 1 Gibbes St.

Jones, Wiswall, Firm of Jones & Smith, res. 58 Meeting St.

Jones, R., Mrs., n. St. Philip St.

Jordan, Antonio, Fruits, 244 King St.

Jordan, Robert, Mill Wright, Chisolm's Mills, Tradd St.

Joseph, Jacob J., Soap & Candle Manufacturer, 74 n. King St.

Joseph, Joseph, 41 Coming St.

Joshua, Peter, Grocer, 35 Market St.

Joye, Daniel G., Firm of Joye, Lawton & Co., Grocers, 57 E. Bay St., res. 57 E. Bay St.

Joye, Ellen, Mrs., 16 Princess St.

Joye, F. S., Grocer, 52 n. King St.

Joyner, William, President St.

Judge, James, Dry Goods, 180 King St.

Juefort, George, Fruits, n. King St.

Jugnot, Charles, 1 Linguard St.

Kain, Christopher, Bricklayer, 154 E. Bay St.

Kain, W. A., Commission Merchant, Fitzsimons' Whf.

Kalb, George, Baker, cr. Washington & Boundary Sts.

Kalb, Jacob H., Baker, 17 Tradd St.

Kaneveugh, Patrick, Carpenter, Boundary St.

Kanstine, Augustus, Cooper, 93 n. King St.

Kearney, Patrick, Line St.

Keast, John, 100 King St.

Keds, Morris, Tailor, n. King St.

Keekley, E., Mrs., 22 Beaufain St.

Keekley, Edward C., Dr., 65 n. King St.

Keekley, J. D., 17 Beaufain St.

Keenan, William, Engraver, 103 Meeting St., res. 123 King St.

Keets, George, Carpenter, Boundary St.

Keggs, Eleanor, Mrs., Boarders, 172 E. Bay St.

Keifar, John, Grocer, 18 Archdale St.

Keils, C. & George, Boundary St.

Keith, Mathew Irving, Register of Mesne Conveyance, res. 3 New St.

Kellers, Carsten, Grocer, 127 Church St.

Kelly, J. A., Boat Builder, 2 Market St., res. 65 Church St.

Kelly, Thomas, Shoe Maker, 58 Broad St.

Kelly, William, Plasterer, 2 College St., cr. Green St.

Kelsey, G. H., Firm of C. & G. H. Halsted, Dry Goods, 5 Hayne St.

Kelsey, James E., Firm of Potters & Kelsey, Carpenters, 17 Anson St.

Kennedy, Dennis, Baker, 46 Queen St.

Kennedy, John, Bricklayer, 10 Queen St.

Kennedy, Mary, Milliner, Market St., above Meeting St.

Kennedy, Patrick, Boarders, 9 Elliott St.

Kennedy, Stewart, Blacksmith, 4 Chalmers St.

Kent, Eden, Reid St.

Kernahrens, John, Grocer, cr. Pinckney & Anson Sts.

Kerneskey, Eliza, 5 Tradd St.
Kerr, George, Firm of Kerr & Smith, Commission
Merchants, Central Whf., res. 20 Laurens St.
Kerr, John C., 179 Meeting St.
Kerr, Thomas J., Commission Merchants, Central Whf.,
res. 20 Laurens St.
Kerrison, C. & E. L. Dry Goods, Merchants, 201 King St.
Kerrison, Edwin L., Firm of C. & E. L. Kerrison, res. 6
Logan St.
Kerrison, William, Capt., Mariner, 2 Stoll's Al.
Kershaw, F., Mrs., 3 Orange St.
Kershaw, Newman, Planter, 10 Lamboll St.
Ketchum, Charles G., Dry Goods, 229 King St.
Ketchum, Joel, Clerk at Kerrisons, cr. King & Market Sts.
Kettleband, George, cr. Columbus & Meeting Sts.
Khen, John C., Grocer, cr. Middle & Laurens Sts.
Kiddle, Arthur, 2 Philadelphia St.
Kiddle, Charles, U. S. Appraiser, res. 35 Broad St.
Kilroy, Patrick, Boarding, 138 Church St.
King, G. W., Merchant, 9 Vendue Range res. 6 Meeting St.
King, George, Carpenter, res. n. King St.
King, John, Agent, Rail Road Depot, Mary St., btw King &
Meeting Sts.
King, John, Shoe Maker, 4 Whim Court
King, John, Sr., 67 Meeting St.
King, Mitchell, Firm of King & Walker, res. cr. Meeting &
George Sts.
King, W. S., Firm of A. S. Willington & Co., Editors,
Courier, 101 E. Bay St., res. 63 Broad St.
King, William A., Blacksmith, 15 Chalmers St.
King, William, Firm of King & Desaussure, Factors &
Commission Merchants, Hamilton's Whf., res. 21
Meeting St.
King, William, Lamp Maker, 96 King St.
King, R., Commission Merchant, Hamilton's Whf.
Kingdon, Rebecca, 37 Wall St.
Kingman, Ann, 15 College St.
Kingman, James, Accountant, cr. Middle & Minority Sts.
Kingman, John, Firm of Kingman, Ney & Co., Grocers,
185 E. Bay St., res. 122 E. Bay St.
Kingman, Samuel, Assistant Clerk, Planters &
Mechanics Bank, res. 8 State St.
Kingman, Sophia, Milliner, 18 Liberty St.
Kingman, Thomas, Carpenter, 15 College St.
Kinloch, Frederick, res. Mrs. Langlois', cr. Montague &
Pitt Sts.
Kinloch, George R., Firm of Kinloch, Phillips & Co., Corn
& Hay, 20 Vendue Range, res. Pritchard St.
Kinloch, Sophia, 15 Bull St., F.P.C.
Kinney, Ann, Boarding, 50 State St.
Kinsey, A., Mrs., Dry Goods, 322 King St.
Kirby, John, Catholic Seminary, 92 Broad St.
Kirkpatrick, John, 34 Broad St.
Kirkpatrick, John, Firm of John Kirkpatrick & Co.,
Factors, Exchange Whf., res. 21 Meeting St.
Kirkwood, William, Port Warden, res. 3 Laurens St.
Kleinback, John, Grocer, 62 Beaufain St.
Klien, John, 92 Wentworth St.
Klint, John, Grocer, cr. Coming & Boundary Sts.
Klint, Nicholas, Grocer, Gadsden's Whf.

Knapp, P. W., Accountant, cr. Church & Queen Sts.
Knee, Harman, Grocer, n. King St.
Knepley, Solomon, Blacksmiths, 82 Meeting St., res. 74
Meeting St.
Knevals S. W., Firm of Hull & Knevals, res. 147 Meeting
St.
Knight, James D., U. S. Navy, res. 20 Mazyck St.
Knowles, Elizabeth, Fancy Store, 184 King St.
Knox, Elizabeth S., Pritchard St.
Knox, W. P., Shipwright, Pritchard St.
Knox, Walter, Mrs., 10 Green St.
Knust, George, 31 Coming St.
Knust, Sarah, 31 Coming St.
Koernreeke, Albert, Grocer, cr. Elizabeth & John Sts.
Kohlman, Hammon, Grocer, 63 Tradd St.
Kohne, Eliza, Mrs., 108 Broad St.
Koster, Jacob, Grocer, 13 cr. Wentworth & Rutledge Sts.
Kouster, Augustus, n. King St.
Kraemer, Philip, Dyer, 111 n. King St.
Kramer, F., Carpenter, n. King St.
Kramer, G., Boot & Shoe Maker, 26 Queen St.
Kruse, -----, Capt., 55 Church St.
Kugley, Martha, 34 Mazyck St.
Kunhardt, W. W., Attorney, 7 Broad St., res. 35 Broad St.
Kunhardt, William, Commission Merchant, res. 35 Broad
St.
Kunze, Philip, n. Meeting St.
Ladson, Gregory, 2nd Lt., Citadel, n. of Boundary St.
Lafitte, A., Firm of A. Lafitte & Brother, Commission
Merchants, Central Whf., res. 49 Church St.
Lafitte, Edward, Firm of A. Lafitte & Brother, Commission
Merchants, Central Whf., res. 49 Church St.
Lafitteau, -----, Madame, 25 E. Bay St.
Lafitteau, S., 25 E. Bay St.
Lafourcade, John B., Confectioner, cr. Market & Meeting
Sts.
Lalan, Alexander, 2 Queen St.
Lalane, P. B., Bank of Charleston, n. King St.
Lamb, James, 199 Meeeting St.
Lambers, Catharine, 43 George St.
Lambert, Charles, Lambert & Brother, Merchants, 197 E.
Bay St.
Lambert, Eliza, 138 Church St.
Lambert, Rachael, 41 Queen St.
Lambert, Robert, Lambert & Brother, Merchants, 197
E.Bay St.
Lambert, W. C., Upolsterer, 41 Queen St.
Lamotte, James, Blacksmith, res. Beaufain St.
Lance, Francis, Broker, 4 State St., res. 11 Legare St.
Lance, Maurice H., Rev., Charlotte St.
Lance, William, Mrs., School, 84 Wentworth St.
Landershine, David P., Ship Carpenter, Marsh St.
Landreth, Robert & David, Seedsmen, 289 & 220 King St.
Lane, William G., Firm of Wiley, Lane & Co., Wholesale
Dry Goods, 3 Hayne St., res. George St., near King St.
Langan, Michael, 20 S. Bay St.
Langley, J. D., Mrs., 39 Queen St.
Langley, William, 39 Queen St.
Langlois, -----, Madame, Seminary, 16 Montague St., cr.
Pitt St.

Lanneau, Bazil, Merchant, 89 E. Bay St., res. 7 Pitt St.
Lanneau, Charles H., Teller, Planters & Mechanics Bank, res. 52 Church St.
Lanneau, F., Firm of G. B. Lock & Co., Commission Merchants, 66 E. Bay St., res. 39 Coming St.
Lanneau, Peter, Firm of Bannister & Lanneau, Dry Goods, 2 Hayne St.
Lapene, John, Gardner, 54 n. King St.
Larkin, John, Grocer, 124 Church St.
Larkin, Patrick, Tailor, 117 Church St.
LaRoche, John G., Notary Public, Meeting St., near Shakspeare
Larousselliere, L., Dr., Pritchard St.
Larousselliere, -----, Madame, 108 King St.
Lassen, Hans, Boarders, 20 Elliott St.
Lathrop, James, 8 Savage St.
Lauchlin, A. M., Firm of John Dunovant & Co., Factors, Fitzsimmons' Whf., res. New Hotel
Laurence, Robert, 30 King St.
Laurens, Ed R., Master in Equity, 38 Broad St., res. 8 Montague St.
Laurens, Henry, Mrs., 188 E. Bay St.
Laurens, Mary, 34 Meeting St., F.P.C.
Laval, Jacinth, Boarders, 17 State St.
Laval, William, State Treasurer, Lower Division, res. George St.
Lawrence, George, Rigger, 3 Motte's Ln.
Lawrence, Sarah, 8 Church St.
Lawton, George, Attorney, 28 S. Bay St.
Lawton, George, Firm of Joye, Lawton & Co., Grocers, 57 E. Bay St., res. 26 S. Bay St.
Lawton, Joseph, Merchant, 40 E. Bay St.
Lawton, R. B., Tavern, 21 Queen St.
Lawton, William M., Firm of Taylor, Lawton & Co., Factors, 13 Southern Whf., res. 12 Lamboll St.
Laypayne, Joseph, cr. Boundary & Wall Sts.
Lazarua, B. D., 80 Tradd St.
Lazarus, Joshua, 202 E. Bay St.
Lazarus, Michael, Broker, King St.
Lazarus, -----, Mrs., 80 Tradd St.
Lea, John, Capt., Pilot, Zig Zag Al.
Lea, W. P., Capt., Pilot, Zig Zag Al.
Lea, William, Capt., Zig Zag Al.
Leader, Mary, 9 Short St.
Leary, Ann, cr. Meeting & Society Sts.
Leaumont, Margaret, 2 Minority St.
Leaumont, R., 98 E. Bay St.
Leavit, William, Boarders, 11 Elliott St.
Lebby, -----, Capt., Mariner, Lower end Church St.
Lebby, N. H., Amen St.
Lebby, Thomas F., res. Amen St.
Lebby, William L., Amen St.
Lebuff, Francis, Painter, 24 State St.
Lecher, Henry, Grocer, cr. Cannon & n. St. Philip Sts.
Lechmore, Henry, Accountant, 14 Church St.
Leckie, David., Firm of Miller & Leckie, Corn & Hay Store, 70 n. King St.
Lee, Charlotte, Mantuamaker, 55 Broad St., F.P.C.
Lee, Edward, Barber, 55 Broad St., F.P.C.
Lee, John, Jones Hotel, 67 Broad St., F.P.C.

Lee, Lawrence, Dr., cr. Meeting & Cumberland Sts.
Lee, Thomas, Mrs., 38 Pitt St.
Lee, W. H., Firm of Lee & Pressley, Attorneys, 90 Church St., res. 77 Broad St.
Lee, William, Teller, Bank of State of S.C., res. Alexander St.
Legare, Daniel, Jr., Dr., 3 Guignard St.
Legare, Daniel, Sr., 3 Guigard St.
Legare, Hugh S., Hon., Attorney, 81 Broad St., res. 32 Bull St.
Legare, J. D., Editor, Agricultural Journal, Office 48 E. Bay St.
Legare, James, Firm of Legare & O'Hear, Factors, Commercial Whf., res. Radcliffborough
Legare, James, Mrs., 128 Bull St.
Legare, James, res. Vanderhorst St.
Legare, John B., Attorney, res. 195 E. Bay St.
Legare, -----, Mrs., 114 Tradd St.
Legare, Sarah, Miss, School, 6 Bull St.
Legare, Thoms, 42 S. Bay St.
Lege, Joseph, Washington St.
Lege, Maria, 69 Queen St.
Lege, William, Grocer, 69 n. King St.
Legge, Maria, 28 Middle St.
Legerix, John P., Firm of Peter Drege & Co., Clothing, res. 139 E. Bay St.
Lehre, Thomas, Col., Ordinary, res. cr. Pitt & Wentworth Sts.
Lehrs, John, Grocer, cr. Anson & Hasell Sts.
Leitch, Jane, 2 Wall St.
Leitch, Martin, Bricklayer, 205 Meeting St.
Leitchstenstein, L., at Dr. Porcher's, Church St., cr. Cunberland St.
Leland, David W., Firm of Leland Brothers & Co., Commission Merchants, Commercial Whf.
Leland, Joseph, Firm of Leland Brothers & Co., Commission Merchants, Commercial Whf.
Lemon, Edward P., Firm of Kingman, Ney & Co., Grocers, 185 E. Bay St., res. Mary St.
Lemon, James, Nassau St.
Lenox, William, Bar Keeper, res. 5 Philadelphia St.
Leonard, James, Blacksmith, Society St., near E. Bay St.
LePrince, A., 113 King St.
LeRoy, E. & N., 156 King St.
Lesesne, Ann, 14 New St.
Lesesne, Daniel, Firm of G. Y. Davis & Co., res. Radcliffborough
Lesesne, Henry D., Firm of Petigru & Lesesne, Attorneys, 12 St. Michael's Al., res. 8 Green St.
Leslie, Oliver, 136 King St.
Levy, -----, & Pascoe, Book Binders, cr. King & Queen Sts.
Levy, A., Dry Goods, 177 E. Bay St.
Levy, D. C., Commission Merchants, Vendue Range, res. 15 Pitt St.
Levy, E. L., 28 Vendue Range, res. 8 Beaufain St.
Levy, Elias, Gauger, res. 28 Lightwood Al.
Levy, Elias, Jr., Accountant, n. King St.
Levy, Emanuel, w. end Beaufain St.
Levy, Isreal, w. end Beaufain St.

114

Levy, L. L., Firm of Levy & Ancker, Clothing, 189 E. Bay St.
Levy, Mark, Firm of Fles & Levy, 190 King St.
Levy, Mary, Clothing, 47 State St.
Levy, Moses, Constable, 21 Berresford St.
Levy, Moses, Mrs., cr. Society & E. Bay Sts.
Levy, -----, Mrs., 9 Short St.
Levy, Thomas, Printer, res. 25 Tradd St.
Lewis, Henry P., Accountant, 107 E. Bay St.
Lewis, Isaac, 27 King St.
Lewis, John, Clerk, 98 Queen St.
Lewis, John, Mrs., 12 Meeting St.
Lewis, John, Shoe Maker, 9 Liberty St., F.P.C.
Lewis, John W., 12 Meeting St.
Lewis, Mary, 8 Magazine St., F.P.C.
Lewis, Phoebe, 12 Philadelphia St., F.P.C.
Lewis, Richard, Carver, 71 king St.
Lewis, Sarah E., Seamstress, res. Burns Ln., F.P.C.
Leyman, C. H., Grocer, cr. Nassau & Mary Sts.
Lieure, Peter, Clothing, 87 E. Bay St.
Lightburn, Eliza, 13 Pinckney St.
Ligneiz, P., French Coffee House, E. Bay St.
Limehouse, Robert, 113 Tradd St.
Lincoln, Sarah, 10 Anson St., F.P.C.
Lindergreen, Charles F., Mariner, 4 Linguard St.
Lindsay, C., Butcher, Cannon St.
Lindsay, R., 1 S. Bay St.
Lindsay, Samuel, 1 S. Bay St.
Lindsay, William, Merchant, 155 E. Bay St.
Lines, James, Jeweller, 151 King St.
Lins, Frederick, Grocer, 113 Queen St.
Little, Robert, Lumber Merchant, Little's Whf., res. Charlotte St.
Lloyd, William, Firm of Carter, Lloyd & Stock, Brokers, 6 Broad St., res. 65 Meeting St.
Lloyd, Joseph, Amherst St.
Lock, G. B., Firm of G. B. Lock & Co., Commission Merchants, 66 E. Bay St., res. 12 George St.
Locklea, John, Carpenter, Wolf St.
Lockwood, Betsey, Phildelphia St., F.P.C.
Lockwood, Caroline, 77 Broad St.
Lockwood, Corinthia, Philadelphia St., F.P.C.
Lockwood, J. A., Wheelwright, 122 Church St., res. 77 Broad St.
Lockwood, Jane, w. end Wentworth St., F.P.C.
Lockwood, Joshua W., Firm of Lockwood & Johnson, Mill Wrights, 4 Hard Al., res. 77 Broad St.
Lockwood, Laura, Philadelphia St., F.P.C.
Lockwood, Thomas P., Teacher, Orphan House, res. 379 King St.
Logan, Ann, 8 Orange St.
Logan, G. W., Attorney, cr. Lynch & Wentworth Sts.
Logan, George, Dr., cr. Wentworth & St. Philip Sts.
Logan, -----, Mrs., 30 Archdale St.
Logan, William, Librarian, Charleston Library, cr. Church & Broad Sts.
Long, Florian H., Shoe Maker, 113 King St.
Long, Joseph H., Firm of Longley & Long, Architects, 43 Queen St., res. 64 Queen St.
Long, R. A., Merchant, Magwood's Whf., res. Tradd St.

Long, S. H., Shoe Maker, 113 Church St., F.P.C.
Longley, James A., Firm of Longley & Long, Architects, 43 Queen St.
Lopez, Aaron, Dr., 7 Meeting St.
Lopez, Catharine, 117 Wentworth St., F.P.C.
Lopez, David, Carpenter, w. end Queen St., res. 12 Short St.
Lopez, -----, Mrs., 22 Cumberland St.
Lopez, William, Barber, 100 Meeting St., F.P.C.
Lord, A. B., Officer of Customs
Lord, Mary E., Boarders, 27 Middle St.
Lord, Richard, 56 Beaufain St.
Lord, Samuel, Firm of Lord & Stocker, Commission Merchants, 84 E. Bay St., res. 1 Maiden Ln.
Losee, Timothy B., Firm of Brown, Oliphant & Co., 287 King St.
Louis, D., 117 Queen St.
Louis, L., Nautical Instruments, 50 E. Bay St.
Love, Frances, 112 Tradd St.
Lovegreen, Andrew, Merchant, 312 King St.
Lovell, H. F., Mrs., 112 Tradd St.
Lowden, G. L., Merchant, 26 E. Bay St., res. 54 Meeting St.
Lowndes, Charles T., Firm of Herkenrath & Lowndes, Commission Merchants, Hamilton's Whf., res. 27 E. Bay St.
Lowndes, Emma, 18 Church St., F.P.C.
Lowndes, James, Mrs., 14 Meeting St.
Lowndes, Pinckney, 6 Short St.
Lowndes, Thomas, 100 Broad St.
Lowther, Thomas, Carpenter & Undertaker, 113 King St.
Lozier, John, Eagle Tavern, 119 E. Bay St.
Lubbock, William, Capt., 35 King St.
Lubet, Caroline, Mantuamaker, 19 Pinckney St., F.P.C.
Lucas, Benjamin, Bricklayer, Savage St.
Lucas, Jonathan, Merchant, Vanderhorst's Whf., res. Cannonborough
Ludson, Thomas, 9 Smith St.
Luken, Henry, Grocer, Cannon St.
Lunquest, John M., 51 Broad St.
Lusher, Joseph O., Dr., 84 Broad St.
Lynah, E., Mrs., 47 Coming St.
Lynah, James, Planter, 194 E. Bay St.
Lynch, F. C., Mrs., Fancy Store, 317 King St.
Lynch, F. C., Tailor, 317 King St.
Lynch, Margaret, 14 Wall St.
Lynes, John R., Painter, res. 10 Friend St.
Lynes, M., n. St. Philip St.
Lyon, George, Watch Maker, 127 E. Bay St.
Lyon, Handford, Firm of Harall, Hare & Co., Saddlery, 4 Hayne St., res. 59 Queen St.
M'Burney, William, Firm of Hyatt, M'Burney & Co., Dry Goods, 9 Hayne St., res. 29 George St.
Macanfuss, Benjamin, President St.
Macaulay, George, 76 Church St.
Macbeth, Charles, Attorney, Firm of Yeaden & Macbeth, res. 9 Legare St.
Macbeth, James, Firm of James Robertson & Co., Merchants, 12 Hamilton's Whf., res. 38 Church St.
Macbeth, Robert, Clerk, Market St., res. 21 King St.

Mack, James, Merchant, King St., cr. Reid St.
Mack, Lewis, Tailor, 49 George St., F.P.C.
Mackay, A. G., Dr., res. Boundary St.
Mackay, -----, Miss, School, n. King St.
Mackie, Louisa, Mrs., 32 n. King St.
Mackie, Margaret, Mrs., 79 Broad St.
Mackie, -----, Mrs., 8 Friend St.
Mackie, Thomas B., Post Office, res. 8 Friend St.
Madden, John, Marble Polisher, 3 Motte's Ln.
Magrath, A. G., Attorney, 23 Broad St., res. 148 E. Bay St.
Magrath, John, Firm of John Magrath & Son, Factors,
   Fitzsimons' Whf., res. 148 E. Bay St.
Magrath, W. J., Firm of John Magrath & Son, Factors,
   Fitzsimons' Whf., res. 148 E. Bay St.
Magruder, T., Rev., Editor, Southern Christian Herald, 71
   Broad St.
Maguire, A., Mrs., 36 Church St.
Magwood, Charles A., Firm of Patterson & Magwood, res.
   5 Smith St.
Main, A. R., Dry Goods, 46 Anson St.
Main, W. B., Ship Carpenter, res. 15 Bull St.
Mairs, Levy, Dry Goods, 229 King St.
Mairs, Samuel, Ship Carpenter, Hasell St., near E. Bay St.
Malcombe, M., Merchant, n. King St.
Mallery, Sarah, Boarders, 76 Broad St.
Malone, T. W., Firm of Rhett & Malone, Attorneys, 64
   Broad St., City Hotel
Mandles, Burley, 33 Church St.
Manigault, Ann H., Mrs., 16 Meeting St.
Manigault, Charles, 6 Gibbes St.
Manigault, Joseph, cr. Meeting & Charlotte Sts.
Manigault, Joseph, Planter, cr. Meeting & John Sts.
Manke, Henry, Boundary St.
Mann, George, Grocer, 22 Bull St.
Mann, John, Bricklayer, 37 Boundary St.
Manson, George R., Ship Carpenter, cr. Vernon & Marsh
   Sts.
Manvel, John, Carpenter, w. end Queen St.
Margent, George, Pinckney St., Neck
Margent, John H., Pinckney St., Neck
Marienhoff, J. M., Tavern, 7 Elliott St.
Marin, Jacob, Blacksmith, res. 27 Coming St.
Marin, Mary, 63 Beaufain St., F.P.C.
Marion, John, Confectioner, 293 King St.
Marion, Maria, Mrs., 12 King St.
Marion, -----, Mrs., Milliner, 135 King St.
Marklay, B. A., Warren St.
Marks, Joseph, Grocer, 8 Queen St.
Marks, William, Auctioneer & Broker, 171 E. Bay St.
Marsellon, F., n. King St.
Marsellon, James, Clothing, n. King St.
Marsh, James, Jr., Firm of James Marsh & Son, Ship
   Wrights, Marsh's Whf.
Marsh, James, Sr., Firm of James Marsh & Son, Ship
   Wrights, Marsh's Whf., res. 138 E. Bay St.
Marshal, Hariet, Mrs., 64 State St.
Marshal, J. T., Baker, 60 Tradd St.
Marshal, James, Grocer, 313 King St.
Marshal, John, Factor, Wharf St., res. Alexander St.
Marshal, Susan, 28 Coming St.

Marshal, T., Wharfinger, res. 101 Broad St.
Marshburn, James H., Officer of Customs, res. 39
   Boundary St.
Martin, Ann, Mrs., Boarding, 30 Elliott St.
Martin, Eliza, 9 Stoll's Al.
Martin, J. B., Shoes, 334 King St.
Martin, John N., Bricklayer, 64 King St.
Martin, Lewis V., Bricklayer, n. Coming St.
Martin, Nicholas, Bricklayer, n. King St.
Martin, Robert, Merchant, Boyce's Whf., res. Charlotte St.
Martin, T. S., Accountant, 87 E. Bay St.
Martin, Thomas, Attorney & Magistrate, 52 E. Bay St.
Martin, William M., Agent, Insurance Co., 9 Broad St.
Masias, S. H., 34 St. Philip St.
Mason, George, Assistant Clerk, Union Bank, res. 22
   Atlantic St.
Mason, Mary, Mrs., Milliner, 138 King St.
Massa, Antonio, Firm of Antonio & Co., Fruits, 106 King
   St.
Massa, Joseph, Firm of Antonio & Co., Fruits, 106 King
   St.
Massot, H., Watch Maker, 4 Queen St.
Massot, Horace, Wharfinger, Central Whf., res. 5 Queen
   St.
Matheissen, Conrad F., 157 King St.
Mathews, Edward W., Firm of Mathews & Habersham,
   Factors, cr. E. Bay St. & Southern Whf., res. 17 E. Bay
   St.
Mathews, Isaac, Livery Stables, 94 Broad St., F.P.C.
Mathews, J. B., Tailor, 61 Boundary St., F.P.C.
Mathews, James, Firm of Mathews & Bonneau, Factors,
   Hamilton's Whf., res. 43 Anson St.
Mathews, Mary, 2 Lamboll St.
Mathews, Nathan, Broker, 17 State St.
Mathews, Simon, 15 Savage St., F.P.C.
Mathews, Thomas, 31 Friend St.
Mathews, William, Planter, Charlotte St.
Mathey, Charles, Watch Maker, 153 King St.
Mathiessen, Eliza, Mrs., 5 Laurens St.
Mathiessen, F. C., Firm of Gourdin & Mathiessen & Co.,
   Commission Merchants, Commercial Whf., res. E. Bay
   St.
Mathiessen, Mathias, 29 Cumberland St.
Mathiessen, William, Firm of Poirier & Matheissen,
   Clothing, 137 E. Bay St., cr Queen St.
Maull, Philip, 36 Beaufain St.
Maxcey, Levi, Moulder, res. 1 Atlantic St.
Maxcey, Virgil, Jr., 1 Atlantic St.
Maxcey, Virgil, Sr., 1 Atlantic St.
Maxey, Flora, 3 Cumberland St. F.P.C.
Maxey, S. T., Bricklayer, Bridge St., Neck
Maxwell, James, Carpenter, 82 Beaufain St., F.P.C.
Maxwell, Mary, Hasell St., F.P.C.
May, Ann, 5 Magazine St., F.P.C.
May, John, Cabinet Ware Room, 66 Queen St.
Mayer, C., Artist, 80 Broad St.
Mayrant, Maria, 163 E. Bay St., F.P.C.
Mazyck, Alexander, Firm of Peronneau, Mazyck & Finley,
   Attorneys, 4 Court House Sq., res. 88 Wentworth St.
Mazyck, William, Jr., Firm of William Mazyck & Son,

Factors, Commercial Whf., res. n. Coming St.

Mazyck, William, Sr., Firm of William Mazyck & Son, Factors, Commercial Whf., res. 88 Wentworth St.

McAlpin, Mary, Mrs., Boaarders, 351 King St.

McAnally, -----, Mrs., 111 Tradd St.

McBeth, Hannah, 27 Wentworth St., F.P.C.

McBride, E., Mrs., Cannonborough

McBride, M., Hat Store, 336 King St.

McBride, Mary, 4 Montague St.

McBride, Mary, Mrs., 46 Church St.

McBride, P., Auctioneer, 28 Vendue Range

McBride, Patrick, Merchant, 192 King St.

McBurnie, William, Firm of Hyatt & McBurnie, Hayne St., res. 29 George St.

McCall, J. B., 14 Mazyck St.

McCall, Joseph, 15 Mary St.

McCall, Susan, Mrs., 8 Legare St.

McCall, William H., Grocer, n. King St.

McCanna, Catharine, 49 Beaufain St.

McCannon, Caroline, Amen St.

McCants, Nancy, 12 Savage St., F.P.C.

McCarter, James J., Firm of James J. McCarter & Co., Bookstore, 112 Meeting St., res. 112 Meeting St.

McCartney, Alexander, Firm of McCartney & Gordon, Hardware Merchants, 15 Broad St.

McCartney, John, Boundary St.

McClentic, M., Mrs., 345 King St.

McClentic, Mary Ann, 8 Coming St.

McClure, John B., 14 Mazyck St.

McCormick, John, Auctioneer, 13 Vendue Range

McCormick, T., Clerk, S. C. Society

McCready, Edward, Firm of McCready & Caldwell, Attorneys, 87 Meeting St., District Attorney, U. S. Court House, res. 4 Anson St.

McCready, Jane, Mrs., 4 Anson St.

McCready, M. C., Milliner, 53 Meeting St.

McCready, Morris, 11 John St.

McDonald, Alexander, Grocer, 302 King St., res. 24 George St.

McDonald, Hugh, Broker, res. 24 George St.

McDonald, -----, Mrs., 62 King St.

McDonald, William H., Pilot, 42 Church St.

McDowall, Andrew, Firm of McDowall, Hayne & Co., Commission Merchants, 30 & 32 E. Bay St., res. 121 King St.

McDowell, Baker, 11 n. King St.

McDowell, Robert H., Hardware, 373 King St.

McFadden, James, Boot Maker, 34 Queen St.

McFeely, -----, Miss, 46 Beaufain St.

McGee, Hall T., Firm of Shannon & McGee, Boyce's Whf.

McGillvry, J. G., Accountant, 16 Atlantic St.

McGillvery, John, 14 Pinckney St.

McGillvery, W. S., Carpenter,16 Atlantic St.

McGinley, Samuel, Blacksmith, 15 Price's Al.

McGinnis, Joseph, Millwright, Charlotte St.

McGinnis, Patrick, Butcher, Cannon St.

McGoveran, Ann, 18 S. Bay St.

McHugh, F. Q., Attorney, 86 Church St., res. 47 Beaufain St.

McHugh, Mary Q., Mrs., 47 Beaufain St.

McI'Lhenny, Planter, Bridge St., Neck

McIntire, John, 136 Tradd St.

McIntire, John, Merchant, 91 King St.

McIntire, Mary, Mary St.

McIntire, -----, Mrs., 136 Tradd St.

McIntire, Peter, Rob Roy House, Market St., near Meeting St.

McIntosh, D. N., w. end Beaufain St.

McIntosh, Donald, Merchant, 45 n. King St.

McIntosh, Sarah, 5 Bull St.

McIntosh, W., Carpenter, President St.

McKee, Abel, Ship Joiner, cr. Market & E. Bay Sts., res. 20 Pinckney St.

McKee, John, Factor, 2 Vendue Range, res. n. King St.

McKeegan, John, Blacksmith, 174 Meeting St.

McKenzie, -----, Butcher, Columbus St.

McKewn, Mary, Henrietta St.

McKewn, Mary, Mrs., 5 Boundary St.

McKinlay, Archibald, 44 Coming St., F.P.C.

McKinlay, George, Tailor, 44 Coming St., F.P.C.

McKinlay, Peter, Grits Mill, Doughty St.

McKinlay, W. & A., 30 King St.

McKinlay,William, Tailor, 44 Coming St., F.P.C.

McKinney, C., 152 King St.

McKinsey, Mary, Pastry, 63 Anson St.

McKinzie, Archibald, Saddlery, 105 Church St., cr. Chalmers St.

McKinzie, Benjamin F., Merchant, 271 King St.

McLaughlin, Edward, Mariner, 2 Chalmers St.

McLean, Diana, 82 King St., F.P.C.

McLean, Hugh, Farmer, n. Meeting St.

McLean, Stephen, Carpenter, 87 Queen St., F.P.C.

McLean, William, Farmer, King St. Road.

McLean, William, Firm of McLean & Whitty, Seedsmen, cr. E Bay & Pinckney Sts., res. Neck

McLeish, Archibald, Pattern Maker, 3 Wharf St.

McLeish, James, Engineer, 1 Wharf St.

McLeish, William, Dry Goods, 90 Church St.

McMillan, John, Commission Merchant, res. 29 Queen St.

McMillan, Thomas, 7 Price's Al.

McMillan, Thomas J., Boat Builder, res. 115 Church St.

McNamara, M., Grocer, 13 King St.

McNamee, James, Boot Maker, 20 Queen St.

McNeill, Ann, 128 Queen St.

McNeill, John, Warren St.

McNeill, Mary, Mrs., 111 Tradd St.

McNeill, Neill, Firm of McNeill & Blair, Grocers, 44 Broad St., res. cr. Broad & Church Sts.

McNellage, John, Sail Maker, res. Reaper's Al.

McNicholas, Patrick, 3 Motte's Ln.

McOwens, Patrick, Accountant, 33 St. Philip St.

McPherson, James, Planter, 263 E. Bay St.

Meacher, Thomas, Miller & Corn Store, 52 Queen St.

Mealy, John, 15 Pitt St.

Mealy, Stephen, Rev., res. Cannonborough

Meazenmuzen, Charles, Columbus St.

Meines, C., Grocer, 34 Tradd St.

Memminger, C. G., Firm of Memminger & Jervey, res. cr. Wentworth & Smith Sts.

Mendenhall, M. T., Firm of Fort, Townsend &

Mendenhall., res. Henrietta St.

Menlove, Edward, Commission Merchant, 10 Fitzsimons' Whf., res. 57 Church St.

Menude, Alexander, Farmer, n. King St.

Mere, James, Accountant, res. New Hotel

Mertins, F., cr. Coming & Vanderhorst Sts.

Messervey, P. J., 17 Broad St.

Metzler, William, Grocer, 71 Tradd St.

Meyer, C., Music, 123 Meeting St.

Meyer, G., Butcher, cr. Cannon & Coming Sts.

Meyer, Henry, Grocer, cr. King & Radcliff Sts.

Meyer, John, City Marshal, 76 Wentworth St.

Meyer, John H., Grocer, Boundary St.

Meyer, Luder, Grocer, 83 n. King St.

Meyers, Jacob, Grocer, cr. Boundary & Coming Sts.

Michell, F., Confectioner, 58 n. King St.

Michell, F., District Coroner, 52 E. Bay St, res. n. Coming St.

Michell, Flora, 103 Queen St., F.P.C.

Michell, John, Notary Public & Auctioneer, 52 E. Bay St., res. n. St. Philip St.

Michell, M. C., Furniture, 37 Market St.

Michell, William, Dr., 78 Queen St.

Middleton, Henry A., Planter, 98 Broad St.

Middleton, Henry, cr. Boundary & Smith Sts.

Middleton, Russell, 117 Boundary St.

Middleton, Thomas, Factor, Hamilton's Whf., res. 10 Meeting St.

Mier, Jacob, Grocer, 25 Boundary St.

Mignot, R., late French Coffee House, res., cr. Anson & Hasell Sts.

Mikell, E., Mrs., n. St. Philip St.

Miles, -----, Capt., 133 Boundary St., cr. Smith St.

Miles, Eliza S., 53 n. King St.

Miles,-----, Printer, 133 Boundary St., cr. Smith St.

Millar, Robert S., Baker, 137 Meting St.

Miller, A. E., Printer, 46 E. Bay St., res. 43 Tradd St.

Miller, Catharine, Mary St.

Miller, Elizabeth, 4 Pitt St.

Miller, Ephraim, Firm of Miller, Ripley & Co., Wholesale Dry Goods, 270 King St.

Miller, F., Grocer, 31 Tradd St.

Miller, George A., 4 Pitt St.

Miller, George N., Firm of Miller, Ripley & Co., Wholesale Dry Goods, 270 King St.

Miller, H., Grocer, 18 State St.

Miller, Horatio, Firm of Miller, Ripley & Co., Wholesale Dry Goods, 270 King St.

Miller, Jacob P, Rope Maker, Vanderhorst St.

Miller, James A., City Marshal, res. 2 Mazyck St.

Miller, John C., Factor, Exchange Whf., res. Mary St.

Miller, John D., Clerk, Board of Fire Masters, res. 14 Cumberland St.

Miller, John M., Wharfinger, Price's Whf., res. 54 Queen St.

Miller, John, Mrs., 31 E. Bay St.

Miller, Martha, 33 Meeting St.

Miller, Martha, Teacher, 83 Meeting St.

Miller, -----, Mrs., 32 Beaufain St.

Miller, Rosanna, 33 Meeting St.

Miller, Samuel Stent, Printer, 50 E. Bay St., res. 7 Wall St.

Miller, William, Firm of Stoddard, Miller & Co., res. cr. Coming & Wentworth Sts.

Miller, William, Jr., Firm of Miller & Leckie, Corn & Hay Store, 70 n. King St.

Milligan, John, n. St. Philip St.

Milligan, William, Old Iron, n. St. Philip St.

Milliken, Adam T., 80 Church St.

Milliken, Edward P., 80 Church St.

Milliken, J. B., Firm of Milliken & Co., Wholesale Grocers, 82 E. Bay St., res. 80 Church St.

Milliken, Thomas, Planter, 80 Church St.

Milliken, William, Firm of Milliken & Walton, Grocers, 108 E. Bay St., res. Commercial House

Mills, Clarke, Plasterer, Mary St.

Mills, James, 30 n. King St.

Mills, James, Mrs., n. King St.

Mills, M., Mrs., 107 Queen St.

Mills, Mary, 3 Montague St., F.P.C.

Mills, O., Firm of O. Mills & Co., Grain & Hay, 10 E. Bay St., res. 91 Meeting St.

Mills, S. S. & Beach, Commission Merchants, 26 Vendue Range

Milne, Andrew, Planter, 12 Rutledge St.

Milnor, J. G., Firm of Milliken & Co., Wholesale Grocers, 82 E. Bay St., res. 38 Broad St.

Minot, Elizabeth, 115 Queen St., F.P.C.

Minsey, Ann, 67 Boundary St.

Mintzing, Jacob F., 20 Friend St.

Miot, Charles H., Planters Hotel, cr. Queen & Church Sts.

Miscally, Daniel W., Accountant, Marsh St.

Mishaw, John, Shoe Maker, 55 Queen St., F.P.C.

Mishaw, Robert, Shoe Maker, 55 Queen St., F.P.C.

Missroon, Henry, Firm of Milliken & Co., Wholesale Grocers, 82 E. Bay St., res. 2 E. Bay St.

Missroon, James, Nautical Instruments, 51 E. Bay St., res. 2 E. Bay St.

Missroon, Margaret, 46 Church St.

Mitchell, Amelia, 25 College St.

Mitchell, Charlotte, 101 Wentworth St.

Mitchell, Charlotte, 162 Meeting St.

Mitchell, George, Boarders, 12 Princess St.

Mitchell, Harriet, Nurse, 2 Burns Ln., F.P.C.

Mitchell, J. S., 120 Wentworth St.

Mitchell, James S., Cooper, 36 E. Bay St.

Mitchell, John, Butcher, 16 Mazyck St., F.P.C.

Mitchell, -----, Misses, Milliners, 167 King St.

Mitchell, -----, Mrs., 8 Short St., F.P.C.

Mitchell, Nelson, Attorney, 8 St. Michael's Al.

Mitchell, Rebecca, 2 Washington St.

Mitchell, Robert, Blacksmith, 23 Boundary St.

Mitchell, S. C., Mrs., Coming St., cr. Boundary St.

Mitchell, Samuel, 61 Anson St.

Mitchell, William M., Boundary St.

Moffett, Andrew, Firm of Moffett & Calder, Merchants, 230 King St., res. 192 E. Bay St.

Moffett, George, n. St. Philip St.

Moise, Aaron, Assistant Cashier, Charleston Bank, cr. E. Bay & Broad Sts.

Moise, Abram, Attorney, 3 Court House Sq., res. 8 College

St.

Molen, Alexander, Dry Goods, 13 n. King St.

Monefeldt, Mary, 14 Mazyck St.

Monefeldt, William S., Dentist, 142 King St.

Mongomery, Andrew, Watchmaker, 296 & 328 King St., res. 8 George St.

Monk, Phoebe, Seamstress, 17 Savage St., F.P.C.

Monpeoy, Honore, Wood Factor, 42 Bull St.

Montesque, R., Tinner, 29 Market St.

Montgomery, Synthis, w. end Wentworth St., F.P.C.

Mood, Edward M., Pump Maker, 192 E. Bay, res. Charlotte St.

Mood, Peter & J., Auctionners & Commission Merchants, 297 King St.

Mood, W. G., Secretary to Sunday School Union, 83 Queen St.

Mood, William G., Firm of McDowall, Hayne & Co., Commission Merchants, 30 & 32 E. Bay St., res. 83 Queen St.

Moodie, J. G., Southwestern Railroad Bank, res. n. St. Philip St.

Moody, Elleanor, 17 Berresford St.

Moony, Ann, Dry Goods, 47 n. King St.

Moore, E., Mrs., Vanderhorst St.

Moore, George A., Printer, 9 Price's Al.

Moore, Hugh, Commission Merchant, Exchange Whf.

Moore, James, Coach Maker, 10 Wall St.

Moore, -----, Mrs., 16 Savage St.

Moore, W. B., Grain Store, 346 King St., res. n. Pitt St.

Moorehead, James, Grocer, 157 Meeting St.

Mordecai, Isaac, Firm of B. P. Colburn & Co., Dry Goods, 216 King St. res. 67 Beaufain St.

Mordecai, M. C., Commission Merchant, 24 Vendue Range, res. 47 Meeting St.

Mordecai, Thomas W., 17 Friend St.

Morgan, Benjamin, Capt., Mariner, 20 Middle St.

Morgan, Mary, 15 College St.

Morilla, N., Tavern, n. King St.

Morris, C. G., Iron Monger, 42 E. Bay St., res. 10 King St.

Morris, Edward, Teller, Union Bank, res. Mrs. Tunis

Morris, James, Rice Merchant, 62 E. Bay St., res. 19 Cumberland St.

Morris, Meekin, Barber, 39 Society St., F.P.C.

Morrison, Jane D., 57 Tradd St.

Morrison, Thomas, Cabinet Maker, 18 Tradd St.

Mortimer, Samuel, Firm of Gantt & Mortimer, Aucioneers & Brokers, 12 State St., res. Hudson St.

Mortimer, Thomas, n. Coming St.

Morton, W. R., Firm of H. W. Connor & Co., Hardware, 8 Hayne St., res. cr. Meeting & Queen Sts.

Moses, Caroline, 181 Tradd St.

Moses, Daniel L., Lodge Al.

Moses, Levy, Jr., Charlotte St.

Moses, Levy, Wolf St.

Moses, Perry, Dry Goods, 150 King St.

Moses, Solomon, Deputy Sheriff & City Marshal, res. 71 Wentworth St.

Mosiman, Julius, Accountant, 34 Chalmers St.

Mosiman, William, Painter, 34 Chalmers St.

Motta, S. A., Mrs., 97 King St.

Motte, F. T., Accountant, 26 Church St.

Motte, Isaac, Mrs., 24 Meeting St.

Motte, Mary W., 26 Church St.

Mottet, E., Firm of Thomas J. Rodger & Co., Commission Merchants, Hamilton's Whf., res. 13 Archdale St.

Moultrie, James, Dr., 16 Montague St.

Moultrie, Mary, 129 Boundary St., F.P.C.

Moultrie, Roxana, Seamstress, 129 Boundary St., F.P.C.

Moultrie, William, Barber, 129 Boundary St., F.P.C.

Mouzon, Charles, 2 St. Philip St.

Mouzon, L. H., Broker, 24 Chalmers St.

Mowry, Edward, Firm of Pringle & Mowry, Factors, Price's Whf., res. Planters Hotel

Mowry, Smith, Jr., Merchant, res. 50 Meeting St.

Muckenfus, Benjamin, 73 Beaufain St.

Muckenfus, Henry W., 73 Beaufain St.

Muckinfus, Henry, 110 Wentworth St.

Muggridge, -----, Mrs., Boarders, 241 King St.

Muhlenbrink, H. & George, Grocers, 146 E. Bay St.

Muir, Asa J., Book, Job & Fancy Printer, 73 E. Bay St.

Muir, Jane, Mrs., Boarders, 24 Broad St.

Muir, Lydia, Mrs., Boarders, 73 E. Bay St.

Mullings, John, Pilot, 1 Stoll's Al.

Mullins, Charles P., Constable, res. 26 Pinckney St.

Mullins, John, Carpenter, 82 Anson St.

Munds, Israel, Rev., 35 State St.

Munn, B. S., Mrs., Corset Maker, 72 Meeting St.

Munn, B. S., Printer, 72 Meeting St.

Munn, Margaret, 46 Meeting St.

Munners, Jane, 7 Smith's Ln., F.P.C.

Munroe, M. E., Merchant, 3 Bedon's Al.

Munroe, Margaret, 46 Church St.

Murden, Eliza, School, 54 Society St.

Murdock, James, Dry Goods, 332 King St.

Mure, Robert, Accountant, res. at Mrs. Tunis'

Murphy, E., Mrs., 13 Back St.

Murphy, John, 89 Queen St.

Murphy, Timothy, 5 Lynch St.

Murray, Ann, 61 King St.

Murray, James, 16 S. Bay St.

Murray, James L., cr. S. Bay & King Sts.

Murray, Patrick & William, Hats, 13 Broad St.

Murray, -----, Plasterer, n. St. Philip St.

Murray, Rachael, 11 Montague St.

Murray, William C., Merchant, res. 13 Rutledge St.

Murray, William, Planter, Thomas St.

Murreli, John J., Factor, Holmes Whf., res. 21 Middle St.

Mushington, E., Pastry, 77 King St., F.P.C.

Musting, William, 26 Berresford St., F.P.C.

Myer, C., Butcher, Columbus St.

Myer, Holtz, Grocer, 37 King St.

Myers, Cord, Miller, cr. Boundary & Coming Sts.

Myers, John, Capt., Mariner, 11 Wharf St., res. Alexander St.

Myers, M., Grits Mill, Warren St.

Nabb, John, 91 Church St.

Nabb, Sarah, Mrs., Fancy Store, 91 Church St.

Nailor, Peggy, n. Coming St., F.P.C.

Naser, Frederick, City Superintendant, Upper Division,

res. 10 Coming St.
Nathan, Myer, Clothing, 333 King St.
Nathans, Hester, 32 Archdale St.
Nathans, Nathan, Merchant, 10 n. King St.
Nayle, Vincent, Baker, 123 Church St.
Neill, Philip, 3 Legare St.
Nell, -----, Mrs., Amherst St.
Nelm, John W., 109 Wentworth St.
Nelson, Charlotte, Mantuamaker, 131 Boundary St., F.P.C.
Nelson, Hannah, 2 Zig Zag Al.
Nelson, Mary, w. end Wentworth St., F.P.C.
Nelson, William, Firm of Nelson & Smith, Tavern, 79 Queen St.
Nesh, William, Green St., cr. St. Philip St.
Neufville, Benjamin, 86 Anson St.
Neville, Edward, Mrs., 10 Short St.
Neville, H. W.
Neville, Joshua, Cabinet Maker, 98 Church St.
Neville, William
Newbold, Samuel, Grocer, 37 E. Bay St., res. 12 E. Bay St.
Newhall, Edward, Merchant, 72 & 128 King St., cr. Queen St.
Newton, Cornelia, 3 West St., F.P.C.
Newton, Susan, 3 West St., F.P.C.
Newton, William, Cannonborough
Newton, William M., 63 Beaufain St.
Neyle, P. A., Firm of P. A. Neyle & Co., Factors, Commercial Whf., res. 3 Legare St.
Nicholas, F., Grocer, Boundary St.
Nicholas, J. F., 9 George St.
Nicholia, J. H., Grocer, Market St., near King St.
Nicholson, Jane, 1 Cumberland St., F.P.C.
Nihans, F., Grocer, cr. Boundary & Smith Sts.
Nixon, J. B., Engraver, Market St., above King St.
Noble, George W., Firm of Tappan & Noble, Builders, Wentworth St., near E. Bay St.
Norman, George A., Mariner, 25 Tradd St.
Norris, James C., 1st Lt., City Guard, Guard House, Broad & Meeting Sts.
Norris, James C., Magistrate, res. Hampstead
Norris, Samuel, Blacksmith, Henrietta St.
North, E. W., Dr., 60 Meeting St., Res, 28 Montague St.
North, Edward, Dr., 60 Meeting St., res. 30 S. Bay St.
North, Priscilla, 3 Back St., F.P.C.
Northrop, C. B., Attorney, 67 Meeting St.
Nowell, J., Planter, Hampstead
Nowlan, -----, Mrs., Milliner, 257 King St.
Nunan, Eliza, 18 George St.
Nye, Albert, Firm of Kingman, Ney & Co., Grocers, 185 E. Bay St., res. 135 E. Bay St.
O'Brien, Jeremiah, 65 Beaufain St.
O'Brien, Stephen, Carpenter, 65 Beaufain St.
O'Brien, Thomas, Firm of Hieronymous & O'Brien, Livery Stables, 100 Church St., res. 101 Church St.
O'Connor, Arthur, Tailor, 63 Church St.
O'Connor, Elizabeth, Mrs., Boarders, 12 Mazyck St.
O'Dena, John, Saddlery, 282 & 339 King St.
O'Discoll, Eliza, Miss, 96 Tradd St.
O'Hanlan, Eliza, Mrs., 15 Middle St.
O'Hanlan, T. Carpenter, Boundary St.

O'Hanlan, William, Barber, Princess St., Victoria House, F.P.C.
O'Hara, Henry, Mrs., 3 Pitt St.
O'Hara, Joseph, n. Pitt St.
O'Hara, Julia, 7 Coming St., F.P.C.
O'Hear, James F., res. Radcliffborough
O'Hear, James, Firm of Legare & O'Hear, Factors, Commercial Whf., res. Radcliffborough
O'Leary, Daniel, Boat Builder, Hard Al.
O'Mara, John, Clerk, 103 Church St.
O'Neal, J., Firm of M. Roddy, Son & Co., 133 E. Bay St.
O'Neal, James, Carpenter, 18 Magazine St.
O'Neal, R., Rev., 92 Broad St.
O'Neill, Edmund, cr. Cannon & Rutledge Sts.
O'Neill, John, Butcher, Cannon St.
O'Neill, Patrick, Planter, Cannon St.
O'Reilly, Charles, Livery Stables, 23 Queen St.
O'Sullivan, Michael, 22 Elliott St.
Oakes, M., Grocer, 47 Market St., cr. Church St.
Oakes, Samuel, 47 Market St., cr. Church St.
Oakes, Z. B., 47 Market St., cr. Church St.
Oakley, R. S., 142 King St.
Oakley, William C., Merchant, 311 King St., cr. George St.
Oates, George, Music Store & Instruments, 218 King St.
Oberhausser, John, Dr., cr. Church & Linguard Sts.
Ogier, Eliza, 130 Queen St.
Ogier, T. L., Firm of Holbrook & Ogier, res. 41 E. Bay St.
Ogilvie, M., Firm of Birnie & Ogilvie, Hardward, 21 Broad St., res. 5 Logan St.
Ohlsen, John C., Grocer, 108 Tradd St.
Ohlsen, John, Grocer, cr. Pitt & Duncan Sts.
Olandt, Deideick, 1 Archdale St.
Olfers, John B., Grocer, 163 E. Bay St.
Oliphant, Edward, Firm of Brown & Oliphant, 287 King St.
Oliphant, Eliza, Mrs., 19 St. Philip St.
Oliver, John, Furniture, 70 Queen St.
Oliver, John G., Firm of Oliver & Ancrum, Tailors, res. 3 Montague St., F.P.C.
Oliver, John H., 25 King St.
Oliver, Nelly, 103 King St., F.P.C.
Oliver, Sarah, 3 Montague St., F.P.C.
Oliver, Susan, 103 King St., F.P.C.
Oliver, Thomas O., Accountant, at Mrs. Tunis', Vanderhorst's Whf.
Olney, George W., Commission Merchant, 11 Vendue Range, res. 33 Broad St.
Oltman, Henry, Grocer, cr. Market & Church Sts.
Oppenheim, H. W., cr. King & Hudson Sts.
Osborn, Catharine, Mrs., 34 S. Bay St.
Osborn, George, Capt., Mariner, 14 Princess St.
Osgood, S. S., Painter, 215 King St.
Ostendorff, John H., cr. E. Bay & Elliott Sts.
Osterholtz, E. H., Grocer, Thomas St.
Otis, -----, & Roulain, Carriage Depository, 195 Meeting St.
Otis, Walter Munroe, Accountant, 46 Church St.
Ottolengue, Abraham, 1 Pinckney St.
Owen, Leslie, Dentist, 136 King St.
Owens, Alexander, Butcher, Cannon St.

Owens, James, Lumber Merchants, N. Y. Packet Whf., res. 17 Lynch St.

Owens, Smart, Carpenter, 40 George St., F.P.C.

Oxlade, Thomas C., Watch Maker, 339 King St.

Oxlade, Thomas, House & Sign Painter, 6 Queen St.

O'Neill, J. F., Firm of M. Roddy, Son & Co., Provisions, 133 E. Bay St., res. State & Queen Sts

Page, James H., New Hotel, Meeting St., cr. Hayne St.

Page, John, 43 George St.

Paine, James, Deputy Sheriff, res. 126 Queen St.

Palmer, Emma, Pastry, 47 Coming St., F.P.C.

Palmer, J., Grocer, 2 Atlantic St.

Pando, Louis, Dry Goods, 336 King St.

Panknin, Charles, Druggist, cr. Church & Tradd Sts.

Pansin, Charles, Firm of Peter Drege & Co., Clothing, 139 E. Bay St., res. 31 Cumberland St.

Parker, Benjamin J., Accountant, 6 George St.

Parker, Charles, Capt., Citadel Guard, res. Citadel

Parker, Elizabeth, 31 Church St.

Parker, Elizabeth, 6 George St.

Parker, Isaac, 41 Beaufain St.

Parker, Mary, 53 Tradd St.

Parker, -----, Mrs., 5 Smith's Ln.

Parker, -----, Mrs., John St.

Parker, Peter, Mazyckborough

Parker,-----, Planter, Elizabeth St.

Parker, Robert L., Accountant, 6 George St.

Parker, S. D., Accountant, 6 George St.

Parker, S. P., Mrs., 1 Legare St.

Parker, William S., Carpenter, 62 Meeting St.

Parkerson, John, Bell Hanger, 90 Meeting St.

Parsals, William N., Furniture, cr. Meeting St. & Burns Ln.

Parsons, William, Planter, Washington St.

Parsons, William S., Painter, w. end Queen St.

Pascoe, John D., Book Binder, 67 Queen St., cr. King St.

Passaleague, Lewis, Baker, cr. Wall & Boudary Sts.

Passenaro, A. B., Grocer, Wolf St.

Patani, Jose, Fruits, 19 Market St.

Patrick, Casmier, Merchant, 38 E. Bay St., res. 3 Middle St.

Patrick, Philip, Jr., Collector, 78 King St.

Patrick, Philip, Sr., Notary Public, 78 King St.

Patten, George, Cabinet Maker, 294 King St.

Patterson & Magwood, Commission Merchants, Magwood's Whf.

Patterson, William, Accountant, 2 George St.

Patton, William, Agent, Steam Packets, 6 Fitzsimons Whf.

Paul, Dunber, Firm of Paul & Brown, Grocers, 47 Broad St.

Payne, James, 3rd Lt., City Guard, Guard House, Broad & Meeting Sts.

Payne, R. K., Civil Engineer, Fireproof Bldg., res. Drake St.

Payot, -----, Madame, Fancy Goods, 169 King St.

Peach, F., Shoe Maker, 89 Queen St.

Pecare, Harriet, n. Coming St.

Pecare, Jacob, Dry Goods, 340 King St.

Pelzer, H., Mrs., President St.

Pemberton, George O., Tailor, 71 Church St.

Pennal, Robert, Merchant, cr. Boundary & King Sts.

Perera, Domingo, Victualer, 14 Market St.

Perey, Ann, 67 n. King St.

Perey, James, cr. Cannon & Corning Sts.

Perkins, Caroline, 3 Philadelphia St.

Peronneau, Catharine, 113 Wentworth St.

Peronneau, Edward, Planter, Charlotte St.

Peronneau, H. W., Firm of Peronneau, Mazyck & Finley, Attorneys, 4 Court House Sq., res. 95 Tradd St.

Peronneau, J. F., Dr., 13 Cumberland St., res. 38 S. Bay St.

Peronneau, William, Import Inspector, res. 38 S. Bay St.

Perram, William, New Theater, Meeting St.

Perry, E., Mrs., n. Coming St.

Perry, James, 21 Montague St.

Perry, Julia, Milliner, 33 Broad St.

Perry, Stevens, Attorney, 81 Broad St., res. Duncan St.

Perry, William, 25 Montague St.

Perry, William, Notary Public, 79 E. Bay St., res. 103 E. Bay St.

Peters, James, Mrs., 39 Church St.

Peters, John, Grocer, Boundary St,

Peterson, George, n. St. Philip St.

Petigru, James L., Firm of Petigru & Lesesne, Attorneys, 12 St. Michael's Al., res. 113 Broad St.

Petit, Charles, Saddler, n. King St.

Petit, N. F., Tinner, 7 Queen St.

Petit, P., 178 King St.

Petsch, William, Engineer & Blacksmith, res. 5 Minority St.

Pettival, -----, Mrs., 128 Wentworth St.

Pezant, E. H., Accountant, 24 Laurens St.

Pezant, Louis, 7 Boundary St.

Pezant, Paul, Ship Carpenter, 7 Boundary St.

Pezant, Peter, Mariner, 24 Laurens St.

Philbrick, Daniel, Capt., cr. Market & Meeting Sts.

Philbrick, Mary A., cr. Market & Meeting Sts.

Phillips, Benjamin F., Firm of Phillips & Simons, Painters, 49 Queen St.

Phillips, John, Attorney, Church St., res. 54 Beaufain St.

Phillips, John, Capt., 4 Atlantic St.

Phillips, Otis, Firm of Kinloch, Phillips & Co., Corn & Hay, 20 Vendue Range, res. 48 Beaufain St.

Phillips, St. John, Dr., res. 52 Beaufain St.

Phin, E. C., Druggist, 31 Broad St.

Phin, Sarah, 1 Motte's Ln.

Picault, F. D., Dry Goods, 51 State St.

Pierce, Phineas, Ice House, Meeting St.

Pinceel, C. G., Shoe Maker, 65 n. King St., F.P.C.

Pinceel, Emanuel, Tinner, 182 Meeting St., F.P.C.

Pinckney, C. C., Engineer, Rail Road Route

Pinckney, Charles, res. 3 St Philip St.

Pinckney, H. L., Hon., Mayor, Council Chamber, res. 3 St. Philip St.

Pinckney, H. L., Jr., res. 3 St Philip St.

Pinckney, H., Miss, 193 E. Bay St.

Pinckney, -----, Mrs., 25 Pitt St.

Pinckney, R. Q., Maj., Surveyor, 38 Meeting St.

Pinckney, Roger, 28 King St.

Pinckney, Thomas, Col., 84 Broad St.

Pinckney, Thomas, Mrs., 9 King St.
Pipard, -----, Sexton, St. Mary's Church, res. 87
Wentworth St.
Plain, W. A., Officer of Customs, res. 36 Church St.
Plumeau, Francis, Coppersmith, res. John St., F.P.C.
Plumeau, J. F., 90 King St.
Pohl, Joseph, Distiller, 8 Coming St.
Poincignon, Anthony, Cooper, 15 Queen St.
Poincignon, E., Tinner, 15 Queen St.
Poincignon, John, Tinner, 3 Wharf St.
Poirier, E., Madame, 118 King St.
Poirier, Peter, Firm of Poirier & Matheissen, Clothing, 137
E. Bay St., cr Queen St.
Police, Francis, 60 Elliott St.
Pond, John, Capt., 21 Mazyck St.
Pool, Edward R., 87 n. King St.
Pool, W. L., Military Store Keeper, 70 n. King St.
Pooser, Matthias, Agent, Southern Methodist Book Room,
Hayne St.
Porcher, C., Mrs., John St.
Porcher, Catharine, 18 N. King St.
Porcher, F. Y., Dr., 131 Church St.
Porcher, H. S., Mrs., 16 Friend St.
Porcher, -----, Mrs., 30 John St.
Porcher, P. J., Broker, 9 State St.
Porcher, Peter, Dr., 49 Tradd St.
Porter, J. Y., Firm of William L. Porter & Son, Grocers, 35
Queen St., res. 33 E. Bay St.
Porter, John, Bricklayer, 33 E. Bay St.
Porter, Sarah, Mrs., 81 Church St.
Porter, William D., Attorney, 68 Broad St.
Porter, William L., Firm of William L. Porter & Son,
Grocers, 35 Queen St., res. 33 E. Bay St.
Post, Reuben, Rev., 26 Meeting St.
Postell, S., Mrs., Alexander St.
Potter, T. R., 229 E. Bay St.
Potter, -----, & Kelsey, Builders, Hayne St., res. 17 Anson
St.
Poulnot, Joseph, Farmer, Wolf St.
Power, J. M., Firm of Beach, Power & Boyce, Shoe Store,
10 Hayne St.
Powers, Thomas, Wolf St.
Poyas, James, Planter, 34 S. Bay St.
Pregnell, Henry, Firm of Alderson & Pregnell, Blind
Makers, res. 16 Tradd St.
Pressly, B. C., Firm of Lee & Pressly, Attorneys, 90
Church St., res. Mrs. Ralston's
Pressley, Margaret Jane, 31 George St.
Preston, James, Commission Merchant, 157 E. Bay St.
Preston, John, Grocery & Provision Store, 103 Church St.
Prett, William, Grocer, Wolf St.
Prevost, Joseph, 7 Pinckney St.
Price, Mary, 55 Coming St.
Price, William, Mrs., 87 Meeting St.
Prince, A. E., Mrs., Midwife, 32 Queen St.
Prince, Edward, 104 King St.
Prince, Edwin, Bricklayer, n. Coming St.
Prince, George, 32 Queen St.
Prince, John, Nassau St.
Prince, Mary, Boarders, 182 E. Bay St.

Prince, William, Book Binder, 104 King St.
Pringle, Ann, 156 Meeting St.
Pringle, B. G., Attorney, 7 Broad St., res. 17 Pitt St.
Pringle, Elizabeth, 156 Meeting St.
Pringle, George, Firm of Pringle & Mowry, Factors,
Price's Whf., res. n. King St.
Pringle, James R., Collector of Customs, res.
Cannonborough
Pringle, James R., Firm of James Adger & Co.,
Commercial Merchants, res. Cannonborough
Pringle, James R., Jr., Firm of James Adger & Co., res.
Cannonborough
Pringle, John J., 64 Tradd St.
Pringle, Robert, Mrs., 17 Pitt St.
Pringle, W. R., n. King St.
Prioleau, Martha, 4 Legare St.
Prioleau, Philip, Dr., 160 Meeting St.
Prioleau, T. G., Dr., Firm of Prioleau & Baron, Meeting
St., res. cr. Charlotte & Washington Sts.
Prior, William, Boot Maker, 117 Meeting St.
Pritchard, C. C., Dr., 233 E. Bay St.
Pritchard, Edward E., Accountant & Notary Public, 213 E.
Bay St.
Pritchard, Margaret, 36 Pinckney St.
Pritchard, Paul, 233 E. Bay St.
Proctor, William, 16 Cumberland St.
Prouten, Charles, Capt., 11 Water St.
Provost, Phillis, 219 E. Bay St., F.P.C.
Purdy, William T., 7 Mazyck St.
Purse, -----, Carpenter, cr. Boundary & St. Philip Sts.
Purse, -----, Gilder, res. 14 Orange St.
Purse, James, 36 Beaufain St.
Purse, R., Cabinet, 1 Coming St.
Purse, R. S., Grocer, cr. Wentworth & Pitt Sts.
Purse, Thomas F., Broker & Auctioneer, 25 Broad St., res.
15 Legare St.
Purse, William, Warren St.
Purvis, -----, Mrs., 119 Broad St.
Purvis, William, 121 Broad St.
Pyatt, Martha, Wolf St.
Quash, Albert, Jr., cr. Queen & Church Sts., F.P.C.
Quash, Albert, Sr., Barber, 2 Anson St., res. 34 Pitt St.,
F.P.C.
Quash, F. D., Planter, 2 Green St.
Quash, Robert H., Factor, cr. Boundary & Coming Sts.
Queery, H., Mrs., Boarding, 160 E. Bay St.
Quinby, E., Mrs., 45 George St.
Quinby, Joseph, House Carpenter, 35 Wall St.
Quinby, Lawrence, Carpenter, 45 George St.
Quinby, Thomas, Grocer, Hampstead
Quirk, William, Dr., Apothecary, 68 Church St.
Rabb, Jacob, Pump & Block Maker, 4 Market St.
Radcliff, John, Blacksmith, res. 103 Wentworth St.
Radcliff, Maria, Mrs., 103 Wentworth St.
Rallston, Sarah, Mrs., 70 Tradd St.
Rambo, S., Dentist, Dr., over Babcock's Book Store, King
St.
Rame, C., Society Rooms, 151 Meeting St.
Ramsay, Susan, 17 Rutledge St., F.P.C.
Ramsay, William G., Dr., 52 E. Bay St., res. 8 New St.

Raney, B., Carpenter, n. Coming St.
Rankin, William, Firm of Sproul's & Co., 16 Hayne St.
Ranlett, Charles H., Firm of H. Johnson & Co., 222 King St.
Ransay, Ellen, Miss, School, 66 Broad St.
Rantin, Caroline, Mrs., 28 Beaufain St.
Ratcliffe, Norman, Bricklayer, Spring St.
Ravenel, C., Mrs., 60 Broad St.
Ravenel, Daniel, President, Planters & Mechanics Bank, res. cr. E. Bay & Water Sts.
Ravenel, E., Dr., 42 Meeting St.
Ravenel, Henry, 2 Short St.
Ravenel, John, Firm of Ravenel & Stevens, cr. E. Bay & Water Sts.
Ravenel, John, Mrs., 69 Meeting St.
Ravenel, William, Firm of Ravenel & Stevens, cr. E Bay & Water Sts.
Raverna, J. D., Linguist, 95 Church St.
Rayne, Paul, Corset Maker, 231 King St.
Rebb, Lewis, Carpenter, 38 George St.
Receli, Carlo, Victualer, 3 Vendue Range
Reddock, Arthur, Carpenter, 3 St. Michael's Al.
Reddy, Ann, 42 Coming St., F.P.C.
Redfern, Edward, Saddler, 119 Church St.
Redmond, W. S., Firm of Green & Redmond, Commission Merchants, Central Whf., res. 67 Church St.
Reed, John Harleston, Planter, 4 Rutledge St.
Reed, Luke, Firm of J. R. Stevens & Co., 272 King St., non resident
Reed, Samuel H., Firm of Shegog & Reed, 57 Market St.
Reed, Sarah E., 14 St. Philip St.
Reeder, Oswell, 76 n. King St.
Reedy, James, Carpenter, 48 Queen St.
Reedy, -----, Mrs., 48 Queen St.
Reeves, M. S., Music Teacher, n. St. Philip St.
Reeves, Solomon, Carpenter, 16 Coming St.
Reicke, George, Grocer, cr. King St. & Burns Ln.
Reicke, Henry, Grocer, cr. Wentworth & St. Philip Sts.
Reid, Andrew, 107 King St.
Reid, C., Mrs., 25 Broad St.
Reid, Elizabeth, 21 Cumberland St.
Reid, George B., 10 Logan St.
Reid, George B., Bookkeeper, S. C. Bank, res. 4 Cumberland St.
Reid, James, Miller, 119 Queen St.
Reid, James, Scavenger, res. w. end Queen St.
Reid, Samuel H., Firm of Shegog & Reid, 57 Market St.
Reid, William, Dr., 31 Meeting St.
Reigne, B., Miss, n. St. Philip St.
Reigne, Louisa, 18 Queen St.
Reilly, H., Mrs., Dry Goods, 84 Church St.
Reilly, James P., Merchant, 165 King St.
Remley, Elizabeth, 16 St. Philip St., F.P.C.
Remley, Paul, Bricklayer, Boundary St.
Remley, Synthia, 16 St. Philip St., F.P.C.
Renbert, Isaac, Mrs., Marsh St.
Renneker, John, Grocer, cr. King & Queen Sts.
Renzy, Joseph, Carpenter, n. King St.
Requier, Elizabeth, Confectioner, 160 King St.
Reverie, J. P., 155 King St.

Reynolds, George N., Jr., Firm of George N. Reynolds & Son, Coach Makers, 93 & 95 Meeting St.
Reynolds, George N., Sr., Firm of George N. Reynolds & Son, Coach Makers, 93 & 95 Meeting St.
Rhett, James S., Firm of Rhett & Malone, Attorneys, 64 Broad St., res. Cannonborough
Rice, Henry S., Accountant, 23 E. Bay St.
Rice, William, Attorney, 65 Meeting St., res. 17 Legare St.
Rich, John, Coach Maker, 36 n. King St.
Richard, -----, Madame, 93 King St.
Richards, Frederick, Firm of Sebring, Egerton & Richards, Tailors & Drapers, 32 Broad St., res. 16 Broad St.
Richards, George R., Ship Smith, 132 E. Bay St.
Richardson, F. D., Firm of Smith & Richardson, Attorneys, 2 Hunt's Range, res. New Hotel
Richardson, Robert & Son, Bell Hangers, 97 Meeting St.
Riche, Samuel, Ann St.
Riggs, John, Saddler, 104 Wentworth St.
Righton, John M., Dr., Hampstead
Righton, Joseph, Sr., Cooper, 4 E. Bay St., res. 5 Water St.
Riley, William, Printer & Bookseller, 41 Broad St.
Rindernath, Joseph, Boarders, 107 n. King St.
Ring, David A., City Lamp Lighter, res. w. end Broad St.
Ring, George E., Auctioneer, 210 King St.
Ripley, N. & F., Ship Chandlers, 6 Vendue Range
Ripley, Samuel P., Firm of Miller, Ripley & Co., Wholesale Dry Goods, 270 King St., res. George St.
Ripley, T., Ann St.
Rippon, John, 18 King St.
Rivers, Carolina, Barber, 84 King St., F.P.C.
Rivers, David, Wharfinger, Exchange Whf.
Rivers, Mary, cr. Whim Court & King St.
Rivers, -----, Mrs., 32 Montague St.
Rivers, Nicholas, Factor, 18 E. Bay St.
Rivers, P. G., Carpenter, 1 Laurens St.
Rivers, W. T., Accountant, res. Mrs. Felders, Beaufain St.
Rivers, William, 121 Wentworth St.
Roach, Edward, City Treasurer, Council Chamber, res. Society St., near Anson St.
Roach, N., Smith St.
Roach, William, Mrs., Boundary St., btw. Pitt & Smith Sts.
Robb, James, Grocer, 186 King St.
Roberts, Owen, Dr., 193 King St.
Roberts, Venus, 11 Burns Ln., F.P.C.
Robertson, Alexander, Firm of Robertson & Thurston, Factors, 18 E. Bay St., res. 15 E. Bay St.
Robertson, Ann, Vanderhorst St.
Robertson, George, Firm of Robertson & Gilfillen, Factors, Magwood's Whf., res. 48 Meeting St.
Robertson, George, Mrs., res. 52 Meeting St.
Robertson, James, 145 E. Bay St.
Robertson, James, Firm of James Robertson & Co., Merchants, 12 Hamilton's Whf., res. 145 E. Bay St.
Robins, A., Fruits, 9 Market St.
Robinson, Adam, Accountant, 5 State St.
Robinson, Alexander, Agent, Augusta Insurance Co., 7 Broad St.
Robinson, Ann, 18 Wall St.
Robinson, James, Ann St.
Robinson, James K., Firm of Robinson & Caldwell,

Factors, Magwood's Whf., res. Judith St.

Robinson, John, Ann St.

Robinson, John, Firm of Robinson & Caldwell, Factors, Magwood's Whf., res. Judith St.

Robinson, Randall, Teller, Charleston Bank, res. Cannonborough

Robinson, Samuel, Firm of Robinson & Smith, Wholesale Grocers, 114 E. Bay St., res. Judith St.

Robinson, Samuel, n. St. Philip St.

Robinson, Stephen, Cashier, Planters & Mechanics Bank, res. Ann St.

Robinson, William James, Accountant, n. St. Philip St.

Rock, John, Grocer, cr. St. Philip & Boundary Sts.

Roddy, John A., Firm of M. Roddy, Son & Co., Provisions, 133 E. Bay St.

Roddy, Martin, Firm of M. Roddy, Son & Co., Provisions, 133 E. Bay St., res. cr. State & Queen Sts.

Rodgers, Charles, 6 Orange St.

Rodgers, Ebenezer, Firm of Blakely & Rodgers, 79 n. King St.

Rodgers, Lewis, Wheelwright, n. Meeting St.

Rodgers, Maria, 10 Stoll's Al. F.P.C.

Rodgers, S. B., Jeweller, 155 King St.

Rodgers, Thomas, Bennett's Mill, E. Bay St.

Rodrigues, B., Dr., Dentist, 213 King St.

Rodrigues, Sarah, Upholstery, 45 Queen St.

Roempke, A. F., Commission Merchant, 7 Hamilton's Whf.

Roger, Thomas J., Firm of Thomas J. Rodger & Co., Commission Merchants, Hamilton's Whf., res. 13 Archdale St.

Rogers, Bethel, res. 124 Queen St.

Rogers, Ebenezer, Firm of Blakely & Rogers, Merchants, 99 n. King St.

Rogers, G., Gilder, 158 King St.

Rogers, George, Head Quarters, cr. Queen & Meeting Sts.

Rogers, John R., Clerk of City Council, Council Chamber, res. 124 Queen St.

Rogers, John R., Jr., Engineer, res. 124 Queen St.

Rogge, Conrad, Grocer, 108 Tradd St.

Rohan, Robert, 5 Gibbs St.

Rolando, F. G., Cooper, 12 Exchange St., res. 9 Magazine St.

Ronan, William, Firm of Holst & Ronan, Country Store, 59 N. King St.

Rondeau, -----, Mrs., 149 King St.

Roorback, O. A., Boarding, 301 King St.

Roosevelt, H. L., Firm of Harris, Roosevelt & Baker, Merchants, 17 Hayne St., res. New Hotel

Roper, B. D., Attorney, 11 St. Michael's Al., res. 23 Legare St.

Roper, R. W., Planter, Battery & E. Bay St.

Roper, Richard, Firm of P. A. Neyle & Co., Factors, Commercial Whf., res. 3 Legare St.

Rose, Arthur G., Cashier, Bank of Charleston, res. 8 John St.

Rose, -----, Capt., Brig. Catharine, res. cr. Church St. & Longitude Ln.

Rose, E., Mrs., Cannonborough

Rose, James, President Southwestern Railroad Bank, res. 267 E. Bay St.

Rose, John, Grocer, Mary St.

Rose, Laurens, Carpenter, Cannonborough

Rose, -----, Misses, Elizabeth St.

Rose, Richard, Grocer, 66 Meeting St., cr. Queen St.

Rosenburg, Moses, Clothing, 13 Anson St.

Ross, Charlotte, 6 College St.

Ross, David, Carpenter, Vernon St.

Ross, David, Measurer, Wood & Coal, Motte's Ln.

Ross, George, Barber, 5 n. King St., F.P.C.

Ross, James L., 337 King St.

Ross, James, Ship Smith, Concord St., 24 Motte's Ln.

Ross, John, Engineer, Rail Road, res. Hudson St.

Ross, Mary, 6 College St.

Ross, Thomas, Wolf St.

Ross, William, Blacksmith, res. 4 Motte's Ln.

Rottereau, Adaline, 140 E. Bay St., F.P.C.

Rottereau, C., 80 King St.

Rottereau, John, Accountant, 80 King St.

Rouchet, Eugene, 54 Tradd St.

Roulain, Abraham, Firm of Otis & Roulain, cr. Anson & Society Sts.

Roulain, Catharine, 57 Anson St.

Roumelat, A., Confectioner, 71 Meeting St.

Roumelat, Eugene, Niagara Garden, cr. Meeting & Wolf Sts.

Roumelat, Ulysses, Confectioner, 52 Broad St.

Roupel, Mary, 102 Tradd St.

Rouse, William M., Silversmith, 178 E. Bay St.

Rout, William G., Outdoor Clerk, Commercial Bank, res. 12 Friend St.

Roux, Ann, 58 Beaufain St.

Roux, Christopher, Carpenter, 18 Vernon St.

Rowan, William, Merchant, n. King St.

Rowland, Robert, Wood Factor, 7 S. Bay St.

Roworth, -----, Mrs., 12 Liberty St.

Roye, Francis, 34 State St.

Ruby, Ann, 42 Coming St., F.P.C.

Ruger, Valentine, Planter, 3 Lamboll St.

Ruggles, Nathan, Shoes, 293 King St.

Rumph, G. H., Wolf St.

Runciman, John, Cannon St.

Runken, S. J., Grocer, Exchange St.

Rusell, John, Charlotte St.

Russ, John, Ship Carpenter, 19 Wall St.

Russ, Mary, 19 Wall St.

Russ, Richard, Bricklayer, 19 Wall St.

Russell, Benjamin, Mary St.

Russell, John, Firm of Russell & Sass, Auctioneers & Commission Merchants, 22 Vendue Range, res. Charlotte St.

Russell, Sarah, 9 Atlantic St.

Rust, John, Grocer, n. King St.

Rutland, Mary, 13 St. Philip St.

Rutledge, H. P., Mrs., 105 Tradd St.

Rutledge, John, Planter, n. King St.

Ryan, G. K., 6 Clifford St.

Ryan, James, 4 Whim Court

Ryan, John, Clerk, Streets & Lamps, res. 70 King St.

Ryan, John S., Wood & Coal Factor, Gibbe's Whf.

Ryan, Lawrence, City Sheriff, City Hall, res. 56 Church St.

Ryan, Thomas, Broker & Auctioneer, 18 State, res. 1 Washington St.

Ryan, William, Grocer, 108 Church St., cr. Chalmers St.

Ryley, Joseph, 19 Bull St.

Salstein, John, Ann St.

Salter, Thomas R., Carpenter, Pritchard St., res. 229 E. Bay St.

Saltus, Francis, Wharfinger, res. Guignard St.

Salvo, Conrad, 92 King St.

Salvo, G., Painter, 58 Broad St.

Sampson, H., Accountant, 131 E. Bay St.

Sampson, S., Clothing, 131 E. Bay St.

Sanders, John, 16 Pitt St., cr. Wentworth St.

Sanders, John, Boundary St.

Sanders, Joseph C., Bricklayer, Vanderhorst St.

Sanders, S., Barber, 43 Broad St., res. 3 St. Michael's Al.

Sankin, Deiderick, Grocer, Boundary St.

Sankster, Alexander, Ship Carpenter, res. 21 Boundary St.

Sargent, John H., res. 7 n. King St.

Sass, Edward G., Assistant Clerk, Market St., res. 57 Queen St.

Sass, Jacob K., Firm of Russell & Sass, Auctioneers & Commission Merchants, 22 Vendue Range, res. 57 Queen St.

Sass, R. F., Accountant, res. 57 Queen St.

Sassard, John, Capt., Mariner, 14 Laurens St.

Savage, Elizabeth, 5 Montague St., F.P.C.

Savage, Henrietta, 82 Anson St., F.P.C.

Savage, Patsey, 5 Montague St., F.P.C.

Savage, Sarah, 18 Savage St., cr. Broad St.

Sawyer, William, 350 King St.

Saxton, Julia, 61 Coming St., F.P.C.

Schachte, John, Grocer, cr. Vanderhorst & King Sts.

Schage, Deiderick, Tavern, Line St.

Scharff, Frederick, Grocer, cr. Boundary & Savage Sts.

Schem, Selina, Fruits, 27 Tradd St., F.P.C.

Scherfesee, A., Grocer, cr. Wentworth & St. Philip Sts.

Scherman, Carsten, cr. Meeting & Reid Sts.

Schirmer, Jacob F., Cooper, res. 120 King St.

Schirras, -----, Dr., res. 66 n. King St.

Schirras, Harriet, 8 Archdale St.

Schlusher, Charles, Mrs., Dry Goods, 33 State St.

Schmidt, Elizabeth, 13 Montague St.

Schmidt, J. W., Dr., 27 Church St.

Schmidt, John, Marion Coffee House, E. Bay St.

Schmidt, Martin, Grocer, 19 S. Bay St.

Schn, Henry, Grocer, Gadsden's Whf.

Schnierlie, John, Col., 11 Friend St.

Schnierlie, John M., Carpenter, 11 Friend St.

Schnierlie, William, Carpenter, 11 Friend St.

Schouboe, Frederick, Furniture, 84 Meeting St.

Schriemer, John H., Bacon Store, Gillon St., res. 231 E. Bay St.

Schrimer, William H., Cooper, res. 3 Linguard St.

Schroder, D., Mrs., Boarders, 180 Meeting St.

Schroder, Frederick, Grocer, Doughty St.

Schroder, George, Grocer, 15 Lynch St.

Schroder, Henry W., Merchant, 379 King St.

Schroder, Jacob, Grocer, cr. Market & Church Sts.

Schroder, Matilda, Dry Goods, 295 King St.

Schroder, William, 62 Anson St.

Schulte, Frederick, Coming St.

Schultze, Charles, Boat Maker, 11 St. Philip St.

Schwerin, Joseph, Firm of Schwerin & Brothers, Dry Goods, 121 E. Bay St.

Schwerin, M., Firm of Schwerin & Brothers, Dry Goods, 121 E. Bay St., res. 13 Broad St.

Schwing, Charles, Grocer, cr. St. Philip & George Sts.

Scott, Charles, 24 Montague St.

Scott, Eliza, Boarders, 357 King St.

Scott, Janes, 2 Montague St.

Scott, Margaret, 9 Pinckney St.

Scott, -----, Miss, Free School, 20 Beaufain St.

Scott, Rebecca, cr. St. Philip & Vanderhorst Sts.

Scott, William, Hair Dresser, 159 King St.

Scriven, Bethia, 57 Coming St.

Scriven, Hannah, Nurse, 12 Zig Zag Al., F.P.C.

Seabrook, Mary, 117 Broad St.

Seabrook, -----, Misses, 2 Logan St.

Seaman, Henry, Firm of Cook & Seaman, Grocers, cr. E. Bay & Tradd Sts.

Seba, B., Grocer, 55 Coming St.

Sebring, Edward, Firm of Dickinson, Sebring & Statham, Importers, 149 Meeting St., res. Cannonborough

Sebring, Edward, Firm of Sebring, Egerton & Richards, Tailors & Drapers, 32 Broad St., res. Cannonborough

Seebeck, Carsten, Grocer, cr. St. Philip & Radcliff Sts.

Segree, Romans, 10 Clifford's Al.

Seigling, John, Music Store, 219 King St.

Seignious, Charles, Coach Maker, res. 346 King St.

Seignious, Francis, Turner, 92 Meeting St.

Selin, Peter, Fruiterer, 11 Market St.

Selinas, C. G., City Hotel, 173 E. Bay St.

Seong, Caty, Pastry, 125 Boundary St., F.P.C.

Seybt, George, Tailor, 136 Church St.

Seyles, John H., Carpenter, 16 Bull St.

Seyles, Samuel, 12 Bull St.

Seyles, Wesner, Carpenter, 12 Bull St.

Seymour, Ann, 41 King St.

Seymour, Robert W., Attorney, 57 Meeting St., res. 7 Back St.

Seymour, William, 109 Queen St.

Shackleford, James M., Commission Merchant, Fitzsimons' Whf.

Shaffer, Frederick, Carpenter, cr. Boundary & Pitt Sts.

Shanks, Charles, Boot Maker, 53 Broad St.

Shannon, Thomas, Rev., Catholic Seminary, 92 Broad St.

Sharp, David, Wagon Yard, n. King St.

Sharpe, W. T., Washington House, n. Race Course.

Shaw, Matthias, Mariner, 2 Vernon St.

Shaw, Sarah, 5 Mazyck St.

Shea, B. F., Farmer, cr. Coming & Cannon Sts.

Shedel, George, Grocer, cr. Pitt & Bull Sts.

Shegog, George, Firm of Shegog & Reid, 57 Market St.

Shegog, Joseph, res. Meeting St.

Sheight, Samuel C., Firm of Henry & Sheight, American Hotel, 83 E. Bay St.

Shelton, -----, Mrs., 62 Archdale St.

Shepherd, Ann, 24 Coming St.

Shepherd, John J., Saddler, 22 Coming St.

Shepherd, William, Saddler, 28 Coming St.
Sheridan, Mathew, 11 Montague St.
Sheridan, Peter, 10 Clifford's Al.
Shilock, George, Mrs., 19 Rutledge St.
Shirer, Charles, Butcher, n. Meeting St.
Shively, C. G., Paints & Oil, 182 Meeting St.
Shoolbred, James, 30 Montague St.
Shoolbred, John, Dr., Boundary cr. Pitt St.
Short, James, Merchant, 89 n. King St.
Short, -----, Mrs., Wagon Yard, 91 n. King St.
Shrewsberry, Edward, Charlotte St.
Shroudy, W. B. T., Accountant, res. Nassau St.
Shulte, M., Mrs., 65 Queen St.
Shultz, George H., Carpenter, Ann St.
Shultz, George, Tavern, 2 Laurens St.
Shultz, John H., Farmer, res. Neck
Siddon, Joseph, Furniture, 53 State St.
Sieman, Herman, Grocer, 93 Queen St.
Siers,-----, Accountant, Warren St.
Siers, Peter, Carpenter, Warren St.
Sifley, Henry, Friend St.
Sifly, John, Bricklayer, Market St., near Meeting St.
Sigwald, John C., Carpenter
Sigwald, Mary, 4 Burns Ln.
Sigwald, Thomas, Carpenter, 4 Burns Ln.
Silcox, Daniel H., Sr., Furniture, 166 King St.
Silliman, -----, Mrs., Boarders, 7 Liberty St.
Simons, Ann, 3 Motte's Ln., F.P.C.
Simons, B. P., Painter, 6 Whim Court
Simons, Bella, 10 Short St., F.P.C.
Simons, Benjamin B., Dr., 14 Middle St., res. 277 E. Bay St.
Simons, Catharine, 93 Wentworth St., F.P.C.
Simons, Edward P., Mrs., 9 Laurens St.
Simons, Elizabeth, 3 Atlantic St.
Simons, Frances, 99 Tradd St.
Simons, Harriet, Mantuamaker, 114 Queen St., F.P.C.
Simons, Harris, Firm of Wragg, Simons & Co., Factors, Commercial Whf., res. Alexander St.
Simons, J. Hume, Dr., Coming St.
Simons, James, 50 Bull St.
Simons, James, Attorney, 51 Broad St., res. Alexander St.
Simons, John A., Planter, Hampstead
Simons, John C., Paints & Oil, 208 King St.
Simons, Joseph M., Editor, Medium, res. 49 Queen St.
Simons, Joseph W., Dr., Thomsonian, 347 King St.
Simons, Margaret, 5 Clifford St., F.P.C.
Simons, Mary, 6 Zig Zag Al., F.P.C.
Simons, Mary, 90 Anson St., F.P.C.
Simons, Morris, Jr., Mrs., 9 Laurens St.
Simons,-----, Planter, 10 Lynch St.
Simons, R. L., Mrs., Thomas St.
Simons, Sarah A., Boundary St.
Simons, Thomas G., Jr., Firm of Simons, Barnwell & Co., Factors, 2 Southern Whf., res. Vanderhorst St.
Simons, Thomas G., Sr., Firm of Simons, Barnwell & Co, Factors, 2 Southern Whf., res. 50 Bull St.
Simons, Thomas Y., Dr., 45 Church St.
Simons, W. C., Wharfinger, Commercial Whf.
Simons, William F., Firm of Phillips & Simons, Painters,
49 Queen St.
Simons, William N., Accountant, 24 Cumberland St.
Simonton, Elizabeth, 38 State St.
Simonton, James, Accountant, 38 State St.
Simonton, John, Accountant, 38 State St.
Simpson, -----, Mrs., Princess St.
Sinclair, M., Mrs., n. St. Philip St.
Singletary, Daniel, Meeting St.
Singletary, John J., cr. Middle & Minority Sts.
Singleton, Tabby, 76 Beaufain St.
Slatterby, Margaret, Dry Goods, 143 King St.
Slaver, Patrick, 10 Clifford St.
Slavin, Patrick, 50 King St.
Slawson, Hamilton, Wharfinger, Gibbes Whf.
Sleight, S. C., Firm of Henry & Sleight, 83 E. Bay St.
Sloman, Eliza, 27 Montague St.
Smallwood, Martha, 17 Mazyck St.
Smallwood, Martha, cr. New & Tradd Sts.
Smith, A. C., District Clerk & Notary, Union Bank, res. 14 State St.
Smith, A., Mrs., Cannonborough
Smith, Aaron, Grocer, 41 Beaufain St.
Smith, Ann, 38 Coming St., F.P.C.
Smith, Ann, Washington St.
Smith, B., 5 East Battery
Smith, B. F., Paints & Oil, 4 Exchange St., res. 9 Atlantic St.
Smith, B. R., Commission Merchant, Magwood's Whf.
Smith, Benjamin, Mrs., 2 Council St.
Smith, E., Mrs., Amherst St.
Smith, Edward, 12 Atlantic St.
Smith, Eleanor, 38 Mazyck St., F.P.C.
Smith, Fowler, Firm of Smith & Bristol, Shoe Store, 214 King St.
Smith, Frances, 99 n. King St.
Smith, Franklin F., School, 16 Wentworth St.
Smith, Henry W., Firm of Smith & Cox, Sail Makers, Little's Whf., res. 43 Beaufain St.
Smith, J. A., Miss, 71 Broad St.
Smith, J., Clerk & Sexton, St. Philip's Church, res. 10 Magazine St.
Smith, James A., Firm of Smith & Bryce, Hardware, 268 King St.
Smith, James, Clerk, Rail Road Depot, res. 81 Boundary St.
Smith, John G., Portrait Painter, 14 Washington St.
Smith, Joseph T., Boat Builder, res. 67 Tradd St.
Smith, Julia, 2 Hard Al.
Smith, Lorent, n. King St.
Smith, M. A., Mrs., 4 Mazyck St.
Smith, Martha, 18 Bull St., F.P.C.
Smith, Mary Ann, 6 Short St.
Smith, Mary G., 70 Broad St.
Smith, -----, Mrs., 63 Coming St.
Smith, -----, Mrs., 68 Broad St.
Smith, Oliver M., Firm of Smith & Richardson, Attorneys, 2 Hunt's Range, res. New Hotel
Smith, Press, Hampstead
Smith, R. C., Firm of Robinson & Smith, Wholesale Grocers, 114 E. Bay St., res. 5 E. Bay St.

Smith, R. P., Firm of Smith & Groning, Dry Goods, 19 Vendue Range, res. 55 Boundary St.

Smith, Rebecca, 38 Coming St., F.P.C.

Smith, Richard, 90 Queen St.

Smith, Robert, 12 S. Bay St.

Smith, Robert S., Firm of Kerr & Smith, Commission Merchants, res. Beaufain St.

Smith, Samuel, Mrs., 75 Broad St.

Smith, Theodore L., President, Fire Co. of Axmen, Hampstead, Neck

Smith, Thomas P., 68 Tradd St.

Smith, Thomas, Tailor, 38 Coming St., F.P.C.

Smith, W. R., Accountant, 24 Wall St.

Smith, W. T., Firm of Nelson & Smith, Tavern, 79 Queen St.

Smith, Whiteford, 76 Beaufain St.

Smith, Whiteford, Rev., Methodist Episcopal Church, cr. Boundary & Pitt Sts.

Smith, William, 43 Beaufain St.

Smith, William, Boarders, 335 King St.

Smith William, Broker, 40 State St.

Smith, William B., Firm of Jones & Smith, Commission Merchants, Dewees Whf., res. Queen St.

Smith, William, Firm of Nelson & Smith, 79 Queen St.

Smith, William J., Officer of Customs.

Smith, William, Mrs., 22 Meeting St.

Smith, William, Ship Carpenter, res. Mazyckborough

Smith, William Wragg, 13 Legare St.

Smylie, A., Mrs., 77 Beaufain St.

Smyth, Thomas, Rev., Spring St.

Smyzer, Henry J., Ship Joiner, N. Y. Packet Whf.

Snowden, William E., Factor, Fitzsimons' Whf.

Sollee, H., 83 Tradd St.

Sollee, Harriet, 73 Church St.

Solomons, A. A., Firm of P. M. Cohen & Co., Druggists, 167 Meeting St., res. King St. Rd.

Solomons, Benjamin, 99 E. Bay St.

Solomons, Eleanor, cr. King & Vanderhorst Sts.

Solomons, Hernson, Firm of Solomons & Hoffman, Clothing, 64 Meeting St.

Solomons, Israel, Mrs., n. King St.

Solomons, M., 64 Meeting St.

Solomons, Sarah, 177 E. Bay St.

Sonnen, Jacob, Tailor, 87 Tradd St.

Sparnick, Henry, Officer of Customs, 25 Queen St.

Spears, William, Rev., Court House Sq.

Speisseger, Edwin, 11 Pinckney St.

Speisseger, Louis, Musical Instrument Maker, 11 Pinckney St.

Speisseger, Theodore C., Grocer, 11 Pinckney St.

Speissegner, John, Music Teacher, 11 Pinckney St.

Spencer, Catharine, 62 Archdale St.

Spencer, Joseph V., Accountant, cr. Queen & Meeting Sts.

Spidle, John G., 10 Archdale St.

Spreigs, Claus, Grocer, 17 Market St.

Springs, A. T., Classical Teacher, 74 Wentworth St.

Sprouls, S. E., Firm of Rankin & Sprouls, Planters Hotel

St. Amand, John A., Capt., City Guard, Guard House, Broad & Meeting Sts., Coach Maker, 173 Meeting St., res. 193 Meeting St.

St. Amand, John P., 167 Meeting St.

St. Amand, M. W., Accountant, 173 Meeting St.

St. Marks, John, Barber, 10 Queen St.

Stagg, John, Wheelwright, 26 Beaufain St.

Stall, A., Mrs., Cannonborough

Stall, Frederick, Butcher, Cannon St.

Stalling J. & Co., Mechanics Coffee House, cr. Market & State Sts.

Stanly, Arthur, 46 Beaufain St.

Stark, Charles, Mrs., 8 Laurens St.

Starr, E. M., Firm of Starr & Williams, Hat Store, 301 King St.

Starr, E. P., Firm of Starr & Howland, Steam Plaining, w. end Beaufain St., res. 122 Wentworth St.

Statham, Barnet, Firm of Dickinson, Sebring & Statham, Importers, 149 Meeting St., res. New Hotel

Stear, Henry, Tailor, 64 State St.

Steed, -----, Dr., Cannonborough

Steedman, John, Mrs., Mazyckborough

Steedman, Thomas, Officer of Customs, res. Charlotte St.

Steekfleet, John, Grocer, cr. Elizabeth & Henrietta Sts.

Steel, Catharine, 6 Magazine St., F.P.C.

Steel, John, Mrs., Boundary St.

Stegin, John H., Grocer, cr. Anson & Society Sts.

Stein, John F., 76 Tradd St.

Steinmeyer, John F., Boundary St.

Steinmyer & Clark, Steam Plaining Mill, w. end Beaufain St.

Steitz, Henry, Cabinet Maker, 1 Philadelphia St.

Stelling, John, Grocer, cr. E. Bay & Elliott Sts.

Stent, John, Carpenter, 23 King St.

Stent, John H., Bricklayer, res. Head Quarters.

Stevens, Arnold H., Capt., 6 Minority St.

Stevens, James R., Firm of J. R. Stevens & Co., 272 King St., res. 32 Beaufain St.

Stevens, Joel, 51 Tradd St.

Stevens, Samuel N., Firm of Ravenel & Stevens, cr. E. Bay & Water Sts., res. 11 George St.

Stevens, Susannah, John St.

Stevens, Thomas, Teller, Union Bank, res. 14 State St.

Steward, -----, Miss, 7 Greenhill St.

Steward, Robert, Carpenter, Radcliffborough

Stewart, Angus, Carolina Hotel, 54 Broad St.

Stewart, -----, Mrs., Dry Goods, 84 Church St.

Stewart, Sarah, 84 Church St.

Stiefvater, Martin, Shoe Maker, 15 Boundary St.

Stiles, Copeland, 23 Pitt St.

Stillman, Charles, Carpenter, 26 Vernon St.

Stillman, J. W., Wharfinger, Boyce's Whf., res. 2 Coming St.

Stillman, James, Officer of Customs, 2 Coming St.

Stock, John Y., Firm of Carter, Lloyd & Stock, Brokers, 6 Broad St., res. 9 Montague St.

Stocker, James M., Firm of Lord & Stocker, Commission Merchants, 84 E. Bay St., res. Washington St.

Stoddard, E. B., Shoes, 317 & 319 King St.

Stoll, Justinus, Accountant, 115 Church St.

Stoll, Margaret, 88 Church St.

Stony, John, Mrs., 24 Hasell St.

Storm, F. H., Exchange Broker, 4 Broad St.

Storm, -----, Mrs., 129 King St.

Straw, Mary, 10 Clifford's Al.

Street, Eliza, 25 College St.

Street, H. G., Firm of Street & Son, Grocers, 85 Church St.

Street, Henry T., Commission Merchant, 64 E. Bay St., res. 9 Society St.

Street, Jesse C., Firm of Street & Son, Grocers, 85 Church St.

Street, Thaddeus, Firm of Street & Boinest, Commission Merchants, 6 Boyce's Whf., res. Hampstead

Strobel, B. B., Dr., 116 Church St.

Strobel, Eliza, 75 Meeting St.

Strobel, John, 33 Mazyck St.

Strobel, Lewis, Bricklayer, 18 Liberty St.

Strobel, Sarah, 5 Back St.

Strohecker, C. C., Clerk, Court of Common Pleas, res. 48 Bull St.

Strohecker, George, 163 Meeting St.

Strohecker, Henry, 72 Anson St.

Strohecker, John, 163 Meeting St.

Strohecker, Lewis, 26 Montague St.

Strong, Daniel, Firm of Jewell & Strong, 45 Society St.

Strong, George, Firm of Jewell & Strong, Cabinet Makers, 45 Society St., res. n. King St.

Stroub, Jacob, Carpenter, 12 Burns Ln.

Stuart, John A., Editor, Mercury, res. Mary St.

Sturkin, John H., Grocer, 31 King St.

Suares, B. C., Tailor, 365 King St.

Suder, Ann, Mrs., 88 Tradd St.

Suder, Peter J., Carpenter, 11 Linguard St.

Sullivan, Casteel, 36 Pitt St.

Sullivan, John, Printer, 5 Whim Court

Sullivan, Mary, Mrs., 72 Anson St.

Sullivan, T., Rev., Catholic Seminary, 92 Broad St.

Summers, P., Mrs., Boarding, 26 Elliott St.

Summers, Rosetta, Nurse, 73 Tradd St.

Surtis, Thomas, Pilot, 33 King St.

Susan, -----, Miss, Midwife, 9 Friend St.

Susportas, Cloe, Clifford's Al., F.P.C.

Sutliff, James, Baker, 185 King St.

Sweegan, Mathew, Grocer, cr. Linguard & State Sts.

Sweeny, Diannah, 3 Longitude Ln., F.P.C.

Sweeny, Thomas J., Book Binder, 78 Anson St.

Swift, Thomas B., State Constable, cr. Motte's Ln & Pinckney St.

Swinton, Ellen, 25 Archdale St.

Swinton, Mary, 69 Beaufain St.

Swizzel, Catharine, Washer, 8 Burns Ln., F.P.C.

Swizzel, Susan, Washer, 8 Burns Ln., F.P.C.

Symmes, Chorlotte, Mrs., Wolf St.

Symms, William L., Clerk, 373 King St.

Symons, John, Rigger, Tradd St.

Taber, W. R., res. Radcliffborough

Taft, A. R., Firm of Howland & Taft, Commission Merchants, 135 E. Bay St., res. 15 Laurens St.

Tally, N., Rev., Methodist Episcopal Church, cr. Boundary & Pitt Sts.

Talvande, -----, Madame, 14 Legare St.

Talvant, Andrew, 100 Broad St.

Tanswell, W. N., Bell Hanger & Locksmith, 20 Chalmers St.

Tapmann, Louis, Commission Merchant, 20 E. Bay St., res. 110 Broad St.

Tappan, Charles B., Firm of Tappan & Noble, Builders, Wentworth St., near E. Bay St.

Tarrant, Joseph, 42 Beaufain St.

Tate, Charles, Saddler, 39 n. King St.

Tate, James, Saddler, 30 n. King St.

Taveaux, -----, Mrs., cr. Alexander & Charlotte Sts.

Taylor, Charlotte, 46 Coming St. F.P.C.

Taylor, George, Firm of O. & G. Taylor, Merchants, 225 King St.

Taylor, George T., Attorney, 16 St. Michael's Al., res. 6 Lamboll St.

Taylor, James H., Auctioneer, res. 210 King St.

Taylor, Joseph, Comb Maker, 39 St. Philip St.

Taylor, Josiah, Firm of Taylor, Lawton & Co., Factors, 13 Southern Whf., res. 6 Lamboll St.

Taylor, Margaret, Fruiterer, 11 Tradd St.

Taylor, Mary, 1 Short St.

Taylor, Oran, Firm of O. & G. Taylor, Merchants, 225 King St.

Taylor, R. R., Firm of Taylor, Lawton & Co., Factors, 13 Southern Whf., res. 6 Lamboll St.

Taylor, Roland, 69 n. King St.

Taylor, Thomas R., Shoes, 233 King St.

Taylor, William, 12 Lamboll St.

Taylor, William M., Firm of Duffus & Taylor, Dry Goods Merchants, 303 King St., res. 12 Lamboll St.

Taylors, -----, Misses, Warren St.

Teague, N., Mrs., Boarders, 325 King St.

Teasdale, Richard, Factor, 6 Southern Whf., res. Cannonborough

Telfair, Robert, Gauger, 7 Tradd St.

Tenbroek, Emily, 15 Berresford St.

Tennant, Ann, 60 Anson St.

Tennant, Joseph, Accountant, 21 Middle St.

Tennant, -----, Mrs., 58 King St.

Tennant, William, 60 Anson St.

Terete, Walter, Farmer, King St Road.

Terry, Daniel, Mariner, 17 Boundary St.

Tew, Ellen, Mrs., 72 Wentworth St.

Tew, Henry S., 159 E. Bay St.

Teystein, Otto, Grocer, cr. Meeting & Henrietta Sts.

Tharin, Theodore C., Wheelwright, 16 n. King St.

Thayer, E., Bonnet Store, 155 Meeting St.

Thayer, Ebenezer, Book Store, 81 Broad St.

Thayer, John D., Grocer, 39 E. Bay St.

Thayer, Susan, 1 Greenhill St.

Thayer, T. Heywood, Broker, 16 Broad St., res. 10 Atlantic St.

Thayer, William H., Accountant, 106 Tradd St.

Thee, John, Grocer, 10 Market St.

Theus, S. B., Mrs., 16 Smith St.

Thoade, F., Grocer, cr. Coming & Duncan Sts.

Thomas, E., Boot Maker, 27 St. Philip St.

Thomas, M., 297 King St.

Thomas, Morris, Bonnet Store, 153 Meeting St.

Thomas, Samuel S., Collector, 2 Montague St.

Thomas, Stephen, Jr., Anson St., Firm of Hillard &

Thomas, Grocers, 7 Vendue Range, res. 31 Pinckney St.

Thomlinson, Joseph, Firm of Trenholm & Thomlinson, Dry Goods Merchants, 22 Hayne St., res. Coming St.

Thompson, Elizabeth, Dry Goods, 88 Church St.

Thompson, George, Bricklayer, 38 Hasell St.

Thompson, Hannah, Court House Sq.

Thompson, James, Locksmith, 88 Church St.

Thompson, Jane, Dry Goods, 142 E. Bay St.

Thompson, John, 1 Bull St.

Thompson, John B., Attorney, Court House Sq., res. 9 New St.

Thompson, Joseph, Firm of Thompson & Wood, Tailors, 32 n. King St., F.P.C.

Thompson, Joseph, Saddler, 45 Broad St., res. 50 Broad St.

Thompson, Lewis, 5 Coming St., F.P.C.

Thompson, Martha, 5 Coming St., F.P.C.

Thompson, Mary C., n. St. Philip St.

Thompson, Robert H., Court House Sq.

Thompson, S. T., Boundary St.

Thompson, Thomas, Accountant, 26 Coming St.

Thompson, William, 14 King St.

Thompson, William, 20 Coming St.

Thompson, William, 40 Meeting St.

Thompson, William, Boarding, 5 Elliott St.

Thomson, Ann, 1 Burns Ln.

Thorn, Philip, Carpenter, 31 Boundary St., F.P.C.

Thrower, Catharine, 10 Pitt St.

Thrower, James, 10 Pitt St.

Thurston, Robert, Firm of Robertson & Thurston, Factors, 18 E. Bay St., res. 19 Pitt St.

Ticken, Henry, Grocer, 11 Clifford St.

Tidyman, H., Grocer, Henrietta St.

Tidyman, Hester, Mrs., 86 Broad St.

Tidyman, Philip, Dr., 2 Ladson's Court

Tileston, William, Dr., 37 State St.

Tilton, N. H., Capt., Mariner, 137 Church St.

Tilton, Rebecca, Boarding, 137 Church St.

Timmons, G. P., Firm of William Timmons & Son, Hardware, 147 E. Bay St.

Timmons, George, Mrs., 4 Smith's Ln.

Timmons, William, Accountant, 147 E. Bay St.

Timmons, William L., Firm of William Timmons & Son, Hardware, 147 E. Bay St.

Tinkin, D., Grocer, 17 Montague St.

Tippet, Thomas, Market St., near Archdale St.

Tityen, Harman, Grocer, cr. Coming & Radcliff Sts.

Tityen, John H., Grocer, cr. Coming & Cannon Sts.

Toalle, Charles, Grocer, Mary St.

Tobias, Abraham, Auctioneer, Vendue, res. 134 E. Bay St.

Tobin, Richard, n. Meeting St.

Toohey, Morris, Boot Maker, 21 Elliott St.

Toomer, H. V., Dr., Office cr. Meeeting & Ann Sts., res. John St.

Toomer, Henrietta, Mrs., 54 St. Philip St.

Toomer, Joshua W., Attorney, res. Ann St.

Torley, M. F., Grocer, 45 E. Bay St.

Tornland, Alexander, Nassau St.

Torre, Peter D., Attorney, 7 Broad St., res. 72 Broad St.

Torrent, John, Rigger, 199 E. Bay St.

Torrey, Ann, 6 New St.

Torrington, Martha, Mrs., Grocer, 7 E. Bay St.

Tortat, H., Boot Maker, 112 Church St.

Toussieger, Eliza, 20 Water St.

Tovey, Henry, Block & Pump Maker, 104 E. Bay St., res. 259 E. Bay St.

Townsend, Isaac, Firm of Fort, Townsend & Mendenhall, Dry Goods, 1 Hayne St., res. New York

Townsend, Mary, 18 Middle St.

Townsend, William, Firm of Fort, Townsend & Mendenhall, Dry Goods, 1 Hayne St., res. New York

Trapier, Paul., Rev., Pastor, St. Stephen's Chapel, Anson St., near Laurens St., res. 39 Meeting St.

Trenholm, Charles L., Firm of Trenholm & Thomlinson, Dry Goods Merchants, 22 Hayne St., res. 4 Friend St.

Trenholm, E. A., Firm of John Fraser & Co., Commission Merchants, Central Whf., res. 4 New St.

Trenholm, Edward L., Firm of Trenholm & Thomlinson, Dry Goods Merchants, 22 Hayne St., res. 66 Wentworth St.

Trenholm, G. A., Firm of John Fraser & Co., res. 4 New St.

Trescot, C., Mrs., n. Coming St.

Trescot, Henry, Teller, State Bank, res. 4 Anson St.

Trescot, Susan, Farmer, back of Race Course

Trezvant, Diana, 12 Orange St., F.P.C.

Trittan, G. H., Market St., n. Meeting St.

Trott, Emma, Mrs., 79 King St.

Trouche, Augustus, Accountant, 47 Church St.

Trout, Thomas, Firm of Leland, Brothers & Co., res. 118 Wentworth St.

Trout, William, Capt., Pilot, 8 Atlantic St.

Truesdale, David, Oyster House, 20 Queen St.

Tucker, H. H., Firm of Hoff & Tucker, Booksellers, 10 Broad St., res. 10 Broad St.

Tucker, J. H., Planter, n. Meeting St.

Tunis, Mary, Boarding, cr. E. Bay St. & Vanderhorst Whf.

Tunno, William, 29 Friend St.

Tupper, S. Y., Firm of T. Tupper & Son, Merchants, Gibbes Whf., res. 52 Tradd St.

Tupper, Tristam, Firm of T. Tupper & Son, Merchants, Gibbes Whf., res. 52 Tradd St.

Turnbull, Andrew, 104 Broad St.

Turnbull, Ann, 1 Legare St.

Turnbull, James, 22 Water St.

Turnbull, -----, Mrs., 1 Logan St.

Turner, -----, 4 Stoll's Al.

Turner, Ann, 3 Short St., F.P.C.

Turner, Eliza, 6 Chalmers St., F.P.C.

Turner, Elizabeth, 19 Archdale St., F.P.C.

Turner, John, Farmer, Cannonborough

Turpin, Jane, 31 Society St., F.P.C.

Tweed, Ellen, Charlotte St.

Tweedy, J. H., Firm of E. T. Hoyt & Co., Clothing, 18 Hayne St.

Twing, Edward, Broker, 10 State St., res. American Hotel

Ulmo, Peter, Firm of Addison & Ulmo, Shipwrights, S. Bay St.

Ummers, -----, Mrs., 53 Beaufain St.

Undal, Andrew, 5 Lynch St.

Underwood, Thomas, Tailor, 18 Tradd St.
Uttermahl, Mary, 10 Burns Ln.
Valentine, Samuel, 4 Clifford St.
Vance, Frances, Mrs., n. Coming St.
Vance, William, Mrs., Vanderhorst St.
Vanderhorst, E. H., Barber, 3 Tradd St.
Vanderhorst, Elias, Planter, John St.
Vanderhorst, Henry, 98 Wentworth St., F.P.C.
Vanderhorst, J., 38 Coming St., F.P.C.
Vanderhorst, Patsey, 98 Wentworth St., F.P.C.
VanDolen, Albert, Grocer, cr. King & John Sts.
Vanmuchi, Francis, Tavern, 33 Market St.
VanRyhn, John M., Mrs., Hampstead
VanWinkle, John, Variety Store, 290 King St.
Vardell, Susan, Mrs., Vanderhorst St.
Vardell, Thomas R., Bricklayer, 36 George St.
Varney, Nicholas, Boarding, 38 Elliott St.
Vaughan, Ann, Miss, 18 Pinckney St.
Vaughan, -----, Mrs., 18 Pinckney St.
Vaulk, Jacob R., 18 New St.
Veilstick, Henry, Grocer, 123 E. Bay St.
Veitch, William, Dr., Drugs & Medicines, Market St., near
    King St.
Velde, John, Country Store, 290 King St.
Venning, J. M., Lumber Merchant, Wharf St., res.
    Charlotte St.
Verner, Henry, 28 Mazyck St.
Vernon, Nathaniel, 1 Greenhill St.
Vernon, William H., 1 Greenhill St.
Veronee, Samuel, Accountant, 35 George St.
Veronee, Samuel, Mary St.
Verree, Caroline, Dress Maker, 6 Pitt St., F.P.C.
Verree, John, 6 Pitt St., F.P.C.
Vidal, John, 1 Smith's Ln.
Vincent, Bosset, Fruits, 8 Wentworth St.
Vincent, Hugh E., Jr., Firm of Hugh E. Vincent & Son,
    Ship Chandlers, 65 E. Bay St.
Vincent, Hugh E., Sr., Firm of Hugh E. Vincent & Son,
    Ship Chandlers, 65 E. Bay St.
Vinro, John W., Factor, 43 E. Bay St., res. 42 St. Philip St.
Vinro, Sarah, Midwife, 42 St. Philip St.
Vinyard, John, Hampstead
Vizzard, H., Shoe Maker, cr. Green & St. Philip Sts.
Vogel & Salvo, Cabinets, King St.
Vogel, Martin, Cabinet Ware, 211 King St.
Vogelsang, E., Grocer, w. end Beaufain St.
VonGlann, Claus, Grocer, Warren St.
Vose, Carsten, n. King St.
Waddy, Anthony, T., Merchant, 323 King St.
Waddy, William, 13 Bull St.
Wade, J. M., Firm of Zealey & Wade, Commission
    Merchants, 120 E. Bay St.
Wade, William Moore, Cabinet Maker, 1 Philadelphia St.
Wagner, E., Planter, 16 New St.
Wagner, George, Bookkeeper, State Bank, res. 19 E. Bay
    St.
Wagner, J., Dr., Wentworth St.
Wagner, John A., Grocer, 67 Market St.
Wagner, -----, Mrs., 46 St. Philip St.
Wagner, S. J., Officer of Customs, res. 118 Queen St.

Wald, Frederick, Grocer, 20 New St.
Walker, Betsey, Pastry Cook, 19 King St., F.P.C.
Walker, E., Firm of Martin & Walker, Factors, Boyce's
    Whf., res. New Hotel
Walker, Edward, 15 Montague St.
Walker, Eliza, Mantuamaker, 31 Wall St., F.P.C.
Walker, George, Shoe Maker, 62 Meeting St.
Walker, Henry D., Carpenter, 16 Magazine St.
Walker, J., Firm of Burges & Walker, 85 E. Bay St.
Walker, J. L., Painter, 173 E. Bay St.
Walker, James E., Firm of James E. Walker & Brothers,
    Stone Cutters, 141 Meeting St.
Walker, James M., Firm of King & Walker, res. 5 Legare
    St.
Walker, John C., Book Binder, 74 Queen St.
Walker, John F., 204 E. Bay St.
Walker, Joseph, Firm of Burgess & Walker, Stationers, 85
    E. Bay St., res. 8 Liberty St.
Walker, Joseph, Merchant, 173 E. Bay St.
Walker, -----, Mrs., 11 Back St.
Walker, R. A., res. Lee's, Broad St.
Walker, R. D., Firm of James E. Walker & Brothers, Stone
    Cutters, 141 Meeting St.
Walker, -----, Rev. Mr., Methodist Episcopal Church, cr.
    Boundary & Pitt Sts.
Walker, Robert, Firm of Martin & Walker, Factors,
    Boyce's Whf., res. Charlotte St.
Walker, W. S., Firm of James E. Walker & Brothers, Stone
    Cutters, 141 Meeting St.
Wall, John 20 State St.
Wallace, Andrew, Capt., 110 Church St.
Wallace, Lavinia, 130 Wentworth St., F.P.C.
Wallace, Mary, 11 Tradd St.
Wallace, -----, Mrs., 85 Boundary St.
Wallace, Thomas, Merchant, 344 King St.
Wallace, W. N., Keeper of Potters Field
Walter, E. W., Firm of Martin & Walter, res. New Hotel
Walter, Jerry, Auctioneer, 8 Vendue Range
Walton, A. Y., Merchant, 300 King St.
Walton, E., Mrs., n. Meeting St.
Walton, J. M., Firm of Milliken & Walton, Grocers, 108
    E. Bay St., res. 35 Coming St.
Walton, J. W. Y., Hardware, 300 King St.
Walton, John 35 Coming St.
Ward, F. S., Clerk, City Court, City Hall, res. 20 Wall St.
Ward, Harrriet, 94 Tradd St.
Ward, John, 2nd Lt., City Guard, Guard House, Broad &
    Meeting Sts.
Ward, John, Wharfinger, Hamilton's Whf., res. 3 Logan St.
Ward, Rose, Pastry Cook, 65 Boundary St., F.P.C.
Ward, Sarah, 24 Church St.
Waring, Francis, 21 E. Bay St.
Waring, H. S., Dr., 59 Meeting St.
Waring, M. A., Firm of Jervey, Waring & White, res. n.
    St. Philip St.
Waring, Morton A., Firm of Jervey, Waring & White,
    Brokers, 18 Broad St., res. n. St. Philip St.
Waring, Sarah, 37 Meeting St.
Waring, Thomas, Merchant, cr. E. Bay & Wharf Sts., res.
    Back St.

Warley, Ann, 79 Tradd St.
Warne, Nancy, Dress Maker, 33 Boundary St., F.P.C.
Warren, Elizabeth, 14 Magazine St.
Warren, G. L., Accountant, 174 Meeting St.
Warren, S. N., Shoes, 57 n. King St & 190 E. Bay St.
Warrren, Susannah, Boarding, 8 Linguard St.
Washington, Maria, w. end Wentworth St., F.P.C.
Waterman, C. O., Carpenter, n. Meeting St.
Waters, Richard, Tavern, 117 Meeting St.
Watkins, Mary, Dry Goods, 299 King St., res. 21 George St.
Watson, John A., Book Binder, 55 Queen St.
Watson, Stephen, Firm of Watson, Crews & Co., Merchants, 28 E. Bay St., res. 9 Archdale St.
Waugh, A. C., Accountant, 142 Meeting St.
Wear, J. S., Wholesale Shoe Store, 171 Meeting St.
Wear, John, Shoe Maker, 6 St. Michael's Al.
Weaver, Joseph, Paints, 21 George St.
Webb, Daniel C., Cannon St.
Webb, M., Mrs., Linen Store, 42 Broad St.
Webb, Michael M., 42 Broad St.
Webb, -----, Miss, 31 St. Philip St.
Webb, T. L., Firm of Ingraham & Webb, Factors, Central Whf., res. Cannonborough
Webb, Thomas L., Firm of Ingraham & Webb, res. Cannon St.
Webber, Sarah, 8 Hard Al.
Weedoe, Jacob, Accountant, 17 Wall St.
Weeks, Joseph, Firm of Weeks & Happoldt, Tavern, 96 Meeting St.
Wehlert, Jacob C., Grocer, 55 Church St.
Weinges, Jacob, 13 Pitt St.
Weissenger, Charles, 81 n. King St.
Welch, John, Reid St.
Wells, Frederick, n. King St.
Wellsman, J. T., Firm of Brown & Wellsman, Factors, 14 Southern Whf., res. 22 Church St.
Welsh, M., 36 Beaufain St.
Welsman, J. T., Firm of Brown & Welsman, 22 Church St.
Werner, G., Blacksmith, 49 State St.
Wesner, Frederick, Master, Work House, res. 10 Mazyck St.
West, C. H., Ship Chandler, 61 E. Bay St., res. 11 Church St.
Westendorffe, C. P. L., Wharf St.
Weston, Jacob, Firm of S. & J. Weston, Tailors, 104 Queen St., F.P.C.
Weston, -----, Misses, Hampstead St.
Weston, Samuel, Firm of S. & J. Weston, Tailors, 104 Queen St., F. P.C.
Weston, Sarah, Mantuamaker, 106 Queen St.
Weston, Thomas, 15 Short St.
Wethers, Mary, n. Pitt St.
Weyman, Ann C., 30 Church St.
Weyman, Robert H., n. Meeting St.
Whaley, William, Planter, Cannonborough
Wheeler, John, Boarding, Meeting, n. Hasell St.
Whitty, Edward, Firm of McLean & Whitty, Seedsmen, cr. E. Bay & Pinckney Sts., res. Neck
Whilden, Elizabeth, 14 Magazine St.

Whilden, L. E., Mrs., Boarders, 83 Broad St.
Whitaker, D. K., Attorney, 9 St. Michael's Al.
Whitaker, William, Grocer, cr. Elizabeth & Henrietta Sts.
White, Alonzo J., Firm of Jervey, Waring & White, Brokers, 18 Broad St., res. 70 Broad St.
White, Edward B., Civil Engineer, 33 Tradd St.
White, Felicity, Fruits, 39 State St., F.P.C.
White, George, Accountant, 8 Washington St.
White, James, City Lamp Lighter, 19 Montague St.
White, John B., Officer of Customs, res. 19 Legare St.
White, John, Stone Cutter, 123 Meeting St.
White, Mary, 24 Mazyck St.. F.P.C.
White, N., 1 St. Philip St.
White, Thomas, Dry Goods, 324 King St.
White, William, Cannonborough
White, William H., Grocer, 64 Queen St.
White, William, J., 15 College St.
Whitemore, C., Tallow Chandler, Radcliffborough
Whitesides, Mary, 20 Wall St.
Whiting, Edward M., Turner, Boundary St., near Anson St.
Whitney, Archibald, 11 Cumberland St.
Whitney, O. L., Dry Goods, 324 King St.
Whitney, Theodore, Collector, 5 Linguard St.
Whitridge, Joshua Barker, Dr., 82 Broad St.
Whitty, Edward, Firm of McLean & Whitty, res. Washington St.
Whyte, Joseph, Teacher, 43 Queen St.
Wienges, Abraham, 126 Queen St.
Wienges, Caroline, cr. Beaufain & Archdale Sts.
Wienges, J. H., 19 Mazyck St.
Wienges, Joseph, Bricklayer, 18 Burns Ln.
Wigfall, Susan, 84 Beaufain St., F.P.C.
Wigfall, Thomas, Planter, Washington St.
Wightman, Jane, 38 Chalmers St., F.P.C.
Wightman, John, Turner, 94 Meeting St.
Wilbur, W. W., Comb Manufactory, 212 King St.
Wilcox, Sarah, Mrs., 23 College St.
Wildman, N. H., Firm of Wildman & Dibble, Hat Store, 169 Meeting St.
Wiley, James, Firm of S. & J. Wiley, Grocers, 361 King St.
Wiley, L. A., Fruits, 171 E. Bay St.
Wiley, L. M., Firm of Wiley, Lane & Co., Wholesale Dry Goods, 3 Hayne St., res. New Hotel
Wiley, Samuel, Firm of S. & J. Wiley, Grocers, 361 King St.
Wiley, William, 20 Atlantic St.
Wiley, William J., Grocer, 342 King St.
Wilkes, John, Factor, Hamilton's Whf., res. 13 Meeting St.
Wilkie, George W., Officer of Customs, 9 Linguard St.
Wilkie, -----, Mrs., 8 Liberty St.
Wilkie, Susan, Mrs., Boarding, 137 King St.
Wilkinson, J. W., Attorney, 4 St. Michael's Al.., res. 58 Meeting St.
Wilkinson, Joseph, 8 Zig Zag Al., F.P.C.
Wilkinson, Willis, Dr., 8 Lynch St.
Will, Robert, Bricklayer, 164 Meeting St.
Williams, Ann, 48 Church St.
Williams, Catharine, 23 Beaufain St.
Williams, Catharine, 81 Church St.
Williams, Dorcas, 64 Beaufain St.

Williams, E. H., Firm of Gibbs & Williams, Steam Saw Mill, w. end Tradd St., res. 6 Coming St.

Williams, Henry W., Firm of Starr & Williams, Hat Store, res. 30 St. Philip St.

Williams, Isham, William's Whf.

Williams, J., Mill Wright, 4 Logan St., F.P.C.

Williams, John, Merchant, Commercial Whf., res. cr. Laurens & Wall St.

Williams, Susan, 48 Church St.

Williams, W. B., Factor, Magwood's Whf., res. 249 Meeting St.

Williamson, E., Mrs., Boundary St.

Williamson, John, Constable, 10 Friend St.

Williamson, John, Engineer, Henrietta St.

Williman, -----, Mrs., Boundary St., near Pitt St.

Willington, A. S., Firm of A. S. Willington & Co., Editors, Courier, 101 E. Bay St., res. Flat Rock, N. C.

Willis, Henry, Broker, 50 Broad St., res. Hampstead

Willis, John George, Boot & Shoe Store, 168 King St.

Wilmot, Samuel, Firm of S. & T.T. Wilmot, Jewellers, 209 King St.

Wilmot, Thomas T., Firm of S. & T. T. Wilmot, Jewellers, 209 King St.

Wilson, Abraham, Planter, Cannon St.

Wilson, Alexander B., Thomas St.

Wilson, Elizabeth, 69 Meeting St.

Wilson, George, Blacksmith St., F.P.C.

Wilson, Hugh, Planter, Cannonborough

Wilson, J., Firm of J. & R. Wilson, Clothing, 94 Meeeting St.

Wilson, James, 23 Friend St.

Wilson, James M., Firm of McDowall & Wilson, 121 King St.

Wilson, James, Seedsman, 34 E. Bay St.

Wilson, Jane, Mantuamaker, 25 Beaufain St., F.P.C.

Wilson, John L., Gov., Attorney, 2 St. Michael's Al.

Wilson, Nancy, 3 College St., F.P.C.

Wilson, R., Firm of J. & R. Wilson, Clothing, 94 Meeting St.

Wilson, Robert, Capt., Mariner, res. Hasell St., near Anson St.

Wilson, S., Mrs., Cannonborough

Wilson, Samuel, Dr., 8 New St.

Wilson, Sarah, Mantuamaker, Smith's Court, F.P.C.

Wilson, Susan, 30 Mazyck St., F.P.C.

Wilson, W. H., Dr., Hasell St., near Anson St.

Wilson, William, Carpenter, 6 Liberty St.

Wilson, William H., 76 Meeting St.

Windsor, Elizabeth, 26 Coming St.

Winslow, Edward, Firm of Winslow & Delius, Commission Merchants, Hamilton's Whf., res. New Hotel

Winthrop, Henry Winthrop, Dr., Shirras Dispensary, 42 Society St., res. 97 Tradd St.

Winthrop, J. A., Factor, Hamilton's Whf., res. 103 Tradd St.

Witherby, Joel, Shoe Store, 103 E. Bay St.

Witherington, Peter, Wood Factor, Gadsden's Whf.

Withers, Francis, Planter, cr. Meeting & John Sts.

Withers, William, Drake St.

Witter, Eliza, Boarding, 30 Tradd St.

Wittpen, -----, Mrs., Nursery, cr. John & Elizabeth Sts.

Wolley, Charles C., Boat Builder, res. 6 Hard Al.

Wood, A. B., Firm of Stoddard, Miller & Co., res. new Hotel

Wood, Edward, Constable, cr. Motte's Ln. & Pinckney St.

Wood, Francis W., 126 Queen St.

Wood, George, Grocer, 100 Meeting St.

Wood, Henry, Firm of Thompson & Wood, Tailors, 32 n. King St., F.P.C.

Wood, Julius L., Dr., Thomsonian, 367 King St.

Wood, -----, Mrs., 139 King St.

Woodly, James, 40 King St.

Woodman, Carsten, Grocer, cr. Rutledge & Bull Sts.

Woodward, E. S., Mrs., 82 Broad St.

Woolf, Isaac, Merchant, 355 King St.

Wotherspoon, Robert, Merchant, 20 E. Bay St.

Wragg, Samuel, Firm of Wragg, Simons & Co., Factors, Commercial Whf., res. Mazyckborough

Wragg, Thomas L., Firm of Wragg, Simons & Co., Factors, Commercial Whf., res. Charlotte St.

Wright, Caroline F., Dry Goods, 32 Broad St.

Wright, Diana, 30 Bull St., F.P.C.

Wright, Elizabeth, 4 Lamboll St., F.P.C.

Wright, Harriet, 164 King St.

Wright, Laughlin, Firm of Wright & Gefkin, Carpenters, W. end Beaufain St.

Wurdehoff, W., Grocer, 60 Elliott St.

Wurdeman, J. G. F., Dr., 12 Queen St.

Yates, David S., 62 Tradd St.

Yates, Elizabeth, 62 Tradd St.

Yates, Francis S., Cooper St.

Yates, Francis S., Discount Clerk, Bank of S.C., res. 28 Church St.

Yates, J. A., 22 King St.

Yates, J. D., Attorney, res. 66 King St.

Yates, James L., Accountant, 5 Zig Zag Al.

Yates, Jane Elizabeth, 5 Zig Zag Al.

Yates, Joseph, 62 Tradd St.

Yates, T. H., House Carpenter, Inspection St.

Yates, W. B., Rev., 5 Meeting St.

Yeadon, William, Col., Arsenal Keeper, Citadel, n. of Boundary St.

Yeadon, Richard, Deputy Cashier, Bank of State of S. C., res. 21 King St.

Yeadon, Richard, Jr., Firm of A. S. Willington & Co., Editors, Courier, 101 E. Bay St., res. 70 Wentworth St.

You, John C., Teacher, Free School, 4 Archdale St.

Zealey, Joseph, Assistant Clerk, Union Bank, res. 3 Minority St.

Zealey, -----, Mrs., Midwife, 45 King St.

Zealey, William E., Firm of Zealey & Wade, Commission Merchants, 120 E. Bay St., res. 45 King St.

Zell, Joseph, Blacksmith, 7 Cumberland St.

Zerlst, Frederick, Farmer, near Race Course

9 780806 346786